*1966*

This book may be kept

# a survey of marxism

## Problems in Philosophy

## and the Theory of History

# A. JAMES GREGOR

*University of Kentucky*

# a survey of marxism

## Problems in Philosophy

## and the Theory of History

 RANDOM HOUSE / NEW YORK

*This book is dedicated to the memory of my father*

A N T O N I O   G I M I G L I A N O

*a worker Italy gave to America*

# Preface

In this book I have attempted two things: (1) to provide within the compass of a single, brief exposition a survey of the wealth and complexity of Marxism; (2) to present not only the principal elements of Marxism as a philosophy and a theory of history but also to suggest some of the criticisms that have been or, in the author's opinion, should be leveled against it.

Several problems immediately arose because the enterprise attempted was so ambitious. To give a brief but authoritative account of a theory which occupied Marx and Engels for upward of fifty years and its exponents and critics for at least another fifty is no mean task. To meet the obligations imposed by such a task, I have gone to the original source material itself and, wherever possible, have provided an exposition in the founders' words. This has made the text cumbersome, not only because of the abundance of direct quotations, but also because each quotation is documented as precisely as possible. All too often quotations taken out of context betray the meaning of the author. Unfortunately the task of documentation is complicated by the fact that there are a multitude of editions of the works of Marx, Engels, and Lenin.

I have tried to use editions which would be most easily obtainable, and whenever an English translation exists, the English-language source is cited. Easiest access to the Russian-language material was to translations into one of the Western European languages, and citations are from such translations as are available. Russian names appear in the text as they are given in the translation employed. Cross-reference in any standard library catalogue will provide the Library of Congress transliteration. Names like Trotsky and Khrushchev have been so written since they have become familiar in that form.

One of the peripheral purposes of this book is to serve as a text for individual or classroom inquiry into Marxism, so all the cumbersome machinery of academic footnoting has been retained. Its purpose is to assist the reader who wants to go back to the primary sources. But the notes are, in general, source references, and the text should be completely intelligible without them. The notes do, of course, further clutter a text already cluttered with extensive quotations. In this regard I can only ask the reader's indulgence. To promote legibility one change in standard procedures has been made. Quotations, irrespective of length, have been incorporated directly into the text and set off by quotation marks.

I have attempted to make the exposition of Marxism as impartial as possible. The words of the original founders are employed wherever possible and I have noted the source. In much of what has been written about Marxism it is often difficult to separate the commentary from the actual Marxist material. It is hoped that the techniques employed in the text, cumbersome though they may be, assist in making the necessary distinctions.

In parts of the exposition, particularly those of the early Marx manuscripts, I have attempted an original interpretation. The interpretations in Chapter One are therefore tentative, but they are advanced as being of interest to the Marx scholar as well as the lay or university student. The reassessment of Marx as a philosopher has only begun. The first and second chapters attempt to outline and distinguish the philosophy of the young Marx from that of Engels, for in order to assess Marx as a philosopher it is necessary to sort out his philosophy from that of his co-worker. It is obvious that the philosophy of the young Marx differs substantially from that of the mature Engels. I have advanced evidence which supports the necessity of making a consistent distinction between the work of the two men. With respect to Marxism as a theory of history I have, in general, made no such distinction. As far as I can determine, both men were in essential agreement with respect to the theory of history. If any distinction is to be made, it is on the grounds that Engels wrote more popular works for the more general reader. For example, Marx's analysis of crises in capitalism includes at least crises of overproduction (or underconsumption), disproportionality crises, and the secular crisis of the falling rate of profit. Engels is aware of these as well, but in his more general expositions he referred almost exclusively to the crises of overproduction.

Not only is a distinction made between some aspects of the thought of Engels and that of Marx, but an attempt is made to establish the contribution which Engels made to Marxism as a philosophy as well as a theory of history. Although Marx and Engels were in essential agreement, many of the final qualifications appended to Marxism as a theory of history came from the pen of Friedrich Engels. The "Darwinian supplement" to Marxism, for example, is almost exclusively Engels' work. There is also good evidence that Engels contributed directly to Marx's increasing concern with political economy during the late forties when the materialist conception of history was being put into its mature form.

Having attempted so much, the book will undoubtedly be found unsatisfactory by some. It is hoped, however, that it will serve as a satisfactory guide to others and that something of value will be found in it for at least the bulk of its readers. Almost the entire text has been directly or indirectly influenced by the work of others. Special acknowledgments should be made to Professors A. G. Meyer, Sidney Hook, Gustav Wetter, J. H. Bocheński, Z. A. Jordan, and S. W. Moore, whose works provide much of the substance of exposition and criticism which have now become standard in the literature. I have attempted to indicate the source of arguments where those arguments are borrowed from a specific authority. Since I can make no claim to special competence in Marxism-Leninism most of that which aspires to originality is to be found in the discussion of classical Marxism.

Acknowledgments should be extended to the members of the Peace Corps to whom I have lectured on Marxism and to those students who have contributed in my seminars in dialectical and historical materialism. Often their searching questions and independent work have suggested interpretations and insights which might otherwise have been missed. Thanks are also due to D. Angus McPherson and Jean McGrath who prepared this text for publication; and finally to my wife, who excised from the manuscript some of its worst literary barbarisms. The work was originally undertaken upon the suggestion of Professor James Gutmann of Columbia University—a good and wise man.

A. JAMES GREGOR

*University of Kentucky*
*Lexington, Kentucky*
*October, 1964*

# Contents

## Part Two   Marxism as a Theory of History

# PART ONE

---

## Marxism as Philosophy

# 1 The Philosophy of the Young Karl Marx

Perhaps no single aspect of Marx scholarship today has aroused more contemporary interest than that devoted to the reconstruction of the thought of the young Karl Marx. The immediate cause of this renewed flurry of academic interest in the philosophy of Marx can be traced to the appearance of the manuscripts he wrote in Paris during the late spring and summer of 1844. These documents have passed into the bibliography of Marxism as the *Economic and Philosophic Manuscripts of 1844*.

After the death of Marx, the Paris manuscripts came into the possession of Engels, but Engels, apparently, was not convinced that they were of interest or importance. Certainly he felt that there were matters more urgent than their publication which demanded his attention. He seemed to consider the Paris documents of only antiquarian interest.[1] Upon his death the manuscripts passed into the archives of the Second International. In 1927 Ryazanov, Director of the Marx-Engels Institute in Moscow, negotiated for their partial publication. They were published in their entirety for the first time in 1932. The advent of National Socialism in Germany and the Second World War precluded most serious discussion of the manuscripts, and it was only with their republication in the postwar period that the academic world undertook a systematic consideration of their content. Now there are countless books and articles analyzing these manuscripts. In 1958 a partial English translation appeared in a volume by Raya

Dunayevskaya,[2] and in 1959 Moscow made a complete English translation available.[3]

The Paris materials are important to Marx scholarship for a number of reasons: (1) They fill a breach in our knowledge of the intellectual history of Karl Marx himself. (2) They document the *values* which Marx entertained at least during the formative years of his revolutionary labors.[4] (3) They shed considerable light on the intellectual relationship between Karl Marx and Friedrich Engels.

Discussion of these manuscripts will, of course, continue. Meanwhile several contesting groups have already emerged: (1) an "orthodox" Marxist-Leninist group which sees the manuscripts as a preamble to the mature Marx, interpreting them in accordance with the established tenets of Soviet Marxism;[5] (2) a "Humanist" group that finds in these manuscripts the "true Marx,"[6] at considerable variance with what has become known as "classical Marxism"; and (3) at least one further contingent, perhaps classifiable as "independent," which sees in these manuscripts evidence of the later Marx, but also unique features that cannot be readily incorporated into Marxism as it has hitherto been known.[7] The discussion within these pages will be of "independent" character, and although there is probably no interpretation which can be considered conclusive, certain elements can be isolated and discussed with some conviction. Finally, the following discussion owes much to the early work of Giovanni Gentile[8] published during the final years of the last century.[9]

### The Intellectual Environment of the Young Marx

Orthodox Hegelianism was committed to the notion that all things in their diversity find their origin in one ultimate source. That ultimate source was, for Hegel, the Absolute. In the effort to explain the diversity of the world of experience Hegel had recourse to a process by which the Absolute could, out of its own intrinsic tensions, produce determinate, although contingent, things. This process he termed the dialectic. He understood it to be the process through which Pure Being gives rise to determinate being. This self-development through categories, the category Pure Being giving rise through its negation (Non-Being) to Becoming, pursues a logic immanent in the Absolute itself. Becoming sublates (*aufhebt*), i.e., abolishes and at the same time preserves on a higher level, Pure Being and Non-Being. This dialectical process, self-differentiation through negation and negation of the negation, continues through more and more determinate categories. The culmination of this process is the Absolute Idea which integrates within itself the entire process through which it attains determinateness. As a stage in this dialectical progression the Absolute as Idea alienates (*entäussert, entfremdet*)[10] itself as the otherness which we come to know as nature. Nature is but a moment in the process toward higher unity and interconnectedness which constitutes the logic of ultimate reality. The Idea returns to itself as Spirit and becomes Absolute Spirit in its final synthesis.

This search for an ultimate reality which contains within itself the motive force of its own development, this attempt to relate all determinate things in the logical nexus of a single Absolute, is the culmination of an intellectual tradition beginning with Kant. It was, perhaps, a search for order in a rapidly changing universe. Whatever it was, it constituted the intellectual patrimony to which the young Karl Marx fell heir. Needless to say, it was an ambiguous legacy. Even before Hegel's death the proponents of Hegelianism each interpreted the Master in accordance with his own lights.[11]

By the time he wrote the Paris *Manuscripts*, Marx himself had already launched a criticism and revision of the philosophy of Hegel. As early as 1837, in his now famous letter to his father,[12] Marx voiced his disquiet with the prevalent philosophical school of his native Germany.[13] His doctoral dissertation, *Difference Between the Democritean and Epicurean Philosophies of Nature* (written in the period from 1839 to 1841), provides evidence that Marx's adherence to Hegelianism was in the process of dissolution. He had become a "Hegelian of the Left." Hegel's Absolute appears in the dissertation only in the garb of "human Self-consciousness."[14] The entire discussion is infused with a Promethean humanism and an almost Romantic peroration to man's self-development rather than the self-development of the Absolute Spirit. Man had become the subject of the dialectical process. Marx came to conceive the developmental process as anthropological rather than ideal.

After the completion of his dissertation in 1841, Marx was occupied with editorial tasks on the *Rheinische Zeitung*, a liberal democratic paper produced in his native Rhineland. Nonetheless, he found the time at the end of 1842 to familiarize himself with the writings of the French Socialists—Fourier, Cabet, Considerant, and Proudhon, probably through the work of Lorenz von Stein.[15] At the end of October, 1843, after the Prussian government obstructed the publication of the *Rheinische Zeitung*, Marx moved to Paris. In Paris he read several essays written by Friedrich Engels and began his study of classical English economy with a detailed reading of the work of Adam Smith.

Such was the intellectual fare of the twenty-six-year-old Karl Marx who in the late spring of 1844 wrote the *Manuscripts*, now so much the focus of attention. He had been, and in part remained, a restive Romantic, a hesitant Hegelian, a convinced democrat—he was an enthusiastic Feuerbachian and a dedicated scholar.

Any effort to interpret the *Economic and Philosophic Manuscripts of 1844* necessarily involves a careful consideration of the impact on the young Marx of the work of Ludwig Feuerbach. That Feuerbach exercised an enormous influence on Marx can no longer be seriously disputed. Not only did Engels recall the far-reaching impact of Feuerbach's ideas on Marx,[16] but Marx himself has left among his published writings explicit references to his commitment to the Humanism of Feuerbach. In January of 1842 he wrote, "There is no other way for you to *truth* and *freedom*, but through a *stream of fire* [a *Feuer-bach*]. Feuerbach is the Purgatory of the present."[17] Moreover *The Holy Family*, written toward the close of 1844, is a defense of Feuerbach's "Real Humanism"[18] against the various Hegelianisms of the period.

## Ludwig Feuerbach and the Young Marx

Marx's reform of the Hegelian dialectic began under the influence of Ludwig Feuerbach and it seems correct to say that "Marx remained, in a certain respect, a disciple of Feuerbach throughout his life."[19] In his preparatory notes for his dissertation Marx singled out a Feuerbachian criticism of idealism which was to provide the basis for his own reform of the Hegelian dialectic. In those notes Marx contended that "common thought always has abstract predicates ready which it has separated from the subject. All philosophers have rendered such predicates subjects."[20]

The full significance of Marx's contention has rarely been appreciated. This theme was to characterize his reform of Hegelianism. Much of the logic of his reform becomes apparent only when this distinctly Feuerbachian tenet is understood.

Feuerbach had advanced the criticism of philosophy in general to which Marx adhered two years before (in 1839) in his critique of Hegelianism.[21] He identified the "inversion" of idealism as the essence of his "revolutionary" philosophy: "We must always render the predicate the subject and, as subject, the object and principle—thereby inverting speculative philosophy to reveal the pure, unvarnished truth."[22]

In essence Feuerbach's reform of Hegelianism turned on the contention that Hegel had reified (*versubjektiviert*) predicates and advanced them as subjects. Speculative thought (either in theology or metaphysics) had progressed only by reifying the attributes of things, by concerning itself with the predicates of things as though they were subjects. All error in speculation arose out of the disposition to abstract qualities and predicates and conceive them as subsistent entities. In religion the attributes of man were reified, shorn of qualification, determinateness, and projected behind the world to become God.[23] "Religion," Feuerbach contended, "is the relation of man to himself, or more correctly to his own nature (i.e., his subjective nature); but a relation to it, viewed as a nature apart from his own. The divine being is nothing else than the human being, or rather, the human nature purified, freed from the limits of the individual man, made objective—i.e., contemplated and revered as another, a distinct being. All the attributes of the divine nature are, therefore, attributes of the human nature."[24] In the worship of the divine being man pays homage to his own attributes projected outward (*entäussert*),[25] lodged now in mystic subsistence.[26] Just as religion sunders man, distinguishing "mere" man and the "divine" man to reunite them in the Godhead, so Hegelian philosophy divests man of his attributes and transposes them into absolute, mystical form, to reunite them in the ultimate Absolute. "The Absolute Spirit of Hegel is nothing other than the finite spirit, abstracted, self-estranged [*von sich selbst abgesonderte*]; just as the infinite Being of theology is nothing other than abstract and finite being."[27] This is the secret (*Geheimnis*), the mystery, of Hegelian speculative philosophy.

Feuerbach's revolutionary reform of theology entailed the reform of the whole of Hegelian philosophy, for he understood speculative philosophy, like theology, as transforming the attributes of man into transcendent subjects, self-subsistent but vacuous.[28] To reveal the true nature of theology and philosophy, Feuerbach held it necessary to expose their mutual "secret." It was necessary to divest the attributes of man of their self-subsistent character and to render them once more determinate traits, predicates, of real subjects.[29] "The essence of theology," Feuerbach held, "is the essence of man made transcendent, set outside man; the essence of the *Logic* of Hegel is human thought made transcendent, set outside man."[30] Predicates had been exalted to self-subsistent subjects (*versubstantialisirt*).[31] The purification of philosophy (and theology as well) required that the predicates be ascribed to *real* subjects. Any alternate course would be a rational mysticism[32] peopled with indeterminate, infinite, and ethereal Beings.

Feuerbach's method of revolutionary reform was to restore Pure Being as a reified subject to the status of a predicate of real beings in space and time.[33] "Philosophy," he argued, "does not rest on an Understanding *per se*, on an absolute, nameless understanding, belonging one knows not to whom, but on the understanding of man. . . . This philosophy has for its principle, not the Substance of Spinoza, not the Ego of Kant and Fichte, not the Absolute Identity of Schelling, not the Absolute Mind of Hegel, in short, no abstract, merely conceptual Being, but a real being, the true *Ens realissimum*—man. . . ."[34] In short, Feuerbach identified his method as the direct opposite (*das direkte Gegenteil*) of that of Hegel.[35]

This reformed Hegelian dialectic became part of the intellectual heritage of the young Karl Marx. In 1844 the twenty-six-year-old Marx was to write, ". . . [It] is only with Feuerbach that *positive*, humanistic and naturalistic criticism begins. . . . Feuerbach's writings [are] the only writings since Hegel's *Phaenomeno-*

*logie* and *Logik* to contain a real theoretical revolution."[36] "Feuerbach is the only one who has a *serious, critical* attitude to the Hegelian dialectic and who has made genuine discoveries in this field. He is in fact the true conqueror of the old philosophy."[37]

Recently Galvano della Volpe has argued that the fundamental premises of Marx's philosophical method, his reform of the Hegelian dialectic, are to be found in the long essay entitled "From the Critique of the Hegelian Philosophy of Right," written in the summer of 1843.[38] Within the text of this manuscript, which remained unpublished until 1927, Marx argued that Hegel had reified predicates and paraded them as subjects. Hegel conceived development as an attribute of the Absolute as consciousness, but consciousness construed as Consciousness, as a subsistent Subject independent of thinking men.[39] The history of the world he conceived as the product of the immanent dialectic of the Absolute Idea—an inversion, according to Marx, of real history, a history standing on its head. Hegel, Marx contended, had reduced to a product, to a predicate of the Idea, that which was actually the subject of history. Man, and not the Idea or Consciousness, was for the young Marx the real principle, the real subject of history.[40] In leveling such criticism Marx reveals himself as a student of Feuerbach.

Marx's treatment of the "patent mystifications"[41] of Hegel's method was, during the years 1842 to 1845, consistently Feuerbachian. At the end of 1843 Marx wrote: "For Germany the critique of religion is essentially finished and the critique of religion is the basis of all critiques. . . . It is the immediate task of philosophy, acting in the service of history, to unmask human self-alienation [*Selbstentfremdung*] in its unholy form now that the holy form of that alienation has been revealed. Thus the criticism of heaven transforms itself into the criticism of earth, the criticism of religion into the criticism of law, and the criticism of theology into the criticism of politics."[42] Feuerbach had undertaken the criticism of religion and theology; Marx assumed the responsibility of the critique of law and politics. During 1843 he announced to Ruge, "Our entire purpose cannot be other than that achieved in Feuerbach's criticism of religion, that religious and political questions be reduced to self-conscious human form. . . . This is the work for the world and for us."[43]

In the criticism of the Hegelian philosophy of right written during that year, the principal features of the reform of the Hegelian dialectic made their appearance. Those features were markedly Feuerbachian. Specifically with respect to the philosophy of the state, Marx argued that for Hegel "the Idea becomes reified [*versubjektiviert*], and the real relationship of the family and civil society to the state becomes conceived as its *inner, imaginary* activity. The family and civil society are the presuppositions of the state; they are the real agents; but in speculation things are inverted. If the Idea becomes reified, then the real subjects, civil society, the family, 'conditions,' 'free will,' etc., become unreal . . . objective moments of the Idea."[44]

About a year later Marx wrote, "If Hegel had commenced with the real subjects as the basis of the state, it would not have been necessary to reify the state in mystic fashion. . . . Hegel reified the predicates. . . . Mystic Substance thereby becomes the subject while the actual subject appears as something else, as a moment of the mystic Substance. Because Hegel begins with predicates in general and not with actual *Ens* [subject] and must find a bearer for these characteristics, the mystic Idea is pressed into service."[45] In the *Manuscripts of 1844* this appears as: "The first [error in Hegel] emerges most clearly in the *Phaenomenologie* . . . [when] for instance, wealth, state-power, etc., are understood by Hegel as entities estranged from the human being. . . . They are thought entities and therefore merely an estrangement of *pure*, i.e., abstract philosophical thinking. . . . The appropriation of man's essential powers, which have become objects—indeed, alien objects—is thus . . . only an *appropriation* occurring in *consciousness*. . . ."[46]

Marx's criticism of Hegel is essentially that of Feuerbach. His words echo what Feuerbach had written in 1842: "Speculative philosophy has seized, in theory, upon the distinction between the essential qualities of men and man himself, and has succeeded in deifying merely abstract qualities as though they were self-existent. . . . Every speculation concerning law, will, liberty, personality outside of man, beyond or above man, is a speculation devoid of unity, of necessity, of substance, of foundation and of reality."[47]

This entire speculative procedure is lampooned by Marx in the *Holy Family*, written in the autumn of 1844, in the section significantly entitled "The Mystery [*Geheimnis*] of Speculative Construction."[48] Within the text of the *Holy Family* Feuerbach is specifically identified as the philosopher who "revealed the mystery of the 'system.' "[49] In the section devoted to "The Critique of the Hegelian Dialectic and Philosophy as a Whole" in the *Manuscripts of 1844*, Marx simply outlines Feuerbach's essential position in treating "the secret of the Hegelian philosophy."[50] The secret is that "Hegel's *Encyclopaedia*, beginning as it does with Logic, with *pure speculative thought*, and ending with *Absolute Knowledge*—with the self-consciousness, self-comprehending, philosophic or absolute (i.e., super-human) abstract mind—is in its entirety nothing but the *display*, the self-objectification, of the *essence* of the philosophic mind, and the philosophic mind is nothing but the estranged mind of the world thinking within its self-estrangement—i.e., comprehending itself abstractly. *Logic* . . . is *alienated* . . . thinking which abstracts from nature and from real man. . . ."[51] The criticism develops in an analysis patently Feuerbachian: "Just as *entities, objects,* appear as *thought entities,* so the *subject* is always *consciousness* or *self-consciousness;* or rather the object appears only as abstract consciousness, man only as *self-consciousness.*"[52] "For Hegel the *essence of man—man*—equals *self-consciousness.*"[53] "It is not *real Man* . . . who as such is made the subject, but only the abstraction of man—self-consciousness."[54] "Real man and real nature become mere predicates—symbols of this esoteric, unreal man and of this unreal nature. Subject and predicate are therefore related to each other in an absolute inversion. . . ."[55]

Thirty years after these criticisms were made, Marx wrote in what sounds like an echo of Feuerbach: "My dialectic method is not only different from the Hegelian, but is its direct opposite [*ihr direktes Gegenteil*]. To Hegel, the life-process of the human brain, i.e., the process of thinking, which under the name of 'the Idea,' he even transforms into an independent subject, is the demiurgos of the real world, and the real world is only the external, phenomenal form of 'the Idea.' With me, on the contrary, the ideal is nothing else than the material world reflected by the human mind, and translated into forms of thought. The mystifying side of Hegelian dialectic I criticized nearly thirty years ago, at a time when it was still the fashion."[56] Written in

1873, this would place the critical years of the reform of the Hegelian dialectic between 1842 and 1845, when Marx was most directly under the influence of Feuerbach.

The Humanism of the young Karl Marx, as it is formulated in the essays of 1843 devoted to the criticism of the Hegelian philosophy of law and the state, in the *Economic and Philosophic Manuscripts of 1844* and in the *Holy Family*, is the positive anthropology of Ludwig Feuerbach. The reform of the Hegelian dialectic, transforming the attributes of the Spirit of speculative philosophy into substantives and its predicates into subjects, is equally Feuerbachian. Man, possessed of all his needs, his sensations, with all his psychological states, man as a person in relation with other persons, distinct from his spirit and in principle distinguished from his general and abstract qualities,[57] is the real subject of philosophy and of history.

Having accepted Feuerbach's analysis, Marx's criticism of his contemporaries turned on their disposition to reify abstractions. His criticism of the Left-Wing Hegelians is that they have made "history . . . a metaphysical subject. . . ."[58] They see "nothing but categories everywhere."[59] Later, in the *Poverty of Philosophy*, he was to level the same charge at Proudhon. Proudhon, "instead . . . of regarding the politico-economic categories as abstractions of the real, transitory, historic social relations . . . thanks to a mystic inversion sees in the real relations only embodiments of these abstractions."[60] By 1847 Marx construed "economic categories [as] only the theoretical expressions, the abstractions of social relations of production. M. Proudhon," Marx went on, "holding things upside down like a true philosopher, sees in actual relations nothing but the incarnation of these principles, of these categories. . . ."[61]

What Marx proposed was a "profane history of the categories,"[62] an effort to "get to the bottom of all these questions . . . to draw up the real, profane history of men in every century and to present these men as both the authors and actors of their own drama."[63] In 1845, in the *German Ideology*, Marx had undertaken to give history a profane, an "earthly" basis, to "bring out empirically, and without any mystification and speculation, the connection of the social and political structure with production."[64] The mystification and speculation to which Marx referred was that consequent upon "all ideology" to see men and their circumstances "upside down as in a *camera obscura*. . . ."[65] In 1843 Engels had indicated that "this inversion is the essence of abstraction. . . ."[66] This was the "mysticism" of German Idealism —and, as Marx frequently points out in this period, it was "Feuerbach, who was the first to describe philosophy as speculative and mystic empirics and proved it to be so."[67]

The development of the profane history of the abstractions which Hegelianism had made the active agents, the self-moving subjects of history, was to occupy Marx for the remainder of his life. In the preparatory notes for the *Contribution to the Critique of Political Economy*, compiled between 1857 and 1859, Marx outlined his dialectic method in a section entitled "The Method of Political Economy."[68] The principal distinction he drew was between the "concrete categories" of his method and the "abstract categories" of Hegel. As long as the study of history, of society, and of political economy proceeds from abstract categories, these categories appear as mystic Subjects, self-subsistent and active outside of man. Real events make their appearance only as derivatives, as the consequence of their mystic and speculative activity. How much influenced Marx's mature work was by this Feuerbachian method, this "inversion" of the Hegelian dialectic, is revealed in the section entitled "The Fetishism of Commodities and the Secret Thereof" in the first volume of *Capital*, published in 1867. The very language of the section recalls the locutions of Feuerbach's criticism of Hegelianism and of theology. As long as the concept "commodity" is employed in an abstract fashion it remains a "mysterious thing."[69] ". . . [A] definite social relation between men . . . assumes . . . the fantastic form of a relation between things. In order . . . to find an analogy, we must have recourse to the mist-enveloped regions of the religious world. In that world the productions of the human brain appear as independent beings endowed with life, [which enter] into relation both with one another and the human race.[70] . . . The categories of bourgeois economy consist of such like forms."[71]

The basis of Marx's reform of the Hegelian dialectic is found in the work of Feuerbach. Even if it were not evident in an analysis of Marx's mature works, Marx indicates as much in the Paris *Manuscripts of 1844*. Feuerbach's central criticism, as Marx understood it in that formative period, was that Hegel had "only found the *abstract, logical, speculative* expression for the movement of history."[72] It was Feuerbach who undertook "the establishment of *true materialism* and of *real science,* since Feuerbach . . . makes the social relationship 'of man to man' the basic principle of the theory. . . ."[73]

Only a "natural scientific" study of the social relations which obtain between men could provide the basis for the ultimate study of the "social relations of productivity," which develop "in conformity with . . . material productivity" to produce the "principles, ideas and categories" which are the "historical and transitory products" to which men have hitherto looked for a speculative explanation of the dynamics of human history.[74] This constituted the reform of the Hegelian dialectic in its social key. Hegel had "mystified" the laws governing social processes by reifying the state, property, civil society, and the will as abstract categories. The real dialectic of society was to be found in the relationship of real persons and groups. Real men in their real relations constitute the real foundation of the state and of society. The concrete study of these relationships permits the articulation of concrete categories, "reflections" of real relations and objective processes in the mind of man.[75] "History ceases to be a collection of dead facts . . . or an imagined activity of imagined subjects. . . ."[76] Marx sought to "set out from real, active men, and on the basis of their real life-process [to] demonstrate the development of the ideological reflexes and echoes of this life process. The phantoms formed in the human brain" he understood as "sublimates of their material life process. . . ."[77]

The young Marx had commenced with Feuerbach's criticism of theology and speculative metaphysics and had pursued the criticism into the philosophy of the state, society, and political economy. He had identified Feuerbach's criticism of religion as "the basis of all criticism." Marx's criticism of Feuerbach in the "Theses on Feuerbach" of 1845 was not of his method but rather of his narrow enterprise. "Feuerbach starts out from the fact of religious self-estrangement, of the duplication of the world into a religious and a secular one. His work consists in resolving the religious world into its secular basis. But that the secular basis raises itself above itself and establishes for itself an independent realm in the clouds can be explained only through the cleavage and self-contradictions within this secular basis. The latter must therefore in itself be both understood in its contradiction and revolutionized in practice."[78] Thus Marx, with his inversion of the dialectic, sought the secular basis for the abstract categories of Hegel. In so doing he remained faithful to Feuerbach's method but extended its application to the secular base in its entirety. The reification of predicates and attributes into self-subsistent categories, behaving like self-moving subjects in the abstract world of Hegelian metaphysics, became concrete social relations.

The young Marx remained faithful to the form of the Hegelian dialectic, but divested it of its idealist, abstract, and speculative content.[79] For that content he substituted the real relations of real men, an "inversion" first undertaken by Feuerbach. Man, instead of being the product, the attribute of the Absolute Idea, becomes in his real relations the producer of ideas. Social relations were understood to "move," to develop as a consequence of their inherent "contradictions." Within the process, components were "negated" only to be "negated" themselves in the subsequent "negation of the negation." Hegelian formulas appear and reappear in the mature writings of Marx, but they are always advanced from the empirically given to abstract generalization to "lawful" formulation.[80]

The reformation of the Hegelian dialectic was thus, in substantial part, the consequence of Feuerbach's positive criticism. The naturalism of Feuerbach conceived men to be the only real subject of the "alienated" and general traits reified in the abstractions of speculative Hegelianism.[81] He understood the world task of the future to be the creation of a critical philosophy which would restore to men their alienated selves and free them from illusions of their own fabrication.[82] It was to be a philosophy that would make of politics a religion: "We must once again become religious—politics must become our religion—but we can succeed in this only if we have an Ultimate in view which can make of our politics a religion."[83] The Ultimate for man was to be man. Marx shared the Feuerbachian vision, for the young Marx held that "the only liberation of Germany that is practical or possible is a liberation defined by the theory that declares man to be the supreme being of mankind."[84] The essentials of Feuerbach's method were to remain with Marx for a lifetime; Feuerbach's vision was to give meaning to his life's labor.

### The Natural Philosophy of the Young Marx

Feuerbach had undertaken the reform of the Hegelian dialectic. This reform had entailed a process of "absolute inversion." The *subjects* of Hegel's mystic dialectic were once more to become the *predicates* of real things. Among Hegel's metaphysical subjects was numbered the broadest and most indeterminate category, that of Pure Being. Feuerbach proposed to restore philosophy to health by reducing abstract Being to the status of concrete, determinate being,[85] in a natural world of human sensuous experience. Philosophy was to begin in the first instance with that which was not philosophical at all[86]—in simple sense perceptions[87] out of which arose the ever-changing distinctions between subject and object.[88] He contended that one must begin with the reality of human sensory experience[89] rather than abstract Being. Such a beginning, he held, obviates the necessity of deriving "otherness" out of "oneself." For the natural concept of self arises out of something other than self. Without such a beginning one is condemned to *remain forever within the confines of the ego.*[90] This ego is then reified to become the Ego of Fichte or the Absolute of Hegel. The Ego then becomes the creator of the world. It was against this exalted Ego that Feuerbach was to contend. The relationship, Feuerbach argued, between the real ego and the objects in its world is reciprocal. The real ego is limited, defined by its encounter with the object which is other than itself, just as the object is determined by the ego.[91] Both arise out of primary sensory experience.

According to Feuerbach, idealism since Kant had been persistently concerned with the abstract and reified Ego as the real and active agent in the cognitive process. The Ego's task was, if not to create the world, then to prescribe intelligible Forms or Categories which make knowledge possible. Feuerbach imagined himself restoring a "natural equilibrium" between the "objective" and "subjective" elements of experience. Feuerbach held that idealist metaphysics and epistemology advanced the ego as an active agent only because it concerned itself with an ego made transcendent and divine. For the real ego, the natural self, is much of the time plainly passive. Hegel, for example, played with the concept "here" in typically idealist fashion.[92] "Here" may be a tree, an object of sensory experience. The subject turns himself about and this "truth" has vanished! The tree is no longer "here." But it has vanished only for Hegel in his *Phenomenology*, where its dispatch costs but a word in a world of abstract forms. In reality the tree continues to stand behind one; to assure oneself of the fact one need but step back![93] The tree limits the *real* ego's free activity—it acts as an agent against which the real ego is, in at least one sense, passive. It is passive in that in sensuous activity one can no more deny the reality of the tree than one can deny the reality of oneself. Sense experience, which does not follow the dictates of our caprice,[94] cannot be denied. We cannot deny the fact that we find ourselves cast in a world wherein we are constrained to labor with the materials at hand.[95]

Hence, it is *practice*, real sensuous experience, which restores philosophy to health. The perplexities which abstract speculation creates are only resolved by practice[96] in the *real* world. To restore vitality to philosophy one must make it "unphilosophical."[97] One must carry it down into the arena of everyday affairs, into practical life.[98] Philosophy must become the intimate concern of mankind. For it is man's suffering which is eloquent testimony to his participation in a world of real being.[99] That man suffers, recognizes the "objective world" as a limit to be overcome, indicates that *real* relations can be established between the "subjective" and "objective" elements of experience. That such relations can exist indicates that they share the same "Being," Nature.[100] Man can operate in nature because he is essentially a natural being.[101] This is the extent of Feuerbach's "realism," his carefully defined "materialism."[102]

Out of the world of sensory experience, thought distinguishes itself; thought is a predicate of being.[103] One might, however, with equal warrant say that matter, too, is a predicate of being because the abstract *concept* "matter" (like the concept "thought") arises only as distinct from that which is other than itself.[104] For Feuerbach was as far removed from materialism as from subjective idealism.[105] Truth lies in neither materialism nor subjective idealism, but in *Man*, in whom all contraries are resolved and contained;[106] man is the secret of philosophy—not man as individual—but Man as species,[107] as universal. The essential nature of the species determines what is true and real.[108] Man, for Feuerbach, is the measure.[109] In avoiding the extreme of subjective idealism one must be equally chary of the extreme of uncritical "objectivism," conceiving sensory experience as a simple "contemplation" of a material world. Man provides the measure of the natural world; the measure of natural philosophy is the human essence.[110]

In order to act in nature man must share with it a common essence. From this it follows that "objects" cannot manifest themselves to the "subject" unless both are conceived as somehow sharing a common unity. Thus every experience with the real world, first conceived as a coming together of mutually independent subject and object in sensation, reveals itself as a process of correlative differentiation through which object and subject distinguish themselves. "In the object which he contemplates therefore, man becomes acquainted with himself; consciousness of the objective is the self-consciousness of man. We know man by the object, by his conception of what is external to himself; in it his nature becomes evident; this object is his manifested nature, his true objective ego; and this is true not merely of spiritual but also of sensuous objects."[111] The "objective world" is "nothing else but the subject's own, but objective nature."[112] Thus every sensory experience with the natural world is an essential expression of self,[113] a "self-alienation."

All the predicates one assigns to nature are ultimately determinations of qualities drawn from one's own nature—qualities in which one, in truth, only projects oneself.[114] Thus the proposition may be applied, "without any limitation . . . the object of any subject is nothing else than the subject's own nature taken objectively."[115]

Each species is for itself the standard. The lifespan of an ephemera is, to us, brief; to the ephemera it is as long as life of years to others. The leaf on which the caterpillar lives is for it a universe, an infinity.[116] But we are conscious of the limitations of the lower order of beings because we are beings of a higher order.[117] We cannot be similarly aware of our own limitations since such an awareness would require that we transcend experience. To speculate upon a "reality" outside, or behind, experience is a vain pursuit.[118] It is a scholastic residual. For the "world-in-itself," the world "independent of sensory experience" is a nonsensical world, without substance and meaning.[119] Man is the

measure of the truth and substance of his world. In the history of
the species this truth and this substance will alter as the complexity of real sensory relations fosters a more complex and intricate world. For an object reveals itself only when one enters into
a real relationship with it.[120] It comes into determinate being as
a consequence of the real sensuous activity of the subject.

A felt need[121] generates a passion[122] which motivates activity
in the search for satisfaction. Objects are defined in the course
of this sensory activity. They are real because they answer an
essential need.[123] Objects confirm the essence and characteristics
of the subject; man establishes a real connection with the real
world when he satisfies a need through his activity. The object
world, then, is a "product" of that activity; nature is provided
determinate qualities. Reality becomes human reality, for only
that is real which is the "product" of man's sensory activity.[124] To
men of limited needs, hence limited sensibilities, the world is cor-
respondingly limited.[125]

The entire process of coming to know the world is a "self-
alienation" (*Selbstentfremdung*), a "self-projection" (*Selbstentäusserung*), a process with which German Idealism had familiar-
ized philosophy. But for Feuerbach it is not the Spirit which
objectifies itself as nature; it is the essence of man as a sensuous
being. Problems are posed by the essential needs of man, solutions
are sought and resolved in activity. Objects which satisfy those
essential needs are real objects.

The early philosophy of Feuerbach was neither materialist
nor idealist. It was a form of radical Humanism. Man is the secret
of the world; his essence is its truth and its reality.[126] His essence
objectified is science and religion. Man projects himself upon the
world and then comes upon his traces everywhere.[127] This was
the philosophy of nature, the revision of German Idealism, which
Feuerbach gave to the young Karl Marx. In it are discernible a
Humanism, the immanence of science and religion in Man, and an
emphasis on sensory practice in the dialectical process of human
self-realization, which make of it a naturalism incorporating
features of the idealism which it rejects.

Our purpose here is not to make this philosophy credible or to
search out its implications and dissect its metaphors. It is to outline a philosophical position, held by Feuerbach at a specific
period of his development, in order to understand the philosophy

of the young Karl Marx in 1844 and 1845. What should be noted here is the central role of the analysis of sensation, by which Feuerbach sought to avoid the egocentric predicament which he felt forever haunted idealism. Sensuous activity establishes a *real* connection between subject and object, a relationship in which both subject and object mutually define themselves. That such a connection is possible indicates, for Feuerbach, that subject and object share a common essence: Nature.[128] Both are limited, concrete entities. Universals, like Mind and Matter, are functions of an abstract summing up of real particulars. Without a tolerably accurate account of Feuerbach's position it is difficult, if not impossible, to understand the position of the young Marx. We have given a summary account of Feuerbach's "Humanism"—it remains for us to trace its influence in the philosophical labors of Karl Marx during the years 1843 to 1845.

The young Karl Marx enthusiastically made the philosophy of Feuerbach his own. He was to defend it during the most critical formative period of his life. For Marx it was Feuerbach who had given Germany the promise of liberation, the only thinker who had advanced a serious criticism of Hegelian Idealism. Echoing Feuerbach, Marx maintained that philosophy must cease its preoccupation with the *Idea*, the *abstract*, the *Spirit*, and must return to the *concrete*.[129] By virtue of its embroilment in the abstract, philosophy had left real human beings in real situations out of its ken.[130] It had been Feuerbach, Marx contended, who had rendered it impossible for philosophy to remain any longer in the heaven of speculation and had compelled it to step down to the depth of human misery.[131] For it is in the real *practice*, which arises out of need and passion,[132] that the problems born of speculation find their resolution.[133]

What is important to note is that Marx is concerned essentially with the *content* of philosophy and not with its method. The entire discussion in the "Critique of the Hegelian Dialectic and Philosophy as a Whole," in the *Economic and Philosophic Manuscripts of 1844*, concerns itself with the *content* of the Hegelian dialectic, not with a critique of the *method* itself. Marx's objection is that the Hegelian dialectic is concerned with *abstract self-consciousness* and not with *real men*.[134]

Man is a limited, concrete, natural entity, subject to needs and engaged in real activity to fulfill those needs.[135] That his needs can be met is evidence of a community of essence between needy man and nature as a source of satisfaction. His needs compel man to real, sensuous activity and in that activity man *creates (erzeugt)* an objective world.[136] But since man is goaded into establishing real relations in the world of nature by need, the object which fulfills that need makes manifest some element of the essence of man.[137] Man finds himself "objectified" in things. Once understood, this thesis reveals nature to us as something sharing a common essence with man.[138] Knowledge of the character of the real connections established in nature protects us from betraying ourselves to materialism *or* idealism. "Nature, conceived abstractly, in itself, fixed in its separation from man, is *nothing* for man."[139] "Reality" is rather, for the young Marx, a "product" of human activity, a product not of Spirit but of sensuous activity.[140] For neither objective nature nor subjective nature are simply *given;*[141] they become distinguished only in practice.[142] To know "reality" one must know man. Man, therefore, is the "secret" of Marx's early epistemology.

This humanistic naturalism resolves, according to Marx, the perplexities of materialism and idealism.[143] Subject and object are continually distinguishing themselves in sensuous practice. The object does not stand as an independent, substantial entity against consciousness; the actuality of the one defines the other.[144] Nature, reality, will be just as complex as are the essential, sensuous activities of man.[145] The implications of such a philosophical position are relatively clear. There is no reality independent of man as species being (*Gattungswesen*). Reality can only be a reality-for-man. Man-in-himself and nature-in-itself are abstract, negative moments of concrete nature.[146] An object without the subject is as inconceivable as the subject without the object.[147] To speculate upon such "being-in-itself" is to speculate meaninglessly.[148] Thought and being, subject and object, are a unity,[149] wedded in sensuous practice, separated only in abstraction. An "ultimate" reality, an "objective" reality is unattainable. An "objective" world would be a meaningless world, for nothing of man would be reflected there. To be known, a world must be a human world, man's "self-projection."

Man dialectically "objectifies" himself in nature, whose essence he shares. He comes to understand the "objective world" because that world is essentially his own creation. "In the working up of the objective world . . . nature appears as his work and his reality. The object of labor is, therefore, the objectification of man's species life: for he duplicates himself not only, as in consciousness, intellectually, but also actively, in reality, and therefore he contemplates himself in a world that he has created."[150]

Within the compass of such a system, truths are relative, determined by the needs and social circumstances of men. As society increases in complexity, and practical experiences multiply, reality becomes more intricate and varied. In place of the passive contemplation of the object which for materialism is the first stage in cognition, the young Marx, following Feuerbach's revisionist program, substituted the dialectic of human sensuous activity. The object can only be understood subjectively, through a comprehensive understanding of the active role of the sensing subject in its determination. Marx proposed to retain the Hegelian dialectic, substituting for its abstract content "real sensuous activity as such." With the discarded abstract content went the universal and infinite Absolute, as Idea and as Spirit. The true subject of the dialectic was man, man conceived as a limited, determinate sensuous entity among equally limited and determinate natural entities.

Such an interpretation makes Marx's obscure first thesis on Feuerbach[151] comprehensible. The "objective world" is not simply "given," but must rather be conceived as a "self-alienation." It is not an alienation of the Idea; it is an alienation which is the consequence of the dialectic of sensuous practice.

We have reconstructed here, in summary form, the metaphysics of the young Marx—relating the philosophy of Marx to his Hegelian and Feuerbachian heritage. Should our exposition and interpretation be correct, it would indicate that Marx's differences with Feuerbach, at the time of the writing of the "Theses on Feuerbach" (1845), were more differences of emphasis than emphatic differences. The young Marx had assumed a position that was certainly more advanced than that of Feuerbach. This is evident even in the *Economic and Philosophic Manuscripts,* where Marx still held himself to be an "orthodox" Feuerbachian. But only when the philosophy of Feuerbach is understood (to the extent to which it is understandable) does Marx's position in the *Manuscripts* become intelligible.

## The Concept of Alienation in the Philosophy of Marx

The discussion of the concept of "alienation" or "estrangement" has only begun. While significant and interesting treatments have been forthcoming, there has been no universal agreement among scholars as to the ultimate role the concept plays in Marxism as a system. The concept functions in many ways in the work of the young Marx and reappears in the manuscripts on which Marx was working when he died.[152] Its use in the early writings is vague and ambiguous. Certainly the interpretation here will be tentative and subject to correction. What can be said with some assurance at this point is that the concept of "alienation" is of fundamental importance in the early writings and that the use of the concept is critical in the maturation of Marx's thought. It can be further said that the concept markedly changes as an explanatory device during the quarter century in which Marx employs it. Any simple treatment of "estrangement" based only on the Paris *Manuscripts of 1844*, as though these documents contained the final essence of Marx's thought, is in error.[153]

Alienation as a concept is rooted in the vastness of German Idealism. In Hegel it shoulders an enormous theoretical load. In the context of his general speculative cosmology, alienation is a descriptive title designating the universal process through which the Idea articulates itself as "nature."[154] The creative life of the Spirit is an activity of self-externalization (*Selbstentäusserung*) by which it takes on objective form. The subject of this process is the Absolute Spirit. Alienation is a necessary process, a logical presupposition of the development of the world.[155] The Spirit as conscious subject, as man, becomes aware of this externalization as "alienation." The external world is experienced as an alien and hostile thing, something opposed to the empirical self. But self-estrangement is transcended (*aufgehoben*) through the realization that the empirical self and the objective world are but moments in the all-embracing, self-subsistent life of the Spirit.[156] This, without doing too much violence to the purport of Hegelianism, might well be termed the metaphysical or ontological dimension of alienation or estrangement.[157] It seems to function as a logically necessary antecedent to development. Since Spirit is one, if there is to be development at all, Spirit must posit the "other than Spirit" out of itself in a "self-estrangement."[158] "The very essence of Spirit is activity; it realizes its potentiality—makes itself its own deed, its own work—and thus it becomes an object to itself: contemplates itself as an objective existence."[159]

The ultimate fulfillment of the Spirit is mediated through the consciousness and will of empirical men.[160] There is thus in history a dimension of alienation which is "empirical."[161] These two dimensions of estrangement seem to possess diverse emotional saliences. Hegel attaches little, if any, negative connotation to the process of the self-estrangement of the Absolute Spirit for such estrangement is necessary if development is to take place at all.[162] Alienations, on the other hand, which afflict men in the course of their history engender what is referred to in the *Phenomenology of Mind* as the "unhappy consciousness" of self-estrangement.[163]

There can be distinguished then, for the purposes of our discussion, at least two dimensions of alienation: (1) the self-estrangement, through logical categories, of the Spirit as a metaphysical process, and (2) the empirical estrangements which involve the consciousness of men as actors in history. As long as a Hegelian Idealism is maintained there seems to be little difficulty in maintaining the distinction between the two dimensions of alienation. The metaphysical process of self-estrangement through logical categories has the Absolute Spirit as its subject. But with the inversion of the Hegelian dialectic, the Idea, the abstract, sacred Subject is recognized as an alienation itself. Man has projected his species traits into a "pure" realm of logic and sees development as the movement of categories.

For Feuerbach, and the young Marx, "Man was the true subject. . . ."[164] This we have identified as the essence of the reform of the Hegelian dialectic. This technique of critical revision, or revolutionary inversion, begun as early as 1841, was consistently and explicitly employed by the young Marx after 1844. In the *Poverty of Philosophy*, for example, instances of its application abound.[165] In his letter to P. V. Annenkov, in December, 1846, Marx specifically identified the treatment of "estranged predicates," "abstractions," and "categories" as "self-moving subjects" as "entirely mystical," as "old Hegelian junk," and a "mystic inversion."[166]

Since Marx made real men the true subject of history, the

cosmic objectifications of the Spirit which constituted the world of empirical things, the alienations in the metaphysical realm, have no home. The alienations and objectifications which Hegel ascribed to the life-activity of the Spirit could only be ascribed to the "true subject" of history, man himself. So, for Feuerbach and Marx, man, not Spirit, *was objectified in nature*. Nature was the unity in which man defined himself through objects—objects which were self-objectifications. The objects of the external world are "objectifications," "self-projections"—objects only when they answer felt needs, when the feelings and passions of men are motivated to seek fulfillment. As Marx articulated this reform of the ontological dimension of Hegelian alienation: ". . . [Man's] *feelings*, passions, etc., are not merely anthropological phenomena in the narrower sense, but truly *ontological* affirmations of essential being. . . . "[167]

In effect Marx abandoned the mystic Subject of Hegel, the Absolute Spirit, and found himself faced with the necessity of providing some plausible account of how development proceeds through concepts and categories. Marx was to come to understand these concepts and categories as logical abstractions "grown entirely indifferent to all real determinateness,"[168] distinct from the particular "forms of existence."[169] The "only substance left"[170] after such abstraction is the ethereal logical stuff of German Idealism, the concepts and the categories. These categories, abstractions from real particulars, are somehow conceived to be logically prior to the particulars by which they are exemplified.[171] What resulted from such a conception was the creation of a metaphysical world from which the world of particular things was derived. Particular things were but aspects of some sort of subsistent metaphysical entities, the empirical working out of abstract concepts.

This analysis of Hegelian categories and concepts *concluded* the period between 1841 and 1845. When the *Manuscripts of 1844* were written this process of clarification was not yet complete. These *Manuscripts* therefore contain residual Hegelianisms. One such residual is Marx's treatment of the *concept* of alienation. Marx continued to speak the Hegelian language and referred to "alienation" as though it were something in some sense prior to the specific forms of alienation which are the product of human enterprise in the empirical world. In the *Manuscripts of 1844* Marx commits himself to a conception of a universal and logically prior alienation from which all empirical alienations derive. He uses the concept of alienation in a broad, generic sense, as a "logical concept" which identifies the process by which man objectifies himself as a species being and thereby creates his world. When Marx tells us that "the object of labor is . . . the objectification of man's species life . . . and therefore he contemplates himself in a world that he has created,"[172] and that "labor is only an expression of human activity within alienation . . . ,"[173] he is obviously using "alienation" as an abstract or metaphysical category in much the same way that Hegel might, as something logically prior to its particular, empirical manifestations.

Thus, there remains in the *Manuscripts of 1844* a "logical concept" of "alienation" which designates the undifferentiated activity, or labor itself, by means of which man objectifies himself and creates his world. The young Marx conceived man's sensuous activity as having the same developmental and dialectical character which Hegel had attributed to the Absolute as Idea and Spirit. "Alienation" is human activity in which "man becomes objective for himself and at the same time becomes to himself a strange and inhuman object . . ."[174] Man has objectified himself in nature and then faces that objective nature as though it were an alien reality. The young Marx refers to that alien reality as "private property."[175] Thus Marx sought to explain the origins of "private property" in its limited, determinate sense, as employed by political economy, by relating it to the broad and abstract "private property" which was a product of metaphysical or ontological alienation. Specific alienation in economic property was the "necessary consequence of alienated labor, of the external relation of the worker to nature . . ."[176] "Alienated labor," activity within alienation, produces "private property" in the undifferentiated or abstract sense. "All human activity hitherto has been labor —that is, industry. . . ."[177] This activity, this "industry" produces, through alienation, the objective world which man conceives as "external." Once the product of his own enterprise is conceived as "external," its alienation in the ordinary sense becomes possible. "Private property," as it is ordinarily used in political economy, exemplifies only one specific form of the *concept* "alienation." Marx conceived "private property" in this limited, economic sense as a consequence of alienated labor, in its abstract or generic sense—"it results by analysis from the concept of alienated labor. . . ."[178]

Marx felt that this kind of analysis, Hegelian in its principal features, answered the fundamental question concerning private property: "How is this estrangement rooted in the nature of human development?"[179] The concept of "alienated labor" seems to refer to human sensuous activity as such. Its product, objective reality, is then spoken of as "private property" in a similarly broad or ontological sense. This "alienation" is "rooted in the nature of human development." It is the logical presupposition of human development itself. Only in such an analysis would it make sense to say: "Private property is thus the product, the result, the necessary consequence of alienated labor, of the external relation of the worker to nature and to himself. Private property thus results by analysis from the concept of alienated labor—i.e., of alienated man, of estranged labor, of estranged life, of estranged man. True, it is as a result of the movement of private property that we have obtained the concept of alienated labor (of alienated life) from political economy. But on analysis of this concept it becomes clear that though private property appears to be the source, the cause of alienated labor, it is really its consequence. . . ."[180]

For the young Marx the alienation spoken of in political economy is only understood when it is seen as an empirical expression of the broad and indeterminate concept of alienation which is in some sense its presupposition. Marx himself realized that the treatment of the empirical alienation of property through the "concept of alienated labor" was Hegelian. "The outstanding thing in Hegel's *Phenomenology* and its final outcome—that is, the dialectic of negativity as the moving and generating principle—is thus first that Hegel conceives the self-genesis of man as a process, conceives objectification as loss of the object, as alienation and as transcendence of this alienation; that he thus grasps the essence of *labor* and comprehends objective man—true, because real man— as the outcome of man's own labor. The *real*, active orientation of man to himself as a species being, or his manifestation as a real species being (i.e., as a human being), is only possible by his really bringing out of himself all the powers that are his as the *species* man—something which in turn is only possible by man's treating these generic powers as objects: and this, to begin with, is again only possible in the form of estrangement. . . . Let us provisionally say just this much in advance: Hegel's standpoint is that of modern political economy. He grasps *labor* as the *essence* of man—as man's *essence* in the act of proving itself: he sees only the positive, not the negative side of labor."[181]

Man objectifies himself, alienates himself as an objective world. The very objective world he creates becomes a strange and alien object: private property. This is the positive alienation—conceivably the "free private property" to which the young Marx obscurely refers.[182] Marx is apparently using "private property" in a broad, undifferentiated sense, something quite other than private property in the narrow sense of political economy. This is evident when he speaks of the *positive* transcendence of private property. ". . . [The] positive transcendence of private property— i.e., the *sensuous* appropriation for and by man of the human essence and of human life, of objective man, of human *achievements* —is not to be conceived merely in the sense of *direct*, one-sided *gratification*—merely in the sense of *possessing*, of *having*. Man appropriates his total essence in a total manner, that is to say, as a whole man. . . . The transcendence of private property is therefore the complete *emancipation* of all human senses and attributes; but it is this emancipation precisely because these senses and attributes have become, subjectively and objectively, human. The eye has become a *human* eye, just as its object has become a social, *human*, object—an object emanating from man for man."[183]

This *positive* transcendence is a complete emancipation of all human senses and attributes and cannot refer to private property in the narrow sense employed in economics. That the young Marx has something like this broad positive dimension of alienation in mind is evidenced by the fact that the transcendence of alienation in political economy through the annulment of private property by collective ownership, Communism as such, is only a preliminary to the next and final stage of man's liberation. "Communism is the position as the negation of the negation and is hence the *actual* phase necessary for the next stage of historical development in the process of human emancipation and recovery. *Communism* is the necessary pattern and the dynamic principle of the immediate future, but Communism as such is not the goal of human development. . . ."[184] Thus the young Marx conceived the liberation of man much more broadly than is generally conceded. "*Communism, as fully developed naturalism, equals humanism, and as fully developed humanism equals naturalism;* it is the *genuine* resolution of the conflict between man and nature and between man and man—the true resolution of the strife between man and man—the true resolution of the strife between existence and essence, between objectification and self-confirmation, between freedom and necessity, between the individual and the species."[185]

Among the notes Marx committed to his notebook in 1845 is this fragment: "The transcendence [*Aufhebung*] of *Estrangement* is identified with the transcendence of objectivity (one side developed by Feuerbach). One's *transcendence* of the given object, of the object as the object of consciousness, [is] identified with the *real objective* transcendence, sensuous *action, practice* and *real activity* which distinguishes itself from thought (to be developed)."[186] The subject of the self-genesis of man is man, rather than the Spirit, as it is in Hegel. But the process is the same: "individuals always project themselves outward [*von sich ausgegangen*], they forever go out of themselves. Their relationships are relationships of their real life processes."[187] In such a context the transcendence of estrangement is identified with the transcendence of objectivity itself. Such a transcendence is achieved through *Communism as a fully developed humanism.*

The tentative interpretation tendered here would suggest that Marx used the terms "alienation," "labor," "economy," "industry," "mode of production," and "private property" in vague and ambiguous ways.[188] There is certainly some evidence that one use of "alienation" as a broad and abstract concept carries in its train an array of equally broad and abstract usages with respect to "industry," "labor," and "private property." Within the general and undifferentiated concept of alienation there are specific empirical alienations. Some of these alienations are described in political economy. "We have considered the act of estranging practical human activity, labor, in two of its aspects: (1) The relation of the worker to the *product of labor* as an alien object exercising power over him. *This relation is at the same time the relation to the sensuous external world, to the objects of nature as an alien world antagonistically opposed to him.* (2) The relation of labor to the *act of production* within the *labor* process. This relation is the relation of the worker to his own activity as an alien activity not belonging to him; it is activity as suffering, strength as weakness, begetting as emasculating, the worker's *own* physical and mental energy, his personal life or what is life other than activity—as an activity which is turned against him, neither depends on nor belongs to him. Here we have *self-estrangement*, as we had previously the estrangement of the thing."[189] A third aspect of estranged labor is "deduced" from the precedent two.[190] Since all of nature is "man's inorganic body," estrangement of man estranges him from his *species life*. This estrangement leads to his estrangement from other men. And the ultimate estrangement of man from man leads to private property in the narrow sense employed by political economy: ". . . [The] product of labor does not belong to the worker . . . it confronts him as an alien power, this can only be because it belongs to *some other man than the worker*."[191] Thus we see, the young Marx concludes, "how in real life the *concept* of estranged *alienated labor* must express and present itself."[192] Through successive applications of a concept from the more general or abstract realm to the immediate, empirical realm, Marx has shown how a concept presents itself in real life.[193] Unfortunately, the successive applications, and the successive meanings of the term, all bear the identification "alienation" or "estrangement." These successive definitions do not bear identifying subscripts or identifying adjectives. Apparently Marx inherited this technique from Hegelianism, abandoning it only after considerable critical reformulation.

There seems to be a real confusion in the *Manuscripts of 1844* and only in 1845 was critical reassessment undertaken. In the spring of 1845 Engels and Marx resolved to "settle accounts with [their] erstwhile philosophical conscience"—to seek "self-clarification."[194] Their enterprise resulted in two large octavo volumes, which remained unpublished until 1932[195] when they appeared as the *German Ideology*.

In the *German Ideology* Marx undertook a concerted effort to concretize the formal abstractions of German Idealism. He sought to establish his revolutionary world-view on the sure foundation of empirical assessment rather than abstract derivation. In the *Manuscripts of 1844* this program was as yet incomplete. His specific charge against the Hegelians was that they "*comprehended* everything as soon as it was reduced to an Hegelian logical category."¹⁹⁶ They understood history as the imagined activity of imagined subjects and their analysis of empirical reality rested not on "existing empirical data," but on the implications of a "concept."¹⁹⁷ In the *German Ideology* the young Marx sought to provide an "earthly" basis for human history, to trace man's history empirically without recourse to the metaphysical concepts and categories of the old and new Hegelians. In the critical treatment of Idealism Marx eschewed treating history through *"categories,"* abandoning even the Feuerbachian category of the "essence of man,"¹⁹⁸ which figured so prominently in the Paris documents. What he had called the "category of alienated labor" received the same treatment.

The "materialist" assessment of history commences with "real" premises: men must produce in order to live; they must reproduce in order to maintain the species; and, as production increases, a division of labor (originally no more than a division of labor in the sexual act) arises on the basis of the natural distinctions among men—differences in predisposition, needs, accidents, and so forth. "This division of labor implies the possibility, indeed the fact, that intellectual and material activity—enjoyment and labor, production and consumption—devolve on different individuals," different classes. "The division of labor and private property are . . . identical expressions," for "with the division of labor . . . is given simultaneously the distribution, and indeed the unequal distribution (both quantitative and qualitative), of labor and its products, hence property. . . ." *Out of these conditions arises "estrangement," "alienation."*¹⁹⁹ The order indicated in the Paris *Manuscripts* is reversed. The division of labor, private property, *causes* alienation. What had been a logical or speculative presupposition in the *Manuscripts* became, in the *German Ideology*, an attempt at empirical analysis, for history "does not have to look for a *category*."²⁰⁰ In the *Communist Manifesto* of 1848 Marx was to mock the "true socialists" who conceived the real activity of political economy in terms of the abstract category, "Alienation of Humanity."²⁰¹

His mockery is evidence of a genuine re-evaluation of his own position of 1844. In Marx's notebooks we find a fragment in which the transition from the abstract treatment of "alienation" as a category is reduced to the empirical assessment of fact. "How is it possible," he asks critically in 1845, "that man's relations become relations standing opposed to him? that the powers of his own life threaten to overpower him? In one word: *the division of labor*, the level of which depends upon the correlative development of the productive forces."[202]

After the critical reassessment of 1845, "alienation" never functions as a general or abstract *concept* or *category*. Where it does appear it is almost invariably used in the sense the young Marx used it when speaking of alienation as a consequence of the division of labor and the differential distribution of private property. This was his use in the *Manuscripts* when he referred to the "empirical" alienations discussed in political economy. "Economy," which in the *Manuscripts* attends "industry" (meaning "human activity"), becomes specifically "political economy," the "anatomy of civil society."[203] Even in the *Holy Family*, written in the autumn of 1844, "alienation" has narrowed to that which is consequent upon the development of private property in the strictly economic sense.[204] "The French and English workers . . . these *massy*, communist workers . . . are most painfully aware of the difference between *being* and *thinking*, between *consciousness* and *life*. They know that property, capital, money, wage-labor and the like are no ideal figments of the brain but very practical, very objective sources of their self-estrangement. . . ."[205] As we have seen, by the time Marx wrote his polemic against Proudhon in 1846–1847, he advocated a "profane history of the categories. . . ."[206]

Between 1844 and 1847 Marx systematically reduced the scope of "alienation" to real or empirical alienation. In its specific meaning it was conceived to be the *consequence* of the division of labor, of private property and the class structure which these antecedent conditions fostered, rather than their cause. This economic alienation was but one of the forms of alienation discussed in the *Manuscripts of 1844*.[207] This is the "alienation" "in the conditions dealt with by political economy. . . ."[208] At that time the young Marx had anticipated a similar treatment of alienation in the state, law, ethics, civil life, and so forth.[209] By the time the *German Ideology* was written (1845–1846) Marx was convinced that political economy constituted the study of the real basis of society. The other proposed critiques could no longer be thought of as distinct from the critique of political economy.[210] Alienation was the consequence of the processes inherent in the process of the material production of life and all other alienations were conceived as subsidiary effects.

The influence of Engels in this redirection, or more specifically, in this empirical and specifically economic reorientation on the part of Marx, has not as yet been determined.[211] Certainly, between 1842 and 1845 Engels had applied himself far more than Marx to the problems of economics and the influence of political economy upon the history of Europe.[212] Although Engels consistently minimized his influence on Marx he did report that prior to his meeting with Marx in 1844 he had decided, as a consequence of his experience with the economic situation in England, that economic facts, long neglected in historiography, "were of decisive historical importance and were the foundation of the real conflict between classes . . . and that they were the basis . . . of all political history."[213]

In November, 1844, after Marx had written the Paris *Manuscripts*, Engels admonished him, "We must begin with the ego, with the empirical, living individual. . . . 'Man' is a spirit figure as long as [he] does not have empirical men as [his] basis. In brief, we must proceed from empiricism and materialism if our thinking and specifically our 'Man' is to be something true; *we must derive the general from the particular, not out of itself or out of the air à la Hegel*. These are all trivialities, which are self-understood, which Feuerbach has already, in part, discussed, and I would not repeat them if not for Hess—who appears to me, to treat empiricism . . . so shabbily. Hess is correct in much of what he says about Feuerbach, but on the other side he has still some idealist evasions—when he speaks theoretically, he proceeds always in categories. . . ."[214]

Whatever the ultimate source there is certainly an abandonment of the use of concepts and categories in explanation on the part of the young Marx. This is nowhere more evident than in his treatment of alienation. After 1845 the concept is used almost exclusively to refer to alienation in the specifically economic sense. The concept occasionally reappears in his writings and it is consistently used in the "empirical" manner of the *German Ideology*. The most careful treatment of this specific use is found in the preparatory notes made by Marx for the *Contribution to the Critique of Political Economy* during 1857–1858. An entire section[215] is devoted to the "Estrangement [*Entfremdung*] of the

working conditions of labor with the development of capital."
Here alienation is discussed in the following manner: "The
objective conditions of labor take up against living labor an ever
increasing independence which reveals itself through its very
extent, and the social wealth in ever increasing dimension stands
over and against labor as an alien and ruling power. *The emphasis
is not applied to the objectification in reality*, but to the alienated,
objectified, projected being, the 'not-for-the-worker,' to the personified productive conditions, that is, the enormous objective
power that belongs to capital that social labor has placed against
itself as one of its moments."[216]

Here Marx seems to be specifically abjuring his treatment of
abstract alienation as it is found in the *Manuscripts of 1844*. The
emphasis should not be applied to the "objectification in reality"
but to the real economic conditions which render the social labor
of the worker an alien capital that stands against him as an opponent.[217] Thus the sense of alienation which survives into Marx's
maturity is the empirical sense of alienation which appeared in
the Paris *Manuscripts* accompanied by the broad sense of abstract
alienation, the "objectification in reality."

This employment of alienation having specific empirical reference makes its appearance in *Capital*. "The laborer therefore
constantly produces material, objective wealth, but in the form of
capital, of an alien power that dominates and exploits him. . . .[218]
"The character of independence and estrangement which the capitalist mode of production as a whole gives to the instruments of
labor and to the product, as against the workman, is developed
by means of machinery into a thorough antagonism."[219] Not only
is the sense of alienation that of limited economic alienation, but
alienation apparently develops specifically under the capitalist
mode of production. "Within the capitalist system all methods for
raising the social productiveness of labor are brought about at the
cost of the individual laborer; all the means for the development
of production transform themselves into means of domination
over, and exploitation of, the producers; they mutilate the
laborer into a fragment of a man, degrade him to the level
of an appendage of a machine, destroy every remnant of
charm in his work and turn it into a hated toil; they estrange
from him the intellectual potentialities of the labor-process in
the same proportion as science is incorporated in it as an inde-

pendent power; they distort the conditions under which he works, subject him during the labor process to a despotism the more hateful for its meanness; they transform his lifetime into working-time, and drag his wife and child beneath the wheels of the Juggernaut of capital. But all methods for the production of surplus value are at the same time methods of accumulation; and every extension of accumulation becomes again a means for the development of these methods. It follows therefore that in proportion as capital accumulates, the lot of the laborer, be his payment high or low, must grow worse. . . . Accumulation of wealth at one pole is, therefore, at the same time accumulation of misery, agony of toil, slavery, ignorance, brutality, mental degradation, at the opposite pole, i.e., on the side of the class that produces its own product in the form of capital.

"This antagonistic character of capitalistic accumulation is enunciated in various forms by political economists, although by them it is confounded with phenomena, certainly to some extent analogous, but nevertheless essentially distinct, and belonging to precapitalistic modes of production."[220]

We have here what the conception of alienation came to mean to the mature Marx. Alienation is stripped of its multiple dimensions. It refers to the alienation suffered by man as a worker within the specifically capitalist mode of production. The very language of this section of *Capital* is taken from Marx's discussion of the specific economic alienation within the concept of abstract alienation in the *Manuscripts of 1844*. Alienation for the mature Marx is the consequence of private property, the division of labor, the accumulation of capital.[221] It is Feuerbach's indictment of religion: "To enrich God, man must become poor; that God may be all, man must be nothing,"[222] transposed into an economic key. In the words of Marx, "All these consequences are contained in the definition that the worker is related to the product of his labor as to an alien object. For on this premise it is clear that the more the worker spends himself, the more powerful the alien objective world becomes which he creates over against himself, the poorer he himself—his inner world—becomes, the less belongs to him as his own. It is the same in religion. The more man puts into God, the less he retains himself. The worker puts his life into the object; but now his life no longer belongs to him but to the object. Hence, the greater his activity, the greater is the worker's lack of objects. Whatever the product of his labor is, he is not. Therefore the greater this product, the less is he himself. The alienation of the worker in his product means not only that this labor becomes an object, an external existence, but that it exists outside him, independently, as something alien to him, and that it becomes a power on its own confronting him; it means that the life which he has conferred on the object confronts him as something hostile and alien."[223]

As a result of successive definition "alienation" has become increasingly specific. In the *Manuscripts* at least two distinct usages can be isolated: (1) There is a broad abstract use which carries with it equally broad usages of terms like "industry," "mode of production," "private property"—it is a category or concept which "expresses and presents" itself in "real life." Its "transcendence" is the "transcendenc of objectivity," the consequence of appropriating the world more humanly, more in accord with the species essence of man. This "alienation" finds its ultimate resolve in "Humanism." (2) There is a narrow usage of political economy, which can be understood only through the employment of ordinary definitions of "industry," "division of labor," and "private property." This specific alienation is transcended through "Communism," the abolition of private property in the sense of "having" and "possessing." This narrow resolution is conceived as preparatory to the advent of the final resolution in Humanism.

In this early period (before 1845) there was much residual Hegelianism; there was an insistent Feuerbachianism; and there was the marked influence of Moses Hess (particularly in the discussion of "having" as distinct from true "human appropriation" in the broad ontological sense).[224] In 1845 Marx began a careful reassessment, eliminating the use of abstract concepts such as the "human essence."[225] In the settling of accounts with his philosophical conscience the young Marx became increasingly critical of analyzing history as though history were the ground in which concepts and categories "presented" and "expressed" themselves. His method became increasingly empirical and his analysis of the historical process became specifically economic, economic in the sense of political economy, a specificity which already characterized the writings of the youthful Engels with whom Marx became intimately associated at that precise time. He thus came to understand alienation specifically as a consequence of the productive relations associated with commodity production in capitalist society. It was to be understood as the consequence of the division of labor and the accumulation of private property in the hands of the capitalist. The conception of the labor theory of value as the process by which man objectifies himself in nature is an application of the concept of *Entäusserung* and *Entfremdung*, which ultimately manifested itself in the writings of Marx as an explanatory device to show how alienation was the inevitable consequence of the capitalist mode of production.

The *Manuscripts of 1844* are youthful writings. They represent Marx's first attempts to develop his world-view with some consistency, and they contain the germ of the ultimate world-view. That ultimate world-view can be understood as a working out of the original Feuerbachian program for the liberation of man in an alienated world.

## Philosophy and Marx

Marx's tempestuous affair with philosophy came to a close, for all intents and purposes, with the *Communist Manifesto* of 1848. He was never again to take up problems of value, epistemology, and metaphysics in any systematic way. His development has been characterized as one from philosophical speculation to political activism.[226] The metaphysics and the natural philosophy of the *Manuscripts of 1844* remain as an interesting fragment of the intellectual history of the nineteenth century. Two themes survive to provide the living continuity to the development of classical Marxism: the reform of the Hegelian dialectic and the development of the empirical significance of alienation. The inversion of the Hegelian dialectic—the transposition of subjects and predicates[227]—is a technique Marx adopted from Ludwig Feuerbach, and refined and applied for the remainder of his life. The concept of alienation, empirically understood and successively defined with increasing precision, forms the core of Marx's subsequent analysis of capitalism. The objects which the worker produces come to stand against him as opponents in the form of alien capital—alien because the property of another man. The more the worker labors the more he impoverishes himself, for as a consequence of his labor capital accumulates, and the weight of this alienated labor bears heavily upon him. That this alienation will ultimately be resolved is the theme of all of Marx's mature work, the explication of the inevitability of its transcendence the preoccupation of his life.

As Marx concentrated more and more on political economy, it was left to Friedrich Engels to articulate the philosophic position of classical Marxism. The principal products of his philosophic lucubrations, generally the result of inter- or intraparty polemics, are contained in the *Anti-Dühring*, published some thirty-odd years after the completion of the *German Ideology* of 1846; in *Ludwig Feuerbach and the End of Classical German Philosophy*, which he wrote only after the death of Marx in 1887; and the notebooks, which have been published under the title *Dialectics of Nature*, dating from the decade 1872–1882. That the philosophy Engels advanced should be different from that of the young Karl Marx is not surprising. A quarter of a century of philosophic reconsideration, of political activity, of development in the natural and social sciences separates them. And then again they are the results of the work of two different men. In the peculiar inversion of roles which was the consequence of their lifelong relationship Engels was left to develop the natural scientific and philosophic components of classical Marxism. Engels—who upon his first encounter with Marx had been the expert in political economy, and whose writings until 1845 were almost exclusively economic tracts—was to become the philosopher of classical Marxism, and Marx—who had earned his doctorate in philosophy and until 1844 knew nothing of political economy—was to spend the rest of his life working in the "dismal science."

What Marx thought of Engels' philosophy we shall probably never know. Certainly the philosophy revealed in the works of Engels is a strange bedfellow to the positive Humanism of the youthful Marx. Engels tells us that Marx read the text of the *Anti-Dühring* (Engels' only expression of classical Marxist philosophy published during Marx's lifetime). But we do not know if Marx approved of it in its entirety, for we have good reason to believe that Marx did not confide *all* his opinions to Engels. What his judgment of the epistemology and metaphysics of his compatriot might have been is a matter of speculation. Marx's daughter took it upon herself to destroy her father's correspondence with his wife, a vandalism undertaken in order to avoid "embarrassment" to Engels.[228] In 1873, when Engels asked for Marx's judgment of his (Engels') treatment of natural science from a "dialectical" perspective, Marx pleaded that he could not judge until he had more time to consider the matter and consult the suitable "authorities."[229] We do not know that he ever found the time. It was left to Engels to develop the philosophy of classical Marxism.

# 2 The Philosophy of

# Friedrich Engels

Friedrich Engels was born in the industrial town of Barmen on the 28th of November, 1820. His early experiences in Barmen, where he observed the consequences of early capitalist industrialization, left a lifelong impression.[1] Marx, born two years earlier in the quiet Rhenish town of Trier, did not deal with the hard facts of economic life until October, 1842, when, as the twenty-four-year-old editor of the first *Rheinische Zeitung*, he took up the question of wood-theft.[2] Engels, on the other hand, in his "Letters out of Wuppertal," published in 1839, had already at nineteen ascribed a whole catalogue of economic abuses to the nascent capitalism he had come to know.[3] In this sense the environments in which Marx and Engels grew seemed to condition their reactions to the problems which beset the Germany of the first half of the nineteenth century. Until 1844 Marx was primarily concerned with philosophic and political criticism, while Engels concentrated on the baleful effects of the specifically capitalist mode of production. It might well be said that during this early period Engels was the more "Marxist" of the two.

Further speculation might indicate that Engels, abjuring the rigidly Pietist faith of his family, turned for consolation to the "immanent God" of German Idealism.[4] Although this point has been made,[5] until the implications of such a statement are competently assessed it can tell us little about the philosophy of Engels and its role in the historical and intellectual development of Marxism. For by 1844 Engels could write, "The question has always been: What is God? and German philosophy has resolved the question in: God is man. Man has but to recognize himself, to measure all of the relations of life against himself . . . not in a beyond, a region without existence, outside of time and space. . . ."[6]

## The Intellectual Environment of the Young Engels

Engels' early years were dominated by his preoccupation in two problems: the wretched conditions which afflicted the working people of his native Germany and the unhappy religion which had governed his childhood. By the end of the 1830's, he had begun to see that the solution of both problems lay in the same direction. A trip to Bremen had permitted him to read and reflect about the opinions of writers then dominating German intellectual circles. He was exposed to the critical *Life of Jesus* by David Strauss and through Strauss to the work of Hegel. On January 21, 1840, Engels wrote to his friend Graeber that "thanks to Strauss," he was "on the high road to Hegelianism." But while Hegelianism might conceivably satisfy Engels' speculative interest in the true "God" with which he had been so preoccupied, it did not mitigate the evident misfortunes which beset the people of his time. The concern with philosophy and the criticism of religion were remote from life, from social problems and politics. Engels sought to remedy the defect by supplementing Hegel with the views of Ludwig Börne (Löb Baruch), a German critic and publicist, whom Engels described as "a titanic fighter for freedom and right."

The amalgam of both stimulated his first literary efforts and testify to his concerted attempt to resolve the problems which were his and those of his time. His writings of the period identify him as an ardent revolutionary democrat who awaits the day when the "old world will tumble in ruins" and the "dawn of freedom" herald the new.

Engels was early associated with the literary radicals around Börne who formed the Young Germany movement and under their influence he sought to change the world through revolu-

tionary verse—poetry which appeared in the organ of the movement, the *Telegraph für Deutschland*. In his revolutionary verse
the young Engels attempted a "synthesis of Hegel and Börne."
In poetry he maintained that wherever "the oriflamme of Freedom
waves," ships should carry grain "which grows to human happiness," and should no longer carry "goods to profit one alone."

When Engels left Bremen in 1841 to undertake his military
service he found himself in Berlin, where the Hegelian Radicals
had organized a group which they called "The Free." To this
group he attached himself. Belonging to it were the Bauer
brothers, Bruno and Edgar, and Max Stirner, all of whom had,
in one sense or another, been influenced by the work of Ludwig
Feuerbach. Their criticisms, couched in the terms of the Hegelian
dialectic, had assaulted philosophy and religion. God was dead,
only Man survived. The Left-Wing Hegelians were to seek a
humanist ethic and to busy themselves only with things of this
world. Counted among these radicals—although not present—
was Karl Marx, who had left the German capital just prior to the
arrival of the young Engels. The two men did not meet until a
year later, in November, 1842.

Friedrich Wilhelm IV, King of Prussia, in an effort to dispel the
Left-Hegelian critics of his state, had appointed Schelling, an opponent of Hegel, to the chair of philosophy at the University of
Berlin. Engels, as a Young Hegelian, was incensed. With an
almost self-conscious awareness of his own presumption, he took
it upon himself to challenge the austere Schelling. During 1841
and 1842 under the pseudonym "F. Oswald," he undertook an
arch criticism of Schelling in a series of articles which appeared
in the *Telegraph* and also as separate pamphlets. In "Schelling
and Revelation," his defense of Hegel was impassioned. For the
young Engels, the Hegelian "Idea" remained charged with
emotion. He saw the resolution of the problems of his nation in
"Hegel renewed."

It was during this period that Engels came under the influence
of Moses Hess. Hess was considerably older than Engels and had
been well known for some time in radical circles in Germany
as the "Communist Rabbi." His *European Triarchy*,[7] in which
he argued for a social and political philosophy of action, had
to appeal to Engels. Hess's efforts to make idealism a philosophy
of revolution involved synthesizing the ethics of Spinoza[8] with the

social theories of Saint-Simon, one of the forerunners of the French sociologist Auguste Comte. It was Moses Hess, then, who introduced the Left-Hegelians, seeking the liberation of man, to the "science" of human society. It was Hess, apparently, who first argued that the Hegelian Idea could work itself out only through the agency of human society itself.[9] He argued that the liberation of the human spirit could not be found in orthodox Hegelianism, for Hegel had seen philosophy as that wisdom to which one has access only after the Spirit has worked itself out in events.[10] Hess argued that philosophy must deduce the future from the course of the past and act as midwife to the birth of the future from the present. "This is a typical Saint-Simonian idea, and later it was to become a cornerstone in the system of Marx and Engels."[11]

In the writings of Hess, the revolutionary classes were somehow equated with an abstract category of distress. Because Hess knew little of the actual proletarians of whom he spoke, the rarefied ethics and the religion of love which he proposed had little to recommend them. But he did give some indication of the role of the rapidly expanding productive forces in generating the contradictions in capitalist society, i.e., he singled out the "contradiction" inherent in a system in which increasing productivity brought only increasing misery.[12] In any event Engels was deeply impressed by the message of the *European Triarchy*[13] and he credited Moses Hess with making Communism "credible and acceptable" to him.

After the meeting of November, 1842, Marx and Engels did not meet again until the end of August, 1844, after Marx had laid aside the *Economic and Philosophic Manuscripts of 1844*. In the interim Engels had begun a systematic study of social and economic conditions prevailing in the industrial centers of capitalist England, the country which Hess conceived as the ground of the "liberating revolution" of the future. He had also begun a study of classical British economics through the works of Adam Smith, David Ricardo, J. R. McCulloch, and John Stuart Mill. He had written several articles for the *Rheinische Zeitung* and had prepared the "Outlines of a Critique of Political Economy" for the *Deutsch-französische Jahrbücher*.[14]

In the "Outlines," a work which was to alter the course of the intellectual development of Karl Marx,[15] one finds the suggestions of an empirical study of the economic basis of capitalist society, and a call to social and political action that bespoke Engels' concern for the dispossessed of his time. But in the company of that empirical assessment are found the turns of phrase and the apocalyptic vision of the "renewed Hegelianism" to which Engels remained faithful. Engels developed the argument out of the "necessary" laws of Hegelianism. "It was *necessary* to overthrow the mercantile system with its monopolies and hindrances to trade, so that the true consequences of private property could come to light. . . . All this lay in the nature of the matter. . . . Once a principle is set in motion, it works by its own impetus through all its consequences, whether the economists like it or not. But the economist does not know himself what cause he serves. He does not know that with all his egoistical reasoning he nevertheless forms but a link in the chain of mankind's universal progress. He does not know that by his dissolution of all sectional interests he merely paves the way for the great transformation to which the century is moving—the reconciliation of mankind with nature and with itself."[16]

Friedrich Engels had taken it upon himself to prove that "Communism was the *necessary* consequence of neo-Hegelian philosophy."[17] This, then, was the man who was the co-founder of classical Marxism, and, from 1844 on, patron and intimate friend of Karl Marx.

### Engels and Classical German Philosophy

After the meeting of Marx and Engels in Paris in 1844 the lives of both men were largely devoted to the articulation of what has become known as historical materialism. They undertook not only intellectual labor but revolutionary and organizational activity as well. In addition, there was always the problem of making a living. The revolution of 1848 had ended in defeat. Marx was expelled from Germany and Belgium and finally took up residence in England where he lived impoverished for most of his life. From 1850 Marx was attempting to lay bare the anatomy of capitalist production in the *Contribution to the Critique of Political Economy*—whose revision, the massive *Capital*, was to occupy him for the remainder of his life.

Engels, in turn, made use of his earlier military experience in the revolutionary army, seeing combat in various sectors. After the revolution he returned to England and the "Egyptian captivity" of industry, first working as a clerk and eventually becoming a partner in the Engels and Ermen Textile Mills. Besides meeting the obligations of business, Engels wrote extensively on military and political matters and threw himself into the organizational and propagandistic work of the First International (which was founded in 1864). By 1870 he was incubating that philosophy of natural science which now bears the name of dialectical materialism.

Dialectical materialism was a curious product. Neither Marx nor Engels during the years between 1845 and 1868 had had time to embark upon a systematic study of natural science. They "could keep up with the natural sciences only piecemeal, intermittently and sporadically."[18] It was only upon his retirement from business that Engels could undertake a systematic study of natural science as it had developed in the generation following the writing of the *German Ideology*. Between the years 1868 and 1876 he made a detailed study of natural science while Marx was occupied with writing the second and third volumes of *Capital*.

The German Social Democratic party was, at that time, in intellectual ferment. Among the foremost of the theoreticians produced in the process was Eugen Dühring, a blind tutor at the University of Berlin. He had developed an "anticratic" socialism which leveled its guns against, among others, Karl Marx, whom it described as a "scientific figure of fun." Both Bernstein and Most, two of the leading intellectuals of the party, were attracted to Dühring's "New Socialism." Liebknecht, who remained faithful to Marx's conception of what the party should be, prevailed on Engels to write a rebuttal. But Engels was not ready to interrupt his studies to make a reply. Finally, in May of 1876, he agreed to write the "sharp snub" against Dühring. At the beginning of 1877, *Vorwärts*, the organ of the German Social Democratic party, began to publish the series of articles entitled "Herr Eugen Dühring's Revolution in Science." In mid-1878 the series was finished and published as the book, *Anti-Dühring: Herr Eugen Dühring's Revolution in Science*.

The volume delivered the first full statement of dialectical materialism, Friedrich Engels' philosophy of natural science. It was written almost thirty-five years after Marx's Paris *Manuscripts* and reveals a conception of philosophy and science markedly different from that of the youthful author of the *Economic and Philosophic Manuscripts of 1844*.

Engels had never lost his conviction that German philosophy, particularly that of a "renewed" Hegelianism, led necessarily to Communism. In his review of Carlyle's *Past and Present*, written in 1844, he lamented that the English Socialists knew nothing of German philosophy,[19] which had wrought a "revolution in thought."[20] In 1874, thirty years later, he wrote, "Without German Philosophy, particularly that of Hegel, German scientific Socialism (the only scientific Socialism extant) would never have come into existence."[21] In 1886 he was still stressing the influence of German philosophy on the development of German Socialism when he wrote that "the German working class movement is the inheritor of German classical philosophy."[22]

Engels, therefore, remained convinced of the importance of Hegelian "theory" in the day-to-day struggles of the international Marxist movement. He conceived a reformed Hegelianism to be the true vehicle of the movement's theoretical rationale. This conviction revealed itself in Engels' disposition to see the world in Hegelian formulations. In a letter to Marx, written on the 14th of July, 1858, Engels reported that he was occupied with studies in physiology and anatomy and required the *Naturphilosophie* of Hegel to see if *"der Alte"* had "anticipated" (*davon gerochen hat*) any of the new developments. Among those developments was the "discovery of cells—in plants by Schleiden and in animals by Schwann (about 1836). Everything is cells." Then he continued, "The cell is the Hegelian 'potential' [*Ansichsein*] and goes through an evolution with the precision of the Hegelian process [*Prozess*], until it develops finally into the 'Idea,' the actual, finished organism."[23]

Hegel remained for Engels "the most encyclopedic mind of his time,"[24] a man "of the greatest genius,"[25] one who had "analyzed the most essential forms of dialectic thought"[26] and "first clearly formulated" the principal laws of the dialectic.[27] Engels was to contend, "Dialectics has so far been fairly closely investigated by only two thinkers, Aristotle and Hegel."[28] After all the criticisms which can be legitimately leveled against Hegelian Idealism have done their work, there remains "Hegelian dialectics."[29] The Hegelian dialectic became the basis of Engels' philosophy of natural science.

## Engels' Philosophy of Natural Science

The philosophy of natural science advanced by Engels as dialectical materialism is found in three major works—the *Anti-Dühring, Ludwig Feuerbach,* and the collection of notes and fragments posthumously published in 1926 as the *Dialectics of Nature.* Engels had been occupied, intermittently, with natural science throughout his life, but it is only with 1873 that we have clear evidence that he contemplated doing an exhaustive book on the subject. By 1875 he had begun to draw up a prospective outline of such a book. But he interrupted this work to take up the obligation of criticizing the "Real Philosophy" of Dühring. With that completed, he returned to his task and on November 23, 1882, he wrote Marx that he hoped to finish the volume on the *Dialectics of Nature* very shortly.[30] He broke off his work again after the death of Marx in March of 1883 to prepare Marx's manuscripts of the second and third volumes of *Capital* for the press. Engels never returned to the volume devoted to the philosophy of natural science. The only remaining work in which he dealt with the problems of the philosophy of natural science was his short *Ludwig Feuerbach,* written in 1886 and published shortly thereafter.

Engels characterized his philosophy as that which sought to "rescue conscious dialectics from German idealist philosophy and apply it in the materialist conception of nature and history."[31] He produced a philosophy of nature in which "both matter and its mode of existence, motion, are uncreatable and . . . therefore, their own final cause."[32] Matter in motion he conceived as indestructible, infinite in space and uncreated in time.[33] Engels held that we come to "'know from experience and from theory that both matter and its mode of existence, motion, are uncreatable and are, therefore, their own final cause."[34]

The conception of matter as its own *final cause* includes the notion that matter *necessarily* develops from its simple aggregate forms to most complex forms, thinking beings.[35] Matter is qualitatively and quantitatively indestructible;[36] consequently in the "eternal cycle in which matter moves" organic life *must* arise and "organic life, once given, must evolve by the development of generations to a genus of thinking beings."[37] "It is the nature of matter to advance to the evolution of thinking beings,"[38] for "we have the certainty that matter remains eternally the same in all its transformations, that none of its attributes can ever be lost, and therefore . . . that with the same iron necessity that it will exterminate on the earth its highest creation, the thinking mind, it must somewhere else and at another time again produce it."[39] "The old teleology has gone to the devil, but it is now firmly established that matter in its eternal cycle moves according to laws which at a definite stage—now here, now there—necessarily give rise to the thinking mind in organic beings."[40]

The laws governing this "new" teleology of the development of "pure matter as such" ("primordial matter"[41]), through its simplest quantitative and qualitative forms to that which becomes thought, are *dialectical*. Dialectics, then, is reduced to the science of the general laws of motion,[42] the modes of existence of matter,[43] comprehending all the "changes and processes occurring in the universe, from mere change of place right up to thinking."[44] As such, dialectics is the "science of universal inter-connection" whose main laws are the Hegelian laws of (1) the transformation of quantity into quality and vice versa; (2) the law of the interpenetration of opposites; and (3) the law of the negation of the negation or development through contradiction.[45]

Dialectics, as objective laws of the essential connection, concatenation, motion, origin, and ending of processes,[46] is reflected in dialectical thought, "so-called subjective dialectics."[47] Subjective dialectics, the product of the human brain, "being in the last analysis also products of nature,[48] do not contradict the rest of nature's interconnections but are in correspondence with them."[49] The "laws of thought and laws of nature are necessarily in agreement with one another";[50] the two sets of laws "are identical in substance, but differ in their expression,"[51] the "dialectics of the mind [being] only the reflection of the forms of motion of the real world, both of nature and of history."[52] "The fact that our subjective thought and the objective world are subject to the same laws, and hence, too, that in the final analysis they cannot contradict each other in their results, but must coincide, governs absolutely our whole theoretical thought. . . . Dialectics is conceived as the science of the most general laws of *all* motion. This implies that its laws must be valid just as much for motion in nature and human history as for the motion of thought."[53]

"An exact representation of the universe, of its evolution, of the development of mankind, and of the reflection of this evolution in the minds of men, can . . . only be obtained by the methods of dialectics."[54] In nature the dialectical laws of motion proceed amid the welter of innumerable changes, governing apparently fortuitous events. These laws ultimately find their way into the consciousness of man. They were first expressed by Hegel in an all-embracing but mystic form. Engels undertook to reveal the form of these laws "clearly before the mind in their complete simplicity and universality."[55]

Divested of their mystic form the laws of the dialectic are the generalizations produced by natural science itself. Men arrive at a dialectical conception of nature "because the accumulating facts of natural science compel" them to.[56] There is no question of building the laws of dialectics into nature but only of discovering them there.[57] Empirical natural science has attained maturity to demonstrate the interconnection of the processes in nature and between particular processes and the whole. Hitherto natural philosophy, in order to provide this comprehensive view, conjured up fancied connections in the place of real, but as yet undiscovered ones, providing a speculative system rather than a scientific one. Today, Engels held, one needs to comprehend the results of natural scientific investigation in their totality in order to arrive at a synthesis for our own time.[58] The dialectical character of this synthesis becomes obvious as science becomes aware that all the processes of nature are systematically interconnected. Such a synthetic natural science delivers an image of the world which "sublates" natural philosophy. This conception "is no longer a philosophy at all, but simply a world outlook which has to establish its validity and be applied not in a science of sciences standing apart, but in the positive sciences."[59] "Natural philosophy is finally disposed of. Every attempt at resurrecting it would be not only superfluous but a *step backwards.*"[60]

Engels' views are markedly positivistic: ". . . [We] all agree that in every field of science, in natural as in historical science, one must proceed from the given *facts,* in natural science therefore from the various material forms and the various forms of motion of matter; that therefore in theoretical natural science too the inter-connections are not to be built into the facts but to be discovered in them, and when discovered to be verified as far as possible by experiment."[61] "It is . . . from the history of nature and human society that the laws of dialectics are abstracted. For they are nothing but the most general laws of these two aspects of historical development, as well as of thought itself."[62] These laws were developed by Hegel, in his idealist fashion, as mere laws of thought. His mistake was to conceive these laws as foisted upon nature and history rather than discovering them there.[63] Once this is understood, the "dialectical laws that look so extremely mysterious in idealist philosophy at once become simple and clear as noonday."[64] For they are the very laws of nature with which empirical natural science concerns itself,[65] laws which are not principles, points of departure, but the end result of investigation.[66]

The compelling awareness of the existence of these laws of process and development is the consequence of the progress of science itself. The discovery of the cell as the unit whose multiplication and differentiation produce the whole of plant and animal bodies reduced the development of all higher organisms to a single general law, and compelled natural science to recognize the dialectical character of biological processes.[67] The second discovery which precipitated the dialectical world-view was that of the transformation of energy. This law demonstrated that all the forces operative in inorganic nature—mechanical force and its complement (so-called potential energy), heat, radiation, electricity, magnetism, and chemical energy—are different forms of manifestations of universal motion. These forms of motion are transformed into one another in definite proportions, so that in place of a certain quantity of the one which disappears, a certain quantity of another makes its appearance; thus the whole motion of nature is reduced to this incessant process of transformation of one form into another.[68] The third great discovery on which Engels based dialectical materialism was Darwin's proof of the organic evolution of species from a few originally unicellular germs that arose out of chemically generated protoplasm or albumen.[69] Engels felt then he could conclude, "Thus we have once again returned to the mode of outlook of the great founders of Greek philosophy, the view that the whole of nature, from the smallest element to the greatest, from grains of sand to suns, from Protista to man, has its existence in eternal coming into being and passing away, in ceaseless flux, in unresting motion and change. Only with the essential difference that what in the case of the Greeks was brilliant intuition, is in our case the result of strictly scientific research in accordance with experience, and hence it emerges in a much more definite and clear form."[70]

Engels believed science could achieve clarity and understanding only by dialectical thinking.[71] The process of attaining such clarity can come about spontaneously by the sheer weight of scientific discoveries or the process can be considerably abbreviated by scientists familiarizing themselves with dialectical philosophy,[72] of which Hegel's was the consummate but mystic form.[73] Today, Engels held, science is compelled to *discover* the laws of transformation and motion, each in its particular domain. "[This] was the legacy which Hegelian philosophy bequeathed to its successors."[74] Contemporary science must conceive thoughts within the brain as "more or less abstract pictures of actual things and processes" in continual dialectical transformation.[75]

The most general expression of the first dialectical law governing dialectical transformation is that quantitative changes in a thing inevitably bring about a change in its quality.[76] Thus a change in the length of a musical string brings about a change in its tonal quality. Change in the length of electromagnetic waves produces waves qualitatively changed to radio waves, infrared radiation, colors, ultraviolet waves, X-rays, and gamma rays. To select an illustration from chemistry, the synthetic substances which figure so prominently in modern industry (plastics and synthetic fibers) are composed of large molecules formed by the combination of many small molecules each of identical composition. This combination of monomers into polymers results in qualitative changes, for polymers exhibit significant qualities that monomers lack.

Such quantitative changes proceed more or less gradually at first, not changing the qualitative character of a thing to any substantial extent. Ultimately the cumulative quantitative change brings about a qualitative change. There is a "leap." Quantity has passed into quality. An illustration of such change in the biological world would be the subspecific variations among organisms of the same species. These minor hereditary modifications ultimately accumulate and what had been variations become species differences.[77] Similarly, the gradual increment of heat transferred to water increases until the boiling point is reached, where quantitative change passes into qualitative change. Water ceases to be a liquid and becomes a gas.

The second law of dialectics, the interpenetration of opposites, is simplified when one considers that hard-and-fast distinctions are incompatible, for example, with the theory of evolution as we have come to understand it. "Even the border line between vertebrates and invertebrates is now no longer rigid, just as little is that between fishes and amphibians, while that between birds and reptiles dwindles more and more everyday. . . . 'Either–Or' becomes more and more inadequate. Among lower animals the concept of the individual cannot be established at all sharply. Not only as to whether a particular animal is an individual or a colony, but also where in development one individual ceases and the other begins. . . . Dialectics, which . . . knows no hard and fast lines, no unconditional, universally valid 'either–or' recognizes also in the right place 'both this–and that' and reconciles the opposites, is the sole method of thought appropriate in the highest degree to this stage."[78]

The plant, the animal, every cell is at every moment of its existence both identical with itself and yet becoming distinct from itself as a consequence of the absorption and excretion of substances, by respiration, by cell formation and decay, by the incessant molecular changes which constitute life.[79] Even life is thus conceived as somehow containing death essentially within itself. "Life is always thought of in relation to its necessary result, death, which is always contained in it in germ."[80]

Opposites and contradictions abound in all the fields of science. Mathematics deals with the opposed operations of addition and subtraction, multiplication and division; mechanics with action and reaction, attraction and repulsion; physics with positive and negative electrical charges; and chemistry with the combination and dissociation of atoms.

The third law of dialectics is the law of the negation of the negation or development through contradiction. Such a law Engels maintained is eminently simple, and nature is alive with illustrative examples. Motion itself, for example, is a contradiction; for even simple mechanical motion can only come about by the virtue of a body being in one and the same instant of time in one place and in another, being in one and the same place and also not in it.[81] There is a contradiction inherent in a thing when that thing "is saddled with its antithesis."[82] There is a contradiction in a thing remaining the same and yet constantly changing. And yet this is the way of the world. Contradiction is "objectively present in things and processes themselves and can be met with in so to speak corporeal form."[83] To anyone who denies the objective existence of contradiction, motion becomes inexplicable, "and in asserting the incomprehensibility of motion, [one] admits against [one's] will the existence of this contradiction, and thus admits the objective presence in things and processes themselves of a contradiction which is more-over an actual force."[84] This force is the motive force of development,[85] for the "continual conflict of the opposites and their final passage into one another, or into higher forms, determines the life of nature."[86] Progression from one form to a higher form is through this conflict of opposites which Engels labels the negation of the negation.

The original notion of this progression through negation is, of course, Hegelian. Hegel had conceived nature as a manifestation of the eternal "Idea" in its alienation.[87] For Engels this conception of progress through "alienation" is "'au fond' something correct."[88] But where Hegel had seen such development as the logic of thinking and as the forms of motion of thought,[89] Engels conceives that which in "Hegel appears as a development out of the thought form of judgement as such [to be] ... the development of our *empirically* based theoretical knowledge of the nature of motion in general."[90] Stripped of its mysticism the process, Engels contends, is eminently simple. The negation of the negation is "a very simple process which is taking place everywhere and everyday, which any child can understand as soon as it is stripped of the veil of mystery in which it was enveloped by the old idealist philosophy."[91]

A grain of barley, to cite an everyday illustration, falls on suitable soil. Under the influence of heat and moisture it germinates; the grain as such ceases to exist; it is negated and in its place has arisen the plant, the negation of the grain. But the plant flowers, is fertilized and once more produces grains of barley. As these ripen the stalk dies; it has been, in its turn, negated. As a result of this negation of the negation we have restored the original grain of barley, but not as a single unit, but ten-, twenty-, or thirtyfold.[92] Not only will there be an absolute increment in number but there will be small qualitative changes of adaptive character, hereditary variations, so that the entire process of negation of the negation can be represented as "progressive development."[93]

"With Hegel, 'in itself' [Ansich] covers the original identity of the hidden, undeveloped contradictions within a thing, and 'for itself' [Fürsich] contains the distinction and separation of these hidden elements and the starting point of their conflict."[94] But the Hegelian distinction which appears in thought as the absurdity of attempting to synthesize contradictions is, according to Engels, "an actual force."[95] Thus we can say that "in the protein granule on its first origin the whole infinite series of higher organisms lies included 'in itself' [Ansich] as if in embryo."[96] Its subsequent development out of itself (Ansich) to final forms (Fürsich) is the consequence of development through contradictions, the process of the negation of the negation. Engels claimed that one can conceive of "heredity as the positive, conservative side, adaptation as the negative side that continually destroys what has been inherited, but one can just as well take adaptation as the creative, active positive activity, and heredity as the resisting, passive, negative activity."[97] Heredity transmits specific characteristics to the filial generations. Adaptation is its negation. But the adaptation is inherited.[98] Thus the negation is negated but the resulting form is more highly evolved than the antecedent. Evolution has progressed through the negation of the negation, through the interpenetration of opposites as a consequence of "the dialectical nature of polar opposites."[99]

This is the philosophy of natural science which we find in the mature writings of Friedrich Engels, the philosophy destined to become dialectical materialism. Engels sees all of nature as composed of differences which gradually merge as all opposites pass into one another through intermediate links.[100] Things and processes harbor in themselves their opposites, their contradiction, as a force generating development. Each successive stage is transitory, the negation of an antecedent stage, only to be negated on a higher level by a subsequent stage.[101] Thus heredity becomes adaptation, and adaptation becomes heredity; cause becomes effect and effect cause. In the history of mankind (primitive) Communism becomes that system characterized by private property holdings and that system in turn is negated by (modern) Communism. The "kernel" of the entire process is the negation of the negation,[102] an "extremely general—and for this reason extremely far-reaching and important—law of development of nature, history, and thought; a law which . . . holds good in the animal and plant kingdoms, in geology, in mathematics, in history and in philosophy. . . ."[103]

Dialectical materialism thus sees the progressive evolution of the world as proceeding in accordance with the fundamental laws of dialectical reason—"nature cannot be unreasonable or reason contrary to nature,"[104] for dialectical reasoning is "the mere reflection of this process in the thinking brain."[105] Nature is the embodiment of reason. Dialectical materialism is Hegelianism "renewed."

## The Epistemology of Engels

Friedrich Engels had remarkably little to say about specifically epistemological problems. Engels simply belongs to the overwhelming majority of thinkers who believe our senses somehow *reflect* the objects of the external world. The "agnostic" admits that all our knowledge is derived ultimately from our senses through reflections. His question is whether we can know that our senses give us correct representations of the objects we perceive through them. He argues that when he talks about objects or qualities he is not literally speaking of those objects or qualities, but rather of the impressions which they have produced through his senses, and that there is no way through which the one can be compared to the other. If we can never compare the "reflection" in the mind with the object out of the mind, which it presumably reflects, how can we speak of a faithful similarity? Engels concedes that this line of argument is "undoubtedly hard to beat by mere argumentation."[106] But he contends that such reasoning is philosophic invention and that human actions had solved the difficulty long before human ingenuity invented it. "The proof of the pudding is in the eating. From the moment we turn to our own use these objects, according to the qualities we perceive in them, we put to an infallible test the correctness or otherwise of our sense-perceptions. If these perceptions have been wrong, then our estimate of the use to which an object can be turned must also be wrong, and our attempt must fail. But if we succeed in accomplishing our aim, if we find that the object does agree with our idea of it, and does answer the purpose for which we intended it, then that is positive proof that our perceptions of it and its qualities, so far, agree with reality outside ourselves. And whenever we find ourselves face to face with a failure, then we generally are not long in making out the cause that made us fail; we find that the perception upon which we acted was either incomplete and superficial, or combined with the results of other perceptions in a way not warranted by them— what we call defective reasoning. So long as we take care to train and use our senses properly, and to keep our action within the limits prescribed by perceptions properly made and properly used, so long we shall find that the result of our actions proves the conformity of our perceptions with the objective nature of the things perceived. Not in one single instance, so far, have we been led to the conclusion that our sense-perceptions, scientifically controlled, induce in our minds ideas respecting the outer world that are, by their very nature, at variance with reality, or that there is an inherent incompatibility between the outer world and our sense-perceptions of it."[107]

The most telling refutation, then, of such agnosticism is practice, that is, experiment and industry. Chemical substances remained unknown "things-in-themselves" until modern industry succeeded in producing them one after another, whereupon the "things-in-themselves" became "things-for-us," hence certifying our conception of the natural process which gives rise to them. Thus Leverrier, utilizing the data provided by the Copernican system, deduced the necessity of the existence of an unknown planet and calculated the position in the system which this hypothetical planet must occupy. Galle subsequently found this planet (Neptune) and the Copernican system was, according to Engels, proved.[108]

Thus *practice*, according to Engels, the ability to make successful predictions, certifies the correspondence of our sense perceptions and the things conceived to be their objective cause. *Cause*, itself, must consequently be assumed to be a component of the world order since the inference from sensory perception to objects and processes in the natural world rests on the validity of such an assumption. Thus the very "activity of human beings *forms the test of causality*."[109] ". . . [If] I am able to make the *post hoc*, it becomes identical with the *propter hoc*."[110] We have, it would seem, not only *practice* providing the confirmation that our perceptions accord with reality (at least in sufficient measure to permit prediction), but *practice* also providing a test for the *necessity of causal sequences*. "The proof of necessity lies in human activity."[111]

Such, essentially, is the epistemology upon which dialectical materialism rests. It is perhaps best described as a form of realism. External objects are more or less what they seem. They are reflected in some sense in the mind, the reflections being only partially correct[112] because they are conditioned by the physical limitations of the sensory organs themselves and circumstances of time and place. "Each mental image of the world system is and remains in actual fact limited, objectively by the historical conditions and subjectively by the physical and mental constitution of its originator."[113] To these limiting conditions must be added actual errors in reasoning, that is, drawing incorrect inferences from perceptions.[114] Limiting conditions and invalid inferences are corrected by careful and controlled observation, and by putting our images of things and processes to the test of practice. These views follow upon the rudimentary causal and representational theory of perception. The things and processes of the external world are objective causes of our perception and the perceptions are reflections of the external world. Engels demonstrates that the material world appears to us as its own effect and that these effects are a true reflection of that world by appealing to predictive success in practice. Thus positive science in its successful operation provides the proof.

## Philosophy and Engels

When we consider the epistemology and the philosophy of natural science found in the mature works of Engels we find a host of problems not easily resolved. First and foremost it is clear that Engels is advancing a form of realist representationalism; that is, he conceives man as possessed of reflections, or images of material objects and processes[115] in the external world. The reflection (*Wiederspiegelung*) is a copy (*Abbild, Abklatsch*) of what is reflected. Such a copy in the mind cannot be conceived of as more than resembling the object or process copied. In that sense the use of the terms "copy" and "reflect" is metaphorical. Engels evidently does not mean to imply a simple relationship between the external world and the reflections we have of it, even if he does lapse occasionally into speaking, for example, of thought as "a *mere* reflection"[116] of the external world. What he seems to mean is that the products of the human brain cannot stand in *contradiction* to the objects and processes of reality, but must in some sense *correspond* to them.[117] Why this should be so poses a number of interesting problems for which Engels does not provide ready solutions.

He argues that a contradiction cannot obtain between the products of the human brain and the external world because both are products of nature,[118] and it somehow does not seem reasonable that one facet of nature would stand in contradiction to another. Once the missing premise of the argument is given it becomes apparent that Engels would be forced to admit either (1) that contradiction as an "objective presence in things and processes," as "an actual force,"[119] does not pervade *all* but only *select parts* of nature, or (2) that the products of the human brain (feelings, thoughts)[120] *can* stand in contradiction to reality. Obviously he wished to hold the former and reject the latter. He is forced to say that contradiction exists only in select parts of nature and does not obtain between reflections and that which is being reflected. If this were not the case, if *all* existence were self-contradictory, Engels would hardly be licensed to say that thought, being a product of nature, *must* correspond to it.

Only select parts of nature involve contradictions. The relationship presumed to obtain between reflections and things reflected is one of "correspondence" or "coincidence." But merely stating that correspondence characterizes the relationship does nothing to warrant the belief. The question here is, What evidence does Engels muster to justify the confidence he places in the pronouncement? This is an epistemological question and Engels, as we have seen, devoted but little space to the questions which other philosophers have felt to be the most essential.

Engels certifies the correspondence by practice. That is, if practice confirms the prediction made on the basis of perceptions, he feels that this warrants the conclusion that the reflection is in correspondence with what it reflects of the external world. This view that reflections serve as a basis for predictions which can be either proved or disproved by subsequent experiment and observation and thereby their "correspondence" has become central to dialectical materialism. But there is an evident difficulty here. Almost all non-Marxist philosophers have held that action that accords with expectation provides an operational criterion of what it means to say that representations are in accord with their objects. The rankest idealists, Berkeley and Hegel among them, have never denied that our perceptions could be tested in subsequent action. *What they did deny was that the predictive success warranted any pronouncements about a reality beyond sense perception or outside experience.* Berkeley argued that *no kind of practice* can accomplish what is required by such a correspondence theory. There is no practice which takes us beyond the products of the human brain, understood as reflections of objects, to the objects themselves. We entertain only the reflections of objects no matter how elaborate our practice. All practice provides is more complex and more varied reflections, which tell us nothing of the nature of the *objects* independent of us that have presumably been reflected. Those who have attempted to show the elementary fallacy involved in such a correspondence theory have argued that predictive success proves nothing more than that we enjoy the faculty of making successful predictions. Predictive success cannot deliver conclusive warrant for maintaining that our reflections deliver adequate images of objects, for we can never experience *objects*. We experience only their *images*. The object and the data of sensory experience are separate and distinct entities which may or may not be related in the manner Engels described. If we can be aware of objects only through reflections, the objects themselves exist only in the realm of inferred knowledge. The validity of the inference is certainly not beyond doubt. Even if the premises employed in such an argument refer to predictive success, they can speak only of the directly given *reflections;* but the conclusion pretends to refer to something else, i.e., to *objects*. Such an argument cannot be construed as yielding a logically valid inference. It can be, and has been, denied in some sense or another without self-contradiction by almost every modern philosopher. That men have derived such a conclusion from such premises tells us something about human psychology but nothing about the logical validity of the demonstration.[121] This is not to say that such a conclusion is not a common-sensical one. It is convenient for us to assume such a correspondence. The conclusion asserts a belief supported by habit and nurtured by convenience and familiarity; it is an alluring, but nonetheless logically defective, hypothesis. Any dogmatically advanced assertion of its "truth" can only be the consequence of an anterior commitment to eliminate "idealist," "skeptical," or "spiritual" propositions from the language.

How much at variance such a correspondence theory of truth is from the humanistic epistemology of the young Marx is immediately evident. For the young Marx there is no reality independent of mankind against which reflections could be measured. Reality could only be a *reality for man*. To speculate upon what exists independently of man is a scholastic residual. Speculations about an objective reality would be meaningless, since nothing of man would be reflected in an "objective world." To be known, a world must be a *human* world, a world humanized. An object without the subject is as inconceivable as the subject (man) without the object. Thought and being, subject and object are a unity, wedded in practice, separated only in abstraction. Truths are relative and transient, determined by the needs and nature of man—they are historical, dialectical. As society increases in complexity, and practical experiences multiply, a more complex reality makes its appearance. The highest truth is the truth entertained by the most highly developed, the most human society, one which fosters the most complex and varied real relations through which both objects and subjects define themselves. The "practice" of which the young Marx speaks is certainly of a different order from that of Engels.

Not only does Engels contend that "practice," understood to mean predictive success, certifies the correspondence of reflections in the mind to the objects and processes of the real world, but he believes that predictive success certifies a view of causality involving such curious characteristics as (1) logical necessity, (2) teleology, and (3) final cause. He tells us specifically that a *post hoc* proves a *propter hoc*, that is, that a cause must somehow necessarily entail its effect! He seems committed to the notion that processes in the natural world follow a *logically necessary development*. This notion also musters in the concepts of teleology and final cause, so that Engels lapses into locutions involving "iron necessity" and "inevitability" when speaking of physical processes in nature. Thus not only does primordial matter in some obscure sense entail the necessary appearance of thinking beings, but it is also the cause of their inevitable recurrence! ". . . [We] have the certainty that matter remains eternally the same in all its transformations, that none of its attributes can ever be lost, and therefore, also, that with the same iron necessity that it will exterminate on the earth its highest creation, the thinking mind, it must somewhere else and at another time again produce it."[122]

Such propositions can never be established by any known scientific procedure. They assert that conditions *must* appear which are necessary for the progressive evolution of matter into mind.[123] Such a causal statement would be of the order that *a* invariably implies *b*. What seems to be involved is a probability law which would be more appropriately stated as *a* is followed by *b* with such and such a degree of probability. The degree of probability would be assigned only after a consideration of the empirical reasons in its favor. An empirical explanation of an event cannot be deduced from universal laws alone. Statements concerning initial conditions must figure in any empirical explanation. The variant initial conditions determine the degree of probability to be assigned to the occurrence of *b* when it is said that *a* is followed by *b*. To talk of the *certainty* and the iron *necessity* of matter giving rise to consciousness does not seem appropriate to science. It is language that is more appropriate to logic or faith. Such a certainty can only derive from the disposition to convert a physical process into a logical necessity. In the West the concept of causation has come to mean predictability according to law (or a set of laws). It cannot legitimately be used to introduce the tortured notions of logical necessity, teleology, and final cause.[124]

The concept of causality in Engels is thus made to carry a metaphysical ballast. Since the time of Galileo the notions of teleology and final cause have been in disrepute, and since Hume logical necessity has been generally abandoned in any serious analysis of causation. Certainly there are few philosophers of science who would support the contention that predictive success alone warrants the introduction of such notions into the scientific conception of causality.

In the course of the discussion we have suggested that Engels could not possibly have meant the logical notion of contradiction exists *universally* in nature as an actual force. If this were not the case Engels would be forced to violate one of the most elementary canons of logic and admit that the conjunction of two contradictory statements was true and that inferences made from contradictory premises would be valid. If such were the case and all correct thinking were a "true reflection" of a contradictory reality, then consistency in thought would constitute a sure sign of error. Science, not to speak of intelligible language, would be impossible.

What Engels is apparently trying to do is to indicate that to meaningfully discuss *certain* processes and things it is necessary to introduce the laws of the dialectic, including the notion of contradiction as something objectively real. But their use must be selective. Apparently the laws do not have universal application. He does tell us that we share with animals all the activity of the understanding, that is, animals employ deduction, induction, abstraction, analysis, synthesis, and experiment,[125] aspects of what might be called traditional logic. These techniques afford predictive success to both men and animals. They are elementary techniques.[126] But dialectics as the "investigation of the nature of concepts themselves" becomes possible only for men at a comparatively high stage of development.[127]

It would seem then that animals and men, even good scientists, can enjoy some predictive success; they can undertake successful practice, without employing the laws of the dialectic. This can only mean that the laws presume the antecedent utility and truthfulness of the traditional logic which employs the principles of identity, of the excluded middle, and of non-contradiction. These principles can only be "transcended" when one seeks more "adequate" understanding, more "appropriate" description. When they are to be used is not clearly stipulated. One can only begin to make such judgments after seeing how dialecticians employ them.

Certainly a law such as the transformation of quantity into quality does not have universal application. The quality of a pile of stones does not seem to alter with the increase in the quantity involved, unless one proceeds to do some curious things with the language. Nor does the law have unequivocal meaning even when it seems to apply. To say that the heating of water involves a quantitative change in temperature until a critical nodal point is achieved and the liquid quality of water is transmuted into the gaseous quality of steam[128] tells us something about how we use our language and about what interests us as human beings, but hardly anything about what is going on in a nature independent of ourselves. The mensurable increase in the temperature of water is expressed quantitatively in metric terms, but water has qualitatively changed throughout the process. Its volume has increased (it is "bigger") and it has become "hotter." Either the law is applicable everywhere and then it is vacuous, or one can identify certain qualities as real and others as unreal. Why should the change of water as liquid to water as steam be more significant than its change in dimension? Certainly the dialectician does not pretend to tell the scientist where to look for the qualitative change, nor does he pretend to predict when a new quality will emerge. This can only be determined by empirical investigation. After the empirical scientist has decided which changes are important for his purposes he can generalize on the fact that certain qualities appear only at some specific point in the course of quantitative change, e.g., a certain specifiable amount of pressure in a boiler will precipitate a qualitative change in the form of the boiler: it will explode. What seems to be the case is that some specifiable qualities vary in some relationships to variable quantities. The variations may be described by continuous or discontinuous functions, certain "leaps" being identified as a consequence of human interest. But it cannot be said that the law is in any legitimate sense universal, that it tells us something ontologically significant, or that a quantity ever becomes objectively transformed into a quality.[129]

What makes this law seem so plausible is that we are aware of qualities in nature and as a consequence of the precision afforded by quantification we reduce qualities to measures of quantity wherever possible. Thus the quality of being hot is reduced to some measure with the use of a thermometer. Consequently quality is in some sense always seemingly attended by quantities. To say that one changes with a change in the other does not tell us very much and may lead to the mistaken idea that one is in some sense identical with the other.[130] To say, further, that one "transforms" itself into the other is certainly to abuse the language.[131] To say that qualitative change can *only* occur by virtue of quantitative addition or subtraction[132] certainly exceeds empirical findings. To further contend that quantity and quality are both the same and yet different would seem to be confusion compounded.

Engels seems to believe that the use of such a "law" imparts clarity,[133] but it certainly does not seem to function in this way. The law in itself is ambiguous and vague, and traffics in metaphors. Nowhere is there any attempt to stipulate the range of its application. What its specific value to science might be is difficult to say.

The difficulties involved in the application of these "laws" become evident when we consider the applications of the law of the negation of the negation, the "kernel" of the dialectic. There are processes in nature, according to Engels, that are essentially "antagonistic," that contain in themselves *a literal contradiction.* They transform themselves into their opposite and the negation of the negation is the "kernel of the whole thing."[134] We have suggested that the antagonisms between quality and quantity cannot be legitimately thought of as contradictory in any strict sense. To say that there are antagonisms in nature is not to suggest that any of them are contradictory. That is, to say that an atom, a unity of positive and negative charges, involves antagonistic components, opposites, is not to say that an adequate description involves affirming the truth of two contradictory propositions. It does not involve a contradiction *in the strict sense* to say that an atom possesses both negative and positive charges since the ascription is made to specific parts of the atom. Nor can it meaningfully be said that this antagonism transforms either attribute into its opposite. Nor, if our language is tolerably precise, can we say that an atom is a contradiction. We can speak, if we like, of a unity of opposites. Certainly if we are aware that our language is necessarily vague, we can appreciate why it is the case to speak of life involving in some sense death. But we are not thereby required to ascribe contradictory attributes to one thing. We say that an organism is alive when it gives evidence of self-conservation by virtue of the physicochemical processes involved in ingestion, digestion, and excretion, which make possible activity in response to stimuli during the time the organism possesses some of the faculties of growth and reproduction. In this life process dead cells are eliminated as a by-product of the process itself. The organism is alive; some of its cells are dead. There is no contradiction inherent in such a notion. It is simply a reasonably adequate description of a process which involves ascribing the attribute "dead" to some parts of the living organism. If this were all that is meant by contradictions in nature, there would be no particular objection; but one might then ask how science or knowledge is advanced by framing one's descriptions in such metaphors.

But Engels has made a more robust claim. He conceives nature as possessed of inherent contradictions which constitute actual forces. Yet the term "contradiction" has no unequivocal meaning in his exposition. Sometimes he seems to consider *distinct* things *contradictory* (quality and quantity) and sometimes he seems to contend that processes involve *contradictions* (living involves dying). All that could reasonably be intended is that, in some vague sense, such processes are a unity of opposites. That is, the process by virtue of which we say something is living involves the regularity of periodic elimination of some of its cells. I am not obliged to assert a contradiction in saying so, nor can we argue as a consequence that nature involves real contradictions. Finally, that we cannot stipulate to everyone's satisfaction when an attribute can be applied (when something is alive or dead) means only that some words in our language tend to be open-textured. Their application has to be the consequence of a decision that rests upon considerations of utility and theoretical fruitfulness in some range of application (in medical, biological, psychological, legal, or common-sense discourse, among others). The proposition "Living means dying,"[135] as such, may brighten the day of some existential philosophers, but it borders on nonsense.

It is the abuse of language which makes such usage possible. The fact that such propositions are uttered is evidence not of contradictions in nature but rather that some descriptive words have applications that have not been fixed, that these must be delimited before they can be confidently employed, that some processes in nature are complex and that any simple summary description does not deliver an exhaustive account. Such considerations make suspect reasonings by means of which the real existence of contradictions in nature is inferred from the occurrence of vague and ambiguous linguistic usage or incomplete explanation sketches.

It would seem that Engels can be charged with such confusion. More than that, there seems to be rank error in some of his proceedings. In the instance of the classic illustration of the "real contradiction" involved in motion we find a case in point. Engels suggests that motion is in and of itself a contradiction since "mechanical motion can come about only through a body being at one and the same moment both in one place and another, being in one and the same place and also not in it."[136] Actually the paradox seems to turn on at least one confusion. If "place" is understood to mean "occupying a space equal to itself" then certainly an object can consistently be said to be in a specifiable place throughout its motion. If "place" is construed to mean something else, i.e., a space which remains, throughout a given period of time, at a constant distance from some determinable marker in some reference system, it can be said that the object in motion cannot remain in *that* "place." Only if one confuses the two meanings can an apparent contradiction result. The contradiction disappears once the ambiguity is made evident. Engels could certainly have described motion as a continuous function of time by means of the classical theory of functions of a real variable, using the perfectly consistent definitions of limit and continuity, of derivative and definite integral, of convergence and continuous function. Such a description of motion does not involve any contradiction.

The suggestion that science cannot describe even simple motion or change without abandoning traditional logic is curious at best. Science employs not only concepts of invariable classes, but also variables like "acceleration," "rate of growth," and so forth which are capable of adequately describing changing aspects of experience. Propositions containing such concepts exhibit relations treated in orthodox propositional calculus. Furthermore, differential and integral calculi provide numerical variables which can be effectively used to represent the instantaneous state and evolution of material systems without having recourse to contradictory formulations.

Certainly Engels could not have used "contradiction" in its

logical sense, for as such only propositions can be contradictory. Since all true propositions must be compatible, it would seem that not only can the processes of nature themselves not be in contradiction, but neither can the propositions describing them. How then is "contradiction" to be understood? Only when the meaning of the concept "contradiction" is given with some specificity can a reasonable assessment be forthcoming.

Similar objections can be raised with respect to the remainder of the dialectical laws. If we consider the law of the negation of the negation, using the illustration provided in the *Anti-Dühring*, its meaning is certainly not at once "simple and clear as noonday."[137] A grain of barley falls on suitable soil and negates itself in a plant. In the course of its normal life process it produces grains of barley and dies. It has negated itself, the negation of the negation. We have the original grain of barley, only on a higher level, that is, increased ten-, twenty-, or thirtyfold.

Engels has given us a description of a particular cycle of an annual in the plant kingdom. There does not seem to be a pretense of delivering any information about the specific process involved.[138] Engels feels he is giving an illustration of a general law of motion. What the import of so describing the life process of an annual might be we shall briefly consider in the further course of the discussion. For the moment there are certain curiosities in this illustration of the negation of the negation that warrant consideration.

Engels has asserted that "every kind of thing . . . has a peculiar way of being negated in such a manner that it gives rise to development."[139] If a thing is negated in an inappropriate way the negation is "bad, barren."[140] No "development" is possible. Thus if I eat the grain of barley I have not undertaken a "real negation."[141] "I must not only negate, but also sublate the negation. I must therefore so arrange the first negation that the second remains or becomes possible."[142] Should all this mean anything, it means that not all change is development and that development is not *inevitable* but depends upon variable initial conditions. Furthermore, development seems to mean change in accordance with the "essential nature" of the thing. That this is an essentially Aristotelian and Hegelian notion involving a covert assumption of final cause seems evident from Engels' value ascriptions. If everything has an essential nature which pursues a natural development, any impediment to that development would be in some sense "bad."

Such a "bad," "barren," or "untrue" negation is "purely subjective, individual. . . . Not being a stage of development of the thing itself . . . nothing can result from it, the negator must be at loggerheads with the world, sullenly finding fault with everything that exists or ever happened, with the whole historical development."[143]

This could only be the consequence of an addiction to the Hegelian notion of the *Ansich* as the "essence" or the "inherently real,"[144] a curiosity to which Engels has frequent recourse. This doctrine would seem to imply, in some sense or another, that some processes observed in nature accord with the *essences of things*. That is, the process going from barley grain to plant to increased numbers (and adaptive change) of barley grains is "good," "true," "fruitful"; while the process beginning with the barley grain and proceeding to milling and resulting in bread is "bad," "untrue," "barren." If the notion is applicable at all, then it would suggest that we can identify *essences*, the *Ansich*, again involving notions of teleology and some sort of logical necessity. Without all this metaphysical machinery all that could be said is that changes come about as a consequence of placing a particular thing under the influence of determinate conditions, but there would be no suggestion that any one change is any more natural or true than any other. We know something of the range of mutability. We know that we can grow barley. We also know that we can grind it and bake it into bread. Why one course is barren, leading its follower to misanthropy, fault-finding, and skepticism, is difficult to say. It would be foolish to attempt to produce an increased number of barley grains by the grinding of barley, but it would be equally foolish to try to produce a loaf of bread by planting barley.

All such talk threatens to lead one to use words in curious ways. Sometimes words and whole phrases are used to no cognitive purpose and look, at best, suspiciously like word-play. To cite only one bizarre example, Engels uses as a prime illustration of the negation of the negation the following: "With the rise of Constantinople and the fall of Rome, antiquity comes to an end. The end of the Middle Ages is indissolubly linked with the fall of Constantinople. The new age begins with the return to the Greeks—Negation of the negation!"[145] If this means anything it means that antiquity bore within itself the rise of Constantinople and that Constantinople as the consequence of some essential contradictions gave rise to its own negation, the Renaissance, and that the Renaissance was inherent in the essence of antiquity. Certainly as it stands such an illustration has no heuristic or cognitive merit. It is doubtful if calling the "new age" the "negation of the negation" assists us in any way in better understanding the history of these periods. Such a schema has all the characteristics of vacuity. Unless we have more in the way of definition of terms and rules for their application, *any* determinate change could seemingly be so described without affording us any predictive advantage or descriptive accuracy.

Engels certainly seems to feel that the comprehensibility of the negation of the negation is a consequence of empirical research and assessment. When the ascription is unpacked it seems to mean nothing more than if one wishes to produce a specific change one has to insure the interaction, under specific conditions, of a specific number of relevant factors. It does not appear to tell one any more than one already knows. To tell one that as a law it applies "everyday and everywhere,"[146] but that it can only be significantly applied *after* the completion of empirical research would seem to materially reduce its scientific interest. After the scientist has established that a process proceeds in a specific way, he can, if he so chooses, refer to that process as obeying the dialectical law of the negation of the negation.[147] The pronouncement of such a law does not tell him how to grow barley. Nor can he, knowing the law but never having grown barley, predict how barley *will* grow because of some privileged insight into its essence. This law, which is certainly "extremely far-reaching," does not immediately give evidence of its scientific or cognitive importance.[148]

There is a great deal more involved in Engels' discussion than is apparent. There are a host of subleties which are never made explicit. Most of them seem to turn on the nature of *causation*. Engels' notion of causation involves all the implications of teleology, and a final and necessary logic of nature. They are all nonempirical notions, the heritage of an idealist tradition. Mixed with them are markedly positivistic elements, empirical prejudices, which complicate and confuse any attempt to systematically represent Engels' thought.

It is difficult, for example, to know what to do with Engels' "empirical" analysis of the status of mathematical axioms. Engels believes that the self-evidence of mathematical axioms derives from the accumulated inheritance, the race memory of a line of ancestors! "By recognizing the inheritance of acquired characters . . . the subject of experience [is extended] from the individual to the genus; the single individual that must have experience is no longer necessary, its individual experience can be replaced to a certain extent by the results of the experiences of a number of its ancestors. If, for instance, among us the mathematical anxioms seem self-evident to every eight-year-old child, and in no need of proof from experience, this is solely the result of 'accumulated inheritance.'"[149] Nor is this simply a lapse. He repeats the same contention in several places,[150] and insists that "Spencer is right in as much as what thus appears to us to be the self-evidence of these axioms is inherited."[151]

The implications of such a notion are staggering. That mathematics and ultimately logic are empirical sciences involves what appear to be insurmountable difficulties. That one inherits ancestral experience smacks of Carl Gustav Jung and would hardly seem compatible with contemporary Marxist thought.

A number of singularly positivistic elements have also been identified in the work of Engels.[152] Max Adler, for example, scrupulously records that Engels—in quite the positivistic fashion —refers to "matter as such" as "a pure creation of thought [Gedankenschöpfung] and an abstraction"[153] and as "nothing but the totality of material things from which this concept is abstracted."[154] Engels even insisted that "atoms and molecules, etc., cannot be observed under the microscope, but only by the process of thought"[155] as "thought determinations"[156] (Gedankenbestimmungen). All of which would suit the positivism of the end of the nineteenth century.[157] But what should also be weighed in estimating Engels' final philosophical position is the fact that he also wrote, "Causa finalis—matter and its inherent motion. This matter is no abstraction. Even in the sun the different substances are dissociated and without distinction in their action. But in the gaseous sphere of the nebula all substances, although separately present, become merged in pure matter as such, acting only as matter, not according to their specific properties."[158] Engels apparently entertained at least two conceptions of "pure matter as such."

The notebooks published posthumously as the *Dialectics of Nature* contain the random thoughts Friedrich Engels collected over a thirteen-year period. The fragments and notes contained in the documents were not meant for publication. That each fragment would be consistent with every other seems too much to expect. The evidence of the notebooks and the somewhat hesitant preface to the second edition[159] of the *Anti-Dühring* suggest that the mature philosophy of Engels was far from being a finished system. The inordinate use of metaphorical language (thought is a "motion"; "opposites" "struggle" in nature), the variable and confused use of the concepts "matter" and "law," the lack of any clearly stipulated rules for the application of the "laws" of the dialectic, all expose real deficiencies in argument and exposition. That as a philosophy it contains a mixture of rationalist, quasi-idealist, and positivist elements never fully integrated seems evident. That there is considerable vagueness and ambiguity seems also evident. That there is real confusion and error is likely.

## Engels and Marxism

How much of the philosophy of natural science, introduced as dialectical materialism into classical Marxism, can be legitimately credited to Karl Marx is difficult to determine. Engels was certainly the prime mover of these concepts. Engels does tell us, in the preface to the second edition of the *Anti-Dühring*, that "it was self-understood" that his exposition of dialectical materialism would not be issued without Marx's knowledge.[160] Marx, then, was apparently aware of its issuance and contributed the tenth part of the chapter on Economics. Whether Marx entirely approved the text's philosophic content is quite another matter. When Engels announced that the idea of the "dialectics of nature" had come to him one morning as he "lay abed"[161] and proceeded to outline the same essential notions that make their full appearance in the *Anti-Dühring* and the *Dialectics of Nature* for Marx's approval, Marx, as we have indicated, could only say that he had to reserve judgment until he could consider the matter and consult the appropriate authorities. In the ensuing years Marx was fully occupied with the preparation of the final volumes of *Capital*, and he nowhere gives evidence of having devoted any systematic study to the subject. In the division of labor which obtained between Marx and Engels, Marx always deferred to the judgment of Engels in matters of natural science. On one occasion, while discussing some feature of natural science in a letter to Engels, Marx went so far as to write, "As you know, things come slowly to me and secondly that I always follow in your footsteps."[162]

Certainly the philosophy of natural science found in the mature works of Engels accords badly even with what we know of the "Theses on Feuerbach," written by Marx in 1845, and is—for all intents and purposes—at complete variance with Marx's natural philosophy in the *Manuscripts of 1844*. The entire notion of thought being a reflection of nature seems to be indistinguishable from a philosophic posture Marx inveighed against in the first thesis on Feuerbach. The conception of "practice" in Marx's early manuscripts is certainly something other than the "practice" to which Engels refers in *Ludwig Feuerbach*. There is only a verbal resemblance between them.

In the Afterword to the second German edition of *Capital*, Marx does speak of the "ideal" as being the "material world reflected by the human mind,"[163] but since the use is patently metaphorical we cannot determine with any assurance what Marx meant by it. Elsewhere he speaks, again metaphorically, of the relationship between life and thought, the latter being a "direct efflux" and an "ideological reflex and echo"[164] of the former. Whether he meant thereby to include all that Engels imputes to the "theory of reflections" we lack the evidence to say. As we have indicated, the wanton destruction of some of Marx's correspondence to his wife, undertaken to protect Engels from embarrassment, may well have contained the answer. As it is, we will probably never be able to determine with any assurance what Marx thought of Engels' philosophy of natural science, which now constitutes one of the prime components of contemporary Marxism.

The twentieth century was the heir of this ambiguous legacy. Among the foremost of the inheritors was Vladimir Ilyich Lenin, leader of the first successful Marxist revolution.

# 3 The Philosophy

# of V. I. Lenin

Vladimir Ilyich Ulyanov, known to history as V. I. Lenin, was born in April, 1870, in the town of Simbirsk on the banks of the Volga. Karl Marx had but a few years before published the first volume of *Capital* and Friedrich Engels was beginning his systematic study of natural science.

Lenin was born to revolution. In 1887, four years after the death of Karl Marx, Lenin's older brother, much beloved by the young Vladimir, was executed in the Schlüsselburg Fortress in St. Petersburg for participating in an attempt on the life of Czar Alexander III. In December of that same year the young Lenin was expelled from Kazan University and arrested for participating in a revolutionary student movement. Still a boy, he was banished to the village of Kokushkino in Kazan Gubernia. It was there, at the age of seventeen, that he read *Capital*. Thereafter the young Lenin undertook the study of classical Marxism in earnest. By 1890 he could read the original German, and he translated the *Communist Manifesto* into Russian. His expulsion from the university did not seriously impede Lenin. He taught himself law and after having been granted permission to take his concluding examinations at the University of Petersburg graduated first in a class of 124. After receiving his law degree in 1891, Lenin numbered himself among the Marxists of St. Petersburg. In April, 1895, he went abroad to contact Russian Marxists in exile. In Switzerland he made the acquaintance of G. V. Plekhanov, with whose works he had been long familiar. In Paris he met Paul Lafargue, son-in-law of Karl Marx, and planned a visit to Friedrich Engels. But Engels was gravely ill and the two never met. Lenin returned to Russia in September and immersed himself in Marxist study and revolutionary agitation. Almost immediately upon his return he was arrested and sentenced to exile in Siberia. Upon his return from Siberia, from 1900 until 1905, Lenin remained outside Russia, until revolution erupted there in 1905.

It was during this period that Plekhanov discussed with Lenin the "philosophical deviations" that had begun to afflict "orthodox" Marxism. While Lenin sympathized with Plekhanov, he did not feel that he could enter the contest because he did "not know enough about philosophy."[1] But the "deviationists" persisted in their efforts to take over the intellectual leadership of the party. Bogdanov published his three-volume opus, *Empiriomonism* (1905–1909) and in 1908 Bogdanov, Bazarov, and Lunacharsky, together with the Mensheviks Yushkevich and Valentinov, produced the *Outlines of the Philosophy of Marxism*. Lenin became convinced that he must speak if he and his faction were not to forfeit intellectual control of the party. The product of this conviction, motivated more by strategic than philosophical reasons, was *Materialism and Empiriocriticism*, published under the pseudonym "Valdimir Ilyin," which went to press at the end of 1908.

The character of the work was almost "scholastic." The ultimate proofs of philosophic assertions are almost always appeals to authority—the authority of Friedrich Engels. For although Karl Marx is referred to scores of times, the ultimate authority is Friedrich Engels. In his polemics, Lenin propounded what he conceived to be the orthodox philosophy of dialectical materialism. The difficulties in his exposition are not only the same difficulties which faced Engels; they are difficulties arising from the development of contemporary science and contemporary thought during the generation since Engels had written on the philosophy of natural science.

We find in *Materialism and Empiriocriticism* not only a restatement of Engel's philosophy of natural science but an attempt to clarify some critical concepts and to deal with the modern problems of thought and of science. If the concept "matter" remained imprecise in the writings of Engels, Lenin undertook its clarification; if the "copy" theory of knowledge remained metaphorical in

Engels, Lenin sought to give it precision; if there was some question as to the nature of truth in Engels, Lenin sought its resolution.

## Lenin's Philosophy of Natural Science

Following Engels' death, it became increasingly evident that philosophy was facing new and crucial issues that would define its tasks for many years to come. That Engels, in his time, could maintain that the issues between materialism and idealism turned solely upon the question of which was prior, "nature" or "spirit," that he could suggest that metaphysics meant nothing more than speculating on "things" rather than "processes," considering objects in isolation rather than within the living context in which they are found, that it was possible for him to seriously formulate these considerations as fundamental philosophical issues, indicates how rapidly philosophy had outdistanced him. The philosopher of science analyzing the concept "matter" has no illusions about "spirit" somehow coming first. To imagine that by rejecting "metaphysics," the positivist was taking sides in the question of whether things are "really" processes or isolated entities is to misunderstand his intent and meaning.

It can be said that in Engels' time some basic philosophical considerations did arise out of the problem of how science was to be understood. Classical Newtonian physics, with its common-sensical materialism, had neatly ordered the celestial reaches, and atomic physics had systematized the world behind the world. It could be said that only the ghost of God remained somehow to disturb the material unity of the scientific world picture. Engels proposed to lay this ghost by prompting each special science to clarify its position in relation to "the totality of things and knowledge." This done, a special science of that totality would be superfluous.[2] Philosophy would be absorbed in science and the graveyard of traditional faith would become a fertile field of science—the specter that haunted matter would be dispelled. Only matter would remain, matter in motion, matter in dialectical motion.

But a generation later the concept "matter" no longer seemed so eminently common-sensical and tidy. The Michelson-Morley experiment had shaken the faith in luminiferous ether, the medium for the propagation of electromagnetic waves. The discovery of the electron imperiled the "compact, impenetrable little billiard balls" of the kinetic theory of gases. The Lorentz transformation and the Fitzgerald contraction threatened to do violence to "mass" and "dimensionality." The neatly ordered common-sensically materialist world of classical physics began to look like the Mad Queen's Croquet Ground where "there don't seem to be any rules in particular or at least no one attends to them."

This was the situation the philosophy of science inherited in the first decade of the twentieth century. It had become increasingly embarrassed by the goings-on in science and as a consequence became more and more chary of "common-sense" beginnings. The philosophy of science became increasingly analytic, and one of the first questions it asked was, "How is the concept 'matter' to be understood?" It was in answer to this question that Lenin wrote his only formal philosophic work, *Materialism and Empiriocriticism.*

No longer could Marxism be content simply to permit science to "absorb"' philosophy, for science appeared to be doing curious things to "matter." Philosophy had to function as a regulative,[3] a control device, to protect science from the depredations of "idealistic religious speculation."[4]

In his search for this regulative discipline, Lenin settled upon the insights provided by Engels in *Anti-Dühring* and *Ludwig Feuerbach.*[5] Of all the elements he found there, it was the "*Abbildtheorie,*" the notion that "matter," the ultimate reality, is "reflected" in the mind, that provided the primary epistemological substance for *Materialism and Empiriocriticism.*

At first view, the system he left us, now almost canonical for Soviet philosophy, is engagingly simple. The "external material world" is posited at the outset.[6] The cognizing intellect is its by-product and knowledge is conceived of as a function of the inter-relation of both.[7] With Lenin, philosophy's task is to "deliberately make the 'naive' belief of mankind the foundation of [the] theory of knowledge."[8] Lenin and his followers have explicitly renounced the search for epistemological "purity"[9] which is so characteristic of contemporary philosophy.

An immediate, material, "objective" world is given, to which our senses relate us;[10] while "objective truth" is a "true reflection" in thought of that objective world."[11] "Absolute truth," in turn, is compounded of relative objective truths,[12] and while this truth is conditioned by man's historical and physiological circumstances, the fact of the existence of "absolute truth" and the fact that we are approaching it continually are equally unconditional.[13]

The concept "matter" is the cornerstone of Marxist philosophical materialism.[14] The external world is composed of matter. Matter is "objective, existing independently of human consciousness...."[15] It is "eternal in time and limitless in space, it has always existed, it exists now and will always exist. It cannot be created or destroyed."[16]

The mind, in its turn, is a function of highly organized matter.[17] It enjoys the capacity of reflecting external reality through the agency of the senses, which "copy," "image," or "photograph" matter in motion.[18]

How the relationship between the "pictures" of reality entertained in the mind and reality itself is to be understood is the fundamental problem of Marxist-Leninist epistemology.[19] The correspondence between ideas and reality is only gradually established and the correspondence is often no more than partial.[20] Such partial ideas are relatively true; they are approximate truths.[21] They reflect but one aspect, one facet of an objective, absolute reality.[22]

Lenin says all this with relative ease and cogency; indeed, there is here a seeming simplicity and directness which is quite engaging. But epistemological difficulties attend each of these three fundamental elements of Lenin's Marxism as a philosophy of nature.

### Lenin and the Concept of "Matter"

In the past, philosophical materialism has always had a substantial meaning.[23] It was essentially a notion that the world is material, i.e., composed of massy, impenetrable (sometimes elastic) particles, generally limited in number, combinations of which give rise to the multiplicity of forms familiar to us in the world of sense perception.[24] The clearest formulations of this position in the ancient world were, of course, those of Democritus, Leucippus, and later Epicurus. For them the world, the Real World of ontology, was reducible to atoms in empty space. Atoms in configuration created objects, while their effects on human sensory apparatus gave rise to sense impressions, that is, to the vexedly veiled picture of the work-a-day world.

The world was thus material, since one could describe its ultimate ontological constituents as massy, impenetrable particles. A similar atomic materialism was revived in the philosophies of Dalton and Boyle; the atom of their chemistry and of classical physics was envisaged as it had been in ancient materialism—as a minute, hard, solid, ultimate particle.

With the discovery of the electron at the close of the nineteenth century a radical revision was made in the philosophy of materialism. The whole mass of the electron, a principal constituent of the ultimate material particle, was found to be its electrical charge. The electron was not matter as matter had been understood; it was an electrical charge. A material particle displaying all the attributes of matter was discovered to be electrical.[25]

The advent of quantum physics, however, has made even more obvious the fact that humans are made aware of the presence of ultimate particles in nature *only* when the particles are disturbed by minute electrical interchanges with some other part of the universe.[26] These interchanges force the atom to indicate a position, a color, and a quantity of heat. What the atom is, what its qualities might be before those disturbances, is quite impossible to say.[27] All the qualities of the atom of modern physics are derived; it has no immediate and direct physical properties at all;[28] all its properties are observed through the screen of the disturbances we create in observing the submicroscopic world.[29]

It becomes otiose to ask what the ultimate particles are independently of our experience of them, for we can never know them in themselves.[30] We succeed in symbolizing their activity in an abstract multidimensional space by a partial differential equation, recognizing always that such conceptions pertain to "atoms-for-us" and not "atoms-in-themselves."[31] For the physicist to transgress the limits of experimental verification, to speculate as to the "essence" of atoms, would be to undermine the autonomy of science and subject it to the vagaries of extraempirical metaphysics.[32] Thus physics does not any longer pretend to be a science of "matter-in-itself," but rather a science concerned with relating phenomena and not with discovering the essence of "ultimate particles."[33]

In order to illustrate the nature of the contemporary concept of the atom Heisenberg draws the analogy between it and the notion of the square root of minus one in mathematics.[34] Although elementary mathematics maintains that among ordinary numbers no such square root exists, the introduction of this square root as a new symbol simplified the most important mathematical propositions. *Its use is justified by this convenience.* Similarly contemporary physics illustrates that atoms cannot exist as simple material objects. Nevertheless only the introduction of the concept "atom" makes possible a simple, coherent formulation of laws governing physical and chemical processes. Thus the criterion for the acceptability of a concept is not whether it "reflects truly" objective reality but rather whether the concept leads to a simpler and clearer survey of observed phenomena.[35]

The physical picture of a discrete particle in a three-dimensional space has been replaced with a collection of mathematical symbols in multidimensional extension. These symbols do not pretend to represent an ontological reality.[36] Rather, such symbolization permits the derivation of laws by which scientists can anticipate, and conveniently formulate, atomic and subatomic behavior.[37] The formulation of such laws, not the pursuit after ontological reality,[38] has been accepted, by and large, as the legitimate task of science.[39]

What can all this mean for philosophical materialism? It means that science, long considered the ally of ontological materialism, can only be neutral.[40] The fact that men have hitherto always transcended epistemological premises behind which they posited a "real world," a "real world" conceived either as "matter" or "spirit," is of biographical and sociological rather than epistemological significance. Convictions concerning the "ultimate nature" of the world are by and large determined not by cognitive preoccupations but by ethical, political, and economic interests.[41]

Against such considerations how are we to understand Lenin's position? The first premise of Lenin's materialism concerned "an objective reality" existing independently of our consciousness. Having posited an objective reality, it is incumbent upon him to prove that it exists. But excusing him temporarily from this philosophical responsibility, we note that in positing an "external reality" Lenin has succeeded not to a materialist position, but rather to a *Realist* acceptance of a "reality" outside us quite independent of our awareness of it.[42] If that is all that Lenin tells us, the immediate objection is that his position cannot be distinguished from that of the Spiritualist who is also a Realist, for the Spiritualist conceives God, Spirit, or *Weltgeist* as existing independently of our consciousness.[43]

If one is to distinguish Lenin's Realism from a Spiritualist or Idealist Realism Lenin will have to qualify the nature of the "ultimate metaphysical substance." At first, Lenin seems unwilling or unable to do this. He tells us that ". . . the *sole* 'property' of matter with whose recognition philosophical materialism is bound up is the property of *being an objective reality*, of existing outside our mind."[44] Further on he says, ". . . the concept matter . . . implies *nothing but* objective reality existing independently of the human mind and reflected by it."[45] We are not to identify matter with any of its known forms or modes.[46] Actually this position is far too exposed to be maintained, and the Marxist-Leninists, following the example of Lenin himself, make haste to introduce physical concepts of matter in order to justify the assumption of the name "materialist."

We have seen that we are expected to accept, on its face, the first premise of an "independent objective reality." Now, in order to retain the designation "materialist," this "reality" must be understood as nothing more than matter in motion—in space and time.[47] Unless we are provided specific rules for the employment, justification, and meaning of such conceptions as "matter," "space," and "time," their use causes real theoretical problems. Unless we are informed as to how they are epistemologically certified, their use is hardly calculated to increase our real knowledge of the nature of the world. The advance of science has made it impossible to make definitive statements about the "external world." In effect this kind of "materialism" demands a return to classical physics.[48]

This seems to be particularly true in the case of space and time. Lenin concedes the "mutability of the conceptions of space and time" but still contends that there is an "absolute space and time" somewhere, toward which our concepts tend.[49] Of course we cannot know what this absolute time and space might be in themselves, any more than we can know what matter-in-itself might be;[50] for absolute space, time, and matter have infinite potentiality[51] and inexhaustible attributes.[52]

We are asked to grant that a "reality" independent of our consciousness exists. Then if we ask what this "reality" might be like, we are told to refer to the scientist. The scientist, in his turn, informs us that his formulations do not concern themselves with the "nature," or "essence" of metaphysical "reality." Rather they are tentative hypotheses employed to order experience and serve prediction, for all constructs have been shown to be transitory—some more, some less, but transitory nonetheless. When we return to the Marxist-Leninist with the objection that the scientist has not been able to tell us anything about the nature of metaphysical "matter," he informs us that "materialism" does not depend on *any* specific property of "matter" (since all properties, for science, are derived.)[53] The *sole* property of matter with which his materialism is concerned is "existence." Reality exists independently of our consciousness. But we could then object that such a "materialism" might paradoxically be a "Spiritualism" (God *is*; He exists independently of our consciousness) unless we are told what the properties of "reality-in-itself" might be.

For a number of reasons which need not detain us here, Lenin accepts scientific information as it stands—with one major proviso. He occasionally ascribes to scientific concepts an ontological character, projecting them into a metaphysical Reality with which a scientist, as scientist, is not concerned. The scientist is *not* concerned with the problem of whether caloric fluid, electric fluid, phlogiston, ether, atoms, electrons, neutrons, neutrinos, positrons, light as a wave or light as a corpuscle *exist in some ultimate reality*.[54] He is concerned with these concepts as working hypotheses, functional notions which lead to new theories, and are useful in organizing experience and successful in prediction.[55]

Questions of "ultimate reality" and metaphysical truth do not enter into the physical scientist's consideration. When he describes physical experience through the medium of the four-dimensional space-time continuum it is not because he intuits such a description to be more "real," more adequately "reflecting" the "absolutely real" space-time, but because it presents physical experience in a simpler, more coherent, more serviceable way than do three-dimensional space and one-dimensional time separately.

To believe, as Lenin seems to, that the contemporary description of things advanced by science is ontologically "real" permits one to apply physical notions to a metaphysics of "matter." It also undermines the independence of science and misrepresents its concerns. It commits one's followers to an absolute faith in the existence of ether as the material medium for the transmission of light,[56] to a "matter" indestructible and uncreated, infinite in time, space, and potentiality,[57] and to the tridimensionality of "real" space.[58]

As a consequence, relativity theory and quantum physics,[59] as well as contemporary astronomy, which all discard ether and tridimensionality and posit the destruction and creation of that which science knows as "matter,"[60] have received only qualified acceptance in the Soviet Union.[61] There are theoretic norms to which concepts of matter must conform in order to be admissible to the Marxist-Leninist. We have here what seems to be a curious inversion of the classical Marxist formula "Being determines consciousness," for now it is consciousness with its regulative principles which determines what can be accepted as the nature of "Being."[62] Had Marxism-Leninism been formulated when the notions of caloric fluid and phlogiston were current, no doubt these would have served as elements of ontological reality.

In his defense against the "new physics" with its "destruction" of the classical notion of matter,[63] Lenin was forced to contend that the *sole* property *his* materialism ascribed to matter was its existence outside the cognizing intellect. When asked to talk meaningfully about his philosophical concept of matter, Lenin seemed to rely on the then contemporary physical formulations (Euclidean tridimensionality and so forth), formulations which science has rapidly left behind.

With the pretension that "materialism'" was to explain *all* phenomena, mental as well as physical, Lenin was forced (almost surreptitiously) to ascribe yet another property to his "matter"— the property "which is essentially akin to sensation, the property of reflection . . ."|[64]

Thus we find the "matter" which Engels left vaguely defined conceived by Lenin as (1) not only independent of us, and (2) having at least some of the characteristics science once ascribed to *its* "matter," but has now abandoned, but (3) also possessing uniformly, in its "foundation," a "faculty akin to sensation."[65]

The first property seems to make this "materialism" a Realism, whether Spiritualist, Idealist, or Materialist. The second qualification seems to make it an obstruction to the free development of hypotheses in science. The third characteristic threatens to make "materialism" a burlesque. To conceive of a matter possessed of the property of reflection is to conceive of a matter possessed of all the principal attributes of Spirit. One can no longer consider himself a materialist in any meaningful sense when he grants that matter intrinsically harbors the quality "essentially akin to sensation, the property of reflection." At best, one is a dualist.[66] A similar theory has long been in currency under the name of panpsychism.

## *Lenin and the "Copy Theory" of Knowledge*

If one has difficulty making sense out of the nature of the material world which Lenin posits at the commencement of his philosophy, one finds no less difficulty in analyzing the relationship assumed to exist between that world and our awareness of it. Lenin, as we have suggested, contends that it is sensation, and sensation alone,[67] which affords us "direct connection" between consciousness and the external world.[68] Sensations are the ultimate and sole source of all knowledge of the world. In fact, it is confidence in the evidence of the senses which generates the belief in matter.[69] It is at this juncture that serious inquiry into Lenin's epistemology can be undertaken. The absolute and unconditional premise of a "material world" existing "infinitely in space and time in eternal motion and obeying the laws of Marxian dialectics," with which Lenin, following Engels, commences, is a singular instance of question begging, for it posits what serious epistemology should attempt to prove.

Indeed the Leninists themselves recognize the critical importance of just such an inquiry.[70] In defining the relationship of the senses to the external world Lenin made some of his most explicit philosophical commitments: "The senses," he contends, "give us *faithful images* of things . . ."[71] and furthermore, "Man's perceptive faculty [is] a *simple reflection* of nature."[72] He maintained that ". . . sensations are *copies* of *images* of . . . objects,"[73] and that "Matter . . . is *copied, photographed* and *reflected* by our sensations. . . ."[74] These statements appear to be admirably unequivocal—but even elementary analysis exposes considerable ambiguity.

A first difficulty arises from a consideration of the simple predicates that we assign to the objects of the external world. What do we mean, for example, when we say of a thing, we sense that it is red? The color red cannot in any significant sense be conceived as a "copy," a "reflection," or a "photograph" of a light wavelength of 6470 A–7600 A. We are all well aware of what we mean when we speak of "images" in the photographic sense. We mean iconic similarity—as when we speak of a portrait likeness. Common features are shared by the portrait subject and the portrait, and a direct comparison of the two is possible. But this obviously cannot be the sense in which Lenin employed the expressions "image," "reflect," "photograph," and "copy," for he specifically refers to the sensation of color (red in this case) as arising from the effects of light waves of specific length upon our sensory apparatus.[75] Our sensation of red can hardly be considered a photograph of a wavelength![76]

If this is the case, then certain critical questions arise concerning the relationship between sensation and the qualities of the external object.[77] Is the relationship a causal one? Do qualities in the object effect a sensation in us which acts as a "representation" or a "signal" of such properties?

An affirmative answer to these questions seems eminently plausible; and philosophers, even in antiquity, had so answered them.[78] Lenin seems to accept this type of representationalism, for he identifies himself with the materialism of the seventeenth and eighteenth centuries.[79] During this period, for example, Hobbes maintained that "the cause of sense is the external body, or object . . . ,"[80] sensation arising as a consequence of some motion in or by this object.[81] He could not conceive of a sense perception that did not find its origin in the external world. In point of fact, although Hobbes continued to use the words "phantasm," "appearance," and "representation," he did occasionally employ the word "image" in referring to sensation—apparently in quite the Leninist manner.

Considerably later, Helmholtz expressed essentially the same conviction concerning the relationship between sense-perception and "reality" by saying, ". . . perceived differences (i.e. color) are the appearances [*Erscheinungen*] of given objective differences in the qualities of the (external) bodies. . . . Sensations are therefore the naturally given, sensory signs [*Zeichen*] or symbols for objective qualities. . . ."[82] But Helmholtz was careful to stipulate that our sensations were not to be considered "similar" in the usual sense to the objective "reality" which caused them. The real relationship of objective "reality" to sensation is a causal one.

Should such an interpretation be utilized by the contemporary Marxist-Leninists to explain the real relationship between objective "reality" and sensations, Lenin could only be charged for using infelicitous and misleading metaphors. The proposed relationship of objects to sensations would be, by virtue of this interpretation, a causal one. The correspondence of "things" to sense perceptions would be causal, not one of similarity.

This interpretation appears to be quite consistent with that offered by a number of English Marxist-Leninists. Maurice Cornforth informs us that sensations only "correspond" in some way "or another" to definite characteristics in things,[83] while D. V. Chaplin, equally explicit, contends that sensations are "signals," "correlates," and certainly not "copies" in any formal sense.[84] It would seem that the analysis reduces to this: Sensations are the "signals," the "correlates," the "signs" of an externally existing object. The use of the words "copy," "photograph," "image," and "reflect" was unfortunate and happier expressions can be substituted, although such substitutions would substantially alter the nature of what had seemed to be a delightfully simple theory.

Unfortunately such a solution runs counter to a number of objections raised by Lenin himself. "Engels," he pointed out, "speaks neither of symbols nor of hieroglyphs, but of copies, photographs, images, mirror-reflections of things. . . . If sensations are not images of things, but only signs or symbols, which do 'not resemble' them, then [the] initial materialist premise is undermined. . . ."[85]

Why should this be so? Because Lenin feels that this view implies "a certain distrust of perception, a distrust of the evidence of our sense organs. It is beyond doubt that an image cannot be identical with the model, but . . . symbol, hieroglyph are concepts which introduce an element of agnosticism."[86]

Obviously Lenin wished to make his position distinct from that assumed by the representationalist realists. Marxist-Leninists consistently criticize the representationalist position. Erhard Albrecht, for example, specifically criticizes Hobbes. "In the current history of philosophy it was Bacon who first represented the subjectivistic tendency. According to him human intelligence cannot achieve an objective knowledge of things because it cannot transcend its own idea-world. Hobbes, too, followed this tendency and declared only that is given in experience which is perceived through the senses and that our sensations and our idea of the external world could not be a picture [*Abbild*] of reality. Our perceptive images are only phenomena, only 'phantasms,' only signs for that which is. . . . This empiricist notion was carried out, by Locke and Hume, to a consistent subjectivism."[87]

Chasschatschich, a leading Marxist-Leninist, contends that the distinction of primary and secondary qualities introduced by the early materialists, including Hobbes,[88] was a concession to idealism. The idea that a rose had color only when observed, that smell and taste are present only for a percipient, is "sheer idealism"![89] "Between human perception and the object which this perception reflects, exists a similarity. Were there no similarity between them we could not, in general, speak of a reflection of the object in human perception."[90] He goes on to say that a ". . . picture must display a certain similarity with the imaged object. A statue, for example, which represents a man, must be formed to a human semblance. For a sign this is not necessary. . . ."[91] "When a man receives a visual sensation, the connection between the outer object and consciousness is 'the picture [*Abbildung*] of the external object in the eye,' that is on the retina. This picture is similar to the picture that we see projected through a biconvex lens upon a screen. . . . Just as a physicist can say that the external object and the picture mediated through a biconvex lens are similar, so a physiologist can say that the external object and its picture on the retina are the same."[92]

Neglecting the obvious fact that Chasschatschich here completely confuses epistemological and natural-scientific concerns, we seem, nonetheless, to be confronted by a naive realist notion of the relationship between the object of sense and sensation. In this context "picture," "copy," and "photograph" seem to be employed in quite the ordinary fashion. The sensory image is a "copy" just as an image on a screen projected through a biconvex lens is a "copy" of an original. That the object and its image are not formally identical arises from the obvious fact that the one is material (objective) while the other is a sensation (subjective).[93]

Thus we find arguments for both a causal correspondence and for a similarity correspondence between sensation and object in Marxist-Leninist literature. The first of these two tendencies within contemporary Marxism has interpreted Lenin's statements in a critico-realist sense, asserting that the *form* of sensation is subjective while its *content* is objective. That is to say, the sensation red is a subjective form of the objective content "wavelengths of 6470 A–7600 A." This interpretation is given by the school of hardheaded English Marxists, who have a long national tradition of empiricism. But this interpretation is open to a number of objections:

(1) If we contend that sensation has a subjective form and an objective content, in the above sense, can we say, significantly, that sensations "reflect," "image," or "photograph" reality? Would it not be more correct to say that sensations, at best, "signalize" reality while the notion of objective content of sensations (light waves, electrons, photons, etc.) is derived only by posterior conceptual analysis and logical construction?[94]

(2) How would such a critico-realist interpretation distinguish itself from the position assumed by the early materialists on this question? It would seem that there could be but trivial differences and yet Marxist-Leninists are quite explicit in their rejection of the analysis made by the earlier materialists. Certainly this cannot be on the ground that the earlier materialists held sensations to be simply subjective, as some Marxists have suggested.[95] Hobbes, by way of illustration again, is quite explicit in maintaining that sensations have a causal dependence upon external motion.[96] The form of sensation (color, sound, taste, etc.), he contends, is subjective, but its content (the motion of material bodies) is objective. Nor are sensations conceived of by these earlier materialists as the "conventional," arbitrary signs Lenin suggests.[97] Sensory "signs" and "symbols" are, for Helmholtz, "natural," that is, they arise as a consequence of the impact of the external world upon our sensory apparatus. "Conventional signs," on the other hand, are arbitrary, belonging to language and not necessarily corresponding to anything in the objective world.

The second of the two tendencies we are here considering suggests a formal identity between object and sensation. Sensation, while being formally identical with the objective world, exists only in consciousness[98] and reflects only a limited view of the world. This seems to mean that the only difference between the sensation and the object is that the object is material and its "reflection" is an element of consciousness.[99]

But such an interpretation of the nature of sensations would founder upon a naive realism which assumes that colors abound when one does not perceive them, that sounds persist when there is no ear to heed them.[100] What status, in such an interpretation, would "light waves" and "sound waves" enjoy? Are they "real" as "color" and "sound" are real? Or are the concepts of sound and light waves provisional scientific constructs?[101]

Actually, Lenin gave us precious little on which to base an intelligent choice between the alternate interpretations—the critico-realist (representationalist) and the naive-materialist. Contemporary Marxist-Leninists provide statements of such dubious cognitive merit as "The similarity between the sense-reflection and the object is not a simple mechanical similarity, but a complicated, *contradictory* similarity."[102] And further, "in its subjective form, in the form of perception the objective quality of a light wave is reflected. Color, thus, has a *relative* similarity with the light stimuli which called it forth."[103] Precisely in what fashion the "relative" and "contradictory" similarity and a "faithful imaging" of color and light waves is conceived is difficult to imagine. Finally, we shall see that whichever interpretation is chosen, it is difficult to find anywhere in Marxist-Leninist literature a serious discussion of the epistemological problems each one entails.

From this juncture we would, by necessity, be embarking upon the path traversed by European philosophy during the modern era, from Hobbes through Locke and Berkeley to Hume. How does one divine the true nature of the object? If one can *never* divine its *ultimate* nature ("Matter is infinite potential," "Matter is not to be identified with any of its known forms," etc.), what is the cognitive status of propositions which purport to speak of that nature?

Lenin, himself, tried to face these problems. Contemporary physics had revealed the "subjective" elements in all cognitive experience. None of those qualities of "matter" which, at one time, passed as "primary" were able to withstand analysis. All revealed a "subjective" element which disqualified them as "absolutely objective." Duration and extension were seen to depend upon convenient, relative, co-ordinating definitions; while color, taste, shape, texture, and impenetrability were seen as conditioned by the sensory apparatus of the perceiving organism.

In the effort to work himself out of this particular representational impasse, generated by and large by science itself, Lenin contended that the philosophy of materialism did not have to assign any definitive qualities to the perceived object other than the attribute of its "categorical existence outside the mind."[104] Little can be said to recommend this attempt to work out of the difficulties of representationalism. If we cannot properly specify any of the objective properties of "matter," why then employ the word in preference to "Spirit"—particularly if one assigns the faculty of "reflection" to it?

Lenin was seemingly conscious of these objections and his insistence upon the use of the words "copy," "photograph," and "image" appears calculated to re-establish confidence in simple perception as an immediate and philosophically credible source of knowledge concerning "matter." If, however, upon further analysis, we find that the *sole* property which can be assigned to the "external object" is its externality, how can we meaningfully employ the terms "copy," "photograph," and "reflect" when referring to the relationship between it and sensation? If we enjoyed the faculty of "photographing" and "reflecting" "matter" in sensation, we could certainly be expected to say something more concerning its attributes than simply that it exists outside of our consciousness.

Even the suggestion of contemporary Marxist-Leninists that the sense-perception is "similar" in a "relative" and "contradictory" manner to the object "reflected" is beset with difficulties, for the first question which springs to mind is—"similar" to what extent and in what fashion? Unless the Marxist-Leninists can specify more clearly the nature of the perceived object as it is independent of our experience of it, "similarity" has as little meaning as "copy," "image," and "photograph." For to speak of "similarity" implies a comparison. But in effect such a comparison would transcend experience. It would be empirically impossible to step outside experience in order to compare the experienced properties of the object with the properties of the object as it exists independently of experience.[105]

It is extremely difficult to assign a precise meaning to the terms "copy," "image," "reflect," and "photograph" as these are used in Lenin's *Materialism and Empiriocriticism*. It seems that Lenin in this "definitive" work conceived of differing meanings in different contexts—either that or his conception of the existing relationship between the sensation of an object and the object sensed was far more subtle than *Materialism and Empiriocriticism* would lead us to believe.

## Lenin and the Conception of Truth

Lenin's pronouncements on truth appear, on analysis, to be no better formulated than those concerning the ultimate material "reality" of our world or those in the ability of the senses to "reflect," "copy," or "photograph" that "reality."

The notion of truth occupies a place of considerable prominence in Lenin's metaphysics. On the one hand the doctrine is conceived as being of critical tactical importance.[106] Unless man is possessed of "objective truth," the argument proceeds, he will not attempt to effect changes in an objectionable social order. Furthermore, Lenin maintained that the principal distinction between Marxism, as he understood it, and contemporary philosophy arises from their respective treatment of truth.[107] For Lenin there must be an absolute, objective truth which is the sum total of all relative truths.

We find that there are deceptively straightforward definitions in Lenin's philosophy. "Objective truth," Lenin tells us, "means nothing else than the existence of objects ('things-in-themselves') truly reflected by thinking."[108] "Truth," we are told, "is the correct reflection of the external world in the consciousness of man."[109]

Having accepted Lenin's contention, contemporary Marxist-Leninists then proceeded to recognize that the acquisition of truth is a gradual process[110] in which one acquires, cumulatively, partial or relative truths, each of which succeeds in only partially reflecting the objective world existing independently of the consciousness of man. This is true because the reflections of objective reality upon which truth depends are conditioned historically as well as by man's sensory apparatus.

Historically our vital interests, the state of economic development and the cultural predispositions of a particular society all condition the nature of truth.[111] Subjectively, perception proceeds only through the senses. As a consequence our observations of "objective things" are conditioned in all manner of ways. Qualities do not inhere in things; the qualities arise only in relation to the observer. Thus not only the "objective" characteristics of objects but also the physical and historic conditions under which they are observed determine what the perceived qualities will be.[112] Nonetheless, according to the theory, there must be a discernible element of objective truth in perception, i.e., a true reflection of some portion or some quality of objective reality—a reflection of that which is true independent of man and of mankind.[113] Absolute truth, in its turn, is understood to be the sum total of all the objective components in relative truths.[114]

This means, of course, that an absolute truth is understood to exist, apart from our knowledge of it, as absolute nature, objective reality[115] to which our relative truths partially correspond. The progress of any science is measured by its increasing approximation to that absolute model.[116]

We can thus distinguish several constituent truths. There is an absolute truth which truly and correctly reflects the "reality"[117] which exists independently of man. There are relative truths which represent the qualities of things in relationship to man, conditioned by the nature of man's society (its interests and vital needs) and man's organic limitations. These latter truths reflect only in part the absolute truth which exists, independently of them, as a model which they only approximate.[118] Having said so much it becomes incumbent upon one to determine how much of the absolute is contained in any relative truth.

As we have seen, the relativity of a truth is determined by the fact that it is conditioned by the circumstances and anatomical limitations of the human percipient.[119] Only the elements of any partial truth which are independent of these conditions would be eternal and absolute.[120]

If the conviction of an absolute truth is to be something more than a faith, instances of such truth should be forthcoming. To satisfy such demands the Marxist-Leninists proffer at least the following illustrations:

(1) Man is unable to subsist on thoughts or beget children through platonic love;[121]

(2) William the Conqueror invaded England in the year 1066;[122] and

(3) The earth *really* goes around the sun in the Copernican fashion.[123]

For our purposes it is sufficient to note that these "truths" could hardly pass muster as absolute or objective under any contemporary philosophical standard. That men subsist on food and succeed in begetting children through intercourse are empirical truths having nothing of necessity or eternality about them. That men may some day subsist on other than food or that women may one day produce progeny parthenogenically are certainly neither logically nor empirically impossible—unusual, perhaps, but certainly not logical contradictions. In accord with contemporary experience such propositions are true, but their truth is neither necessary nor eternal. Ascriptions of necessity and eternity are appropriate only to logical tautologies.

This limitation of truth is all the more the case with historic fact since the evidence is far less immediate and since propositions concerning time are conditioned, furthermore, by a variety of co-ordinating definitions which lend consistency to our statements. That in the future time may be measured by a different periodic process than that presently employed which would alter our calculations of the past is certainly conceivable, and that future inquiries into the evidence for William's landing may controvert hitherto existing historical evidence is most assuredly within the realm of the possible. Such is equally the case with respect to the propositions concerning the rotation of the earth around the sun. That the Copernican system may one day be superseded by another system, just as the Ptolemaic system was superseded by it, must certainly be entertained as a possibility. Ascriptions of eternity and necessity are simply inappropriate in these contexts.

What, then, can be the absolute components within any relative truth? This is one of the most critical questions which can be asked of Lenin's epistemology. And ultimately the answer must be that absolute truth must be found among the propositions of science and experience. But if the propositions selected are empirical then they can lay no claim to finality, for they can be controverted by subsequent empirical evidence. If they are truths of logic or definition then they can make no legitimate claim to being true of a real world independent of the thought and experience of man. It seems quite pointless to have a faith in absolute truth if one can never identify it. And yet this seems to be the position in which the Marxist-Leninist finds himself. There is absolute truth but our knowledge is *always* relative.[124]

What we have here is a difficulty arising from an attempt by Lenin to maintain the traditional, materialist, common-sensical definition of truth suggested by Engels, i.e., that truth is the correspondence between our ideas and an external world, in the face of the increasing inability of materialist epistemology to offer a convincing theory of verification. The correspondence theory of truth certainly affords us no comfort. We must, first of all, accept the unconditional existence of an absolute model to which all our knowledge approximates. We can have empirical, experiential acquaintance only with the approximations. And such reflections constitute all our knowledge. What role, then, does the absolute model play? What service does it perform? How is it to be employed? What disabilities would science suffer through its absence?

As a matter of fact such absolute models no longer play any serious role in science,[125] either heuristically or as a goal toward which science aspires.[126] This is the critical distinction between Marxism-Leninism and contemporary epistemology. Contemporary epistemologists are content to endow experimental, empirical elements with priority, relegating self-existent models to the level of derived constructions which alter with the alteration in the experimental data. Lenin, on the other hand, seems to give precedence to the self-existent model to which all knowledge must somehow approximate. Beyond empirical knowledge, Lenin asks us to entertain a faith in the existence of an absolute, unalterable model of the real world which we can never come to know in its entirety. We are asked to support this faith in order to avoid skepticism and agnosticism.[127]

But while such a faith (like any and all faith) acts as a deterrent to skepticism it does (like any and all faith) create problems for science. If every truth is composed, at least in part, of objective absolute truth, then one should be able, in principle, to have confidence in the permanence of some empirical truths. Lenin gave evidence of such confidence. He selected, as an illustration, the existence of ether as an empirical absolute truth.[128] An unfortunate choice! About the time Lenin was affirming its existence as an objective and absolute truth, science was abandoning it as a serious physical concept.[129]

Lenin committed himself to the real existence of ether,[130] to the three-dimensionality of real space, and to the indestructibility of matter—all provisional, empirical truths which can lay no unassailable claim to necessity or to finality. What durability these concepts seem to display resides in the constancy of the perceptible elements out of which they have arisen.

If the luminiferous ether was an acceptable hypothesis for science, it must have been true. If true, according to Lenin, it must have approximated the absolute model of reality existing independently of it, as required by the correspondence notion of truth.

Actually science has abandoned every notion of correspondence in its selection of truths. Few assume the existence of a model to which the scientific hypothesis must correspond. The appropriate question is not whether a truth "reflects," "copies," or "photographs" an absolute reality outside experience, but rather whether a truth is *adequate*, whether it is capable of synthesizing in a comprehensible way observed phenomena as well as providing ground for prediction.[131]

## Lenin's Philosophical Notebooks

During 1929–1930 there were published in the collected works of Lenin some miscellaneous fragments which included the reproduction of marginal jottings in books he had read, and brief exploratory speculations on a wide range of philosophical topics. These were ultimately collected into book form and published as Lenin's *Philosophical Notebooks*.

The bulk of the material collected in the *Notebooks* was written by Lenin during the years 1914 and 1915, that is, about six years after he had completed his *Materialism and Empiriocriticism* in

1908. Lenin was in exile at the time, and the First World War had provided him with the involuntary leisure necessary to read, for probably the first time, Hegel and Aristotle with some care. Thus, these *Notebooks* represent something of an afterthought to that "definitive" philosophical work, *Materialism and Empiriocriticism*. It seems likely that the *Notebooks* constituted the preparatory material for a special work on materialist dialectics—a work which Lenin had no opportunity to write.[132]

The *Philosophical Notebooks* are even less than notebooks. They are a jumble of fragments without sequence or structure, marginal notes to his reading of a variety of volumes concerned with a variety of problems. But they do unquestionably give evidence of increased philosophical sophistication on Lenin's part. Where in *Materialism and Empiriocriticism* he could bring himself to write that man's perceptive faculties delivered "simple reflections of nature,"[133] and that man's sensations were "true copies . . . photographs . . . of objective reality,"[134] in the *Notebooks* he was to say that "the approach of the (human) mind to a particular thing, the taking of a copy ( = a concept) of it *is not* a simple, immediate act, a dead mirroring, but one which is a complex, split into two, zig-zag like, which *includes in it* the possibility of the flight of fantasy from life. . . ."[135] Elsewhere he notes, ". . . [First] of all impressions *flash by*, then *Something* emerges. . . ."[136]

It is evident that the "reflection theory of cognition" has undergone a radical change. The metaphorical use of "reflection" permits its signification to change without a corresponding change in terminology. The talk of "reflections" remains but the process of "reflecting" the objective world is no longer spoken of as a "simple reflection," "a true copy," "a photograph." Impressions, for the more sophisticated Lenin of the *Notebooks*, *flash by*, our approach to a particular thing is spoken of as formulating a "concept," the consequence of a complex, zigzag procedure ( a zigzag mirroring! ). All the machinery of concept formation, of abstraction and generalization is introduced to render credible the notion that the senses "reflect" the objective world. The use of metaphors attempts to conceal this fact, but it is immediately evident.

It is difficult to argue with any assurance that Lenin intended his *Notebooks* to be read by contemporary Marxists or that he further expected them to attempt to synthesize the views advanced with those of his polemical *Materialism and Empiriocriticism*. Nonetheless, his *Notebooks* have been published, and it has been left to contemporary Marxists to make Lenin's fragmentary ideas intelligible. Among the foremost obligations that the contemporary Marxist-Leninist has assumed is the responsibility of making Lenin's fragmentary *Notebooks* consistent with his simplistic theory of "reflections" as it is found in *Materialism and Empiriocriticism*. Since at least 1930, this has been the self-imposed task of Marxism-Leninism.

Nor is the theory of "reflections" the only difficulty which faces Soviet Marxism. We have considered Lenin's notions concerning "matter" as they are found in the earlier document. They appear confused enough. To that seeming confusion the contemporary Marxist-Leninist must add a new element: Lenin's apparent conviction in the *Notebooks* that "knowledge of matter must be deepened to knowledge (to the concept) of Substance. . . ."[137] Lenin seems convinced that "matter" must be conceived as "substance" having "within it an active force, a never-resting principle of activity." "For this," he tells us, "Marx valued Leibnitz."[138] Thus the Marxist-Leninist is left with a conception of "matter" which includes at least (1) a matter whose *sole* attribute is that it exists independently of consciousness; (2) a matter which objectively possesses some of the attributes empirical science ascribes to it; (3) a matter which possesses, already in its inorganic *fundamentum,* some kind of susceptibility which is analogous to sensation; and (4) a matter which now, in some manner, is connected with the traditional category of "substance," the active "first principle" of the universe.[139]

The *Notebooks* add a still further difficulty. In *Materialism and Empiriocriticism* Lenin speaks of law and causality as expressing "a natural connection . . . between natural phenomena. . . . There is no doubt that there exists a natural, objective interconnection between the phenomena of the world."[140] As long as the "theory of reflections" could be construed to mean that sense perception somehow "simply" and "merely" "copied" or "photographed" the objective world, the word "phenomena" could with some plausibility be used to mean either the "phenomena" entertained in sensation *or* the object of sensation, the "phenomena" of nature. But once given the increased sophistication of the *Notebooks*, the suggestion that there is any formal similarity between the two fails because coming to know any particular thing is not a simple process, not a mere reflection or photograph. The "impressions" merely "flash by." A recognition of law and causality as the "natural connection" between "phenomena" can only mean that the knowledge of law and causal necessity must somehow involve a "deep" knowledge, an insight behind the fleeting impressions of the senses to some kind of *essence* of phenomena and the interconnections between *essences*. And such apparently is the case. In the *Notebooks* we are told that "law is relation. . . . Relation of essences or between essences."[141] "Law is the enduring (the persisting) in appearances."[142]

Lenin contended that according to the "theory of reflections," regularities formulated in thought as "natural laws" by means of abstraction and generalization must, in some sense, directly correspond with regularities in the objective world. The "reflection" cannot obtain between the fleeting impressions of sense and the objective world since Lenin has become aware of the fact that in order to speak meaningfully about cognition it is necessary to interpose something between "phenomena" as objects of sense impression and "phenomena" as natural things or processes. That "something" has apparently become the *essence* of phenomena. We have in the *Notebooks* a philosophy of *essences!* Lenin tells us that "law and essence are concepts of the same kind (of the same order), or rather, of the same degree, expressing the deepening of man's knowledge of phenomena, the world, etc."[143] To discover essences, thought must traverse the path of *concepts* and *categories*. In some sense there is a "coincidence of concepts with . . . the sum, summing up of empiricism, sensations, the senses. . . ."[144] But these concepts are "hewn, treated, flexible, mobile, relative, mutually connected, united in opposites, in order to embrace the world."[145] Further, "if everything develops, does not that apply also to the most general *concepts* and *categories* of thought?"[146] "Man is confronted with a *web* of natural phenomena. Instinctive man, the savage, does not distinguish himself from nature. Conscious man does distinguish, categories are stages of distinguishing, i.e., of cognizing the world, focal points in the web, which assist in cognizing and mastering it."[147]

This can only mean something like the world exists as a "web" of natural phenomena and "instinctive man" perceives the world "falsely" in some sense, not being able to distinguish enduring essences from fleeting impressions. He perceives "reflections" which are at best only partially "true." Knowledge of the world is the *history* of the development[148] of *concepts* and *categories* which correspond to the *essence* of the impressions we receive. If they are true, concepts and categories represent the essences of phenomena in nature, objective phenomena. The subjective phenomena and the objective phenomena are, in some sense, made to correspond through concepts and categories. The nature of the "correspondence" is not immediately clear. Lenin employs simile and metaphor to describe the relationship. "A river and the *drops* in this river. The position of *every* drop, its relation to the others; the direction of its movement; its speed; the line of the movement—straight, curved, circular, etc.—upwards, downwards. The sum of the movement. Concepts, as *registration* of individual aspects of the movement, of individual drops ( = 'things'), of individual 'streams,' etc. There you have [approximately] the picture of the world according to Hegel's *Logic*."[149] Concerning this "picture of the world" he tells us, "If I am not mistaken, there is much mysticism and empty pedantry in these conclusions of Hegel, but the basic idea is one of genius: that of the universal, all sided, vital connection of everything with everything and the reflection of this connection . . . in human concepts. . . . Continuation of the work of Hegel and Marx must consist in the *dialectical* elaboration of the history of human thought. . . ."[150]

This is the "dialectical" conception of the world and its "reflection" through "concepts" and "categories" in the mind found in the fragments of Lenin's *Philosophical Notebooks*. In it are notions of a "theory of reflections" far more complex than anything in *Materialism and Empiriocriticism*. There are suggestions of some notion of self-moving substance and the "reflection" of its self-movements in thought through the categories and concepts which fathom its essence and express it in terms of laws and necessities.

By 1930 contemporary Marxists were faced with a mass of material delivered by an intellectual and philosophic tradition then almost a century old. The inheritance included Engels' *Anti-Dühring*, in which he advanced what he characterized as only "indications" of a systematic epistemology and philosophy of nature. The "indications" were hardly further advanced in his

*Ludwig Feuerbach*. The *Dialectics of Nature* was left in a fragmentary and incomplete state. Lenin had, in turn, left the mixed elements of the *Materialism and Empiriocriticism* and the sentence fragments and marginal notes of the *Philosophical Notebooks*. Out of these diverse and heterogeneous elements contemporary Marxism, particularly in the Soviet Union, assumed the responsibility of articulating "a harmonious, integral system"[151] which provides "a scientific solution of all the basic questions of philosophy."[152]

## The Synthesis of Contemporary Marxism

To render the mass of inherited material "harmonious," contemporary Marxists have had to face an enormous number of problems, and their attempts to solve them have produced most singular results. It is no longer possible to determine what Lenin had in mind when he insisted that the senses "copy" or "photograph" the objective world. Certainly he came to mean by these terms something other than what is normally meant. His meaning in the *Notebooks* is sufficiently clear so that no one can legitimately doubt that his use of "photograph" and "reflection" could only be understood in the vaguest metaphorical sense. But since Soviet philosophers in their efforts to "harmonize" have refused to abandon the term, their results are often grotesque. F. V. Konstantinov, who was principal author of one of the recently published (1958) official Soviet texts on philosophy, can still say, "Sensations and perceptions are *copies*, photographs or images of material objects,"[153] that our sensations deliver "faithful images" of things,[154] and that sensation is "a *direct* and *immediate* reflection of the material world."[155] And yet he goes on to tell us that our senses often provide ambiguous data which we must "decipher" with "thought."[156]

M. M. Rosental, perhaps the Soviet Union's foremost methodologist, can write that "our sensations, impressions . . . of things are reflections, images, copies of the existing objects themselves."[157] Yet in the subsequent discussion Rosental tells us that our "sense organs" cannot give us any knowledge about the essence of things, and that as a matter of fact the appearances they deliver often do not "correspond with the essence of an object, but stand in direct contradiction to it."[158] For example, the "appearance" of color is in direct contradiction to the common essence in electromagnetic waves shared by *all* colors.[159]

Rosental is suggesting that our sensory impressions cannot inform us directly of the electromagnetic waves of specific frequency which produce the sensation of color, and Konstantinov indicates that even the simplest garden variety sense impression must be assessed against the "apperceptive mass," right reason, and the mutual evidence of the various senses. Once all this is granted one wonders why the misleading locutions about "photographs," "copies," and "faithful images" are retained. Some Soviet Marxists have gone so far in their attempt to defend the use of "reflection" in characterizing the relationship assumed to exist "immediately" between the data of sense and the external world that they have argued that the "similarity" which the term "reflection" inevitably connotes should be understood in the sense that "changes in the reflecting body [are] . . . coded properties of the acting (reflected) body." "Similarity" cannot be understood to mean "physical similarity" which would "significantly narrow the sphere of the properties being reflected."[160] The notion of "reflecting," "photographing," or "copying" of the objective world in sense perceptions must rather be understood as a relation of "mathematic isomorphism . . . in which the attributes of the original and the model are commensurable."[161] Such an analysis makes of "reflection" a "signal," which, out of apparent respect to Engels and Lenin, is called a "signal-image."[162]

In these circumstances contemporary Marxism in its Marxist-Leninist form is compelled to speak a strange language. To "photograph" has come to mean to produce a "mathematical isomorphism." Sense perceptions provide "faithful images" which may "contradict" the "essence" of "appearances." The "faithful images" must be "deciphered" by the mind to avoid error.

We have earlier indicated that such a position cannot be distinguished from that of the representationalist realists who argued that features of the object world causally arouse in us specific responses in the form of sensations. To the Soviet Marxist these sensations "correspond" to the object world, but they must be "deciphered." They are the basis of knowledge,[163] but do not, in and of themselves, constitute knowledge. The path to true cognition is long and tortuous.[164] The employment of the expressions "copy," "image," and "photograph" adds nothing to the analysis, since Soviet Marxists simply maintain that sensation and perception are but "the first stage" in the "complex process of cognition."[165]

That "reflection" has come to mean something most singular is evident. Konstantinov talks of the "universal" faculty of "reflection" possessed by "matter" itself. This seems to mean no more than that there is interaction in the material world. In nature a material object can provoke a "reflection" in another by acting upon it, that is, a physical reaction in one object is regularly associated with the external influence of some other object. The illustration given is that of the response of an electron to the field in which it operates, varying its velocity and emitting electromagnetic radiation accordingly. This is called the "physical form of reflection," a mode peculiar to the inorganic world.[166] Similarly a magnetic field produces change in the properties of iron. This is also considered a "reflection." Albuminoid bodies which possess the property of irritability are gifted with "a new form of reflection." Under the influence of external stimuli the physical and chemical properties of albumin are more or less modified. This is the "biological form of reflection." What all this has to do with reflections or with cognitive reflections which "photograph," "copy," or "faithfully image" the objective world is difficult to say.

What seems to be meant is that there is interaction in the world and that specific interactions can be studied with some success. Certain isolated interactions may then be reduced to a formula which expresses the regularities observed. But to say that these formulas mean that iron "reflects" a magnetic field and that electrons "reflect" the field of which they are a component is to do violence to the language. The addiction to the picture language of Engels' and Lenin's "classics" of Marxism is explicable on grounds other than philosophic relevance.

## The Process of Cognition

Real differences between representationalism and dialectical materialism begin to appear only when contemporary Marxists commence an exposition of the "complex process of cognition." At that point they begin to be concerned with the human faculty of abstraction and generalization, the formation of concepts and categories, and the discovery of necessary laws in the natural world. The impetus, of course, is again derived from Engels and Lenin. "From living perception to abstract thought, *and from this to practice,*—such is the dialectical path of cognition of *truth,* of the cognition of objective reality."[167]

In the perception of individual things, their most general attributes are impressed upon us with more regularity than their more casual and accidental traits,[168] providing us with a general image which subsumes a number of particulars.[169] This, of course, sounds deceptively like the process of abstracting the general or universal from the particular with which nominalists, since at least the Middle Ages, have made us familiar. Locke suggested the apparently similar operation of abstracting a core of common qualities in order that this abstraction might represent a whole range of particulars. In such a conception the number of particulars included under a given abstraction would increase in inverse proportion to the number of traits considered. The less specific and the fewer in number the class-defining properties, the wider would be the class subsumed. Such is assuredly not what the Marxist-Leninists mean when they begin to discuss the abstractions which give rise to concepts and categories. The process of "concrete abstraction" is conceived to differ fundamentally from the process of generalizing and abstracting which Locke, Berkeley, and Hume tried to describe and analyze.[170]

The nominalist would say that a statement containing a general term, an abstraction, can only be equivalent to a conjunction of statements about individual things. When we ascribe a common property to two different things we are not postulating the existence of something called a "common property"; we are reporting a perceived similarity. What nominalists reject is the notion that universals have as a referent something other than the similarities perceived in particulars. That is, the world is not composed of particular things *and* some objectively real universals.

The young Marx seems to have accepted something like this position: ". . . [It] would be a contradiction to say, on the one hand, that all ideas have their origin in the world of the senses and to maintain, on the other hand, that a word is more than a word, that besides the beings represented, which are always individual, there exist also general beings."[171] Engels seems to say something very similar in proposing that "matter, as such, is a pure creation of thought and an abstraction. . . . Matter, as such, as distinct from definite existing pieces of matter, is not anything sensuously existing. When natural science directs its efforts to seeking out uniform matter as such, to reducing qualitative differences to merely quantitative differences in combining identical smallest particles, it is doing the same thing as demanding to see fruit as such instead of cherries, pears, apples, or the mammal as such instead of cats, dogs, sheep, etc., gas as such, metal, stone, chemical compounds as such, motion as such."[172]

Lenin, on the other hand, in the *Notebooks,* apparently under the influence of Aristotle and Hegel, introduces a distinction between abstract universals and concrete universals unknown to either Marx or Engels. The concrete universal, according to what Lenin called "a beautiful formula," is one "which comprises in itself the wealth of the particular, the individual, the single (all the wealth of the particular and single!)! *Très bien!*"[173] One such concrete universal is apparently "matter," for it is one of the "abstractions [which] reflect nature more deeply, truly and completely." Such a concrete abstraction comprises within itself all the wealth of the particular; Lenin goes so far as to contend that in the concrete abstraction the individual *is* in some sense the universal.[174] Thus Lenin conceived of some cognitive process which yields concrete universals, concepts and categories that have as referents some *objectively real essences* in some sense distinct from particulars. The concepts and categories derived through concrete abstraction truly "reflect" the essence of the real world. That essence is an interconnection of things and processes. According to this thesis "Hegel actually *proved* that logical forms . . . are not an empty shell, but the *reflection* of the objective world."[175]

Contemporary Marxist-Leninists in the Soviet Union have attempted to render such notions intelligible. Some simply employ the term "universals" to cover "categories," and the Soviet *Brief Philosophical Dictionary* defines "categories" as the "basic logical concepts which reflect the most general and most essential qualities . . . of the objects and phenomena of reality."[176] They are in some sense generically related, representing various levels of concrete abstraction from particulars. They are reduction products or complexes of reduction products which "reflect" the general and essential qualities, aspects and relations of the real world.[177] They are more "real" than immediately perceived particulars.

The concrete universals as categories and concepts are understood to truly "reflect" not only the objective essence of the world but the objective and essential interconnections of things as well—essential interconnections which constitute the objective basis of the laws of nature. There is therefore a radical distinction between the abstract universals with which philosophers have been long familiar and the Marxist-Leninist concrete universal. The abstract universal "man," for example, increases its extension with the reduction in the number of its defining characteristics. Such a universal does not reveal an essence, nor does it serve to provide the basis of natural law. The concrete universal of the Marxist-Leninist, on the other hand, is conceived as performing precisely those functions. Thus the universal, "man," treated in a "concrete" manner is understood to apply to man's *essential* characteristic: his capacity to produce his own means of subsistence. Such a universal serves as a "scientific concept" to which other "concepts" can be related to restore "concreteness." The relationship understood to obtain between concepts reveals all the contradictions, the interpenetration of opposites, and *the necessary development inherent in them.*[178] The relationship reveals the "inner, inherent connections,"[179] the "logic" of development obeying the three principal laws of the dialectic—the change of quantity into quality, the interpenetration of opposites, and the development through contradiction. Only the "principles" of this dialectical "logic," revealed in the relationship of concrete universals can be, according to contemporary Marxist-Leninists, formulated, for it would be a "monumental task to work out the system of a dialectic materialist logic."[180]

What we have in this conception of concrete universals as categories and concepts and their intrinsic interconnection is the "logic" of dialectical materialism—not a "logic" in any recognizable sense of the word at all. Its tasks are those which could only be competently undertaken by scientific techniques and are singularly "alogical." Dialectical logic pretends to explore the causal relationships which obtain between phenomena; it is concerned with the development of solar systems, the evolution of species and processes of thought. Its subject matter is all or anything in the universe—anything that can legitimately be made the subject of human inquiry. But such inquiry is the task of empirical science which seems to do eminently well without the concrete universals of dialectical materialism.

When we consider the illustrations Soviet philosophers offer of various "concrete concepts" it becomes obvious that they are little more than hypothetical constructs used in a theoretical explanation sketch. Chasschatschich cites Stalin's definition of a "nation" as an instance of a concrete concept.[181] Rosental cites Lenin's definition of "imperialism" as another.[182] To call such concepts "concrete universals" which reflect the objective essence of things, revealing the "necessary development inherent in them," is to generate considerable confusion. What we have in these cases are definitions which do service in an explanation by virtue of which certain variables are selected out of the richness of observed phenomena in the effort to achieve theoretical understanding. This is simply the method of empirical science and has precious little to do with concrete universals which comprise in themselves "all the wealth of the particular," and which relate themselves in "logical forms."

Certainly Marx seemed to harbor no such notions. He left us a fairly concise account of his own "concrete" treatment of universals in his preliminary drafts for the *Contribution to the Critique of Political Economy*, where we find written in the section "The Method of Political Economy": "It seems to be the correct procedure to commence with the real and concrete aspect of conditions as they are; in the case of political economy, to commence with population which is the basis and the author of the entire productive activity of society. Yet on closer consideration, it proves to be wrong. Population is an abstraction, if we leave out e.g. the classes of which it consists. These classes, again, are but an empty word, unless we know what are the elements on which they are based, such as wage-labor, capital, etc. Capital, e.g., does not mean anything without wage-labor, value, money, price, etc. If we start out, therefore, with population, we do so with a chaotic conception of the whole, and by closer analysis we will gradually arrive at simpler ideas; thus we shall proceed from the imaginary concrete to less and less complex abstractions, until we get at the simplest conception. This once attained, we might start on our return journey until we would finally come back to population, but this time not as a chaotic notion of an integral whole, but as a rich aggregate of many conceptions and relations. . . . The concrete is concrete, because it is a combination of many objects with different determinations [*Bestimmungen*], i.e., a unity of diverse elements."[183]

This simply outlines a program of analysis and empirical verification, apparently not different in any substantial respects from the hypothetico-deductive system employed in any scientific inquiry. What this has to do with universals which make "logic, dialectics and the theory of knowledge . . . one and the same thing . . ."[184] is difficult to say. To say that in this conceptual scheme of interlocking categories and concepts we have discovered "that negativity which is the *inherent pulsation of self-movement and vitality*"[185] may be lyrical but not very informative. To further say that "concepts" are "all-sided, vital connections of everything with everything," like "drops in a river," "flexible, mobile, relative, mutually connected, united in opposites," does not seem to make any sense.[186] In 1901, before Lenin exposed himself to Hegel, he certainly seemed to think that such notions concerning concepts were nonsense, for he tells us that the "attempt to include into a general concept all the partial symptoms of single phenomena" is "meaningless,"[187] yet after an exposure to Hegel he was to maintain that the "individual is the universal."[188]

The attempt to make the "logic of categories" of Hegel reflect the "logic of the world" seems to have led Lenin into an incredible muddle of logic and empirical science. What could it mean to say that a "concept" develops, that a "concept" moves?[189] To say that a new species has historically developed does not imply that the "concept" "species" has developed! It is not a matter of the species concept having developed, but rather of organisms having developed so that they no longer are numbered among a specific species. We can develop new explanations of how the change took place, but the logical conception "species" has not changed.[190] The confusion seems to be the consequence of conceiving the logical conception of "class" or "category" as identical with an aggregate or collection.

Soviet Marxists seem to have taken up the entire "logic" of Hegel (which is not a "logic" but a "metaphysics") when they contend that "concepts" and "categories" mirror the real internal connections of universal relations and mutual interaction in the world of natural phenomena, revealing that a particular thing is not just an instance of a universal, a concept, but an evolving complex whole, a unity of *all* things, the essence of which is discoverable in each particular! This is of course the doctrine of "internal connections" that is expressed in the formula in which the "concrete concept" reveals the "essential relations," a particular becoming more and more transformed into a complex of universals. This entire tortured business involves a conception of an interrelated whole which seems to exhibit characteristics distinct from the properties of its parts taken severally and collectively, a whole whose regularities are irreducible to those of which each of its parts or processes is subject. Such a notion is "metaphysical" and subject to no conceivable sort of confirmation. It gives rise to notions of *necessary* development, *inevitable* laws and of "matter" which is a "substance," which is the *cause of itself,* and which *must inevitably* develop all the properties, qualities, things, and processes *inherent* in it. All of this transcends any possible empirical verification, for the "whole," the totality of all things, is by definition impossible of investigation.

For the Marxist-Leninists the "knowledge" of the "whole" is somehow equated with "absolute knowledge" toward which our current knowledge can only "approximate."[191] This is the "absolute model" toward which knowledge aspires. As a consequence the knowledge we actually possess is "always necessarily relative." It could not be otherwise.

This "absolute knowledge" would somehow exhaust the "whole," and the "whole" seems to be nothing more than "matter" as a "philosophical category," possessed of "inherent pulsation of self-movement and vitality." For Lenin had "far transcended Engels" with his "definition" of "matter."[192] In his "creative development" of Marxism, Lenin provided "a profound, exhaustive and scientific definition of matter."[193] It is a definition of matter not content with simple realism (i.e., that matter exists independent of consciousness), but includes ontological and metaphysical attributes as well. Matter is a "substance" which is its own cause and in which all things are contained *in potentia.* In some sense this "definition" of matter contains in it the "principles of its development."[194] That a definition is understood to somehow "reflect" development is curious at best. To say that such a definition reveals the "essence" of a thing is more curious still.

The attempt to speak of a "logic" of the dialectic leads contemporary Soviet Marxists to talk of natural laws as "necessary and inevitable," as the "relationship" obtaining between "essences," and of these essences as somehow locked into a complex system of "essences" which compose a "whole." It gives rise to such statements as: "Dialectical materialism means by necessity that which has in itself its own cause, that which occurs inevitably and with the force of a law of its own essence, the internal nexus of things, of processes and events which are forced to occur in a given manner and no other."[195]

Such a conception of necessity and inevitability seems appropriate to logic or mathematics where specific conclusions follow necessarily as the consequence of the administration of valid rules of inference. But such locutions hardly seem appropriate to empirical science.

The notion of "law [as] essential appearance"[196] is the Hegelian conception of law as an inner tendency on the part of phenomena themselves. But such a notion was not a "logic" but a "metaphysics," a "transcendent hypothesis," which (in principle) defies confirmation. To infuse such a metaphysics with the language of logical discourse is to talk of necessities and inevitabilities when science only warrants probability statements. If an empirical "law of development" were *necessary*, it would have a closed class of events as a referent. Since future events could not constitute members of such a class, such a law could only refer to past and present events. We would certify our statement about "necessity" on the evidence that such a development had taken place. But it would be an inconclusive argument, because it would assume that no other development *could* have taken place. If we pretend that we can utter predictions about future events that have the force of *necessity* and *inevitability* we seem to be referring to some holistic conception of the universe whose "essence" we know and whose interconnections can be deduced. Such a "whole" which could serve as subject for such notions is forever outside the range of human wisdom. Only a Hegel could contend that he had some knowledge of such a "whole," such an "Absolute," because mind was, in some sense, the "Absolute."

The Marxist-Leninist in accepting Lenin's conception of matter as a "category," has ascribed to matter all the attributes of Hegel's Absolute. It is its own necessary, sufficient, material, and final cause and looks suspiciously like God. Actually, whatever the Marxist-Leninist can tell us about matter he derives from the empirical sciences; whenever he pretends to advance one step beyond their precincts he utters statements which are patently metaphysical.

In effect the "dialectical logic," if it means anything at all, means that to have a knowledge of things and processes we must consider them in their various aspects. In meeting our needs we employ techniques in a regular and specifiable fashion in order to produce desired results. This is the program of empirical science. As long as techniques and applications satisfy our requirements, they are retained; when we develop more adequate techniques, they are abandoned. Within the range of our abilities, and relative to the complexity of any given problem, we devise laws which permit us to make predictions of a probabilistic sort. As the range of our experience increases, we revise the laws to cover an increased number of phenomena.

This seems to be all that Engels means when he talks of the laws of science.[197] That Engels, however, fails to distinguish "logic" from "science" involves the whole discussion in a number of gross confusions. He talks, for example, of the proposition "All men are mortal" as being a genuine and immutable truth. If the statement is conceived of as *necessary* then it can only function as a definition; that is, should we find a "man" who is not mortal he would be classified as something other than a man. We would not consider the *necessary* truth of the proposition "All men are mortal" in any way compromised. The statement would operate as an analytic proposition. But if we should conceive the statement to be "empirical," that is, that man is mortal and that every man we will ever find will be mortal, we can only consider this a probability statement based on induction. The class of such men remains open. Every man has not been empirically tested— and such a test would seem to be eminently fatal.

Some such confusion pervades much of the discussions in Marxist-Leninist literature. When Konstantinov admits that "dialectical logic does not have its own proper and specific laws distinct from the laws of the dialectic,"[198] he seems to be saying that the "logic" of the dialectic is no "logic" at all, but the sum of very general statements which in some way relate to the laws discovered by empirical science. Whether such "laws" as the transformation of quantity into quality, the mutual interpenetration of opposites, and the negation of the negation have any heuristic or predictive value seems determinable only after science has inquired into a specific thing or process. Because the words which give expression to the "laws" can mean almost anything, instances where they are seen to apply abound. If Adoratsky can seriously contend that the development of the animal kingdom "proceeds by contradictions and the conflict of opposites (the struggle for existence, procreation by sex, etc.),"[199] then almost *anything* can be said, and the "laws" of the dialectic are unfalsifiable. As such they are of no interest to science and of no cognitive interest to man.

Contemporary Marxism-Leninism is faced with the problem of synthesizing a body of heterogeneous material. Some of the material is in an unfinished and disorderly state. Some Soviet thinkers concede development within the corpus of the Marx-Engels-Lenin material, but in general the body of literature is treated as though it were a unitary mass. Contemporary Marxist-Leninists usually concede that Lenin "creatively developed" the thought of Marx and Engels,[200] yet maintain that this was accomplished without significantly modifying that thought in any respect. Not only does this not seem to be the case but there is good internal evidence that Lenin, in the course of time, abandoned or significantly modified some of his own earlier positions. In the *Notebooks* Lenin nowhere speaks of sensations "photographing" or "faithfully copying" the objective world. He speaks of achieving real or essential definitions through concrete concepts and categories, and he talks of a "logic" which is both an epistemology and a philosophy of nature. What has resulted in Lenin's case has been an attempt on the part of contemporary Soviet commentators to force a marriage between the "photograph" theory of sensation and the "concept" theory of cognition.

Lenin, finally, commits himself to a far more exposed position than Engels. Engels, in turn, entertained a philosophical position far different from any to which Marx made explicit commitment. What the actual relationship between the philosophical positions of the three men might have been we will perhaps never know. That they are not entirely compatible seems obvious.

# 4 Contemporary Marxism as Philosophy: A Brief Survey of Problems

We have briefly considered some of the variegated, complex, and ambiguous components which make up Marxism in our own time. To speak of "contemporary" Marxism is not precise, for there are as many Marxisms as there are countries with Marxists; one might almost say that there are as many Marxisms as there are Marxists. Even a brief consideration of the various trends which have developed out of classical Marxism could not be undertaken within the confines of this discussion. But that there have been a host of interpretations, developments, and revisions of the philosophy of classical Marxism should be borne in mind. Among the most prominent has been the positivistic trend that characterized German Marxism until the Second World War, typified in the writings of Marxists like Karl Kautsky,[1] Eduard Bernstein,[2] Max Adler, and Josef Dietzgen and his few followers.[3] A variety of Marxist and quasi-Marxist trends have developed in France and Italy.[4] Russia herself has produced a variety of interpretations of classical Marxist thought—not the least of which is that of Plekhanov.[5] Even India has produced an "orthodox" Marxist philosopher whose system can only with some difficulty be made consonant with that dominant in the Soviet Union.[6]

Because the Soviet Union is the center of contemporary Marxist discussion for a great many reasons (only a few of them philosophical), we shall largely restrict the following considerations to the "orthodox" philosophy of Marxism-Leninism as it is represented in Soviet philosophical speculation, and consider only briefly the development of that philosophy in countries within the Soviet orbit.

## The Course of Marxism-Leninism

From 1917 until the death of Lenin in 1924, Marxist-Leninist philosophy in the Soviet Union was unsystematic. The philosophical thinking of the period seldom directly concerned itself with the natural sciences, its practitioners, or their institutions.[7] A relatively tight rein, however, was held on philosophers by the highest party organs,[8] and it was clear that philosophy was tied to party aims. Nonetheless there was less than unanimity of opinion. One form of mechanistic materialism was advanced by Emmanuel Enchman and S. Minin, and a more sophisticated form by Bukharin and Bogdanov.[9] Even Trotsky's notion that the ultimate reality (material particles) to which science, "in the last analysis," would reduce all inorganic, organic, natural, social, or intellectual phenomena, was "mechanistic."[10]

In opposition to the mechanists, an idealistic tendency developed, which placed increasing weight on the Hegelian elements in Marxist philosophy. Abram Moiseevich Deborin was welcomed by a considerable number of philosophers in the Soviet Union during the late twenties as the man who "revealed an understanding of the philosophical tasks of the epoch." While "neither Marx nor Engels nor Lenin, in spite of their desire to do so, left . . . a systematized theory of materialist dialectics," Deborin was understood to have begun such a work. Deborin was concerned with laws which would reveal "the universal connection of everything with everything." He argued that matter was a universal substance which possessed the quality of the physicist's ether and elementary particles on the microscopic level of organization, but had further qualities at the macroscopic levels of organization which were irreducible to the regularities of the simpler levels. His monistic materialism was expressed in Hegelian language.[11]

At the time of Lenin's death there does not seem to have been any particular emphasis placed upon his philosophic "contribution," his "creative development" of Marxist philosophy. Bukharin, for example, commemorated Lenin's death with an encomium which spoke of Lenin as a Marxist, but said nothing of Lenin as a philosopher. Even Stalin's lectures in 1924 on *The Foundations of Leninism*[12] did not direct attention to Lenin's contributions to philosophy.

In 1926 Engels' *Dialectics of Nature* made its appearance, and was used as a cudgel by the idealist faction, the Deborinites, against the mechanists. The publication of Lenin's *Philosophical Notebooks* in 1929 seemed to further support their Hegelian interpretation of the dialectic.

The Deborinites conceived the dialectic as an independent discipline, "leading" the natural sciences. This seemed justified by Lenin's pronouncement that not a single science could advance without it. Yet the mechanists argued that Engels had clearly left no place for such a "separate" discipline independent of the "positive sciences."[13] Dialectics was nothing more than a generalization of the results of empirical science.

Lenin's position did little to clarify the situation. In his "Testament" Lenin had referred to Bukharin, one of the principal mechanists, as the "most important theoretician of the party"; but he quickly qualified this endorsement by adding, ". . . [But] his theoretical views can only with the very greatest doubt be regarded as fully Marxist, for there is something scholastic in them (he never has learned, and I think never has fully understood, the dialectic)."[14] Lenin's position, while confused in the *Philosophical Notebooks*, seemed clearly to support the Deborinite faction.

By 1931 Stalin had codified the doctrines of the party; the mechanistic and idealistic differences were overcome by fiat. By 1932 philosophers had begun weaving quotations from the classics, the works of Marx, Engels, Lenin, and Stalin, into their writings to exemplify their Stalinist orthodoxy.[15] The philosophy of dialectical materialism was specifically codified in Stalin's *Dialectical and Historical Materialism* of 1938.[16] While Stalin was long celebrated as a philosopher who had made immeasurable contributions to the discipline, his major material contribution is limited to this article of about three dozen pages in length. His other works which tangentially touch on philosophic matters,

"Anarchism or Socialism,"[17] *Marxism and Linguistics*, and *Economic Problems of Socialism in the U.S.S.R.*,[18] are each of them not much longer.

Stalin's philosophical education was meager. There is no evidence that he had devoted any time to the systematic study of philosophical problems, and his philosophical postures can almost always be ascribed to the political considerations which motivated him.

But whatever his political motives, Stalin formulated the outline which philosophy in the Soviet Union followed without reflection for a decade. Stalin devoted the introduction of *Dialectical and Historical Materialism* to what we would call ontology, for in it he discusses the nature of the real, objective world, independent of man's consciousness. But since he identified what we would call ontology with idealistic metaphysics, he conceived his own pronouncements about the ultimately real world as part of the theory of science. Stalin grouped his exposition under seven principal features, four devoted to the dialectical method and three to philosophical materialism.

The four principal features of the dialectical method included these conceptions: (1) Nature was not to be regarded as an accidental agglomeration of things but as an integral whole "in which things, phenomena, are organically connected with, dependent on, and determined by, each other."[19] (2) Nature is in a state of continuous movement and change; "something is always arising and developing; and something always disintegrating and dying away."[20] (3) The process of change is not a simple process of growth, but one in which quantitative changes lead to qualitative changes in a "leap."[21] (4) This process of development is the consequence of the "struggle between opposites," for "dialectics holds that internal contradictions are inherent in all things and phenomena of nature . . . they all have their negative and positive sides. . . ."[22]

Stalin's formulation of the fundamental bases of dialectics was not notable for its brilliance, but it did contain a rather singular feature. No mention of the law of the negation of the negation was made. From 1938 until Stalin's death, this law, which Engels had understood to be the "kernel" of the dialectic, found no place in the philosophical literature of the Soviet Union.[23] The outline devoted to "Dialectical Materialism" in the *Great Soviet En-*

*cyclopedia* of 1952 makes no mention of this neglected law. In the portion devoted to "The Marxist Dialectical Method," the four principles of Stalin are dealt with. One mention of the law of the negation of the negation is to be found in the *Encyclopedia's* treatment of the history of the dialectic wherein Engels' *Dialectics of Nature* is specifically referred to, but the editors were careful to add that "J. V. Stalin raised the Marxist dialectic to a new, higher level. In his classic work, *Dialectical and Historical Materialism*, J. V. Stalin generalized and systematized the teachings of Marx, Engels and Lenin concerning the dialectic, developed it further and gave a complete and profound characterization of the Marxist dialectical method."[24]

Upon the eclipse of Stalin's influence, discussion broke out almost immediately. The specific precipitating cause of the controversy was the textbook *Dialectical Materialism* by G. F. Alexandrov. A congress was called, at which one of the specific charges leveled against Stalin was neglect of the law of the negation of the negation. From April to June, 1954, the issue was debated. Kedrov, Malzev, and Gaidukov contended that the neglect of the negation of the negation could not be justified. Georgijev, defending the position taken by Stalin, argued that neither Marx, Engels, nor Lenin had employed the law of the negation of the negation. The defense was, of course, grotesque. Nor could the law of the negation of the negation be subsumed under the struggle of opposites. The founders of Marxism had made a distinction between them. Not only had Engels considered this specific law the essence of the dialectic, but Lenin committed himself to it as well.[25] In the 1955 edition of the *Great Soviet Encyclopedia* the law of the negation of the negation was restored to the triumvirate of dialectical laws, reaffirming the classical metaphysics of Engels.

B. M. Kedrov, who had led the opposition to Stalin's "creative development" of Marxism, assumed the charge of restoring dialectical materialism to the form it had attained before Stalin's modifications of 1938. In 1955 he co-authored an exposition, "Toward a Fundamental Exposition of Lenin's Philosophical Heritage," which had the unmistakable approval of the Central Committee of the Party. In 1956 he specifically repudiated the attempt to synthesize the three fundamental laws of the dialectic into the four fundamental principles of the dialectical method. "The law of the 'Negation of the Negation' has a completely independent character and cannot be covered by any other law of the dialectic." The reformulation given by Stalin was rejected and the dialectic was again conceived in the manner which Engels had bequeathed it.

Why Stalin should have troubled himself with modifying the traditional laws of the dialectic remains a mystery. It is quite possible that the law was simply unintelligible to him. An alternative explanation would be that he read, in such a law, the challenge of continued revolutionary change and, as such, a threat to his regime. In any event he saw fit to delete the law in his official account of dialectical materialism.

But Stalin had, wittingly or unwittingly, also initiated a new phase of philosophical development in the Soviet Union. The publication of Stalin's *Marxism and Linguistics* in 1950 had a far-reaching impact on the development of Marxism-Leninism. Stalin argued that language was not a class-bound product. It arose out of the necessity of social co-operation and consequently served all classes equally. But it was quickly noted that if language could be free of class character because it served the interests of all classes and was necessary for productive activity, natural science could demand, on equal grounds, the right to class-free character.[26] Engels had frequently pointed out the value of science in production, as well as its service to the collective well-being of mankind. The dictum on language threatened to spread to all the natural sciences.

In the earlier editions of their *Dictionary* Rosental and Iudin had been able to say that "the forms of ideology are political concepts, science, morals, art, religion, and so forth. All the ideologies are reflections of social being. They express and defend the interests of classes in opposition."[27] Science was explicitly identified as an element of the superstructure of society which reflects a particular economic and class base.[28] The interpretation of Lenin's advocacy of partisanship in ideological matters was understood to mean that there was a bourgeois science and a proletarian science.[29] Such a conception of partisanship had actually fostered an attempt in the Soviet Union to devise a socialist logic to replace bourgeois logic.[30]

Stalin's exemption of language from class partisanship seemed to provide an opportunity for the rehabilitation of science. Logicians were not slow to avail themselves of the opportunity provided by Stalin's dispensation. Logic was declared to be an "auxiliary" of production, free of a class character and in the service of humanity.[31] The repercussions of this thesis resounded throughout the theoretical structure of contemporary Marxism. Konstantinov wrote, "Some lecturers and authors of popular Marxist pamphlets usually unreservedly treated all forms of social consciousness, including all spheres of science, as a part of the superstructure. The superstructure was often enough conceived too broadly and was erroneously thought to include the language. This was a gross mistake. . . . Firstly, all sciences, both natural and social, have it in common that they are intended to provide us, and do provide us, with objective truth existing independently of man and mankind. Both natural and social sciences are called upon to discover the laws governing processes that take place independently of man's will. Secondly, science progresses from ignorance to knowledge, from less complete truths to truths more complete, and from relative to absolute truths. Hence, there is continuity and interconnection in the development of all sciences, and every new generation of scientists carries on the work of their predecessors. This law-governed process is inherent in equal degree in all spheres of knowledge."[32] In the Soviet Zone in Germany Fred Oelssner contended, "The natural sciences are not the product of a determinate [economic] base, but rather the results of a steady progress in the knowledge of mankind."[33] In 1956 Kedrov summarized the results of the discussions which followed Stalin's dictum on language in the following manner: "One of the most serious errors among some of our philosophers finds its explanation in their erroneous interpretation of partisanship in philosophy. This interpretation held that the scientists, including natural scientists, of the capitalist countries, who in their philosophical utterances argued from an idealistic and agnostic standpoint, were not in a position to contribute anything in physics, chemistry, biology and so forth. Consequently some of our philosophers and physicists sought to dismiss the theory of relativity as the product of 'physicalistic' idealism with the argument that the author of the theory, A. Einstein, was under the influence of Machism. Actually the theory of relativity constituted an important advance in modern physics."[34]

This new interpretation of science should be contrasted with the Stalinist doctrine of "two camps" which was expressed by

Zhdanov. The Central Committee of the Party was apparently dissatisfied with the prevailing circumstances on the ideological front. Zhdanov, speaking at the Congress held at the Philosophical Institute of the Academy of Science on the 24th of June, 1947, announced that he spoke in Stalin's name and in the name of the Central Committee. He chastised the philosophers for not having the "fighting spirit" of the party and for not having assessed problems from the vantage point of Lenin's partisan spirit. Marxism-Leninism was the only true science against which other sciences were to be measured. These pronouncements led to the critical discussions on music, biology, and psychology in 1948, at which time the party line was laid down. Zhdanov had suggested that because of its lack of partisan ardor philosophy had become sterile. Thirty years after the victory of Marxism-Leninism in the Soviet Union, many questions still remained philosophically unresolved. Zhdanov demanded increased diligence in the areas of ethics and aesthetics. He demanded that the "dialectical lawfulness" of scientific development be assessed and subjected to "self-criticism."[35]

The 1956 interpretation must be compared with the conception of partisan science advanced in Zhdanov's 1947 speech. Between 1947 and 1956 physics had given evidence of an inability to effectively operate within the confines of a science bound by partisan constraints. By 1955 it had as a consequence received permission to operate with the theoretical tools of "bourgeois" relativity physics. Logic, grammar, and cybernetics had similarly been given relative independence by the Central Committee.

In order to conform to the presupposition of dialectical materialism, the measure of independence achieved by formal logic, which made possible studies in mathematical logic and cybernetics, was qualified by the insistence that logic must have a "material base," that is, that logic must be understood to be, in some sense, an empirical science. The partial liberation of the sciences from the trammels of "partisanship" in 1955 was quickly qualified by the recognition that the *social* sciences, economics, history, sociology, and philosophy, could not be conceived of as free of class bias.[36] "Taken as a whole," Lenin had advised, "the professors of economics are nothing but learned salesmen of the capitalist class, while the professors of philosophy are learned salesmen of the theologians."[37]

By 1958 a further reaction reduced the relative independence of science. Konstantinov, now the principal editor of an official text on philosophy, stated, "The natural sciences . . . do not occupy themselves with the social being of man, but rather with objective nature. In this sense their fundamental content does not belong to the forms of ideology. But certainly one must not exaggerate the distinctions which separate the natural from the social sciences. One like the other develops in answer to the necessities of man's social being. They develop on the basis of a given economic system and stand in the service of this system and the social forces to which it gives rise. The general conception of the world of this or that class influences the natural sciences. In this respect these sciences do not differentiate themselves from the other forms of social consciousness."[38] Thus in the last analysis it has been left to the ideological leadership class of the Soviet Union to decide when a natural science is concerning itself with "objective nature" and when it is under the influence of the "general conception of the world" of one or another class.

Such a responsibility is, of course, difficult to discharge. Those burdened with such a charge are not only obliged to protect the integrity of the system but its viability as well. The further developments of science have made it increasingly difficult to effect both.

S. Mueller-Markus has indicated the importance the discussion on relativity theory has had in the development of Marxism-Leninism. The first reactions to relativity theory turned on its specifically philosophic implications. Einstein was attacked as a bourgeois partisan of subjectivism, conventionalism, and positivism. But the criticism was extended to a rejection of the content of the theory. Some of the objections achieved the extraordinary crudity of rejecting not only the Einsteinian principle of relativity of lengths and intervals, but also the relativity principle of Galileo which maintained that *all* mechanical processes occur in exactly the same manner, whether the reference system is stationary or in uniform rectilinear motion.

Einstein had extended this principle, which described mechanical phenomena, to optical or electromagnetic processes. Out of this concept came the special theory of relativity, based upon two principles: that the laws of nature are valid for all bodies uniformly in rectilinear motion and that the speed of light remains constant for bodies moving uniformly in a straight line. From the relativity of spatial and temporal intervals of events the non-existence of absolute space (or "ether"), absolute time, and absolute motion follows. The general theory of relativity developed out of the special theory. Both were concerned with motion in space and time employing a "four-dimensional" space-time continuum. The seeming rejection of absolutes, the rejection of ether, the talk of a four-dimensional world, sounded exceedingly suspicious to Marxist-Leninists. How matter as substance, endowed with the faculties of self-movement, existing in space and time, with attributes of mass and extension, having in its fundamentum the faculty akin to sensation, would fare at the hands of such a theory was a serious concern.

Some of the objections directed against Einstein turned on his conception that mathematics was a formal (logical) and not an empirical science, since for the contemporary Soviet Marxist mathematics must be, in some sense, a "reflection" of the objective world.[39] The very suggestion that the acceptance of an absolute inertial motion was impossible seemed to threaten the notion of self-moved matter. Since the principles of relativity obtain with respect to motion, any absolute system of co-ordinates for such motion becomes impossible and the attribution of "mass" and "extension" in any absolute sense becomes meaningless. In the further course of the discussions it became also apparent that contemporary physicists were obliged to consider "material particles" as force fields. Although these force fields were referred to as the "form of matter," there is no meaningful equivalence. Space and time, some physicists contended, could not be the "mode of existence of matter," but rather "matter" was the mode of existence of space and time. The discussions clearly indicated that experimental physicists were pursuing independent formulations of the category of matter.[40]

The objections to the theory of relativity itself thus included "philosophical" and "substantival" criticisms, and ranged from its incompatibility with the "proletarian world view" to mistaken principles of verification and definitions of "simultaneity."[41] Maksimov led the most vocal opposition. The philosophers Kuznecov and Stejnman attempted an alternative interpretation of relativity phenomena on the basis of the relativity interpretation of Lorentz—a thesis that had already been rejected by physicists. In a conference held in Kiev in 1954 this alternative explanation was rejected. And in 1955 the theory of relativity was officially recognized and its principal opponent, Maksimov, was removed from the editorial staff of *Voprosy filosofii*. Fok and Aleksandrov, perhaps the most advanced of the supporters of the theory of relativity, were given the responsibility of formulating the theory's compatibility with dialectical materialism.

In general the contemporary Soviet position is to see in the theory of relativity a "brilliant confirmation" of dialectical materialism where several years before a goodly number of Marxist-Leninist philosophers had rejected it as "bourgeois science."[42] Certainly the philosophers of dialectical materialism had long conceived relativity physics as fundamentally opposed to philosophical materialism. And in general it seems that the philosophers opposed the admission of Einsteinian relativity physics while the physicists insisted that without its mathematical and theoretical devices science could not proceed. The very concept of atomic energy rested on the Einsteinian law of the equivalence between mass and energy. The theoretical tensions which the rejection of Einsteinian physics would cause would have serious consequences for the scientific program of the Soviet Union.

That the philosophers of Marxism-Leninism could neither anticipate the theory of relativity nor its ultimate acceptance by Soviet science seriously compromises many of their claims. It would seem that science advances irrespective of the notions of Marxism-Leninism; or it might mean that contemporary Soviet philosophers have no generally accepted interpretation of the full implications of their philosophy of nature. It might also conceivably mean that all scientists are unconsciously dialectical materialists. If the first is true then it becomes difficult to maintain that "dialectical materialism is the most advanced, the *only* scientific conception of the world."[43] If the second is true then one could not say, with any persuasive force, that "genuine science can always foresee the new"[44] and that Marxism-Leninism is that science which "gives us an instrument with which to look into the future. . . ."[45] Finally, if all scientists are unconsciously dialectical materialists then the propagation of dialectical materialism, if not a positive hindrance, does not seem to be necessary since an "unconscious" dialectical materialist,[46] i.e., Einstein, devised a "brilliant confirmation" of Marxism-Leninism before any "conscious" dialectical materialist recognized it as such.

### Logic and Marxism-Leninism

Of all the problems which have beset dialectical materialism in the Soviet Union that which is most intrinsically interesting is the problem of the relationship between formal and dialectical logic. Engels, using arguments borrowed directly out of Hegel's *Logic*, argued that an adequate description of the world required that one utter literal contradictions. Plekhanov had taken essentially the same position. He argued that the laws of formal logic were applicable only within "certain limits" outside of which the "laws" of the "logic of contradiction" obtained.[47] Traditional logic had only marginal utility. An adequate description of natural processes required the strict application of contradictions—a yes and a no answer to precisely the same question.[48]

Lenin in his turn, after his study of Hegel's *Logic*, leveled similar criticisms at the "old logic."[49] The "old formal logic" was for Lenin "mystic," "idealist."[50] Nature was contradictory and only contradictory locutions could adequately describe it.

During the twenty years which followed Lenin's death in 1924, the relationship between "formal" and "dialectical" logic remained obscure. "Formal" logic was conceived as, at best, a marginal and subsidiary component of a system called the "logic of contradiction." At its worst, as Rosental and Iudin contended in the early editions of the standard Soviet *Brief Philosophical Dictionary*, "the laws of formal logic oppose themselves to the laws of dialectical logic."[51]

In 1946, however, the Central Committee of the Communist party decreed that traditional logic be once more introduced into the school curriculum. Because of the lack of textbooks of formal logic, provisional permission was given for the use, in revised form, of a prerevolutionary textbook by Chelpanov. From that date a number of logic textbooks appeared but they were all systematically condemned as "idealist" or "formalist." An entire edition of a collection of essays on formal logic was actually confiscated by the Ministry of Higher Education. The discussions concerning the status of formal logic with respect to the logic of contradictions continued without results until the publication of Stalin's letters on *Marxism and Linguistics* published in the summer of 1950.[52] In the letters Stalin criticized the late N. Y. Marr, who had conceived language as a derivative, as a component of the ideological superstructure of society. Stalin took the position that grammar was a science yielding abstract, general rules for the formation of words and sentences which could be considered independently of the content of the words and sentences expressed. Grammar, as a science, could be appraised independently of class interests. Grammar, as such, did not serve the ends of any specific class in society and consequently could be evaluated independently of class interest. In effect, grammar could be assessed by formal and universal rules that would be as binding on the proletariat as they were on the bourgeoisie. Stalin argued that language was created precisely to serve society as a whole, to serve as the common vehicle of expression for an entire people, irrespective of class differences.[53] Once proposed, such an argument provided a ready rationale for considering formal logic, the "rules of thought," independently of class interest, and logicians began their discussions almost immediately.[54] Drawing out the implications of Stalin's analysis occupied Soviet philosophers and logicians for upwards of two years. Nor was the quickened interest restricted to the Soviet Union. In November, 1951, a philosophical conference devoted to the question of logic was convened in Jena,[55] as a result of which it was decided that formal logic did not possess a class character.[56] In Poland Stalin's *ukaz* on language and logic simply accelerated the process of reassessment.[57] Actually as much might well be said of the development in the Soviet Union itself. As early as 1949 Soviet mathematicians reported extensively on their work in the area of mathematical logic. While their account was almost apologetic in tone, they did indicate the importance of investigating the logical algebra of relay systems. They indicated that mathematical logic had revealed the elementary logical connections to which various complex logical operations which form the basis of relations in relay and electronic systems are reducible.[58]

Thus, while there had been prior development, Stalin's letters did precipitate a reconsideration of the nature of formal logic and its relationship to "dialectical" logic. A discussion was organized under the auspices of *Voprosy filosofii*. A systematic attempt was made to find a *modus vivendi* which might permit the autonomy of both formal and "dialectical" logic. Actually the discussion was exegetical—most of the dispute turning on competing "interpretations" of the texts of the founders of Marxism-Leninism.[59] The editors of *Voprosy* concluded the discussion with a restatement of Lenin's position that formal logic constituted "the elementary laws and form of correct thought" and dialectical logic coincided with the theory of knowledge of Marxism. By 1956, in a discussion with the editors of *Voprosy*, K. S. Bakradze and N. I. Kondakov, both eminent Soviet logicians, gave evidence that considerable objection had arisen with respect to the official solution. Bakradze contended that there cannot be *two* logics, one formal and other dialectical, both operating with distinct laws and in part actually contradictory of one another. Formal logic cannot be understood to deal with the simple, abstract relations while dialectical logic devotes itself to concrete and complex relations. In the strict sense there can only be *one* logic, having as its object the investigation of the rules of inference governing propositional operations.[60] Dialectical logic, Bakradze held, is not a theory of the laws of valid inference; the classical founders of Marxism-Leninism identified dialectical logic with dialectics and epistemology. Lenin had contended that the "logic, dialectics and the theory of knowledge of materialism [are] one and the same thing. . . ."[61] Consequently, dialectics could be understood to be concerned with formulating the most general empirical laws governing processes in the natural world. As such its subject matter would be entirely different from that of formal logic. Yet in speaking about the general laws governing the motion of all things from history to human thinking (as a psychological process) the laws of formal logic would have to be binding. Dialectical logic would be no logic at all, but an epistemology, a theory of the higher laws of development in nature, society, and human thought. Any discussion about such laws would have to accord with the rules set forth in formal logic.

In the last decade philosophers in the Soviet Union have evinced an increasing interest in formal logic. In 1955 the Institute of Philosophy published a collective volume in which several articles were devoted at least marginally to mathematical logic. But the most important development in this area seems to have been the consequence of the conference organized by the Institute of Philosophy of the Academy of Sciences of the U.S.S.R. in April, 1958, "On the Question of Dialectical Contradictions in the Light of Contemporary Science and Practice."[62]

The discussants separated themselves into two relatively well-defined groups. One group defended the Hegelian conception of real contradictions in nature as providing the impetus of development and argued for the technical necessity of contradictory formulations in which these real contradictions are reflected. Another group, led by Ernest Kolman, while committing itself to the existence of real contradictions in nature, attempted to define contradiction in a manner which would make contradictory locutions compatible with the rules of formal logic. Kolman, a Czech by birth, had come to philosophy through the empirical sciences and had in 1948 presented a critical discussion of mathematical logic dealing with the relevant literature from Leibniz through Boole, Peano, Frege, Russell-Whitehead, to Tarski, Church, and Quine. In the course of his presentation at the 1958 conference, Kolman drew on this background and contended that no judgments concerning real contradictions could be forthcoming until "contradiction" was defined with some specificity. Kolman provided instances of contradictions rooted in nature: the contradiction between living and dead matter, between repulsion and attraction, between positive and negative charges, between north and south. It is interesting to note that no mention was made of the distinction, common among logicians, between contradictory, contrary, subcontrary, and polar opposition.[63] What is more interesting is Kolman's contention that these real contradictions in nature could only be adequately described in language which conformed to the principle of non-contradiction common to formal logic. Specifically, he contended that "the laws of formal logic, including the law of non-contradiction, are binding upon dialectical logic."[64] "Although," he went on, "it reflects reality, formal logic is not concerned with reality itself but with propositions concerning reality. Thus the interdiction of formal logic against affirming contradictions concerns propositions, not contradictions which obtain between two different aspects of reality."[65] Thus when Lenin had described the atom as a contradiction he had not violated the rules of formal logic. He had been rather adequately describing a submicroscopic entity, ascribing negative charge to some of its parts and positive charge to other of its parts. He had not been affirming a contradiction in the formal sense.[66]

Kolman's position seems to make eminent good sense. He maintained that consistency is a necessary condition of truth. Science would be impossible if contradictory propositions were permitted to infect its system as truths. The principle of non-contradiction is prompted by formal considerations. Its purpose is to exclude from a deductive system pairs of propositions which cannot be true in conjunction. A formal deductive system which includes such a pair of contradictory propositions could include any propositions whatsoever. All contradictory systems would be identical and their productions sterile. We could not formulate correct rules of inference by discovering invalid ones. Consistency, in a deductive system, certainly seems to be at least a necessary condition of truth.

Thus Kolman contended that whenever, in any concrete instance, Engels illustrates the dialectical logic he is describing different aspects of one and the same phenomenon, ascribing positive and negative poles to a magnet, living and dead cells to a body. It would be an error to suppose that in so speaking, one is ascribing contradictory attributes to one and the same entity in one and the same sense at one and the same instant. The ascriptions are made to different components of one and the same entity.

The importance of the discussion in 1958 is evident from a brief survey of contemporary Soviet Marxist philosophy texts. Almost without exception the universal applicability of the laws of formal logic is admitted. Konstantinov, for example, maintains, "All the laws of formal logic must necessarily be observed in all thinking with respect to objects."[67] In the most recent edition of the Brief Philosophical Dictionary, Rosental and Iudin reverse their original commitment to a dialectical logic which opposes the principles of identity and non-contradiction. They insist that formal reasoning necessitates strict observance of these principles. "(1) Thought must respect the principle of identity. The law of identity provides that we identify and distinguish things accurately and not substitute one thing for another. In reasoning . . . a notion must be employed with the one and the same signification throughout. (2) Reasoning must not be contradictory. The law of non-contradiction forbids self-contradiction in the course of an argument or the analysis of a problem. It is necessary to distinguish between the inadmissible contradictions of fallacious arguments and those of real life—dialectical contradictions."[68] The distinction between the contradictions of formal logic and "dialectical" contradictions is clearly drawn. Meliujin is careful to indicate: "Objective [dialectical] contradictions can and must be conceived as non-contradictory from the point of view of logic."[69] An adequate account of phenomena cannot affirm the conjunction of two mutually exclusive propositions.[70] "In effect, scientific theories cannot contain logical contradictions; should they do so they would not adequately reflect reality."[71] This seems to imply not only that it is inadmissible to permit formal contradictions in descriptions of reality but that nature itself cannot be conceived as contradictory in any formal sense. A true description correctly "reflects" reality. Since correct descriptions must be logically consistent, nature must be logically consistent as well. In pursuing this reassessment K. Ajdukiewicz, A. Ossowski, and S. Schaff in Poland,[72] J. Bartos in Czechoslovakia,[73] and E. Kolman in the Soviet Union[74] have argued that Engels was in error in maintaining that the local motion involved a literal contradiction and that its description necessitated the affirmation of the conjunction of mutually exclusive propositions.

The distinction between formal contradictions and dialectical contradictions is made explicit in contemporary Soviet texts: "In formal logic contradiction refers to the incompatibility between the signification of propositions while in dialectical materialism it refers to the process of interaction between objective tendencies."[75] Formal logic functions as a kind of grammar governing correct reasoning; it is concerned with the valid rules of inference. "In speaking of 'contradictions,' materialist dialectics is concerned primarily with the contradictions existing in objective reality. These, of course, must be distinguished from contradictions that arise from inconsistent thinking and confused ideas. When someone asserts something in the process of reasoning, and then proceeds to deny it, he can be justifiably accused of a logical contradiction that is not permitted by the laws of formal logic. Contradictions due to incorrect thinking should not be confused with the objective contradictions existing in objective things. Although the word 'contradiction' is the same in both cases, it means different things."[76]

Marxist-Leninist philosophers seem ready to grant that intelligible discourse cannot contain literal contradictions. The contradiction of dialectics is carefully distinguished from that of formal logic. Any description of the world, either in common sense or scientific discourse must accord with the rules of formal logic. In effect, Soviet dialectical materialism has all but abandoned the logic of contradictions bequeathed it by Friedrich Engels.

For our purposes we can best understand dialectics as having nothing to do with logic as such, but rather as a loose collection of extremely general "laws" which characterize the "motion" common to thought, and the physical and social processes. At their worst, the "laws" of the dialectic are "transcendental hypotheses" about the "origins" of motion. Dialectical logic seems to entail nothing more than a concern with "laws" which reveal "the universal connection of everything with everything"—a preoccupation Hegelian in essence and explicitly metaphysical in character.

### Marxism-Leninism as Philosophy

Since approximately 1950 there have been a number of changes in the interpretation of the relationship between dialectical materialism and the sciences which it is conceived to incorporate. Most of these changes seem to have been prompted by practical necessity. The decision to divest language of its class character may have been prompted by many mutually interacting factors.[77] The "declassifying" of logic and grammar followed. That logic was conceived to be a non-political science seems to have been as much a consequence of the necessity of developing mathematical logic in the work with computer systems as of anything else.

But more than that, in time certain terms in the body of Marxism-Leninism as philosophy have considerably altered their meaning. "Reflection," as we have seen, has come to mean "mathematical isomorphism," while the locution "The senses photograph reality" is retained solely as a metaphor. "Matter" is sometimes conceived as a "force field" divested of attributes, a mode of existence of space-time, and at other times as a "philosophical category."

Since 1950 it has become impossible to describe the philosophy in the Soviet Union as a monolithic ideological system. Philosophy in the Soviet Union can more appropriately be understood as being composed of at least three components:[78] (1) a fixed system of basic commitments, e.g., that development upward and onward from capitalism through Socialism to Communism, obeying the laws of historical materialism, is necessary and inevitable; (2) a relatively systematic philosophy incorporating the doctrine that the world is material in its inmost nature and that its development obeys the laws of the dialectic, laws which can be cognized as a consequence of their "reflections" in the sensory apparatus and mind of man; and (3) special disciplines which apparently have been accorded apolitical status, the most important of which are logic, mathematical logic, Einsteinian relativity physics, and certain aspects of quantum mechanics.

We have seen that there has been some manipulation within the body of the systematic doctrines. Stalin had even neglected one of the basic, perhaps the most basic, of the dialectical laws, the negation of the negation. But even within the system the meaning of words and phrases can be, and has been, significantly altered in the course of time and discussion. The picture language and metaphors of classical Marxism, of course, lend themselves to this form of development. The vocabulary may remain constant but the armory of ideas is stocked with markedly different materials. The laws of the dialectic, even when the trinity is retained, are so loosely formulated that they cover all observed phenomena indiscriminately. Dialectical logic is no longer a "logic" in any literal sense, but a metaphysics, a theory of knowledge and the sum of current scientific thinking about the world. The attempt to propound a formal "dialectical logic" has been abandoned, and the "theory of categories" seems to be in flux.[79] Apparently it has not been systematically formulated.[80]

Within the range of the "declassified" doctrines the picture is not consistent. Some of the sciences have been conceived as "apolitical." Which are and which are not, at any particular time, seems to turn on decisions by the Central Committee of the Communist party. They must ultimately decide which sciences, or which component parts of the sciences, are not "class bound" and hence are "apolitical." These decisions seem to be based on considerations of practical necessity and ideological tension. But where the practical necessity is pressing, ideological considerations seem to have little weight. This is nowhere more evident than in the freedom accorded physics. Some of the central notions of relativity physics threaten the materialism of Marxism-Leninism, but physicists have been permitted their use although no fundamental discussions about their ontological implications have been undertaken. Where present programs are not of such urgency, as seems to be the case in genetics and psychology, ideological considerations seem foremost.

The interaction of all these forces seems to determine the course of Marxism-Leninism in the Soviet Union. That the variables involved are so multidimensional and disparate makes any prediction of the subsequent course of philosophical and scientific development hazardous. The fact that the decision of the Central Committee of the Communist party in the Soviet Union has assumed the responsibility of ultimate arbitration increases the difficulty of prediction. It is difficult, if not impossible, to know which problems might generate reconsideration of the sciences, a particular science, or the components of any particular science. It is similarly difficult to anticipate which specifically ideological considerations might be conceived as critical at any given time.

Soviet philosophers conceive the basic propositions of Marxism-Leninism to have been confirmed, *en bloc*, by world-historical and social events.[81] As a consequence of success in practice, i.e., successful revolutions, Marxist-Leninist philosophers feel justified in using the "classics" of Marx, Engels, and Lenin (Stalin is rarely mentioned in current philosophical literature) as canonical in the assessment of the truth of a philosophical position. The logic of this kind of confirmation seems to be that the philosophy of Marxism-Leninism has provided the "intellectual weapon" for the successful revolutions of nearly half the world's population, and therefore Marxist-Leninist conjectures on ontology, metaphysics, and epistemology are "true." That the logic of the argument is defective is, of course, apparent. Nonetheless Soviet philosophers are, in one way or another, committed to it. Hence we find their arguments conclude with citations from the "classic" authors as definitive proof of their truth. An alternative "proof" of Marxism-Leninism is that afforded by its "confirmation" by all the scientific advances of the century. Since the language of Marxism-Leninism is so loose, it can be made to fit almost *any* scientific development. To see this as a virtue and not as a vice is a curiosity.

In any event the total commitment to Marxism-Leninism is evident in the body of contemporary Soviet literature. But within the commitment we have seen that many lines of development are possible. The course of development is subject to the control of the Central Committee of the party. The fact that the theory of Marxism-Leninism is "confirmed" by the historic success of the Communist party is conceived as sufficient warrant for its assumption of the role of final arbiter in ideological matters. The recent textbook of the fundamentals of Marxist philosophy states that "for the Communist Party questions of the conception of the world have never been and cannot be considered the 'personal affair' of certain of its members. . . . The Communist Party regards the defence of the theoretical, philosophical basis of Marxism as a Party affair. . . ."[82] Such statements can be multiplied almost without number.[83]

But while the party retains ultimate authority to correct "error," there have been recurrent admissions that some component parts of classical Marxism can be, and have been, abandoned. Lenin, for example, in his "creative development" of Marxism-Leninism did as much.[84] Into the elaboration of dialectical materialism Lenin brought "much that was new."[85] There is then a "creative" change possible within Marxism-Leninism. Stalin himself had, in his time, introduced "creative" changes. Subsequent reconsideration has, perhaps, conceived them as less "creative" than they were at one time thought to be—but continued change, per se, is admitted as a real possibility. Such an admission creates a difficulty for Marxist-Leninists. The difficulty arises from the inability of Marxism-Leninism to distinguish a "creative" change from a "revision" or a "deviation." This problem within the Soviet Union is resolved by fiat from the Central Committee of the party. Such a resolution seems less effective where Socialist thinkers outside the Soviet Union are concerned. In some respects, for example, the developments in Poland have taken an independent course.[86] The discussions have been more fundamental and more far-reaching in their implications.

That a more critical attitude toward Marxism-Leninism has become manifest is evidenced in the appearance of an articulate faction among Polish Marxist-Leninists who demand a "return to the young Marx" and a reformulation of Marxist epistemology on the basis of the "anthropological naturalism" of the *Economic and Philosophic Manuscripts of 1844*.[87] Kolakowski, the most persuasive spokesman of a group which includes Helena Eilstein and Zdzislaw Kochanski, has forcefully argued for a reconsideration of the early Marx *Manuscripts*.[88] His principal opponent is Adam Schaff, who has had a long history of orthodoxy in Marxism-Leninism.[89]

It is difficult to know how far such a development can proceed without precipitating tensions within Marxism-Leninism of such an order that the fundamental theoretical structure of the system would be jeopardized. For the time being a return to the philosophical position of the young Marx does not seem possible within the Soviet Union and few of the other countries within the Soviet orbit seem to display as much philosophical independence as Poland.[90]

The difficulty in determining with any objective index when a change in the fundamental doctrines of Marxism-Leninism constitutes a "creative evolution" and when it constitutes a "deviation" seems to be of critical importance for Marxist-Leninists, particularly since Communist China has taken it upon herself to challenge the "changes" which the contemporary leaders of the Communist party in the Soviet Union have introduced into the body of theory.

Marxism-Leninism is of necessity committed to a self-characterization which must include "development and enrichment" as a consequence of "changing historical conditions."[91] That it will change cannot be gainsaid. How it will change will be determined by the whole complex of forces which act upon the ideology itself.

## Marx, Marxism, and Marxism-Leninism

The doctrine which Karl Marx founded has run a strange course. It began in the struggle the young Karl Marx undertook to divest Hegelianism of its mysticism, to see the earth and man and society in their mundane shape, to conceive nature and history as somehow the product of *man's* labor rather than the working out of categories and concepts of some absolute substance behind the world. Today that doctrine seems to be all that Marx as a philosopher could not suffer. Again there are "categories" working themselves out in nature, man, and society. For the "categories" for Lenin are "reflections" of the "essences" of things. The "categories" of Hegel have once again been conjured up to serve as *demiourgos* of the world.

Both the young Marx and the young Engels had inveighed against the Hegelian "categories," only, apparently, to fall victim to them in their most pernicious form. Marx had sought to concretize the abstract categories of Hegel, which he conceived as reified predicates of real subjects in a real world. He contended that Hegel had not taken account of real natural or social phenomena and was incapable of explaining either their origin or their course of development. Hegel appeared to Marx as a kind of thaumaturge who, with the verbal magic of the "negation of the negation," could posit or sublate, create or destroy, conserve or abolish, scientific and social reality. In the "categories" the act of thought was sundered from the human subject, and in an inverted world hypostatized thought became the absolute Subject.

Marx, as we have seen, clearly distinguished his dialectical method from that of Hegel. But he openly avowed himself a pupil of Hegel; and while his method was the "direct opposite" of that of the great German Idealist, he even "here and there . . . coquetted with the modes of expression peculiar to him."[92] But Marx clearly distinguished the "method of presentation" from that of "inquiry." "The latter," he tells us, "has to appropriate the material in detail, to analyze its different forms of development, to trace out their inner connexion. Only after this work is done, can the actual movement be adequately described. If this is done successfully, if the life of the subject-matter is ideally reflected as in a mirror, then it may appear as if we had before us a mere *a priori* construction."[93]

Marx's clear intention was to proceed with his work in a radically empiricist manner. He studied the "development of the economic structure of society as a natural historical process" by making inquiry into the "social antagonisms which arise from the natural laws of capitalist production." In order to study this development under its most advanced conditions he chose the whole of England as his laboratory. He was well aware that in the course of his inquiry he would have to entertain abstractions in order to isolate the processes governing the development with which he was concerned. These processes might then be conveniently described in Hegelian terms.

The techniques Marx followed were, by and large, those of the empirical science which was maturing during the last half of the nineteenth century. But the "coquetry" with Hegelianism, if that was all that it was, had a disastrous effect. His description of social processes was cast in terms of inevitability and necessity. This addiction to "inexorabilities" led to a conception of things which saw them in some sense *logically* connected. The Hegelian *logos* seemed to cast its long shadow over his whole system.

Marx's criticism of the Hegelian method seems to have been restricted to a substitution of *content* without a radical assessment of the implications of the *form*. This was certainly evident in his *Philosophic Manuscripts of 1844*. Engels, in turn, apparently remained convinced that Hegel had achieved a brilliant insight into the ultimate nature of the world and embarked upon a program of "Hegelianizing" the natural sciences. But where the young Marx had made man the bearer of all the attributes Hegel had ascribed to the Absolute, Engels made *Matter* the reified subject and man one of *its* attributes. Lenin proceeded one step further in restoring the Hegelian world-view. Man, and his thoughts, were conceived as the highest development of Matter, a Matter which is its own cause and final form, a Matter which contains inherent within itself all the phenomena of nature, history, and the Spirit.

Lenin, it would seem, ultimately became more of an Hegelian than a Marxist in philosophy. We even find this curious remark in his *Notebooks*. "It is impossible completely to understand Marx's *Capital*, and especially his first chapter, without having thoroughly studied and understood the *whole* of Hegel's *Logic*. Consequently, half a century later none of the Marxists understood Marx!!"[94]

The implications of such a remark, should it be taken in complete seriousness, are staggering. A great deal of Lenin's Marxist writings antedate his familiarity with Hegel. One wonders if we are to conclude that Lenin is suggesting that *he* did not understand Marxism prior to the end of 1914? Dunayevskaya argues that the exposure to Hegelian dialectics produced "nothing short of a restoration of truth to philosophic idealism against vulgar materialism to which [Lenin] had given the green light in 1908 with his work on *Materialism and Empiriocriticism.*"[95] The essay he wrote during that time entitled "Karl Marx"[96] contains a section on "Dialectics." Discussing the philosophy of "Marx and Engels," he tells us that "the revolutionary side of Hegel's philosophy was adopted and developed by Marx," and that "according to Marx, dialectics is 'the science of the general laws of motion—both of the external world and of human thought. . . .' "[97] *And yet every single reference in the brief section is to a work by Engels.*

Lenin's Hegelianism had its source in the writings of Engels. Marx had ceased to occupy himself with specifically philosophical problems after 1848. In 1857 and 1858 Marx returned to the "leafing through" of Hegel's *Logic.* In a letter dated the 14th of January, 1858, he mentioned to Engels that if he could find the time he would like to write a brochure devoted to an exposition of the rational components of the method which Hegel had discovered but had "mystified." We have indicated that it was left to Engels to undertake this "exposition." And it is Engels who is responsible, by and large, for the formulations which today fill Marxism-Leninism with Hegelianisms. "Hegel remained for Engels the pinnacle of philosophical achievement, the very embodiment of philosophy."[98]

Engels proceeded to apply the Hegelian dialectic to nature. Marx had done something similar in the *Manuscripts of 1844,* but the results were markedly different. Subsequent to 1844 Marx's application of the "dialectical method" to history was exemplified only by his socioeconomic studies, particularly in the *Contribution to the Critique of Political Economy* and *Capital.* What he left to philosophy was by and large a legacy of economic, social, and historical theories. Marx himself was to leave no finished work on epistemology, ethics, or metaphysics, only the incomplete *Manuscripts* of Paris of 1844 written when he was twenty-six years old.

Since that time a world of literature has been written about his philosophical position. The Marxist-Leninists have been content to hyphenate "Marx-Engels" and treat the speculations of Engels as those of Karl Marx. Lenin went a step further to Hegel himself. We have briefly considered some of the results. A little Hegel is a dangerous thing.

# PART TWO

---

# Marxism as a Theory

# of History

# 5 Classical Marxism

## as a Theory of History

There are few documents in the intellectual history of the West that have had the impact of the *Communist Manifesto*. Written little more than a century ago, the *Manifesto* has been instrumental in directly changing the lives of over a third of the world's population. While its most significant function has been to animate revolutionary movements, it has also provided the point of departure for innumerable expositions, inquiries, and assessments. The literature devoted to the *Communist Manifesto* of Karl Marx and Friedrich Engels is enormous. The treatment has varied from cavalier dismissal to canonical exegesis. Our purpose here will be exposition, treating the *Manifesto* as perhaps the most succinct statement of classical Marxism as a theory of history, for the document contains all the essentials of the view of history of Marx and Engels. Moreover it signals an important juncture in Marx's intellectual development. It is the culmination of his preoccupation with philosophy and marks the commencement of a systematic study of political economy. To the *Manifesto* Engels brought a concern for, and a knowledge of, the working-class movements of Germany and England. He brought to it a perhaps more detailed knowledge of political economy than that possessed by Marx at that time. The finished document is the work of two men, but of two men who had come to understand the workings of history in essentially the same way. They had come to that understanding by different paths, but the essential oneness of their thinking can be traced in their earlier and certainly in their later writings on the processes of history, the nature of the state, and revolution.

The twenty-seven-year-old Marx had been expelled from Paris at the beginning of 1845 upon the orders of the Guizot government. Marx, with his wife and their infant daughter, sought refuge in Brussels. There he was joined by the twenty-five-year-old Engels. Both men lost no time getting in touch with various German working-class organizations, among them the German Workers' Educational Association, which was affiliated with a federation called the Communist League. The Communist League was the successor to the League of the Just, which had been a secret revolutionary society with a loosely formulated program influenced by Wilhelm Weitling.

The Communist League asked Marx and Engels to rework the program of the original League of the Just and reformulate the doctrine upon which such a program would rest. In 1847 Engels wrote the first draft of the new doctrinal statement, the *Foundations of Communism*. It was couched in the form of questions and answers to conform to the tradition established by the League of the Just. Marx felt, however, that the form traditionally used in prior publications by the League would not permit him to organize his exposition to greatest advantage. He therefore rewrote the *Foundations* putting the material in the form of a manifesto, the *Manifesto of the Communist Party*.

The *Manifesto of the Communist Party* is a program manifesto of unmatched power and eloquence. For more than a century it has been read as a revolutionary hymn, a statement of brilliant historical insight, a document of compelling intellectual force, and a candid program of antisocial design. Few thinkers have seen fit to neglect it.

### The Communist Manifesto

On a narrow canvas the *Communist Manifesto* paints a broad picture of an entire epoch in man's history. With consummate skill and artistry broad historical theses are employed as a background for the surface features of the contemporary history of the mid-nineteenth century. Together they provide a picture which purported to reveal the essence of the modern as well as the outline of the future world.

On the surface of history is recorded the struggle of classes. Even this surface history was only gradually revealed to the men of the modern world. Its revelation was the consequence of the simplification of class antagonisms in the bourgeois world of the nineteenth century. The epoch of the bourgeoisie is exemplified by one distinctive feature—the progressive simplification of class antagonisms to a contest between two great hostile camps, the bourgeoisie and the proletariat.

This epoch of the bourgeoisie is the product of a long historical development, of a series of revolutions in the modes of production and exchange. Within the very confines of the old feudal society a new class gradually developed. The feudal system, with its constraints upon industrial productivity, rapidly revealed itself incapable of coping with the economic demands which followed the discovery of the New World, the development of foreign markets, and the expansion of trade. A new aggressive and revolutionary manufacturing class rose to meet the demands of a new situation. The revolutionary bourgeoisie created the complex economic system required by the situation, but its every advance was harassed by the vested classes of the old, moribund order. Working with one hand to create the new order of industry, the bourgeoisie was compelled to defend its advances with the other. Each step in its development was accompanied by a correlative political struggle. Ultimately the bourgeoisie captured exclusive political control of the state; the executive of the modern state became a committee for managing the common affairs of the entire entrepreneurial class.

Every form of feudal, patriarchal tie which related man to man in conformity with the old order of production and exchange was pitilessly rent asunder. The only relation which bound men together was money payment. Every "natural" tie was severed. Personal worth, honor, and family ties were reduced to mere money relations. The driving force of bourgeois vigor is egotistical calculation.

Within the feudal society itself the means of production and exchange had developed to the point where they were no longer compatible with the feudal organization of agriculture and manufacturing industry, that is, the feudal relations of property became fetters on the rapidly developing productive forces. Only free competition, calculation for personal profit, could permit the full and untrammeled development of the productive forces. To meet the increasing demands for produce the rising bourgeoisie was compelled to constantly revolutionize the instruments of production. This protracted revolution in production produces a constant disturbance of social conditions. All fixed relations with their attendant prejudices and opinions are shattered. Man is forced to face, without illusion, the hard reality of his life, of his relations with his kind. The very conditions which obtain in production produce the ideas men entertain, codified in law, morality, and religion. The ideas of an epoch are the ideas of its dominant class, those who control the forces of production. The law is their will made law and their will is in its essential character determined by the economic conditions which ensure the continued existence of that class which masters the processes of production.

But to mobilize the revolutionized instruments of production, the rising bourgeoisie required the services of men as sources of labor power. The rise of the bourgeoisie necessitated the commensurate rise of a class of workingmen who, shorn of their feudal ties, become abjectly dependent upon the sale of their labor power in order to survive.

The conditions which prevail in production determine the relationship which will exist between the bourgeoisie and the proletariat. The continual expansion of production and the necessary improvement of the instruments of production require the continual expansion of capital investment. An industrial system based essentially upon such conditions requires that the relationship between entrepreneur and worker be one of calculation. The bourgeoisie will purchase labor power at its value, as a commodity. As a commodity labor power is purchased only so long as it increases capital. And as a commodity, the cost of labor power is almost entirely restricted to the means of subsistence that is required for its maintenance and for the propagation of the race of workers. As machinery is increasingly introduced, the cost required for the maintenance of workers is reduced. Wages fall. Workers must compete for the opportunity to sell their labor power and are subject to all the vicissitudes of competition and market fluctuation.

As capital increases, the economies of large-scale production drive more and more of the lower strata of the middle class, the petty tradespeople, the artisans, the shopkeepers and peasants, into the proletariat. Their diminutive assets are at a competitive disadvantage in the rush of modern industry. Gradually society splits into two large hostile camps. The bourgeoisie enrolls living labor in the service of the machine, but it will continue to do so only so long as it is profitable. The existence of the working class depends on its value to the bourgeoisie as a source of profit. The increase of profit provides the capital for the expansion and extension of industry, further precipitating the remnants of the lower-middle class into the proletariat while concentrating more wealth in the hands of the capitalist class.

The very contradiction of bourgeois society is revealed in the absurdity of overproduction. As the productive forces mature there is too much civilization, too much means of subsistence, too much industry, too much commerce. Bourgeois society enters a period of crisis. Society cannot consume, profitably for the bourgeoisie, all that society can produce. Foreign markets are sought abroad while masses languish at home. The misery of the working class grows. As wealth accumulates among the ruling class, and industry develops, poverty among the working population increases. Their existence is precarious, the unceasing improvement of machinery increasingly simplifies their tasks, making their daily toil burdensome and monotonous. The competition among the bourgeoisie makes the wages of labor increasingly unstable.

But the very conditions which prevail ensure that the proletariat will become increasingly organized. They are brought together in vast urban centers. Life within the ranks of the working class becomes more and more uniform and organized. Improvement in machinery reduces their labor uniformly to one of attendance insofar as there is continual reduction in skill required. Nearly everywhere wages are reduced to the same low level. And everywhere the proletariat is concentrated in larger and larger numbers, their number continually increased by recruits from the lower strata of the middle class, ruined by the expansion and competition of modern industry. As the number of the bourgeoisie is reduced, its absolute wealth increases.

The two classes face each other. The proletariat has increased in size and organization. The meanness of labor and compensation embitter it. The threat of poverty haunts it. Periodic crises threaten it with starvation. The bourgeoisie accumulates greater and greater wealth while reducing its number. Its control over the machinery of the state becomes more and more brazen. More and more frequently the working class collides with the bourgeoisie. The working class begins to form combinations in the service of its interests. More and more frequently the exchanges with the bourgeoisie take on the character of organized protest. The combinations of the working class take on a more and more permanent and extensive character. The rapidly developing means of communication permit different localities to maintain permanent liaison. Local struggles take on the character of national struggles between classes. The class struggle becomes a political struggle. Impoverished elements of the middle class sink into the proletariat and make more articulate its demands, more cogently formulate its policies. These are the men who have raised themselves to the level of comprehending theoretically the historical movement of the modern epoch as a whole.

Finally the struggle enters its decisive phase. The proletariat has become a self-conscious, independent movement of the immense majority. The bourgeoisie has produced its own gravediggers. The fall of the bourgeoisie and the victory of the proletariat are inevitable.

### The Background of the Communist Manifesto

Like all intellectual products, the *Manifesto* of the Communist party drew upon intellectual materials available in the funded ideas of its time. Individual ideas, generalizations, even turns of speech can be identified as those of precedent or contemporary thinkers. The doctrine of the class struggle, for example, had become an almost commonplace idea in a time which still remembered the bitter class strife of the French Revolution. Writers such as Quesnay, Voltaire, Rousseau, Helvetius, Mably, Raynal, Necker, Turgot, among others, employed the class struggle as an explanatory device to render intelligible the political history of their period. Raynal in his volume *Histoire philosophique et poli-*

*tique des établissements et du commerce des Européens dans les deux Indes,* which appeared in 1771, argued that the dynamics of his period could be explained by the tensions which existed between the "rich" and those they sought to "exploit." Turgot, in 1766, had argued in a similar vein in his *Reflexions sur la formation et la distribution des richesses:* ". . . [The] entire class which is concerned with the infinitely complex industrial processes necessary to meet the demands of society is divided into two segments: first, the entrepreneurs, manufacturers, those possessed of capital . . . and secondly the workers, who have nothing other than their ability to work to insure them a livelihood."[1]

Jean Paul Marat identified each political party with the class interest it represented. He interpreted the French Revolution in such categories. The various political groups aligned themselves in accordance with their "various class interests." Marat defined the opposing forces in class terms. François Auguste Mignet and Henri de Saint-Simon used similar techniques in their analyses. The Marxists have long understood that such conceptions were part of the heritage they inherited from their intellectual forebears.[2]

By the turn of the nineteenth century, F. R. de Lamennais could write that nations were divided into two classes, the owners of property and government officials on the one hand and the working people on the other. The workers had no assurance of personal liberty, for hunger placed them in a position of abject dependence upon the capitalist class.[3] These ideas came to the attention of Marx early in his intellectual career. He was probably directly influenced by the work of Saint-Simon, for the disciples of Saint-Simon were extremely active in Germany during that period. One such disciple, Ludwig Gall, who lived in Trier while Marx was completing his high-school education there, published, in 1835, a pamphlet on *The Privileged Classes and the Working Classes.* Gall was a member of the literary circle to which Marx's father belonged, and it was probably through its members that Marx became familiar with the ideas. Furthermore Eduard Gans, one of Marx's lecturers at the University of Berlin, was a dedicated Saint-Simonian.[4]

Moses Hess, one of Marx's early mentors, was also a Saint-Simonian of sorts, and it was probably he who called Marx's attention to Lorenz von Stein's *The Socialism and Communism of*

*Contemporary France.*[5] Von Stein's study, based on his own observations in France and drawn partly from secondary sources, asserted that political struggle could only be understood by an analysis of "contradictions" in the class relationships of society.[6] Revolutionary movements could only be understood in terms of the relationships of classes (what von Stein called "estates" or "orders," *Stände*).[7] Wealth tended to accumulate in the hands of a few, and the many tended to become increasingly miserable in a process which seemed irreversible.

Marx, himself, never pretended that the concept of the "class struggle" was original with him. In his letter to Weydemeyer of March, 1852, he clearly stated that "no credit is due me for discovering the existence of classes in modern society, nor yet the struggle between them. Long before me bourgeois historians had described the historical development of this struggle of the classes. . . ."[8]

Intimately bound up with the concept of the class struggle was the concept of the continual "immiseration [*Verelendung*] of the proletariat." This idea, too, had become all but commonplace by the middle of the nineteenth century. As early as 1774 the Venetian Giammaria Ortes had advanced the thesis that where one finds the greatest wealth one also finds the greatest poverty. The level of the one is in inverse proportion to the level of the other.[9] If Marx was not familiar with Ortes' works at the time of the writing of the *Manifesto*, he was certainly familiar with them by the time he completed the first volume of *Capital*, in which he makes reference to Ortes.[10] In 1818, Nebenius argued that the economic conditions in England had concentrated wealth in increasingly fewer hands, while at the same time steadily increasing the misery of the working population.[11] Parisi could write in 1840 that "we see that there is a general correspondence between the maximization of power and opulence of the few and the maximization of misery and degradation of the masses."[12] As wealth increased the conditions of the working class became more precarious, beset by misery, degradation and hunger.[13] In England, Charles Hall hypothesized that the rich became richer and the poor, poorer—a hypothesis which became central to the thought of Robert Owen. Owen's work was certainly known to both Marx and Engels prior to the writing of the *Manifesto*. Owen had argued that increasing industrialization had reduced the value of labor which was sold as a commodity. The consequence was that the situation of the working class was becoming increasingly hazardous.

Almost all these authors thought that the increasing misery of the working class would drive them to revolution.[14] Driven by desperation, the working classes were expected to rise up and strike down their oppressors. By 1835 Georg Büchner was so convinced of this that he could write: "The uniquely revolutionary factor in the world arises out of the relationship between the rich and the poor. The only god of liberty is hunger."[15] As early as 1780 Gaetano Falangieri had contended that society had become divided into two "irreconcilable factions, the propertied and the non-propertied."

Similar ideas matured in the thought of Charles Fourier and Sismondi. Alive in all these discussions are the notions of class struggle arising from the interests of the classes in society and of the increasing misery of the working class as opposed to the increasing concentration of wealth in fewer and fewer hands—mutually interacting processes which generate revolution.

The surface features of history were political, but every political event was made intelligible by an analysis of social problems. Such a conception was again commonplace among Marx's intellectual collaborators. Hess had argued in the *Rheinische Zeitung* that the revolutionary catastrophe which threatened England was explicable only upon the analysis of the problems which were, in essence, social.[16] Lorenz von Stein had, at about the same time, offered a similar thesis.

The role of increasing technological improvement in the growth of unemployment, in the diminution of wages, and in the reduction of man to an "appendage of the machine"[17] was known to Ferguson, Owen, Fourier, and Sismondi. The idea that in the course of capitalist development man's relation to man was reduced to one of "cash payment" was advanced by Hess in 1837 in his *The Holy History of Mankind*.[18] The conception that this arose out of "free competition" was similarly advanced by Hess—as was the idea that such circumstances bred the "absurdity of crises of overproduction." These latter two ideas were expounded in his "On the Nature of Money,"[19] a work with which Marx was familiar.

Even the concept that man's material existence conditions his ideas was a hypothesis advanced by the French materialists as early as the eighteenth century.[20] In England, Adam Ferguson had held that man's place in the processes of production determined his psychology and fashioned his conceptions of the world.[21] How many of these ideas directly influenced Marx's thought is difficult to document, but they had been in currency since the end of the eighteenth century.[22]

The writings of Victor Considerant, with which Marx *was* familiar,[23] contained so many ideas advanced in the *Manifesto* that Tscherkesoff[24] maintained that Marx and Engels had "plagiarized."[25] Considerant had maintained that the disorder which prevailed in society was the consequence of the developing productive processes. Free competition had concentrated wealth and the means of production in the hands of a small possessing class, a process which left behind it factories on the one hand, but an impoverished mass of working people on the other. The consequence was that the civilized nations were sinking beneath a superfluity of capital and manufacture. The crises of over-production were driving nations all over the world in a frenetic search for markets. "The industrial nations," Considerant contended, "are driven to supplement with foreign markets the market for their produce. Under the burden of overproduction . . . England has made superhuman efforts to market the surplus of its factories . . . while masses of working men perish for want of sustenance because of the senseless system of competition. . . . Society is dividing itself more and more clearly into two great classes: a small group which possess almost everything in the realm of property, of commerce and industry, and the great mass that possesses nothing, who live in absolute and collective dependence upon those who possess the capital and the instruments of production and who are compelled to sell their efforts, their talents and their strengths, for an ever sinking wage, to the feudal barons of modern society. . . . Capital and labor oppose each other in a literal state of war. . . . The function of the gigantic capitalistic system of exploitation precipitates, every day, new elements of the middle class into the ranks of the proletariat and renders this proletariat, by virtue of the bitter competition in the labor market, every day more miserable. . . . Industrialism with free competition is . . . a monstrous mechanism which extracts unceasingly the wealth of the nation to concentrate it in the reservoir of the new aristocracy and creates starving legions of paupers and proletariat."[26]

The fact that Marx and Engels were steeped in the literature of French social criticism and French Socialism has been recognized for some time.[27] One need but compare the vision of the future society entertained by Marx and Engels: "In place of the old bourgeois society . . . we shall have an association, in which the free development of each is the condition for the free development of all"[28] with that advanced by Rousseau: ". . . a method of associating . . . which will defend and protect, with all collective might, the person and property of each associate, and in virtue of which each associate, though he becomes a member of the group . . . remains as free as before"[29] to appreciate the extent of the similarities. Often there were more than general similarities. The expression "The proletarians have nothing to lose but their chains" was taken from Marat, as was "The workers have no country."[30] Bazard is responsible for the expression "the exploitation of men by men."

Both Marx and Engels admitted that their conception of history had been anticipated, in part, by the theoreticians of French Socialism[31] and the bourgeois historiographers of the French Revolution.[32] In his letter to J. Weydemeyer, dated March 5, 1852, Marx said, ". . . [No] credit is due to me for discovering the existence of classes in modern society, nor yet the struggle between them. Long before me bourgeois historians had described the historical development of this struggle of the classes, and bourgeois economists the economic anatomy of the classes."[33]

There was an obvious debt to the classical English economists, particularly Adam Smith and David Ricardo. The labor theory of value and the concept of a subsistence wage for workers is in large part borrowed from Smith.[34]

The originality of the *Manifesto*, then, does not derive from its *content*, some elements of which were available for more than a century. The originality of the *Manifesto* derives from its form.[35] In the *Manifesto* the elements are given a sustaining *logic*. Theses are connected in a compelling account. Engels saw the originality of the *Manifesto* in its core of central theses: (1) Economic production and the structure of society which it determines in every historical period constitute the basis for the political and intellectual history of that period. (2) Economic production (at least since the dissolution of primitive Communist production) has rested upon the division of exploiters and the exploited, of dominating and dominated classes, and history finds expression in the struggle of these classes. (3) In our own period class struggle has reached a stage where the exploited and oppressed class, the proletariat, can no longer emancipate itself from its oppressors without at the same time freeing the whole of society from exploitation, oppression, and class struggle.[36]

In the *Anti-Dühring*, Engels expressed similar theses in the following fashion: "The materialist conception of history starts from the proposition that the production of the means to support human life and next to production, the exchange of things produced, is the basis of all social structure; that in every society that has appeared in history, the manner in which wealth is distributed and society divided into classes or orders is dependent upon what is produced, how it is produced, and how the products are exchanged. From this point of view the final causes of all social changes and political revolutions are to be sought, not in men's brains, not in man's better insight into eternal truth and justice, but in changes in the modes of production and exchange. They are to be sought, not in the *philosophy*, but in the *economics* of each particular epoch. The growing perception that existing social institutions are unreasonable and unjust, that reason has become unreason, and right wrong, is only proof that in the modes of production and exchange changes have silently taken place with which the social order, adapted to earlier economic conditions, is no longer in keeping. From this it also follows that the means of getting rid of the incongruities that have been brought to light must also be present, in a more or less developed condition, within the changed modes of production themselves. These means are not to be *invented*, spun out of the head, but *discovered* with the aid of the head in the existing material facts of production."[37]

The theoretical substance of these theses had been clearly formulated before the *Manifesto* was written in 1847. Evidences of the development are found in the individual writings of Marx and Engels from 1840 until 1847. During these years Marx and Engels, as scholars and as students of the society of their time, processed, critically analyzed, interrelated, sculptured, one might say, the materials available to them into the form in which they are found in the *Manifesto*.


## *The Genesis of the* Communist Manifesto


It is generally conceded that Karl Marx had taken the philosophy of Hegel as a point of departure.[38] Engels indicated as much in the opening pages of *Ludwig Feuerbach*.[39] Nonetheless, while Marx's intellectual debt to Hegel must be acknowledged, Marx was never a Hegelian in any literal sense. In his letter to his father in 1837, when he was only nineteen, Marx indicated that he sought to resolve the "contradiction between that which is and that which should be" by seeking the "Idea" of Idealism in "reality."[40] He undertook a systematic study of Hegel with this thought already in mind.

We have briefly considered the influence of Hegel's epistemological and ontological notions on the work of the young Karl Marx. Here it is only necessary to indicate that Marx's concern with politics and society was equally rooted in Hegel. Hegel's discussion of "civil society" was Marx's point of departure in his criticism of what he ultimately called "bourgeois society." In his preface to the *Contribution to the Critique of Political Economy*, Marx indicates the relationship.[41] "Civil society" is the sum total of the material conditions of life, the basis of society and history.

Even a cursory inspection of Hegel's *Philosophy of Right* reveals insights which proved suggestive to the young Marx. Hegel had, for example, indicated that civil society was organized to satisfy human needs[42] and that human needs differ from animal needs in that the former multiply and develop. There is a multiplication of needs and means of satisfying them and then a differentiation and division of concrete needs into single parts and aspects which in turn become different needs. This process goes on *ad infinitum and constitutes the empirical motive force of development*. In the "infinitely complex, criss-cross, movements of reciprocal production and exchange, and the equally infinite multiplicity of means therein employed"[43] groups crystallize into classes. When civil society is in a state of unimpeded activity it is expanding internally. The process of industrial expansion promotes the accumulation of wealth on the part of a given class. At the antipode "a large mass of people falls below a certain subsistence level—a level regulated automatically as the one necessary for a member of the society—and when there is a consequent loss of the sense of right and wrong, of honesty and . . . self respect . . . the result is the creation of a rabble, of paupers. At the same time this brings with it, at the other end of the social scale, conditions which greatly facilitate the concentration of disproportionate wealth in a few hands. . . . [The] evil consists precisely in an excess of production and in the lack of a proportionate number of consumers who are themselves also producers. . . . It hence becomes apparent that despite an excess of wealth civil society is not rich enough, i.e., its own resources are insufficient to check excessive poverty and the creation of a penurious rabble. . . . This inner dialectic of civil society thus drives it—or at any rate drives a specific civil society—to push beyond its own limits and seek markets, and so its necessary means of subsistence, in other lands which are either deficient in the goods it has overproduced or else generally backward in industry. . . ."[44]

Hegel had found the resolution of the antagonisms of civil society in the "ethical state" which mediates between collective private interests in the service of the whole of society. Both Marx and Engels were aware of the antagonisms Hegel had isolated within civil society. What failed to convince them was Hegel's resolution of the tensions through the mediation of a neutral state. The manifest contradiction between the Real and the Ideal could not be resolved by state interference motivated by good will. Marx, as we have seen, accepted the Feuerbachian criticism of Hegelianism. He had come to consider Hegelianism a compensatory projection in which men sought the illusory solution of their real problems in the realm of abstract categories. "Philosophy," Feuerbach had contended, "is the recognition of that which *is*. To recognize things and essences *as they are*—that is the highest law, the highest task for philosophy."[45] In 1843 Marx echoed this judgment when he said, "Philosophy does not stand outside the world."[46] Men have confused themselves because they created a false dichotomy between the "material" world and its needs and the "thought" world.

Marx understood that philosophy conceived the state as "the realization of rational freedom"—but it was not only philosophy's task to so *conceive* it, it was also philosophy's task to *realize* it.[47] Its task was a ruthless criticism of all that impeded this realization. His subsequent criticism of the state indicated that the young Marx had already developed some of the characteristic themes of mature Marxism. He found, for example, that the state was hardly the neutral mediator of conflicting interest, but rather that it had been "degraded" to serve special interest.[48] As early as 1842 he criticized the Rhenish Landtag for having become the "executive force" of "private interests."[49]

More significantly, because of its influence in the development of later Marxism, he indicated, during this same early period, that in the "study of political [*staatlicher*] conditions one too easily overlooks the *real nature of relations* and seeks to explain everything as a consequence of the *will* of persons concerned. *There are relationships which determine the activities of individual men and separate groups that are as independent of them as breathing.* If one places oneself in this real perspective ... one will perceive the effects of relations where upon first view only persons were conceived as active forces. As soon as it is pointed out that relations necessarily produce the event, it will not be difficult to determine under which external conditions the event must actually manifest itself in life and under which it cannot, even though there exists a need for it. One could determine this with almost the same certainty as a chemist can determine under which external conditions matter undergoes combination."[50]

We have here the elements of Marx's mature method. His criticism of Hegelianism, that it was unable to bridge the contradictions in the society of his time with *thought categories*, prompted him to inquire into the *real conditions* which prevailed in the world. His criticisms indicated that he had come to understand the state, at least in specific circumstances, as the executive arm of the possessing classes and, further, that its behavior was to be ascribed not to the will of individuals, but to objective relationships which determined the activities of individual men and groups in social interaction. These relationships could be studied with the same precision with which one studies natural science. This conception of studying the real relationships which operate in society as a natural science had, by 1847, matured into the study of "social relations of production," which develop "in conformity with . . . material productivity" to produce the "principles, ideas and categories" which are the "historical and transitory products" to which men have hitherto looked for an explanation of the dynamics of human history.[51]

The principles governing the study of the real relations which obtained in society were laid down as early as 1845 in the *German Ideology*. The study of these relations provided the basis of the *Manifesto* by 1847. In 1859 the principles employed in Marx's method were summarized in the preface to the *Contribution to the Critique of Political Economy*. In *Capital* the application of these principles resulted in the "laying bare of the economic laws of motion of modern society."[52]

This constituted the reform of the Hegelian dialectic in its social key. Hegel had mystified the laws governing social processes. The real dialectic of society was to be found in real persons and groups and the objective relationships which obtained between them. "The state is an abstraction," Marx argued in 1843. "The people alone are the concrete."[53] The real foundation of the state, of its constitution, is real people,[54] and their "earthly being."[55]

Feuerbach had indicated the path of such criticism. It was Feuerbach who established "true materialism" since he "[made] the social relationship 'of man to man' the basic principle of the theory. . . ."[56] While Feuerbach never achieved the critical insight Marx was to attain in the analysis of the social relations (the sum of which constituted the "human essence"),[57] he had been sufficiently astute to note the "commencement of a new historic epoch" which would dawn with the revolution of an "oppressed mass or majority" against a ruling caste or class.[58]

Marx had begun with Feuerbach's criticism of theology and speculative philosophy, and had extended the criticism into the philosophy of the state. In his concern with the "real, material problems" of the German state as he knew it, he became convinced that philosophy could divine the real processes, the social relationships, which gave rise to the overt behavior of men and groups. He came to understand that the contradiction between reason and reality, between the *conception* of man as a creature to whom rational freedom should be accorded and his *reality* as a "degraded, servile, neglected and contemptible being,"[59] could only be overcome in a "radical revolution . . . the revolution of radical needs."[60] Such a radical revolution requires a class possessed of radical needs. Such a class would exemplify "all the defects of society." That class, "in radical chains, a class which finds itself in bourgeois society, but which is not of it, an order which shall break up all orders, a sphere which possesses a universal character by virtue of its universal suffering . . . which stands not in a one-sided antagonism to the presuppositions of the German community, a sphere finally which cannot emancipate itself without emancipating all the other spheres of society, which represents in a word the complete loss of mankind, and can therefore only redeem itself through the complete redemption of mankind. The redemption of society reduced to a special order is the proletariat. . . . Just as philosophy finds in the proletariat its material weapons, so the proletariat finds in philosophy its intellectual weapons. . . ."[61] For the task of philosophy is not to conjure up "new principles" of society but rather to make the world conscious of the conditions which make struggle a necessity.[62] In the autumn of 1844 he wrote *"Private property . . . drives itself in its economic movement towards its own dissolution, only however, through a development which does not depend on it, of which it is unconscious and which takes place against its will, through the very nature of things. . . .* Since the conditions of life of the proletariat sum up all the conditions of life of society today in all their inhuman acuity; since man has lost himself in the proletariat, yet at the same time has not only gained theoretical consciousness of that loss, but through urgent, no longer disguisable, absolutely imperative *need*—that practical expression of *necessity*—is driven directly to revolt against that inhumanity; it follows that the proletariat can and must free itself. It cannot abolish the conditions of its own life without abolishing all the inhuman conditions of life of society today which are summed up in its own situation. Not in vain does it go through the stern but steeling school of labor. The question is not what this or that proletarian, or even the whole of the proletariat at the moment *considers* as its aim. The question is *what the proletariat* is, and what, consequent on that *being*, it will be compelled to do. Its aim and historical action is irrevocably and obviously demonstrated in its

own life situation as well as in the whole organization of bourgeois society today."[63]

In the *Economic and Philosophic Manuscripts* Marx had analyzed the material conditions which drove the proletariat ineluctably to revolution. He had accepted Adam Smith's analysis
of the wages of labor as that necessary for minimum subsistence
(a notion which Hegel had also accepted).[64] Marx had gone on
to analyze the nature of the capitalist productive process, based
on "avarice" and greed.[65] The prevailing mode of production produced circumstances in which "even in the condition of society
most favorable to the worker, the inevitable result for the worker
is overwork and premature death, decline to a mere machine, a
bond servant of capital, which piles up dangerously over against
him, more competition, and for a section of the workers starvation
or beggery."[66] Free competition among capitalists jettisons more
and more of the peripheral members of the middle class into the
proletariat. When "wages, which have already been reduced to a
minimum, must be reduced yet further, to meet . . . new competition—this then necessarily leads to revolution."[67]

Thus by 1847 Marx had formulated all the ideas Engels had
identified as original in the *Manifesto*. None of the ideas were
simply taken up mechanically from predecessors; they were critically elaborated. The ideas had become increasingly well defined
in the years between 1842 and 1847. As a consequence of successive critical assessments of the society of his time Marx had produced the essentials of revolutionary Socialism.

Friedrich Engels had made significant contributions to this
enterprise. His essay "Outlines of a Critique of Political Economy,"
published by Marx in the *Deutsch-französische Jahrbücher*, had
a profound impact on Marx, for it was this essay which directed
him to the study of political economy. In that essay, and in the
essays written during that same period, Engels explicitly outlined many of the theses that were to characterize historical materialism. He contended that the science of political economy
"unfolded" the "laws of private property," something which lay
"in the nature of the matter."[68] "Greed," "selfishness," and an
"obsessive mania" to accumulate wealth by expanding industry
lay in the nature of private property. The expansion of industry
required the creation of a permanent, propertyless working class.[69]
The culmination of the process of industrial expansion in the serv-

ice of private wealth was the "division of mankind into capitalists and workers—a division which daily becomes ever more acute, and which . . . is bound to deepen."[70] Competition produces the concentration of wealth in fewer and fewer hands. Wealth is reinvested in technological improvement and industrial expansion. The consequence is an increase in products which cannot be effectively marketed. Trade crises appear regularly. "There is so much superfluous productive power that the great mass of the nation has nothing to live on . . . the people starve from sheer abundance."[71] As early as 1842, his observations in England had led him to this conviction.[72] In 1845, in the volume he wrote on the conditions of the working class in England, he had already indicated that "the enemies are dividing gradually into two great camps—the bourgeoisie on the one hand, the workers on the other."[73] These classes were represented in political parties.[74] To the question "Who rules England?" Engels answered "Property rules."[75] "The middle class and property rule; the poor are without rights, they are oppressed and degraded . . . the war of democracy against aristocracy in England is the struggle of the poor against the rich."[76]

Engels' first draft, the *Foundations of Communism*, contains almost all the essential ideas of the *Manifesto*. By the time it was written Marx and Engels had synthesized their views into an articulate system. That system was their own, fashioned out of their experience and out of their familiarity with the vast literature of their time. It was rooted in Hegelianism and transmitted by Feuerbachianism. It constituted an attempt to lay bare the inhuman reality so much at variance with the Hegelian ideal of man developing to his full potential in a society of rational freedom. Marx came to his convictions through a criticism of politics and law, and his experience as a journalist in the Rhineland— Engels as a consequence of his experience in English industry, the most highly developed industrial system in Europe. These convictions were incubated in France where Marx and Engels developed close contact with the French and German working-class movements. In 1845 the theory appeared, in all but its final form, in the *German Ideology*.

## The Theory of History of Classical Marxism

Perhaps the most lucid exposition of the materialist conception of history is that which Karl Marx provided in 1859 in his preface to the *Contribution to the Critique of Political Economy*. Despite its shortcomings, it is perhaps the only place in his writings where Marx provided the outlines of his theory of history in its essential entirety.

"[1] In the social production of their life, men enter into definite relations that are indispensable and independent of their will. . . .

"[2] [These] relations of production . . . correspond to a definite stage of development of their material productive forces.

"[3] The sum total of these relations of production constitutes the economic structure of society. . . .

"[4] [This is] the real foundation, on which rises a legal and political superstructure and to which correspond definite forms of social consciousness. [This] mode of production of material life conditions the social, political, and intellectual life process in general. It is not the consciousness of men that determines their being, but on the contrary, their social being that determines their consciousness.

"[5] At a certain stage in their development, the material productive forces of society come into conflict with the existing relations of production. . . . From forms of development of the productive forces these relations turn into their fetters. Then begins an epoch of social revolution."[77]

This constitutes, in essence, historical materialism, the theory of history of classical Marxism. The exposition is relatively clear and the careful reader will discover that the determining forces of historical development are the material productive forces.

Productive or social relations (property relations) are "independent" of the will of man but must "correspond" to the "material productive forces" which are in the process of development. In the *Poverty of Philosophy* of 1847 Marx had written, "In acquiring new productive forces men change their mode of production; and in changing their mode of production, in changing the way of earning their living, they change all their social relations."[78]

Social relations (determined by the stage of development of the productive forces),[79] coupled with the productive forces themselves, constitute the "real foundation"[80] (the mode of production) which determines the consciousness of men.[81]

It is only when the material productive forces can no longer freely develop within the confines of the existing social relations (which correspond to the conditions of an earlier stage in the development of the productive forces) that history "moves" by means of social revolution. Thus revolution, by virtue of which qualitative historical change occurs, is precipitated by changes in the forces of production. In the final analysis the "productive forces . . . are the basis of all . . . history."[82] Social or productive relations which had developed to facilitate production become, as the productive forces outgrow them, fetters on production. The result is a qualitative change in the social order, a "leap" in historical progression, the ultimate consequences of prior gradual quantitative changes in the economic structure of society. The "material productive forces," therefore, constitute the demiurge of world history[83]—the productive forces stand behind the social history of man, and only through their development is world history comprehensible.[84]

Since these forces occupy such an essential position in the theory of history, it is necessary to determine precisely what constitutes them.[85] Neither Marx nor Engels ever gave an explicit definition. Some authors have conceived the productive forces as simply "the economic system,"[86] while others contend that the productive forces include "all forces which contribute toward the manufacture of products."[87] Stalin defined the productive forces as "the instruments of production . . . the people who operate the instruments of production . . . [and] a certain productive experience and labor skill. . . ."[88] Henri Lefebvre argues that the productive forces include geographic conditions, technology, and the division of labor.[89] Heinrich Cunow gives the most elaborate exposition. He divides the productive forces into animate and inanimate categories, listing human and animal labor under the first heading and the forces of nature (wind, water, electricity, etc.), the nature of the soil, and the technological forces (the instruments of production) under the other.[90] Plekhanov, while bringing geographic differences into the picture to explain the local variations in the forces of production, entertains the view that the instruments of production themselves constitute the productive forces.[91]

This array of the component parts of the productive forces comes from the formulation given by Marx in the first volume of *Capital*, where he tells us that "The elementary factors of the labor process are (1) the personal activity of man, i.e., work itself, (2) the subject of that work and (3) its instruments. The soil (and this, economically speaking, includes water) in the virgin state in which it supplies man with necessaries or the means of subsistence ready to hand, exists independently of him and is the universal subject of human labor. All those things which labor merely separates from immediate connection with their environment, are subjects of labor spontaneously provided by nature."[92] To this should be added the "natural" division of labor which attends human effort—the natural division of labor which arises from the physical differences which distinguish men from women, children from adults, and the weak from the strong.[93] If we combine these accounts, the productive forces, which constitute the motive lever of all history, include technological forces (instruments of labor), geographic factors (including natural forces and resources), and human labor divided on the basis of age, sex and strength—including productive experience and skill.

The productive forces, which constitute the basis of history, are essentially dynamic, since Marx uses them to explain development in history. But it becomes immediately evident that not all the components of the material productive forces are dynamic, for some, like the geographic environment, are essentially passive. Historic change is far more rapid than alterations in the geographic environment.[94] Marx consistently spoke of nature as remaining the subject of labor, something upon which labor operates.[95] It is only technological advance, employing the skill of man, that can fully utilize the free gifts of nature.

In a search for the dynamic components of the material productive forces we, in our efforts at interpretation, are left with the instruments of production and human labor. While Marx and Engels introduced the "natural division of labor" as one of the "presuppositions" of the system, all subsequent divisions of labor were clearly identified as the consequence of the development of the productive forces.[96] They understood the division of labor to be, essentially, the consequence of the development of the material productive forces and its influence is thus derivative rather than original. We are left with two possible ultimate determinants—the instruments of production and the skill and experience of men employing them.[97] Thus the motive force of history must, in the last analysis, stem from (1) technological development, (2) man's skill and inventiveness, or (3) a combination of both.

Some of the most heated controversies concerning the Marxist theory of history, involving Marxists and non-Marxists alike, have raged around this problem. In assessing all the passive, but necessary, components of the material forces of production, investigators have sought the active ingredient which produces historical evolution. The language of Marx and Engels is never fully explicit and their turns of speech are often rendered even more obscure by an addiction to Hegelianisms.

While the geographic, natural environment is a necessary precondition for any development of the productive processes, it can hardly be conceived as a dynamic ingredient.[98] The division of labor imparts only a derived impetus, having received its original impulse from changes deeper in the economic structure of society itself. The division of classes, and the subsequent class warfare, is only a surface manifestation of the changes going on at the base of the productive structure.[99] We must, in summary, discover the active element in either the technological development of the instruments of production or in the skill and experience of man, or, finally, in some sort of union of the two.

Any analysis requires a review of the relevant statements made by Marx and Engels on this issue. This is rendered difficult because there is internal evidence to indicate that their interpretation changed in the course of time. In his earliest writings, for example, Engels seemed disposed to conceive the "spiritual element of invention, of thought,"[100] as functioning in a dynamic fashion in the "material base" of society. And yet in some of his final remarks on the subject of human inventiveness, Engels indicated that inventiveness is, in some critical sense, the consequence of dynamic need.[101] Priority would be attributed to need rather than to inventiveness. This latter position seems more consistent with the mature Marxist view. The mature view seems to be that men must be in a position to meet the elementary needs requisite to life before they can commence to make history. Consequently the "first historical act is . . . the production of the means to satisfy these needs, the production of material life itself."[102] Man, before he can make history, is compelled to enter into production in order to provide himself with the necessities his nature demands.[103] "The first thing of which the laborer possesses himself," in this production, "is not the subject of labor but its instrument."[104] Man is a "tool-making animal."[105]

"Technology," Marx contended, ". . . lays bare the mode of formation of man's social relations, and of the mental conceptions that flow from them."[106] He goes on to inquire, "Does not the history of the *productive organs of man* [the instruments of production] . . . *the material basis of all social organization*, deserve . . . attention?"[107] Marx seemed prepared to commit himself to a modified form of technological determinism. "Relics of by-gone instruments of labor," he argued, "possess the same importance for the investigation of extinct economical forms of society, as do fossil bones for the determination of extinct species of animals. It is not the articles made, but how they are made, and by what instruments, that enables us to distinguish different economical epochs. Instruments of labor not only supply a standard of the degree of development to which human labor has attained, but they are also indicators of the social conditions under which that labor is carried on."[108]

In the discussion of contemporary history, both Marx and Engels are emphatic in their designation of the instruments of production as the essentially dynamic component of the material basis of society. Marx maintained, "The starting point of modern industry is . . . the revolution in the instruments of labor."[109] In the early manuscripts of 1845 Engels argued that "the history of the proletariat in England begins with the second half of the last century, with the invention of the steam engine and of machinery for working cotton. These inventions gave rise, as is well known, to an industrial revolution, a revolution which altered the whole civil society. . . ."[110] The fullest statement of what appears to be a "technological theory of history" is found in Marx's *Poverty of Philosophy*, written immediately before the writing of the *Manifesto*. "In acquiring new productive forces men change their mode of production; and in changing their mode of production, in changing the way of earning their living, they change all their social relations. The hand mill gives you society with the feudal lord; the steam mill, society with the industrial capitalist. The same men who establish their social relations in conformity with their material productivity, produce also principles, ideas and categories, in conformity with their social relations."[111] We find this same emphasis on technology in the *Manifesto* itself: ". . . [The] bourgeoisie cannot exist without constantly revolutionizing the instruments of production, and thereby the relations of production, and with them the whole relations of society,"[112] a conception repeated by Engels in the *Anti-Dühring* over a generation later.[113]

Classical Marxism seems to have chosen technological development as the *causa causans*, the dynamic determinant within the complex of the material productive forces. Certainly this is how many Marxists, for example the Indian Marxist S. Dange, have interpreted the materialist conception of history: "In the change-over from one stage to another, the revolutionary factor is the instruments of production. The peculiarity of the instruments of production is that they are never static and are constantly changing, undergoing change due to man's social productive activity and the needs of human society. The changes in the instruments of production, the productive forces, are the key to the revolutionary changes in the structure of society."[114] Dange seems to equate the instruments of production with the productive forces.

Konstantinov, one of the foremost Soviet Marxists, interprets the theory in the following way: "The first thing that changes in the development of social production are the productive forces and above all the instruments of production. . . ."[115] This interpretation follows that of Stalin.[116] Plekhanov had argued in a similar vein: "In the implements of labor man acquires new organs, as it were, which change his anatomical structure. From the time that he rose to the level of using them, he has given quite a new aspect to the history of his development. . . . Since that time it has become first of all the history of the perfecting of his artificial organs, the growth of his productive forces."[117] Plekhanov seemed to equate the "perfecting of his artificial organs," the implements of labor, with "the growth of his productive forces."

An impressive number of Marxists have come to understand human social evolution in the following fashion: (1) Technological development is the ultimate dynamic component of the material productive forces (some Marxists seem to lapse into locutions which suggest they are, in some significant sense, equivalent) and provides the motive force of historical change. (2) Technological change comes about "necessarily" independently of the will of man who is its mediating agency (Marx and Engels explicitly argued that the "bourgeoisie" "cannot exist" without mediating this development). (3) Technology determines corresponding social relations which in turn determine the nature of "mental conceptions" entertained by a particular society. Technological development for many Marxists is, then, at the root of historical change: "The hand mill gives you society with the feudal lord; the steam mill, society with the industrial capitalist."[118]

There seem to be singular stylizations which appear in the exposition of the theory of history. The productive forces are usually spoken of in an active sense,[119] as "developing" and not being developed; we are told that a social relation, "the cooperative character of the labor-process [is] . . . dictated by the instrument of labor itself,"[120] as though the instruments themselves are active and determinant; and human beings, although energizing agents, remain passive in the sense that initiative somehow rests with the productive forces.[121] The technological forces at the base of the entire superstructure of human history do not, apparently, depend for their development upon the will or initiative of man. Marx indicated that "it is superfluous to add that men are not free to choose their productive forces—which are the basis of all their history. . . ."[122] If men are not free to choose their forces of production—forces which, in turn, determine their very consciousness—we are left without a clear understanding of how the entire process began its dialectical development and how it is sustained.

The process seems eminently Hegelian in conception. We have seen that Hegel conceived "civil society" as an organization for the satisfaction of needs, and that these needs developed in a dialectical fashion in "infinitely complex, criss-cross, movements of reciprocal production and exchange." Marx and Engels similarly argued that the "first historical act is . . . the production of the means to satisfy . . . needs," and that this production creates new needs which man is compelled to satisfy.[123] "The second fundamental point," Marx argued in the German Ideology, "is that as soon as a need is satisfied (which implies the action of satisfying, and the acquisition of an instrument), new needs are made. . . ."[124] Thus, once begun, the necessary development of the productive forces seem to require continual readjustment on the part of man. Man is launched upon an historical career which seems to develop with an intrinsic logic of its own. "What, in this connection, can we ask of sociology?" Plekhanov inquires. "We can ask it to explain why men who are seeking to satisfy their needs . . . enter, sometimes into these relations, and sometimes into those. Well, sociology (with Marx as spokesman) explains this with reference to the condition of the forces of production. But does the condition of these forces depend upon the will of human beings and upon the ends after which they strive? Sociology, still speaking through the mouth of Marx, answers that there is no such dependence. If there is no such dependence, this signifies that the forces of production are the outcome of a necessity determined by extant conditions external to man."[125]

The addiction of Marx and Engels to Hegelian locutions permits this kind of interpretation. When Engels tells us that some piece of machinery "gave rise to the agricultural proletariat"[126] there seems to be an unnecessary suggestion of "entailment," of "necessity." When Marx tells us that some feature of the labor process is "dictated by the instrument of labor itself" or that the steam mill "gives" us the capitalist, there seems to be implicit a kind of necessity inappropriate in an empirical assessment.

Men, of course, are not free to meet their needs in whatever fashion they choose. A primitive community must satisfy its primitive needs with a primitive mode of production, but a primitive mode of production could be construed to be the consequence of a primitive mentality rather than its cause. Whatever the mode of production, primitive or developed, further needs might well develop which men attempt, in some manner or other, to satisfy. To say this much provides a loose theoretical structure with reference to which investigations can be pursued. But much of what Marx and Engels say seem to suggest that these needs follow a remorseless logic, compelling men through various determined developmental stages so unalterably linked that a primitive community need but observe a more highly developed society in order to see its future self. "The country that is more developed industrially only shows, to the less developed, the image of its own future."[127] "Tendencies" are construed somehow as "working with iron necessity toward inevitable results."[128] Production proceeds through the action of "immanent laws"; production "begets with the inexorability of a law of nature, its own negation. . . ."[129] Social change can be predicted with the certainty of "a mathematical or mechanical demonstration."[130] "Modern industry develops . . . the conflicts which make absolutely necessary a revolution in the mode of production,"[131] in conformity to the "inexorable natural laws of their particular form of production."[132]

There seems to be a conviction that laws in general, natural or social, are to be understood in the strict sense of logical entailments. Development is "inexorable," "inevitable," "necessary," "immanent." This confusion is the consequence of seeing history in terms of a "logic." But the Hegelian "logic" is no logic at all. It is a metaphysic; it is, at best, a transcendent hypothesis. Marx frequently admonished Marxists not to apply "laws" mechanically, but to assess each historic situation empirically in all its complexity. He clearly rejected the transcendent logic of Hegel, yet he seems to have remained convinced that history possessed a Hegelian form in that its "logic" was immanent.[133] Marx contended that Hegel's "logical categories [come] damn well out of 'our intercourse.'. . ."[134]

In other words, the employment of the first tool carried within itself the germ of the subsequent divisions of labor, increased productivity, exploitation of man by man, and the entire history of class-warfare, culminating in the Communist abolition of classes and exploitation. This seems to be nothing more or less than the Hegelian accession to rational freedom through the logical categories of economic development rather than the logical categories of the Absolute. But the "logic" remains, nonetheless, inherent in "the nature of things." As heirs to such a conviction contemporary Marxists can write, "Unlike animals, which passively adapt themselves to the external environment, man exercises an active influence on his environment, and obtains the material values needed to his life by means of labor, which presupposes the use and making of special instruments. Society cannot arbitrarily choose these instruments. . . . [The] *development* . . . *follows a definite sequence.*"[135]

Classical Marxism as a theory of history has a great many suggestive insights. It has influenced the thoughts of some of the finest sociologists and historians of our time. No longer can students of history or society neglect the productive forces and the relations within which these forces operate. Many subtle and important works have developed from insights provided by Marx and Engels.[136] The principal difficulty seems to arise out of the obscure but pervasive connection Marx and Engels retained with the Hegelian dialectic. The addiction to Hegelianism led them to the conviction that there were *necessary* and *inevitable* laws which history pursued and which permitted them to make predictions with "mathematical certainty." How much of an impairment this addiction was is evident in many places. Engels, for example, could write in 1845: "Prophecy is nowhere so easy as in England, where all the component elements of society are clearly defined and sharply separated. The revolution must come. . . . I think the people will not endure more than one more crisis. That next one, in 1846 or 1847, will probably bring with it the repeal of the Corn Laws and the enactment of the Charter. . . . By the time of the next following crisis, which, according to the analogy of its predecessors, must break out in 1852 to 1853 . . . the English people will have had enough of being plundered by the capitalists. . . . The proletarians, driven by despair, will seize the torch which Stephens has preached to them; the vengeance of the people will come down with a wrath of which the rage of 1793 gives no true idea. . . .[137] [The] middle class dwells upon a soil that is honeycombed, and may any day collapse, the speedy collapse of which is as certain as a mathematical or mechanical demonstration. . . ."[138] The treatment of "social movement as a process of natural history, governed by laws not only independent of human will, consciousness and intelligence, but rather, on the contrary, determining that will, consciousness and intelligence,"[139] coupled with the Hegelian conviction that "laws" involved logical entailments, led Marx and Engels to make "prophecies," which were almost always unfortunate. There were successive predictions of imminent revolution throughout the forty years following the *Communist Manifesto*. Few of them were realized. Conceiving laws in Hegelian fashion led Marx and Engels to employ unfortunate locutions about "inevitability" and "ineluctability" when all they could have conceivably meant was "tendency," or at best "probability" of a high or low order.

Engels later admitted that perhaps Marx and he had been guilty of overstatement, but such disclaimers do little to clarify their position. The complexity of historical progression is admitted by Engels, but he still argued that "the economic movement finally asserts itself as necessary,"[140] and that "*ultimately* economic necessity asserts itself."[141] "The whole vast process," Engels argued, "goes on in the form of interaction—though of very unequal forces, the economic movement being by far the strongest, most primeval, most decisive—that here everything is relative and nothing absolute—this [critics] never begin to see. Hegel has never existed for them."[142] Engels, as a Hegelian, can say that everything develops with an inevitable logic in which the economic factor is ultimately decisive and yet everything is relative and nothing absolute. Hegel, of course, might very well say as much. But this does not seem to be a recommendation, and that Marx and Engels would think so is unfortunate.

If classical Marxism advances its method as a hypothesis, then it would be, like all hypotheses in science, subject to proof and disproof. Notions of necessary development and inevitable happenings would not be appropriate. If classical Marxism as a theory of history is a scientific hypothesis and a suggestion for research in social science, then it is part and parcel of the scientific machinery of our time. Descriptions in which the instruments of production are spoken of as "giving rise" to one or another form of social relations obscure rather than clarify, and defy scientific confirmation. Expressions like ". . . [It] was necessary to overthrow the mercantile system with its monopolies and hindrances to trade, so that the true consequences of private property could come to light,"[143] ascribe a purpose and a logic to a process— they animate history with a preternatural design. This kind of locution afflicts much of classical Marxism. Under such influence Engels could write, "There is no great historical evil without a compensating historical progress."[144] One wonders how one could verify such a pronouncement. Similarly one wonders what would confirm Engels' conviction that if "Napoleon had been lacking, another would have filled the place," and that if Marx had not discovered the "materialist conception of history" someone else would have because it "simply *had* to be discovered."[145] Finally, Engels informs us that "scientific socialism" is "nothing but the reflex, in thought of [the] conflict" between "the new productive forces" and "the capitalistic mode of using them."[146]

These curiosities are clearly the consequence of residual Hegelianism, and Engels identifies it as such. He tells us that the "great merit" of the Hegelian system is that it conceived "for the first time the whole world, natural, historical, intellectual . . . as a process, i.e., as in constant motion, change, transformation, development; and the attempt is made to trace out the internal connection that makes a continuous whole of all this movement and development,"[147] a development which proceeds through "inner law."[148] He can then speak of "the solution of social problems" lying "hidden in undeveloped economic conditions. . . ."[149] Marx can contend that "no social order ever perishes before all the productive forces for which there is room in it have developed; and new, higher relations of production never appear before the material conditions of their existence have matured in the womb of the old society itself,"[150] and "even when a society has got upon the right track for the discovery of the natural laws of its movement . . . it can neither clear by bold leaps nor remove by legal enactments, the obstacles offered by the successive phases of its normal development."[151] It was with some such conviction that Marx introduced the four successive historic modes of production —Asiatic, ancient, feudal, and modern bourgeois, a classification he took directly out of Hegel's *Philosophy of History*.

The attempt to formulate the "necessary laws" of "universal progress"[152] is an enterprise which transcends any known historiographic or sociological technique. If we restore to historical and sociological study all the complexity of each given situation, the interaction of the multiplicity of forces, it is difficult to isolate with any assurance the "inner, hidden laws" which "assert themselves as the ruling ones in the history of human society."[153] Both Marx and Engels seem ultimately to have become aware of this. We have indicated that Engels had recognized the danger of conceiving Marxism not as a "guide to study," but a "lever for construction à la Hegelianism. All history," he insisted, "must be studied afresh, the conditions of existence of the different formations of society must be examined in detail before the attempt is made to deduce from them the political, civil-legal, aesthetic, philosophic, religious, etc. notions corresponding to them. Up to now but little has been done here because only a few people have got down to it seriously."[154]

## Engels and the Materialist Conception of History

We have traced, in brief outline, the theory of history of classical Marxism. It was the joint product of Marx and Engels. In the course of their four decades of collaboration the theory underwent considerable change. By 1880 it had attained the sophistication with which history has come to identify it. Less well known than the components of the classical theory with which we have been concerned are the addenda to Marxism which were advanced by Engels after the death of Marx. Engels survived Marx by twelve years, and in that period he brought forth what might be called the Darwinian supplement to classical Marxism.

By the time Darwinism made its appearance Marxism had reached its maturity. Marxism had already become that view of history "which seeks the ultimate cause and the great moving power of all important historic events in the economic development of society. . . ."[155] It was in the context of this theory of history that Darwinism, as a theory of organic and social evolution, was to be considered. Marxism, like Darwinism, conceived the world in dynamic evolutionary terms. But Marxist evolutionism had been won through philosophical speculation rather than natural science.

Marx and Engels at first welcomed the new theory as a corroboration of their dialectical world-view.[156] But it soon became evident to both Marx and Engels that Darwinism created special problems for the materialist conception of history. Darwinism spoke of human history in terms of evolutionary epochs, in terms of hundreds of thousands of years, against which the few thousand years of recorded history diminished conspicuously in significance.

The *Communist Manifesto* of 1848 commenced with the confident pronouncement that "the history of all hitherto existing society is the history of class struggles." Forty years later Engels was forced to amend that pronouncement with the qualification— "that is, all *written* history. In 1847, the prehistory of society, the social organization existing previous to recorded history, was all but unknown."[157] To fill in the gap in the theory, a gap which involved something like a million years of human prehistory, Engels pressed into service a Darwinian theory of social evolution formulated by the American ethnologist Lewis Henry Morgan.[158] The artificiality of the attempt immediately became evident.

The original thesis was that man's social relations were determined by the prevailing processes of production. Indeed, Marx had gone so far as to suggest that one need possess but the instruments of production, the dynamic component of the economic base employed in a given prehistoric epoch, to reconstruct the prevailing social relations of the period. But in 1882, immediately preceding Marx's death, Engels announced the necessity of far-reaching modifications in this original thesis. He confided to Marx that all the evidence compelled him to admit that "at [the prehistoric level] the mode of production is less decisive than the degree of dissolution of the old blood groupings and the old opposing sexual communities in tribes."[159] No reply to this letter is extant. Marx died on the 14th of March, 1883, apparently without having reconsidered the original thesis and its proposed modification.

So it was left to Engels to make the necessary revisions in the theory. In 1884, Engels published the *Origins of the Family, Private Property and the State,* the proposed revision of the Marxist theory of history designed to conform to the new perspective of Darwinism. This work and an unpublished and fragmentary manuscript of 1876 entitled "The Part Played by Labor in the Transition from Ape to Man"[160] make up the Darwinian supplement to the theory first explicitly formulated in 1847.

The discrepancy between them must have been obvious to Engels. The original theory held that the ultimate determinant of man's social relations—as well as their ideological expression, man's intellectual life in general, as well as the legal relations governing the organization of the family, private property and the state—was the mode of material production and specifically "the development of . . . material productive forces." But in 1884 Engels said that "according to the materialistic conception, the determining factor in history is, in the last resort, the production and *reproduction*[161] of immediate life. But this itself is of a twofold character. On the one hand, the production of the means of subsistence, of food, clothing and shelter and the tools requisite therefore; on the other, the production of human beings themselves, the propagation of the species. . . . The old society [was] based on sex groups. . . ."[162]

We no longer have social life determined by the development of material productive forces. Now we have, among the determining factors in history, sexual reproduction and the formal sex groupings in which men undertake that reproduction! Engels plays on the verbal similarity of the words "production" and "reproduction" to smuggle through a fictive "synthesis."[163] "The social institutions under which men of a definite historical epoch and of a definite country live *are conditioned by both kinds of production*:[164] by the stage of development of labor, on the one hand, and of the family, on the other. The less the development of labor, and the more limited its volume of production and, therefore, the wealth of society, the more preponderatingly does the social order appear to be dominated by ties of sex."[165]

For Marx, history and social life were in the last analysis determined by the processes of material production, mediated by human labor, meeting the human demand for sustenance, raiment, and shelter.[166] For Lewis Henry Morgan, from whose work the new supplement to historical materialism was substantially derived, the organic basis of human society was the procreative instinct. Its historic form was determined by man's disposition to organize himself in breeding communities governed not by immediate fertility but by self-imposed rules of exogamy and endogamy.[167]

Engels produced a modified historical materialism in the attempt to incorporate this radically incompatible social Darwinian conception of Morgan.[168] Man's social life, for the hundreds of thousands of years of prehistory, was determined not by the production of material goods but by the complex rules governing sexual reproduction. Engels makes evident throughout the text of the *Origin of the Family, Private Property and the State* that these rules evolve independently of the material forces of production.[169] It is difficult to conceive how this disposition to formulate and obey rules governing breeding practices, and its religious and ethical appurtenances, which determined man's social relations in evolutionary time, could suddenly fall under the determining influences of the material productive forces some few thousand years ago.[170] It would seem more credible to maintain that the disposition to control breeding practices in accordance with law, as Morgan and others suggested, is part of man's evolutionary heritage and must be recognized as an independent variable in any adequate appraisal of his history and his social life.

But Engels wrestled with a still more fundamental problem. As we have seen, according to classical Marxism, all man's history is ultimately determined by the development of the material productive forces. Of those forces the truly dynamic factor is technological development.[171] All other factors are passive in the sense that they are exploited by technology.[172]

The productive forces, at the base of which are the instruments of production, are the motive forces of social evolution. But the instruments of production do not discover themselves. All creatures are afflicted with the same elementary needs which must be met. Yet man alone is the creator of tools—tools which set him upon the course of a truly *historical* evolution. Conceivably man's needs could have been met satisfactorily by employing the same means available to lesser creatures—creatures who meet their needs perennially in the same fashion—creatures having no tools, no "ideological superstructure," and no social and historical development. Of all animate things it is only man who, driven by his needs, *creates* his means of subsistence.[173] Even among men there are sects, classes, whole peoples, who remain "primitive," who evince but little initiative and creativity.

Darwinism ascribed man's greater creativity to the fact that man was a more highly developed organism, that his cerebral cortex was thicker, that there was a quantitative difference in the size of man's thinking organ, the brain. In such a theory, the motive force of history could no longer be found in material production, but must be sought in organic evolution. Unless Marxism was capable of producing an argument that would establish that man's cerebral development, his inventive genius, was somehow a function of his economy, then its interpretation of history would be sadly deficient. Engels undertook to produce just such an argument.

If man distinguishes himself as a tool-making animal, his ability to invent tools must be the consequence of some real difference between himself and related primate species. This is the issue Engels faced in the 1876 and 1884 revisions of the materialist conception of history. A careful reading of those manuscripts indicates that Engels rested his case on two suspect theses: (1) the inheritance of acquired characteristics, and (2) a notion that the mating of two inbred lines produces offspring superior to both.

What we have, in fact, is a half-formulated theory of organic evolution to supplement what had been an economic interpretation of history.[174] In order to successfully accommodate Darwinism and explain intra- and interspecific differences in creativity, Engels argued that the *ultimate* determinant of man's organic, social, and creative evolution was his economy.[175] To defend this thesis, he displayed some spectacular theoretical gymnastics, for he had to maintain that, in some meaningful sense, "labor created man himself."[176]

According to his explanation, the anthropoid antecedents of man, in response to the demands made by arboreal life, had assigned different functions to the hands than to the feet. Consequently, when these primates found themselves forced to adjust to living on the ground they could adopt bipedal gait, freeing their hands for an increasing number of functions. The hands, freed by the adoption of an erect carriage, attained ever increasing *dexterity, which was subsequently inherited.* "Only by labor, by adaptation to ever-new operations, by inheritance of the thus acquired special development of muscles, ligaments and, over longer periods of time, bones as well, and by the ever-renewed employment of this inherited finesse in new, more and more complicated operations, has the human hand attained the high degree of perfection that has enabled it to conjure into being the paintings of a Raphael, the statues of a Thorwaldsen, the music of a Paganini."[177]

The development of the hand increased the occasions of mutual enterprise among men. Increased co-operation, in turn, necessitated increased communications: ". . . [Men] arrived at the point where *they had something to say to one another. The urge created its organ;*[178] the undeveloped larynx of the ape was slowly but surely transformed. . . ."[179]

Under the stimuli of labor and speech the brain developed apace. The increasing creativity which was consequent upon this development permitted man to fashion fishing and hunting implements, and thus make the transition from a purely vegetable diet to a meat diet. "The most essential effect . . . of a meat diet was on the brain, which now received a far richer flow of the materials necessary for its nourishment and development than formerly, and which, therefore, could develop more rapidly and perfectly from generation to generation."[180]

According to Engels, men reduced to an almost exclusively vegetable diet have a smaller brain.[181] He uses this conjecture to explain the cultural eminence of specific races of men.[182] Thus, while admitting that *race* was an economic factor,[183] he went on to explain racial characteristics as the consequence of conditions surrounding the prevailing mode of production.

This account was supplemented by a curious notion of hybrid vigor. According to this notion, men, becoming increasingly repelled by consanguineous mating, excluded a wider and wider circle of blood relatives from marriage, finally restricting marriages to individuals from non-consanguineous groups—marriages which "tended to create a more vigorous stock physically and mentally. When two advancing tribes are blended into one people . . . the new skull and brain would widen and lengthen to the sum of the capabilities of both."[184]

It seems evident that Engels felt that only in some such fashion could the classical Marxist theory of history be salvaged—and observed differences in inventive capacity be adequately explained. How adequate this explanation is need not concern us here. What is important is the fact that Engels found it necessary to make significant alterations in the materialist conception of history in order to accommodate the new data of empirical science. It is more to our purpose to pursue two concepts which have had enormous consequence because of their influence upon Marxism as a political-action program: the dynamics of political insurrection and the conception of the state and society.

## The Mechanics of Revolution

In the *Communist Manifesto* the impending revolution is clearly conceived as the outcome of two necessary and sufficient conditions: (1) the increasing misery of the proletariat and (2) their clear awareness of the causes of their misery. The same necessary and sufficient conditions are cited in the works of Marx and Engels throughout their entire lives. In 1842 Engels asked, given the conditions in England, ". . . [What] remains for the workers to do but revolt?"[185] In the *Foundations of Communism* of 1847 he indicated that the necessary condition of revolution was the reduction of wages below the subsistence minimum.[186] Misery is directly correlated with revolutionary activity. The proletariat is "driven" to insurrection[187] by the intolerable conditions in which it finds itself. "The workers must therefore strive to escape from this brutalising condition . . . [they] can save [their] manhood only in hatred and rebellion against the bourgeoisie."[188] He maintained that "The majority of the proletariat . . . has no other choice than to starve or to rebel,"[189] a sentiment he had voiced as early as 1842.[190] More specifically, Marx argued that capitalism must eventually lead to a reduction of wages below the minimum for subsistence and that this "necessarily leads to revolution."[191] In 1854 Engels repeated that "economic crisis and hunger" might at any time provoke revolution.[192]

At the same time Marx and Engels argued that the conditions prevailing in the bourgeois society had sufficiently simplified the relationship between classes to allow the working class clearly to understand the situation. Engels outlined the conception briefly in his work of 1845. "The commercial crises [will] continue and grow more violent, more terrible, with the extension of industry and the multiplication of the proletariat. The proletariat [will] increase in geometrical proportion, in consequence of the progressive ruin of the lower middle class and the giant strides with which capital is concentrating itself in the hands of the few; and the proletariat [will] soon embrace the whole nation, with the exception of a few millionaires. But in this development there comes a stage at which the proletariat perceives how easily the existing power may be overthrown, and then follows a revolution."[193] The consciousness of class interests is interpreted by Marx to be the inevitable consequence of economic development. "Economic conditions had first transformed the mass of the people of the country into workers. The combination of capital has created for this mass a common situation, common interests. This mass is thus already a class as against capital, but not yet for itself. In the struggle . . . this mass becomes united, and constitutes itself as a class for itself. The interests it defends become class interests. . . . The struggle of class against class is a political struggle."[194] Years later Engels was to hold: "Modern socialism is nothing but the reflex, in thought, of this conflict in fact; its ideal reflection in the minds, first, of the class directly suffering under it, the working class."[195] In Engels' last introduction to the Manifesto, in 1890, he clearly maintained: "For the ultimate triumph of the ideas set forth in the *Manifesto* Marx relied solely and exclusively upon the intellectual development of the working class as it necessarily had to ensue from united action and discussion."[196]

Clearly Marx and Engels attempted to predict Socialist revolution as the consequence of the two necessary and sufficient conditions: (1) the increasing misery of the proletariat which necessarily leads it to insurrection, and (2) the real class consciousness of the working class. Both, of course, are the consequence of maturation within the economic substructure of society.[197] As we have indicated, both Marx and Engels held that the consciousness that social institutions had become unreasonable and unjust "was proof" that the institutions had been outgrown, "that other economic facts [had] made their appearance, owing to which the former [had] become unbearable and untenable."[198] Consciousness was an "efflux," an "echo," of the material conditions of life.

The relationship between the economic base and political consciousness was construed as eminently simple. In contemporary society a contradiction has developed between the material productive forces and the capitalist mode of distribution (the social or property relations). The capitalist class "personifies" the prevailing social relations and the working class "personifies" the material productive forces.[199] Classes have been personified with such abstractions as "productive forces," to the extent that Engels lapses into locutions which make the "productive forces" themselves active agents. In *Anti-Dühring* he tells us that "these productive forces themselves, with increasing energy, press forward to the removal of the existing contradiction, to the abolition of their quality as capital, to the practical recognition of their character as social productive forces."[200] He refers to this as the "rebellion of the productive forces. . . ."[201]

The conception being advanced is clearly that the consciousness of a class is "determined" by its conditions of life. The proletariat "perceives" the contradictions in the capitalist system because those contradictions exist in its very material conditions of life. The workers "know" that "property, capital, money, wage-labor and the like are . . . the . . . very practical, the very objective sources of their self-estrangement and that they must be abolished in a practical, objective way. . . ."[202] The proletariat is "misery conscious of its spiritual and physical misery."[203] This simple one-to-one relationship is expressed in the *German Ideology.* "We set out from real, active men, and on the basis of their real life process we demonstrate the development of the ideological reflexes and echoes of this life process. The phantoms formed in the human brain are . . . necessarily sublimates of their material life process . . . all of ideology . . . thus no longer retain[s] the semblance of independence . . . men developing their material production and their material intercourse alter . . . their thinking. . . . Life is not determined by consciousness, but consciousness by life."[204]

In the early period of Marx's theoretical activity, his belief in the simplicity of the relationship between the material conditions of life and the political consciousness is apparent in his discussions of the various workers' movements of his time. In 1847 he argued that class consciousness was the necessary consequence of prevailing economic conditions. Marx felt that the theoretical echo of these conditions was so clear that "the workers *know* that the abolition of bourgeois property relations is not brought about by the maintenance of feudal property relations. They *know* their own revolutionary movement can only be accelerated through the revolutionary movement of the bourgeoisie against the feudal orders and the absolute monarchy. They *know* that their own struggle with the bourgeoisie can only break out on the day the bourgeoisie triumphs. . . . They do not share . . . middle-class illusions. They can and must take part in the middle-class revolution as a condition preliminary to the labor revolution. But they cannot for a moment regard it as their objective."[205] Marx ascribes this politically mature class consciousness to the English working class. He even seems to ascribe such a consciousness to the wretched Silesian weavers who undertook an abortive revolution in Germany in the early forties of the last century.[206] Engels, as early as 1842, expressed this same conviction of the sapience of the working class.[207] And in 1845 he contended, "The workers are coming to perceive more clearly with every day how competition affects them; they see far more clearly than the bourgeois that competition of the capitalists among themselves presses upon the workers too, by bringing on commercial crises, and that this kind of competition, too, must be abolished. They will soon learn *how* they have to go about it."[208]

The development of class consciousness in the proletariat is understood, in the *Manifesto,* to be a function of the reduction of all workers to the same mean level of income and life circum-stance.[209] Even national differences and antagonisms are abolished in the course of industrial development,[210] further accelerating the development of a uniform class consciousness. There is a "spontaneous class-organization of the proletariat."[211]

This "spontaneous" "reflex" activity of the proletariat is ex-pressed in its class consciousness and finds practical expression in political action, either through a political party or in spite of it. "Revolutions are not intentionally and capriciously made, but rather have universally been the necessary consequence of con-ditions completely independent of the will and leadership of the individual parties and entire classes."[212] At the same time the parties clearly and simply represent class interests.[213] "The parties [in England]," Engels maintained in 1843, "are identical with social levels and classes."[214]

This simple account of the mechanics of revolution underwent significant revision in the subsequent work of both Marx and Engels. When they applied their theory of history to actual historical situations there is compelling evidence that their early assessments were substantially modified. Marx's and Engels' most significant efforts to apply their theory cover the intermediary period from 1848 to 1851 and involve the works *The Class Strug-gles in France* and *The 18th Brumaire of Louis Bonaparte* by Marx and *Germany: Revolution and Counter-Revolution* by Engels.

In *The Class Struggles in France* and *The 18th Brumaire*, Marx was faced with a historical situation in which economic develop-ments and social classes interacted to produce the surface flow of events. In his treatment Marx actually proceeded to employ two distinct though connected methods. In *The Class Struggles in France* he found it necessary to include in his account of the day-to-day history of the period the workings of political institutions, of established traditions, and of groups afflicted with "false ideologies." As a consequence, the "simplified class structure" proclaimed in the *Manifesto* becomes enormously complex. We find different social groups identified as the "finance aristocracy," "the industrial bourgeoisie," "the petty bourgeoisie of all grada-tions," "the peasantry," "the industrial working class," "the lumpenproletariat," and a proliferation of subgroupings like "the big landed proprietors," "domestic servants," "shopkeepers," "tradesmen," and the "military."

The relationship between class consciousness, class interest, and manifest political behavior becomes complicated. We find, for example, that "French industrialists . . . in order to secure the advancement of their interests as against the remaining factions of the bourgeoisie . . . take the lead of the movement and simultaneously push their class interests to the fore; they must follow in the train of the revolution, and serve interests which are opposed to the collective interests of their class."[215] Furthermore, "in France, the petty bourgeois does what normally the industrial bourgeois would have to do; the worker does what normally would be the task of the petty bourgeois; and the task of the worker, who accomplishes that? No one."[216] There seems to be a real difficulty in relating overt political behavior with "objective" class reality. The simple one-to-one relationship between the objective economic role which defines a class and that class's consciousness of its "objective" interests is no longer seriously maintained. The relationship is complex and often *paradoxical*. *The 18th Brumaire*, on the other hand, which deals with the same events two years later, speaks in terms of standard theory. The analysis is more "logical" than historical. Much the same can be said for Engels' *Germany: Revolution and Counter-Revolution*. Engels does not treat the political events of the period; instead he deals with putative economic and social groups whose overt behavior he finds easy to analyze in retrospect.

This seems to be true for at least some of the theoretical efforts of both Marx and Engels. In December, 1851, Marx wrote to Engels, "I have let you wait for an answer, for I have been quite bewildered by the tragicomic events in Paris. . . . It is difficult, indeed, impossible, to prognosticate in a drama whose hero is Crapulinski" (Marx's derogatory name for Louis Napoleon). Yet in *The 18th Brumaire*, written shortly thereafter, Marx declared, "If ever an event has, well in advance of its coming, cast its shadow before, it was Bonaparte's coup d'état."[217]

Despite the disposition to read the *logic* of history into history in retrospect, the impact of the class struggles in France was not lost on Marx, particularly when, in the years following 1850, the class consciousness of the European proletariat did not manifest itself spontaneously out of the material conditions of production. In the early Marx-Engels manuscripts there is an almost naive conviction that the proletarian consciousness was somehow a simple "echo" of its life circumstances. Certainly by 1860 both Marx and Engels had been forced to reconsider the putative relationship between the life circumstances of a class and its class consciousness. In a letter to Kugelmann on March 28, 1870, Marx could confide: "The English have all the material conditions necessary for a socialist revolution. What they lack is the spirit of generalization and the revolutionary passion." Nor was this written in a fit of pique. After the first elections under the new franchise laws in England, millions of workers had, for the first time, gone to the polls. And the results were a sad commentary on their "class consciousness." Engels termed the results "a hopeless certificate of destitution for the English proletariat. The parson has shown unexpected power and so has the cringing to respectability. Not a single working-class candidate had a ghost of a chance, but my Lord Tomnoddy or any parvenu snob could have the worker's vote with pleasure."[218] The difference becomes manifest when we compare this with Engels' statement of 1845, "English socialism affords the most pronounced expression of the prevailing absence of religion among the working men, an expression so pronounced indeed that the mass of the working men, being unconsciously and merely practically irreligious, often draw back before it. But here, too, necessity will force the working men to abandon the remnants of a belief which, as they will more and more clearly perceive, serves only to make them weak and resigned to their fate, obedient and faithful to the vampire property holding class."[219]

In 1845 Engels had been convinced that the working class would be, by virtue of its objective class interests, increasingly disabused of its religious ideology. The working class will "more and more clearly perceive . . ."; "necessity will force them to abandon . . . " By 1868 not the working class, but Engels, seems disabused of faith. Early classical Marxism anticipated the spontaneous rise of revolutionary class consciousness as a derivative of the objective economic developments in the material base of society.[220] The later Marxism was faced with the necessity of explaining the lack of such "consciousness" among the proletariat of the most advanced capitalist country in Europe.[221]

As early as 1858 Engels told Marx that England, the country

once conceived (in 1845) to be on the brink of proletarian rebellion, had created for itself a "bourgeois proletariat"— a proletariat with a bourgeois social consciousness.[222]

More and more frequently both Marx and Engels, in their explanation of the lack of class consciousness, had recourse to the stratagem of ascribing "corruption," "venality," "foolishment," "wretchedness" to at least the leaders of the proletariat in Germany, Italy, Spain, England, and France.[223] The correspondence between Marx and Engels during the last decade of Marx's life gives ample evidence of their disillusionment. While Engels, even toward the very end of his life, could maintain that "particular political parties . . . [are] more or less adequate political expression of . . . classes and fractions of classes,"[224] the impact of thirty years of trial are evident in his private correspondence. The mature writings of Karl Marx give evidence of a similar reassessment. Instead of the "consciousness" of the proletariat becoming increasingly uniform and explicit as a consequence of the maturation of capitalism, we find, in the third volume of *Capital*, talk of "an infinite fragmentation of interests and rank created by the social division of labor among laborers, capitalists and landlords."[225] The relationship between conceived conscious interests and putative objective economic interests is infinitely complex. On occasion workers will act "like sheep,"[226] rather than class-conscious proletarians.

The objective conditions necessary for revolution were still evident. The creation of a relative surplus population, an army of unemployed, was still conceived as inseparable from the technological development of capitalism.[227] The notion that "conflict must continually ensue between the limited conditions of consumption on a capitalist basis and a production which forever tends to exceed its immanent barriers,"[228] which "periodically . . . seeks vent in crises,"[229] and necessary expansion into foreign markets[230] was still argued. Capitalist production still "move[d] in contradictions."[231]

The increasingly social aspects of production continued to be emphasized by Marx. Stock companies, he argued, arise which separate the function of the capitalist as manager from the ownership of capital. Cartels expand, giving further emphasis to "socialization." There is the "abolition of the capitalist mode of production within capitalist production itself, a self-destructive contradiction which represents on its face a mere phase of transition to a new form of production."[232] Finally, the entire first volume of *Capital* was a detailed catalogue of factors increasing the physical and spiritual misery of the proletariat.

And yet while all the objective conditions necessary for social and political revolution were present in England the revolution was not forthcoming. In 1890, in the effort to tender an explanation, Engels wrote, ". . . [a]ccording to the materialist conception of history, the ultimately determining element in history is the production and reproduction of real life. More than this neither Marx nor I have ever asserted. Hence if somebody twists this into saying that the economic element is the *only* determining one, he transforms that proposition into a meaningless, abstract, senseless phrase. The economic situation is the basis, but the various elements of the superstructure: political forms of the class struggle and its results, to wit: constitutions established by the victorious class after a successful battle, etc., juridical forms, and then even the reflexes of all these actual struggles in the brains of the participants, political, juristic, philosophical theories, religious views and their further development into systems of dogmas, also exercise their influence upon the course of the historical struggles and in many cases preponderate in determining their *form*. There is an interaction of all these elements in which, amid all the endless host of accidents (that is, of things and events, whose inner connection is so remote or so impossible of proof that we can regard it as nonexistent, as negligible) the economic movement finally asserts itself as necessary. . . . History is made in such a way that the final result always arises from conflicts between many individual wills, of which each again has been made what it is by a host of particular conditions of life. Thus there are innumerable intersecting forces, an infinite series of parallelograms of forces which give rise to one resultant—the historic event."[233] Only *ultimately*, and in the *final analysis*, does the "economic factor" finally assert itself as "necessary." Labriola calls this kind of determinism "derived, reflex and complex."[234]

If one persists in calling historic events "necessary" and "inevitable" after conceding that history is made by an "endless host of accidents," "innumerable intersecting forces," and an "infinite series of parallelograms of forces," the choice of words can not be much more than personal preference. To say that "ultimately" the economic movement asserts itself is to attempt a proof by pronouncement or to commit oneself to a thesis so vague that it can forever escape confirmation or disconfirmation. When Marx discussed contemporary history he seemed to employ all the tools of analysis of empirical historiography, but when he interpreted history in retrospect it took on an *a priori* logical form. The predictions which would have at least partially confirmed the tightened form of the materialist conception of history that both Marx and Engels advanced prior to 1850 were never realized. Proletarian class consciousness did not come to characterize the proletarian class. When faced with the necessity of explaining contemporary behavior, both Marx and Engels seem to have modified the simplistic "echo" or "reflex" theory of consciousness which is found in the early statements. Consciousness in the more mature documents is derived, complex; interests are multivaried and multidimensional. In explaining overt political or social behavior the simple conception of society being divided into two classes is abandoned. "In England," Marx writes in the third volume of *Capital*, "modern society is indisputably developed most highly and classically in its economic structure. Nevertheless the stratification of classes does not appear in its pure form, even there. Middle and transition stages obliterate even here all definite boundaries. . . ."[235]

In every analysis "class" is always qualified by some reservation until finally a period is only accurately described when it is understood to result from an interaction between a multiplicity of groups having real or presumed interests to advance or defend. These interests may be "objective" in the classical Marxist sense, rooted in the real economic situation, or they may be fancied. The working class can be led astray by "corrupt" labor leaders in England or "police spies" in Germany. In any event the simple interpretation of history in which each class comes to "more clearly perceive" its "objective" interests is more than significantly modified, for the proletariat of the advanced capitalist countries still pursue fancied, imaginary or partial interests.

Classical Marxism never seems to have resolved the vexed question of the relationship between the material conditions of life and the social consciousness of the class which was to be the protagonist in the drama of world history. Yet it will be seen that classical Marxism's conception of the good society rests implicitly upon the conviction that the proletariat, as a class, has attained full consciousness, that the liberating Socialist revolution will ideally be the act of the "vast majority" of men acting in responsible concert in the interest of all men.

## The State and Society in Classical Marxism

We have suggested that there is more than a "flirtation" with Hegelian terminology in the mature Marx. In turning our attention to the Marxist conception of the state and society we shall argue that its source lies in the neo-Hegelianism of Karl Marx's youth, for the values which animated his work are those which conceive the ultimate aims of mankind to be liberty and rationality —and the true state "the realization of rational freedom."[236] These values are essentially Hegelian and were all but universally shared by the Young Hegelians who were the companions of the young Marx.

Marx saw in philosophy the uncompromising defender of man's ultimate liberty and rationality; and in the true state he saw the realization of that liberty and rationality. Marx felt that rational freedom could only be the consequence of a correct appraisal of the nature of man—and the conformity of the state to that nature.[237] Man was the "real principle of the state"[238] and the state which sought the realization of rational freedom must consider men concretely, in all the complex interpersonal relationships which constitute their essence as men.[239] The state must not consider men abstractly, but rather as members of a community (*Gemeindemitglieder*).[240] For the human essence is a "communal essence" (*Gemeinwesen*), a "communist essence" (*kommunistische Wesen*).[241] Man attains true humanity only in so far as he establishes real relations with other men in a community.[242]

Only men related in an association governed by reason can attain true freedom. "Contemporary philosophy," the young Marx argued, ". . . sees the state as a great organism in which legal, moral and political freedom has attained realization and the individual citizen, in obeying the laws of the state obeys only the natural laws of his own reason, human reason."[243] In such a state the individual finds fulfillment in the collectivity and the collectivity in the individual.

For Marx this true community (*Gemeinschaft*) distinguished itself from a mechanical aggregate (*Gesellschaft*).[244] The former implied an organic community of mutual and abiding interest—the latter a commercial association. A good state would be one which rested upon the full awareness that the nature of man is that of a social being, a "real generic being."[245] The true state would be the "essence of the community,"[246] and consequently would fully reflect the essence of man.

Animated by such an essentially neo-Hegelian conviction, the young Marx undertook a critique of the political institutions of his time. Marx's criticisms, in turn, can only be understood against the background of Feuerbach's analysis of man's alienation in religion. Marx, as we have indicated, was a dedicated Feuerbachian between 1841 and 1845, when he leveled his first criticisms against the bourgeois state.

Feuerbach was, and remained, primarily a critic of religion and of Hegelian idealism—but some of the specifics of his method materially influenced (and to some extent remained intrinsic to) the social and political philosophy of Karl Marx. His analysis of man's religious alienation became paradigmatic for Marx's analysis of man's political alienation.

Feuerbach had understood religion to be an alienation of man, a projection of human attributes (predicates) into an absolute realm where those characteristics were reified into an Absolute Subject. Such projections he conceived to be *compensatory:* ". . . [R]eligion abstracts from man, from the world but it can only abstract from the limitations . . . in short, from the negative, not from . . . the positive. . . ."[247] Whatever deficiencies man finds as his human lot are compensated for in the process of projecting his attributes into the eternal. Hegel had succeeded in resolving man's needs by seeing them sublated in the Absolute—and the Absolute was only the pedant's way of saying God. Hegel's resolution of man's needs was a mystic resolution. God or Spirit, Feuerbach indicated, possessed everything man cried out to possess: wisdom, truth, righteousness, and liberty.[248] "Every deficiency in man stands opposed to a fulfillment in God: God is and has what man is not and has not."[249] Every deficiency man suffers from thus finds its speculative fulfillment in God.[250] "The less God is, the more man is found to be; the less man is, the more is God."[251] Thus only "in the mouth of need, of misery, of deficiency has the word God any weight, seriousness and sense. . . ."[252] For God is man's fulfillment, but a fulfillment in fancy alone. Religion, as Marx contended, accepting Feuerbach's analysis, is "the fantastic realization of the human being, inasmuch as the human being possesses no true reality."[253] The more man, in reality, realizes himself, the less significance, for him, has God and religion. Religion offered men the *idea* of fulfillment, but fulfillment purchased at the cost of a loss of fulfillment in fact.

For the young Marx this insight provided "the basis" for all subsequent criticism. "The abolition of religion, as the illusory happiness of the people, is the demand for their real happiness. . . . The immediate task of philosophy, when enlisted in the service of history, is to unmask human self-alienation in its unholy shape, now that it has been unmasked in its holy shape. Thus the criticism of heaven transforms itself into the criticism of earth, the criticism of religion into the criticism of right, and the criticism of theology into the criticism of politics."[254]

Thus Marx, using the Feuerbachian technique, launched his radical criticism of the bourgeois state. He criticized the Hegelian conception of the state "because and in so far as the modern state itself makes abstraction of real men or only satisfies the whole man in an imaginary manner."[255] For Marx, political alienation, like religious alienation, was the consequence of attempting to resolve real problems through speculation alone. Hegel had rendered the predicates of man independent (*"Hegel verselbständigt die Prädikate"*), and in the rarefied reaches of political mysticism the predicates of man appeared in the "state as Person, as 'Subject.' "[256] So conceived, the "state," the "Subject" is divested of those deficiencies which characterize *real* subjects, real men. In the realm of abstract reason the state becomes fulfillment of man, just as in religion God becomes his fulfillment. In order to resolve the real miseries and deficiencies of society a state is thought of as possessing the idealized attributes of man as a social being.

"The political constitution was heretofore the religious sphere, the religion of the life of a people, the heaven of its communality [*Allgemeinheit*] over against the *earthly being* of its reality. The political sphere was the only . . . sphere in which the content as well as the form constituted a species content [*Gattungsinhalt*], a true communality. . . ."[257] The state will cease to be a religious object, a fetish, for mankind when it ceases to be an abstract compensation for real human miseries, when mankind is understood to be its "real principle."

For Marx the criticism of religion had revealed that religion could only be understood as the inverted consciousness of real misery in the observable, historic, and empiric world of men. "The existence of religion indicates the presence of a defect, the source of this defect may only be looked for in the nature of the state. . . . We do not transform secular questions into theological questions. We transform theological questions into secular questions."[258] Marx conceived his task as the reform of the inverted consciousness of men, "not through dogmas, but rather through an analysis of the mystical and unreal consciousness which manifests itself as only religious or political," in order that men should possess in reality that which they have only possessed, in the past, in abstract speculation.

Marx understood the modern political state to be a compensatory projection, an inverted image, of the conditions which prevailed in bourgeois society. Such a state provided man, in an abstract fashion, the human, social essence of which bourgeois society had deprived him. "The political state is related to bourgeois society as spiritualistically as heaven is to earth. It occupies the same position of antagonism toward bourgeois society; it subdues the latter just as religion overcomes the limitations of the profane world, that is, by recognizing bourgeois society and allowing the latter to dominate it. Man in his outermost reality, in bourgeois society, is a profane being. Here, where he is a real individual for himself and others, he is an untrue phenomenon. In the state . . . where the individual is a generic being, he is the imaginary member of an imagined sovereignty, he is robbed of his real individual life and filled with an unreal universality."[259]

Civil or bourgeois society is characterized by egoism, the desire for individual material accumulation. "Bourgeois society [is] the sphere of egoism, of the *bellum omnium contra omnes*."[260] But man is in his essence a social being, a "real generic being."[261]

Bourgeois society, the realm of individual egoism, seeks freedom for man, but its freedom is "not based upon the connection of man with man, but rather on the separation of man from man. . . . None of the so-called rights of man, therefore, goes beyond the egoistic individual, beyond the individual as a member of bourgeois society, withdrawn into his private interests and separated from the community. Far from regarding the individual as a generic being, the generic life, society itself, rather appears as an external frame for the individual, as a limitation of his original independence. The sole bond which connects him with his fellows is natural necessity, material needs and private interest, the preservation of his property and his egoistic person."[262] Man as a social being is degraded to the level of man as bourgeois.

But man is not an atom.[263] The unity of the human essence is "man's consciousness of his species and his attitude toward his species . . . the practical identity of man with man, i.e. . . . the social or human relation of man to man."[264] The fact that man cannot be man without establishing real relations with other men[265] finds alienated expression in a projection, in the possession of abstract citizenship in an abstract political community. "The members of the political state are religious by virtue of the dualism between the individual life and the generic life, between the life of bourgeois society and the political life; they are religious inasmuch as the individual regards his true life to be the political life beyond his real individuality. . . ."[266] The political state in such an inverted order is endowed with the qualities lost to the real individual. Political citizenship gives man the semblance of fulfillment. As a citizen of the state, the individual is conceived again as a social being, but only in a fantastic and alienated manner. Just as God is the alienated compensation for man's real needs and deficiencies, the political state is the alienated compensation for man's social and civil impoverishments. "True man," a social, generic being, "is only recognized in the shape of the abstract citizen."[267]

Men come to imagine the political state as "holding together" the atoms of bourgeois society. Only in the political state can men find true manhood. As a matter of fact the truth is that it is "natural necessity, *essential human properties,* however alienated they may seem to be, and *interest* that hold the members of civil society together: *civil*, not *political* life is their *real* tie. It is therefore not the *state* that holds the *atoms* of civil society together, but the fact that they are atoms only in *imagination*, in the *heaven* of their fancy, but in *reality* beings tremendously different from atoms. . . . Only *political superstition* today imagines that social life must be held together by the state whereas in reality the state is held together by civil life."[268]

That men have become increasingly aware of political alienation was evident to Marx. The events of the French Revolution were evidence that political superstition was being dispelled. "In the moment of its heightened consciousness, the political life seeks to suppress . . . bourgeois society and its elements, and to constitute itself as the real and uncontradictory generic life of the individual."[269]

The state which the young Marx opposed was the state based upon the "contradiction between public and private life, upon the contradiction between the general interest and individual interests."[270] Political life is alienated because secular life is based upon a false conception of man. Real, radical revolution begins with the conviction that man is a social, communal being. Such a revolution would restore to man in reality what speculation has provided him in the form of a dream, in the form of abstract citizenship in the political state. For the young Marx the bourgeois political state had become the dream fulfillment of man's social alienation.

The thinkers of the French Revolution had attained, in Marx's estimation, a heightened awareness of these considerations. The source of political alienation was sought not in the maladministration of the state bureaucracy, but in society itself.[271] Since Marx conceived man to be essentially a social creature,[272] a social order which separated the individual from the community of men was degrading. Bourgeois society, predicated on individualism, creates material conditions of life in which the individual is compelled to envisage himself an atom among atoms having no real relations with others except in the abstract realm of the philosophy of the state. Bourgeois society with its "modern division of labor, the modern form of exchange, competition, concentration," and so forth, degrades man.[273] To establish a true state, in which man is no longer degraded, requires that history should have produced "the material conditions which would render necessary the abolition of the bourgeois mode of production. . . ."[274] For the modern political state rises upon the foundation of the material life processes of civil society.

Bourgeois society is predicated upon "practical needs or egoism," whose God is money;[275] it dissever[s] all the generic ties of the individual, set[s] egoism in place of these generic ties, and dissolve[s] the world into a world of atomized, mutually hostile individuals."[276] In attempting to resolve the contradiction between what the individual is and what he should be, bourgeois political theory paints the vain picture of abstract citizenship in which the individual realizes his social essence in political abstraction. This, according to Marx, characterizes the political philosophy of Hegel. It is the lie of his system. "There can . . . no longer be any question about an act of accommodation on Hegel's part *vis-à-vis* . . . the state."[277] Hegel's solution of the problem of the relationship between the individual, civil society, and the state is an abstract solution. It is "merely formal."[278] Man's alienations in the bourgeois world of egoistic atoms are resolved in the realm of abstract thought with the contention that man somehow, as citizen, participates in a rational and free "political life." The contradiction between what man is and what he should be reappears as the contradiction between private and public life.

Bourgeois political philosophy contended that the state stood above private interests; in practice the state was the executive agent for those interests. The more exalted the state became in theory the more debased it was in practice. It could not, for Marx, be otherwise. Men find themselves in real, material relations, which come to govern their overt behavior. The very conditions of their life determine the breadth of vision they possess as members of political society. Their political liberality extends only as far as the liberality of their real life conditions. Because bourgeois life is predicated on private gain it conceives society only in terms of an arena in which one is free to accumulate wealth. This is conceived as "natural." The so-called "natural rights of man" as distinguished from the rights of the citizen are "nothing else than the rights of a member of bourgeois society, that is of the egoistic individual, of man separated from man and the community."[279] The bourgeoisie finds it impossible to "raise property or labor to the level of social elements" but can only conceive them in "their separation from the political whole and constituted . . . as special societies within society."[280] Thus in the bourgeois state the individual "was not freed from property: he received freedom of property. He was not freed from the egoism of industry; he received industrial freedom."[281]

With this conception of men as social atoms rather than members of a "human community," man's inhumanity to man—man's degradation itself—is construed as the consequence of natural disaster or individual frailties.[282] In actual fact men are inhuman and degraded because the real circumstances governing their real life activities are themselves inhuman and degraded. An entire social order rests upon the "slavery of middle class society" and the existence of a degraded state is its necessary consequence.[283] If the contemporary state wishes to abolish human degradation, it would have to abolish the "present day mode of living. If it wishes to abolish this mode of living, it would have to abolish itself. . . ."[284]

Marx conceived the abolition of the state as a consequence of the abolition of the mode of production which made such a state a necessity. But he did not conceive the abolition of either the consequence of an "act of suicide" on the part of the ruling class. Such an abolition would be the consequence of economic development. The development of modern industry had produced conditions in which the vast majority of men[285] are separated from the real community of men, a community which is "life itself, physical and intellectual life, human morality, human activity, human enjoyment. . . ."[286] Hegel was, of course, aware of this. "The poor," Hegel argued, "still have the needs common to civil society, and yet since society has withdrawn from them the natural means of acquisition and broken the bond of the family . . . their poverty leaves them more and more deprived of all the advantages of society, of the opportunity of acquiring skill or education of any kind, as well as of the administration of justice, the public health services . . . and so forth."[287] His solution was that ultimately state administration must resolve social dislocation. Marx's argument was simply that the contemporary state by its very nature was incapable of performing such a function. The state was, in practice, a medium for the expression of private interests and only in theory did it concern itself with the generic human being. To truly abolish social ills the bourgeois state would literally have to abolish itself, and "suicide is unnatural."[288]

The resolution of man's political alienation can only come from radical revolution by a class of men afflicted with radical needs, by men who have suffered all the degradations of bourgeois society, whose alienation is complete, who have a world to win and nothing to lose but their chains. That class in "radical chains" is the proletariat,[289] and its radical chains are the "necessary consequence of modern industry. . . ."[290] The revolution in which that class throws off its chains, leading to the abolition of "all conditions in which man is a degraded, servile, neglected, contemptible being . . ." is a *social* revolution which abolishes "bourgeois property relations."[291] For with their abolition are resolved all the "antagonisms which are produced by the great industry, the development of the world market and of free competition."[292]

The bourgeoisie as a class arises upon the foundation of "economic conditions independent of [its] will."[293] These economic conditions compel the bourgeoisie to produce, again against its will, the ultimate conditions for the victory of the proletariat.[294] With the victory of the proletariat the true state emerges as that form of association in which the "free development of each is the condition for the free development of all."[295] When the "real, individual man is identical with the citizen, and has become a generic being in his empirical life, in his individual work, in his individual relationships, [when] man has recognized and organized his own capacities as social capacities, and consequently the social force is no longer divided by the political power . . . then will human emancipation be achieved."[296]

With the revolution the democratic socialist state will wrest "all capital from the bourgeoisie, to centralise all instruments of production in the hands of the state, i.e., of the proletariat organized as the ruling class. . . ."[297] Credit and the means of communication and transport will both be centralized in the hands of the state and there will be an extension of factories and instruments of production owned by the state. There will be an equal liability of all to labor, including the establishment of industrial armies, especially for agriculture.[298]

The conception of society and the state advanced by Marx and

Engels in 1848 had its source in the neo-Hegelianism of the young Marx. Marx had resolved the contradiction between civil society and the political state by ultimately identifying the two. Society *was* the *true* state, and the *true* state *was* society. There will no longer be political power as such, interposed between man as a generic being and the society in which he manifests his essence. For "political power, properly so called, is merely the organised power of one class for oppressing another."[299] In the democratic Socialist state all such antagonisms will have been resolved. The individual whose essence is an ensemble of social relations will find his fulfillment, his human liberation, in a state predicated on the conviction that man is a *social* being.

We find this expressed in the *Poverty of Philosophy:* "The working class, in the course of its development, will substitute for the old civil society an association which will exclude classes and their antagonism, and there will be no more political power properly so-called, since political power is precisely the official expression of antagonism in civil society."[300]

That such a state would be democratic is never doubted. The revolution is undertaken by "the immense majority in the interests of the immense majority"[301]—in the interests of nine-tenths of the population. In the *Foundations* Engels maintained that the revolutionary state would have a "democratic constitution,"[302] and would be characterized by the direct or indirect dominance of the proletariat.[303]

Both Marx and Engels retained such a conception of the state, society, and radical democracy until the end of their lives. The major departure in the original theory arose as a consequence of their reassessment of the essence and character of the state. In the Introduction to *The Civil War in France,* written in 1891, Engels maintained that "the state is nothing but a machine for the oppression of one class by another, and indeed in the democratic republic no less than in the monarchy; and at best an evil inherited by the proletariat after its victorious struggle for class supremacy, whose worst sides the victorious proletariat . . . cannot avoid having to lop off at once as much as possible until such time as a generation reared in new, free social conditions is able to throw the entire lumber of the state on the scrap heap."[304] Here the state is identified with what had been called "political power" in the *Manifesto*. In the Preface to the German edition of 1872, Engels specifically referred to the sections of the *Manifesto* where allusions had been made to the role of the state subsequent to the revolution. "That passage would, in many respects, be very differently worded today. In view of the gigantic strides of modern industry in the last twenty-five years, and of the accompanying improved and extended party organization of the working class, in view of the practical experience gained, first in the February Revolution, and then, still more, in the Paris Commune, where the proletariat for the first time held political power for two whole months, this programme has in some details become antiquated. One thing especially was proved by the Commune, viz., that 'the working class cannot simply lay hold of the ready-made state machinery, and wield it for its own purposes.' "[305] Later Engels was to predict that society will "organize production on the basis of a free and equal association of the producers [and] will put the whole machinery of state where it will then belong: into the Museum of Antiquities, by the side of the spinning wheel and the bronze axe."[306]

In the later conception, the state is equated with what had earlier been called the "political power."[307] Society was to resolve the disparity between the ideal of rational freedom and the painful shortcomings of bourgeois society in a society of free and equal productive association. By revolution the means of production are transformed into public property. "By this act," Engels maintained, "the proletariat frees the means of production from the character of capital they have thus far borne, and gives their socialized character complete freedom to work itself out. Socialized production upon a predetermined plan becomes henceforth possible. The development of production makes the existence of different classes of society thenceforth an anachronism. In proportion as anarchy in social production vanishes, the political authority of the state dies out. Man, at last the master of his own form of social organization, becomes at the same time the lord over nature, his own master—free."[308] The free association of workers, the social organization, is thus identified with what Marx had originally called the true, the good, state.

In the *Anti-Dühring* of 1877 the entire relationship of the state to society is summarized. "The modern state, no matter what its form, is essentially a capitalist machine, the state of the capitalists, the ideal personification of the total national capital. The more it proceeds to taking over of the productive forces the more does it actually become the national capitalist, the more citizens does it exploit. The workers remain wage-workers—proletarians. The capitalist relation is not done away with. It is rather brought to a head. But, brought to a head, it topples over. State ownership of the productive forces is not the solution of the conflict, but concealed within it are the technical conditions that form the elements of that solution.

"This solution can only consist in the practical recognition of the social nature of the modern forces of production, and therefore in the harmonizing of the modes of production, appropriation, and exchange with the socialized character of the means of production. And this can only come about by society openly and directly taking possession of the productive forces which have outgrown all control except that of society as a whole. . . . The social anarchy of production gives place to a social regulation of production upon a definite plan, according to the needs of the community and of each individual.

". . . [Whilst] the capitalist mode of production more and more completely transforms the great majority of the population into proletarians, it creates the power which, under penalty of its own destruction, is forced to accomplish this revolution. . . . The proletariat seizes political power and turns the means of production in the first instance into state property.

"But, in doing this, it abolishes itself as proletariat, abolishes all class distinctions and class antagonisms, abolishes also the state as state. . . . It becomes the real representative of the whole of society [and] renders itself unnecessary. . . . State interference in social relations becomes, in one domain after another, superfluous, and then withers away of itself; the government of persons is replaced by the administration of things, and by the conduct of processes of production.

". . . [With] the seizing of the means of production by society, production of commodities is done away with, and, simultaneously, the mastery of the product over the producer. Anarchy in social production is replaced by plan-conforming, conscious organization. . . . Man's own social organization, hitherto confronting him as a necessity imposed by nature and history, now becomes the result of his own free action. The extraneous objective forces that have hitherto governed history pass under the control of man himself. Only from that time will man himself, with full consciousness make his own history—only from that time will the social causes set in movement by him have, in the main and in a constantly growing measure, the results intended by him. It is the ascent of man from the kingdom of necessity to the kingdom of freedom."[309]

In mature Marxism the state is understood to be the political machinery for class oppression. Its function is to defend existing property relations against the changes made necessary by the development of the material productive forces. The productive processes become increasingly social while the processes of distribution are governed privately. The coercive machinery of the state is employed in the effort to resolve the contradiction by force. An ominous situation results. Society is driven by class differences. Those who produce wealth receive only a subsistence compensation while a small minority of capitalists garner the rewards. In the effort to control the inflammatory situation, the state poses as mediator, prepared to mete out impartial justice.[310] The impartiality of the state becomes part of the ideology of the ruling class. The greater its shortcomings in fact, the more the state is compensated in theory. As the real relations of men become more precarious, their disposition more egoistic, the state becomes more invested with qualities men, in reality, no longer possess. The state loses these compensatory attributes, and ceases to be a state, only when society finds the means of expressing directly the truly social relations which obtain between producers. Society expresses this reality when it organizes itself as a free association of producers who control the processes of distribution.

For mature Marxism the state was identified with what Marx had earlier conceived as the "degraded" state—the state in the service of private interest—what had been referred to as "political power." Mature Marxism remained true to the conception of the good state by identifying it with the free association of producers.

While the details of this association of producers were never described by either Marx or Engels, they did commit themselves to certain propositions. Engels contended that "society cannot free itself unless every individual is freed. The old mode of production must therefore be revolutionized from top to bottom, and in particular the former division of labor must disappear. Its place must be taken by an organization of production in which . . . productive labor, instead of being a means of subjugating men, will become a means of their emancipation, by offering each individual the opportunity to develop all his faculties, physical and mental, in all directions and exercise them to the full—in which, therefore, productive labor will become a pleasure instead of being a burden. Today this is no longer a fantasy, no longer a pious wish."[311]

This feature of the true society of men sounds like a more sophisticated restatement of the view of Communist society advanced in the *German Ideology* of 1845. "The division of labor offers us the first example of how, as long as man remains in natural society—that is, as long as a cleavage exists between the particular and the common interest—as long, therefore, as activity is not voluntarily but naturally divided, man's own deed becomes an alien power opposed to him, which enslaves him instead of being controlled by him. For as soon as labor is distributed, each man has a particular, exclusive sphere of activity which is forced upon him and from which he cannot escape. He is a hunter, a fisherman, a shepherd, or a critical critic, and must remain so if he does not want to lose his means of livelihood; while in communist society, where nobody has one exclusive sphere of activity but each can become accomplished in any branch he wishes, society regulates the general production and thus makes it possible for me to do one thing today and another tomorrow, to hunt in the morning, fish in the afternoon, rear cattle in the evening, criticize after dinner, just as I have a mind. . . ."[312]

These ideas are considered compatible with a "society which makes it possible for its productive forces to dovetail harmoniously into each other on the basis of one single vast plan. . . ."[313] Perhaps the most interesting notion concerning the true society in which "productive labor" would offer every individual the opportunity to develop all his faculties, both physical and mental to the fullest—within, of course, a single vast plan—is the medium through which it is to be effected. Both Marx and Engels saw in the Paris Commune the model of the future society.[314] The system of society was to be organized on the lines of a "free federation of all . . . Communes . . . a national organization which for the first time was really to be created by the nation itself."[315] Marx describes the character of the Commune in the following manner: "The Commune was formed of the municipal councillors chosen by universal suffrage . . . responsible and revocable at short terms. . . . Like the rest of public servants, magistrates and judges were to be elective, responsible, and revocable. . . . The Commune was to be the political form of even the smallest country hamlet. . . . The rural communes of every district were to administer their common affairs by an assembly of delegates in the central town, and these district assemblies were again to send deputies to the National Delegation in Paris, each delegate to be at any time revocable and bound by the *mandat impératif* [formal instructions] of his constituents. The few but important functions which still would remain for a central government were not to be suppressed, as had been intentionally misstated, but were to be discharged by Communal and therefore strictly responsible agents. . . . While the merely repressive organs of the old governmental power were to be amputated, its legitimate functions were to be wrested from an authority usurping pre-eminence over society itself, and restored to the responsible agents of society. Instead of deciding once in three or six years which member of the ruling class was to misrepresent the people in Parliament, universal suffrage was to serve the people, constituted in Communes. . . . Nothing could be more foreign to the spirit of the Commune than to supersede universal suffrage by hierarchic investiture. . . . United co-operative societies are to regulate national production upon a common plan, thus taking it under their own control, and putting an end to the constant anarchy and periodical convulsions which are the fatality of capitalist production. . . ."[316]

This is the political structure of society which follows hard on the revolution, the period of the "revolutionary dictatorship of the proletariat."[317] For Engels tells us that if we "want to know what this dictatorship looks like, look at the Paris Commune. That was the Dictatorship of the Proletariat."[318]

There are, of course, evident difficulties in maintaining all such theses in conjunction. We have on the one hand the individual's free and full physical and mental development, and on the other a society organized on the basis of one vast plan and subject to controlling authority.[319] "The workers," Engels tells us, "must therefore . . . come to an understanding on the hours of work: and these hours, once they are fixed, must be observed by all, without any exception. Thereafter particular questions arise in each room and at every moment concerning the mode of production, distribution of materials, etc., which must be settled at once on pain of seeing all production immediately stopped; whether they are settled by decision of a delegate placed at the head of each branch of labor or, if possible, by a majority vote, the will of the single individual will always have to subordinate itself, which means that questions are settled in an authoritarian way. The automatic machinery of a big factory is much more despotic than the small capitalists who employ workers ever have been."[320]

If this is true with respect to the individual how much more so would it be with respect to the locally organized communes which must be integrated into the single vast plan which is to govern the true society? It is difficult to imagine how a single vast plan of social production could be organized and administered by delegates possessed of only a short-term mandate (always subject to recall) and bound by explicit instructions. Others have, of course, devoted more space to these evident difficulties. For our purposes here it is more important to indicate that ultimately the conception of the state and society advanced by classical Marxism was one in which the state became simply the administrative apparatus of a self-conscious, essentially democratic socialist society.[321]

Marx and Engels concluded their analysis of the state and society where they had begun, with a Feuerbachian critique of Hegel. Under capitalism the state is held in superstitious awe, endowed with the attributes denied real men, while in fact the state is a machine created for the coercive control of the oppressed majority. In "bourgeois society men are dominated by the economic conditions created by themselves, by the means of production which they themselves have produced, as if by an alien force."[322] The "universal emancipation"[323] of man is accomplished only "when society, by taking possession of all means of production and using them on a planned basis, has freed itself and all its members from the bondage in which they are now held by these means of production which they themselves have produced but which confront them as an irresistible alien force . . . only then will the last alien force . . . vanish. . . ."[324] So, too, will the state vanish. "There will no longer exist a government nor a state opposed to society itself."[325] In its place will arise the true community of men, the "true state" of the young Karl Marx. The mature Engels could therefore write with conviction, "We would therefore propose to replace state everywhere by community [*Gemeinwesen*], a good old German word which can very well represent the French word commune."[326]

Whatever else they were, both Marx and Engels were democrats who saw in the future society the fulfillment of what they had found in Hegelianism only as a dream—the realization of man's rational freedom.

## Classical Marxism as a Heritage

This was the theory of history left to contemporary Marxism. Rich in suggestive power, brilliant in individual insight, as a system it left a certain obscurity surrounding the ultimate nature of the propulsive forces of historical development. History seems to move through men. Men were somehow its unwilling and unwitting agents. Classical Marxism seemed committed to a conception of history that pretended to "prove concretely how in capitalist society the material, etc., conditions . . . *compel* the workers to lift" the social curse of capitalism,[327] that the proletariat was "ineluctably," "inevitably," "inexorably" driven to institute the revolutionary dictatorship of the proletariat. It used the concept of social class as an explanatory device without defining it with any precision. The proletariat was variously defined as comprised of those who, "having no means of production of their own, are reduced to selling their labor power in order to live,"[328] "of working men," of "wage-laborers," of almost anyone who "toils" for wages. But in given historical situations, these "working men" fall into various interacting and seemingly independent groups: "the lumpenproletariat," "the corrupt labor leaders," "workers who were police-spies," "working-class mem-

bers without class consciousness," and so forth. Society was conceived as divided into two classes, sometimes three classes, and
sometimes into a host of "intermediate" and "transitional" classes.

At times the theory was formulated simply in terms of an
"economic base" giving rise to "a social superstructure," in
language which affirmed that social consciousness must necessarily reflect the material conditions of life. The economic base
seems to have been conceived as possessing the instruments of
production as its dynamic component. Yet, at times, it was contended that "of all the instruments of production, the greatest
productive power is the revolutionary class itself."[329] Under such
circumstances the social consciousness becomes part of the effective economic base of society—and yet it would seem to become
so only as a consequence of a complex form of determinism;
for we are told that "the organization of revolutionary elements
as a class supposes the existence of all the productive forces
which could be engendered in the bosom of the old society."[330]

It was argued that the objective conditions generated by the
capitalist mode of production created the necessary understanding and determination among the working class to create social
revolution. Capitalism produces the very social consciousness
which will effect its destruction. Yet both Marx and Engels
found it necessary to try to explain the failure of the proletariat
to achieve the class consciousness necessary for revolution, for
they remained convinced that the objective conditions were in
accord with their original theoretical formulations. The misery
of the working class increased with its increasing physical and
spiritual exploitation. This coupled with periodic crises of overproduction and the ultimate stagnation of the system as a consequence of the fall in the rate of profit provided the necessary
and sufficient conditions for revolution—and yet there was no
revolution.

By the turn of the century, on the other hand, a number of
Marxists had suggested that the answer to the problem of the
missing revolution was to be found in the fact that the objective
conditions did not correspond to the theory of increasing misery
of the proletariat. What was suggested was that the picture classical Marxism had drawn of capitalist economy was oversimplified.
The theory of history was substantially correct. The social
consciousness of the working class *did* reflect its material life

conditions—but those life conditions, whatever else they were, included a real rise in the standard of living for the proletariat. The proletariat was not being driven to revolution, it was advocating reform—and the propertied classes were making real concessions. The theory of history was to be salvaged by forsaking revolution. The workers were to arm themselves with a vote and the Socialist revolution was to be fought in the ballot box. "The time of surprise attacks," Engels himself had already conceded, "of revolutions carried through by small conscious minorities at the head of unconscious masses, is past."[331] But whatever the change and however it was to be effected one issue seemed clear. Where it is a question of the entire transformation of society either through revolution or evolution the masses must be fully conscious of what is entailed. Since the advanced bourgeois states have granted the working classes the ballot, Engels maintained, their success, given their conscious awareness of issues, is assured. Only by violating the principles of its own political constitution could the bourgeoisie attempt to avert the inevitable. Such brazen imposture could only lead to their violent overthrow by the vast majority of socially and politically conscious working people.[332]

Such consciousness seemed clearly predicated on the maturity of the economies of the advanced capitalist countries.[333] In those countries the workers would have been schooled in labor organization and industry to a full conciousness of issues and responsibilities. Only in an economy where all the productive potential had matured would the consciousness of the working class qualify them for rulership. Both Marx and Engels had argued that a theory, no matter how correct, could not be a substitution for the actual and objective economic maturity of a society.[334] A people, even if possessed of correct theory, could not "clear by bold leaps, nor remove by legal enactments, the obstacles offered by the successive phases of its normal development."[335]

Only with the fully matured material potential of advanced capitalism could the transition to a classless society be made. "The separation of society into an exploiting and an exploited class, a ruling and an oppressed class [is] the necessary consequence of the deficient and restricted development of production. . . ."[336] Certainly this was how the majority of Marxist theoreticians understood classical Marxism before the First World War. A free society could not arise on the immature base of restricted productive potential. By and large, this was the materialist conception of history inherited by Lenin. Armed with this ambiguous legacy, Lenin made a revolution.

# 6 V. I. Lenin and the

# Materialist Conception

# of History

From the evidence provided by their early writings it appears that both Marx and Engels believed that the world revolution of the proletariat was imminent at the time they wrote the programmatic *Manifesto of the Communist Party* in 1847. They seemed convinced that they were expressing the class-conscious sentiments of the vast majority of oppressed mankind. The consciousness of the proletariat was conceived as a reflection of its material conditions of life, and its material conditions were those of "radical chains." The proletariat was nothing; it demanded to be everything.[1] Only the most thoroughly miserable members of the moribund social order could raise the demand for complete humanity. Only *they* were fully conscious of the contradictions in modern society.

The failure of the revolutions of 1848 to attain their ends and the subsequent failure of the proletariat to develop the consciousness which classical Marxism argued history demanded of them led to an increasing sophistication in historical, social, and political interpretation. The simple dichotomies of the early period became the complex interplay of forces, the diffusion of interests, the asymmetrical impact of factors of the mature theory. The class consciousness of the proletariat was no longer conceived as the simple spontaneous reflection of objective economic conditions.

In the years which followed the revolution of 1848, Marx and Engels became increasingly concerned with the apparent lack of maturity of the working classes, particularly the urban proletariat. Prior to 1848 both were convinced that class consciousness, an explicit awareness of its *real* interests, would arise spontaneously among the proletariat as a reflection of its very life conditions. After 1850 the analysis became increasingly sophisticated. By 1858 Engels realized that the most advanced proletarians in the world, the English, were becoming increasingly "bourgeois" in sentiment, aspiration, and political orientation. The real interests of the proletariat, formerly considered so obvious to everyone, were now understood to be obscured by the complexity of the real socioeconomic situation. Issues were veiled by ideological subterfuge, by political manipulation, and by the very stupidity of the working classes themselves. Working-class organizations were afflicted with utopian Socialism, anarchism, and a vulgar trade-union mentality. Both Marx and Engels, at least in their private correspondence, were aware of the lack of class consciousness among the proletariat of capitalist Europe.

By the time of Engels' death the only working-class organization substantially influenced by Marxian ideas was the German Social Democratic party. But the very character of that party aggravated the crisis in Marxism as a theory of history. The German working-class leadership continually "vulgarized" Marxism. Both Marx and Engels found themselves forced to substantially criticize the various programs advanced by the party toward the end of the nineteenth century, for it had gradually become reformist in sentiment and behavior. It became increasingly evident to them that whatever the Social Democrats said in terms of revolutionary Marxist theory had little relevance to the party's reformist practice. Upon the death of Engels, Eduard Bernstein, in whom Engels had placed much confidence, attempted to restore the unity of theory and practice by indicating that proletarian class consciousness corresponded reasonably well with the real conditions which prevailed in the material life of the working class. In his *Presuppositions of Socialism* Bernstein argued that the reformist mentality of the working class should be understood as a reflection of the altered social and economic circumstances in which it found itself at the turn of the twentieth century. He argued that the middle class had not given way to two mutually opposed classes in modern capitalist society. He further contended that real gains had been made in the living standards of the working classes and that the thesis of the increasing misery of the proletariat could not be supported by the facts. Since both the division of society into two antagonistic camps and a real decline in the wages of the working class were necessary conditions for revolution, Bernstein argued that revisions in the original theory had to be undertaken. Furthermore, since the Franco-Prussian War, Europe had suffered no serious political crises. Even the crises of capitalism had apparently been damped by the increasing organization of industry, the rise of cartels, and an elastic credit system.[2]

The failure of classical Marxism to accurately predict the proletarian revolution was explained by providing evidence that the objective conditions of the modern working class in Europe conduced to reformism rather than revolution. The theory that man's consciousness was a reflection of his material life conditions was saved by what Bernstein felt to be a more accurate description of the real-life conditions. Even ultimate revolution could be saved by making a distinction between the real as distinct from the momentary interest of the proletariat. The working class was activated by its *immediate* interests, the theoreticians of the party spoke in the name of its *ultimate* interests. The party serviced the immediate needs of the proletariat in the name of Socialism. For Socialism was the ultimate goal. The "revolution" was to be peaceful.

Friedrich Engels died in 1895. Three years later Bernstein's revisions of classical Marxism shook the Social Democratic movement throughout Europe.


### The Russian Background of Leninism


In the last quarter of the nineteenth century, Czarist Russia was the most reactionary state in Europe. Its economy was essentially agrarian; its political structure basically feudal. The onerous weight of autocracy had provoked successive local peasant rebellions and had mobilized anti-Czarist tendencies among the Russian intelligentsia who were ashamed of Russia's political and economic backwardness. A small class of professionals and intellectuals agitated for reform. The peripheral development of modern industry provoked further ferment by creating an urban working class, which gradually increased in number in the last decade of the nineteenth century.

Revolutionary sentiment in Russia had spoken the language of the utopian Socialism of Fourier and Saint-Simon. In the 1840's Feuerbach had made an impact on the Russian intelligentsia. Herzen, Chernyshevsky, Dobrolyubov, and Pisarev had advanced a revolutionary "realism" calculated to "reorganize consciousness" in order to transform the world in accordance with scientific principles.

The sense of urgency, the recognition that change was imminent, led the intelligentsia to "go to the people" (*v narod*), in order to loose the revolutionary impulses pent up within the peasant masses which would sweep away the old order and establish a social order of freedom, equality, and justice. In the middle of the 1870's hundreds of young Populists "went to the people" to act as a goad to rebellion. Their experience was almost always disheartening. Frequently these visionaries were met with open hostility, often with indifference. Police repression further disheartened them. Even the attempt to cater to the peasants' prejudices and predilections brought no real result. As a consequence, the revolutionary Populists were singularly ineffective in introducing revolutionary change. In a desperation borne of a conviction that the peasants would remain passive, many intellectuals abandoned Populism and had recourse to violence in the form of sporadic individual attacks on the agents of the state. "Direct action," terrorism, was mustered into the program of revolutionary activities. The major organizations directing this campaign were the terroristic *Narodnaya Volya* (the People's Will) and the *Chernyi Peredel* (the Black Partition).

March 1, 1881, marked the day of the greatest triumph for the *Narodnaya Volya*. On that day it succeeded in assassinating the very embodiment of absolutism, the Czar himself. But the price of success was the capture and execution of practically its entire Executive Committee. The path of terrorism was hazardous not only for the victims of terror, but for its advocates as well.

During the last quarter of the nineteenth century a rapid change had altered the class structure of Imperial Russia. The landed gentry were becoming gradually impoverished while a new entrepreneurial class made its appearance. The alliance of this new class with the old bureaucracy followed much the same pattern as that which characterized the development of capitalism throughout the West. The government and the new entrepreneurs collaborated to introduce industry. In the 1880's this alliance between the government and the bourgeoisie had serious implications for revolutionary theory. Already excluded from participation in Russian national life by the exclusiveness of the decaying society of estates, the intelligentsia also found itself excluded by the rising bourgeoisie. The new capitalist class was prepared to buttress the old absolutism in exchange for economic privilege and protection.

In the face of this accommodation G. V. Plekhanov, in the early 1880's, had advanced two theses: (1) that capitalism was to be the fundamental form of productive relations in the new Russia, and (2) that capitalism was the revolutionary link between the moribund feudal order and the future Socialist state, and the agent of that future order was the revolutionary proletariat.

The intellectuals who organized around Plekhanov called themselves *Osvobozhdenie Truda* (Emancipation of Labor) and advocated an orthodox classical Marxism. In 1894 Plekhanov authored *The Development of the Monist View of History* under the pseudonym of N. Beltov and the Czarist censor permitted its publication in 1895. In his volume Plekhanov expressed his conviction that the course of history followed a rational and determinate progression. Capitalism would destroy the feudal order and ultimately absolutism, both incompatible with the newly developed productive forces of Russian society. In the process capitalism must necessarily draw the Russian peasantry to the manufacturing centers, transforming it into an urban proletariat. This urban proletariat would be the bearer of the ultimate social revolution. The proletariat was the only social class capable of organizing a truly Socialist party which would assure a future of liberty and equality to all men.

During the period 1896 to 1899 a weighty tome was written to certify the accuracy of Plekhanov's conviction that capitalism had come to Russia. The volume was published in 1899 and entitled *The Development of Capitalism in Russia: The Process of the*

*Formation of a Home Market for Large Scale Industry.* Its author was a twenty-nine-year-old, who for seven years had been a convinced and dedicated Marxist. His name was V. I. Ulyanov—better known to history as Lenin.

## Lenin and the Role of Consciousness in History

Classical Marxism had left much to be desired in the analysis of the nature and dynamics of revolutionary consciousness and class organization. The history of the working-class movement in Central and Western Europe did not seem to fit theoretical expectations. Finally, the peculiar history of revolutionary activity in Russia was to produce two radically diverse assessments of revolutionary consciousness and organization of the masses.

There were those Russian revolutionaries whose faith in the revolutionary spontaneity of the masses had been destroyed. They saw the masses as essentially passive and mass violence as simply destructive. The masses were not "conscious." Having lost faith in the masses many of these agitators gave themselves over to a doctrine of terrorism. The revolution would be made by small, tightly organized bands of professional conspirators committing acts of terrorism.

Other groups, like the *narodniks,* believed that revolution lay at the heart of the Russian masses. They saw revolution as the destiny of the Russian people. In its more sophisticated expressions this view became a conviction in the revolutionary spontaneity of the masses. A revolutionary consciousness would necessarily manifest itself. Much of the history of Russian Social Democracy could be written around these two assessments of the revolutionary potential of the masses.

Developments in Central and Western Europe made the problem of revolutionary class consciousness of pressing practical and theoretical importance. The organization of the proletariat had not produced the revolutionary ardor necessary to inaugurate the Socialist millennium. While classical Marxism seemed convinced that class consciousness would mature with the maturity of large-scale industry, the overt political behavior of the working classes, organized in trade unions and political parties, seemed to belie the thesis. The working class of Central and Western Europe seemed to respond to their immediate rather than what Marxists felt to be their "ultimate" interests. They seemed more pre-occupied with increasing their present wages through trade-union agitation and extending their political liberties through legislative reform than in overthrowing the capitalist social order.

On the one hand classical Marxism seemed to argue that revolution would be the necessary consequence of economic development; and yet on the other hand, there was an unqualified insistence upon the importance of correct theory in the service of revolution. Revolution was inevitable, but correct theory was, in some crucial sense, necessary. Most of Engels' writings during his maturity, for example, were polemics against the leaders of the working class, charging them with theoretical errors which could only impair the progress toward Socialist revolution. And in his inaugural address before the Working Men's International Association in 1864, Marx had argued that the workers possessed one element of success—numbers; "but numbers weigh only in the balance, if united by combination and led by knowledge."[3] While Engels did write that Marx "relied solely and exclusively upon the intellectual development of the working class, as it necessarily had to ensue from united action and discussion," the *Communist Manifesto* had already implied that Communist theoreticians were distinguished from the proletarian movement in general in being able to advance the ultimate interests of the international proletariat as distinct from the more national and immediate interests of the local movement.[4] These theoreticians, of bourgeois origin, have "raised themselves to the level of comprehending theoretically the historical movement as a whole."[5] This segment of the bourgeoisie apparently functioned in some crucial way, but that function was never clearly formulated in the classical theory.

This combination of theoretical considerations and historical circumstances led Plekhanov to define the role of the petty-bourgeois intelligentsia as one which was devoted to "actively . . . develop and consolidate the class-consciousness of the pro-letariat."[6] The proletariat were destined to develop the requisite revolutionary consciousness; the bourgeois theoreticians could assist in its rapid manifestation. Plekhanov saw the proletariat as the truly revolutionary class in Russia. The function of the intelligentsia was to make clear to the revolutionary workers their historic role. That such a role was determined by the processes immanent in history Plekhanov never doubted. The very mechanisms of capitalist production would produce a revolutionary working class and the conditions surrounding the intelligentsia would qualify it to function as the philosophic arm of rebellion. The proletariat would be lent the sure consciousness of what it was striving for by the revolutionary intelligentsia, and the intelligentsia would assist in constructing the organization which would fashion the proletariat into an effective fighting force in the course of historic events. For Plekhanov this course of history was necessary and inevitable. He had inherited from classical Marxism an inalienable conviction that history, in the lockstep of the dialectic, was moving ineluctably toward the rational Socialist order. "When a class longing for emancipation brings about a social revolution, it acts in a way which is more or less appropriate to the desired end; and, in any case, its activity is the cause of that revolution. But this activity, together with all the aspirations which have brought it about, is itself the effect of economic revolution, and therefore, is itself determined by necessity."[7] He would later state, "Let our intelligentsia go to the workers; *life itself will make them* [the workers] *revolutionaries.*"

There seems to be some evidence that Lenin shared at least the essentials of such a faith in the spontaneity of class consciousness among the nascent proletariat. In his pamphlet of 1894, *What the "Friends of the People" Are and How They Fight the Social Democrats,* he seemed to commit himself to a strict determinism. "Marx's basic idea," he argued, was "that the development of the social-economic formations is a process of natural history. . . . By what means did Marx arrive at this basic idea? He did so by singling out the economic sphere from the various spheres of social life, by singling out *production relations* from all social relations as being basic, primary, determining all other relations."[8] Since Lenin accepted this proposition, he went on to argue that "the course of ideas depends on the course of things" as the only conclusion "compatible with scientific psychology."[9] The ideological superstructure was to be explained "*exclusively* through production relations."[10]

The logic of this commitment led him to reject the "absurd tale about free will,"[11] and to argue that the "necessity of the present order of things . . . proves the necessity of another order which must inevitably grow out of the preceding one regardless of whether men believe in it or not, whether they are conscious of it or not. . . . If the conscious element plays so subordinate a part in the history of civilization, it is self evident that a critique whose subject is civilization, can least of all take as its basis any form of, or any result of, consciousness."[12]

In the years immediately following the publication of *What the "Friends of the People" Are,* the Russian Marxists developed significant theoretical differences among themselves. In 1895 the Okhrana, the Czarist police, arrested Lenin along with almost all the major figures of the Petersburg movement of the Social Democratic party. The remaining Social Democrats increasingly gave themselves over to what Lenin termed "the path of least resistance," the path of "spontaneity." In essence what this tactic involved was a conviction that the workers would develop a spontaneous class consciousness as a consequence of their class struggles against the industrial bourgeoisie and its political collaborators. Thus during the workers' strikes of 1895 and 1896, the Social Democrats had insisted that the theory and practice of Social Democracy should be the outgrowth of the self-consciousness and independent activity of the working class. The members of the party who collected around the journal *Rabochaya Mysl* argued that Social Democracy does not create a specific class consciousness among the workers but rather the workers' class consciousness provides the theoretical content of Social Democracy.[13]

Various Marxist groups voiced similar sentiments. The Economists were convinced of the spontaneity of class consciousness. The Legal Marxists sought to legally publish their books and tracts by studiously neglecting the insurrectionary character of Marxism. They justified this neglect by arguing that working-class consciousness had not matured to the point of countenancing revolutionary demands. That these notions lent themselves to reformism can hardly be gainsaid. The conviction that objective economic conditions determine the course of revolutionary agitation made the Social Democratic party more and more a vehicle for the expression of the workers' *immediate,* as distinct from their *ultimate,* interests. The concern for *immediate* interests led to piecemeal, reformist demands. The *ultimate,* revolutionary interest receded to await the maturing of "objective circumstances." In effect, Bernstein's revisionism made its appearance in Russia.

To the Old Guard of the Social Democratic party, among whom the thirty-year-old Lenin was numbered, the issue seemed clearly defined. Either the struggle against the oppressing classes followed the course dictated by the "spontaneous" reactions of the working class in the service of its immediate interests, or the struggle pursued a strategy prepared by Social Democratic theoreticians in the service of the apocalyptic revolution. The Old Guard, and Lenin, opted for the latter alternative. In choosing such a course Lenin was compelled to modify the strict determinism to which he had committed himself in 1894. In 1900, in the first issue of *Iskra*, the journal founded to defend revolutionary Marxism from reformism, Lenin advanced a thesis which became central for the Bolshevik party: "Isolated from Social Democracy, the working-class movement becomes petty and inevitably becomes bourgeois."[14] In 1901 he added the supplement to the first thesis: the call "for the formation of a strong well-organised party, whose aim is not only to win isolated concessions but to storm the fortress of the autocracy itself. . . ."[15]

In December of 1901 Lenin formulated his thesis with still more precision: ". . . [The] 'ideologist' is worthy of the name only when he *precedes* the spontaneous movement, points out the road, and is able ahead of all others to solve all the theoretical, political, tactical, and organisational questions which the 'material elements' of the movement spontaneously encounter. . . . One must be able to point out the dangers and defects of spontaneity and to *elevate* it to the level of consciousness."[16] He argued that the "spontaneous awakening of the masses" must be led by "ideologists" "sufficiently trained theoretically to be proof against all vacillations. . . ."[17] The revolution demands "a strong and centralised organisation of revolutionaries" who would provide the "conscious element" necessary to direct the "spontaneous element."[18]

In the autumn and winter of 1901, Lenin provided a full account of his position in *What Is to Be Done?* In this book he endeavored to settle accounts with the various reformist trends which had developed out of the question of revolutionary consciousness. The question which sought resolution was that which concerned itself with the origin and nature of revolutionary consciousness. Lenin had earlier argued that the peasantry was not to be trusted to realize the Socialist revolution. The development of capitalism in Russia had precluded such a possibility. The peasant economy was being gradually and inevitably eroded, yet the peasantry, in their desire to retain their small holdings, were attempting to stay the hand of history. They demanded reforms which would ensure, rather than socialize, private property. They desired a reformed capitalism, one in which the threat to their petty holdings would dissipate.

By 1901, it had become evident to Lenin that the petty-bourgeois democrats, while they were "natural and desirable allies of Social Democracy" during the period of "bourgeois democratic revolution," could not lead the Socialist revolutionary movement either. Both the peasantry and the petty-bourgeois democrats were animated by reformist interests. Thus, not only peasant leadership was to be abjured, but Socialists must impress upon the revolutionary proletariat that in the last analysis "its interests are diametrically opposed to the interests of the bourgeoisie" as well.[19] The Socialist revolution must be proletarian, and the proletariat must possess a clear revolutionary consciousness. And this could only be the consequence of possessing a clear revolutionary theory. "Without a revolutionary theory there can be no revolutionary movement."[20] Lenin defined the fundamental issue as that which raised the problem of the "relation between consciousness and spontaneity."[21]

Lenin expressed his own position without qualification. "We have said that there could not yet be Social Democratic consciousness among the workers. *It could only be brought to them from without.* The history of all countries shows that the working class, exclusively by its own effort, is able to develop only trade-union consciousness, i.e., the conviction that it is necessary to combine in unions, fight the employers and strive to compel the government to pass necessary labor legislation, etc. The theory of Socialism, however, grew out of the philosophic, historical, and economic theories that were elaborated by the educated representatives of the propertied classes, the intellectuals. According to their social status, the founders of modern scientific Socialism, Marx and Engels, themselves belonged to the bourgeois intelligentsia. In the very same way, in Russia, the theoretical doctrine of Social Democracy arose quite independently of the spontaneous growth of the working-class movement, it arose as a natural and inevitable outcome of the development of ideas among the revolutionary socialist intelligentsia."[22] Lenin explicitly rejected the thesis that the "pure working-class movement" could formulate an independent *revolutionary* ideology for itself. Such a conception constituted a "profound mistake."[23] He proceeded to assume the position of Karl Kautsky who argued that "Socialism, as a doctrine, has its roots in modern economic relations. . . . But socialism and the class struggle arise side by side and not one out of the other; each arises under different conditions. Modern socialist consciousness can arise only on the basis of profound scientific knowledge. . . . The vehicle of science is not the proletariat, but the bourgeois intelligentsia. . . . Thus, socialist consciousness is something introduced into the proletarian class struggle from without, and not something that arose within it spontaneously."[24]

Lenin thus concluded that the spontaneity of the working class inevitably led it into "bourgeois ideology." The task of Social Democracy, then, was to "*combat spontaneity,* to *divert* the working class movement from this spontaneous, trade-unionist striving to come under the wing of the bourgeoisie. . . . A *fierce struggle against spontaneity* was necessary. . . ."[25] There was thus drawn a clear distinction between the immediate interests of the workers, which would lead them to develop a "trade union mentality," and their ultimate interests, with which they could be made familiar only by the revolutionary theory of the Socialist ideologist.[26] Only the Socialist revolutionary could raise the level of the spontaneous consciousness of the working class to the level of the program of Social Democracy. "The spontaneity of the masses demands a mass of consciousness from . . . Social Democrats."[27]

Since Lenin conceived the situation in this way,[28] his demand was for a highly organized, centralized vanguard party of revolutionary Marxists with a membership restricted to professional revolutionaries[29] capable of lifting the working class consciousness to full Socialist class consciousness.[30]

Furthermore, such an organization, highly centralized and necessarily secret, could offer little scope for what Lenin called "primitive democracy." The members of the central committees of the party could hardly, in an autocracy and under surveillance by the Czarist police, be elected to office in accordance with "broad democratic principles."[31] Such a procedure would be suicidal. It would facilitate the work of the police in searching out the leaders of the party. Periodic rotation of the leadership would promote amateurishness among them. Finally, the party leadership had more to do than draw up "detailed 'paper' rules for election systems."[32]

The party leadership must be self-selected and self-perpetuating. The organizational hierarchy must be entrusted, therefore, with the responsibility of purging itself of irresponsible or inept members. There was in fact, Lenin argued, a fairly well-developed sense of discipline which governed revolutionary circles, sternly and ruthlessly punishing every departure from the duties of Socialist responsibility.

Thus, Lenin had clearly outlined the Bolshevik vision of revolution and of revolutionary organization. He had distinguished between the "elemental destructive force of the crowd" and the "conscious destructive force of the organization of revolutionaries."[33] Socialist consciousness could only be brought to the working class through the agency of professional revolutionaries possessed of the most advanced theoretical awareness of the ultimate interests of the proletariat. Where such leadership was lacking the working class would inevitably become bourgeois. Lenin had stipulated the conditions governing the development of class consciousness among the "toiling masses." Left to their own devices not only the peasantry, but the working class as well, would become bourgeois. Only the consciousness of the professional revolutionary, expressed by a highly organized, self-perpetuating body, could insure the continuity and theoretical consistency, and the ultimate victory of the Socialist revolution.

It is significant that this first full statement of Bolshevism should bear the title of *What Is to Be Done?* Valentinov, who knew Lenin during during this period, informs us that Lenin was emphatic in his admiration of Nicholas Chernyshevsky, the author of *Chto Delat'?* (*What Is to Be Done?*), a novel written in the 1860's. The work was also the favorite of Lenin's brother Alexander, who was executed in 1887 as a consequence of the attempted assassination of Alexander III, and it was immediately after his brother's execution that Lenin read Chernyshevsky's novel. Lenin "read it in earnest and spent on it, not days, but weeks on end."[34] Chernyshevsky was to become, for Lenin, "the greatest and most talented representative of socialism before Marx." Valentinov suggested that Chernyshevsky, more than any other writer—more than Engels, or Plekhanov, or Marx himself— had influenced the decisive years of Lenin's revolutionary development. Throughout the 1880's Lenin returned to the work of Chernyshevsky, and it was probably this work that convinced Lenin that the "new age" demanded the exertion of "strong personalities"—rare men of vision, who could impose their will upon the course of events and upon the "chaotic movement of the masses." It is difficult not to see in Lenin's own *What Is to Be Done?* the reflection of Chernyshevsky's distinction between "chaotic movement" and "conscious will." Lenin, like Chernyshevsky, saw victorious Socialist revolution as the consequence of the submission of the elemental and spontaneous movement of the masses to the implacable will of a self-conscious and strong minority of professional revolutionaries. That such a conviction accorded with Chernyshevsky's work and with the traditions alive in Czarist Russia is undoubtedly true. The question that sundered the unity of the Social Democratic party was whether such a view was consonant with classical Marxism.

During the last six months of 1901, Plekhanov prepared a draft program for the Russian Social Democratic party. At the beginning of 1902 the draft program was presented to the party comrades for their inspection and criticism. Lenin wrote marginal notes on the draft program, which indicate his growing irritation with Plekhanov and his interpretation of classical Marxism. Among Lenin's major criticisms was a reminder to Plekhanov that in Russia and many other countries the "proletariat is not the majority. . . ."[35] He cited Plekhanov's lack of clarity, his lack of forcefulness. But his fundamental criticism was that while the rise of discontent was a spontaneous occurrence, an elemental destructive force, the development of the proletarian consciousness could only be "introduced by *us*," the intelligentsia of the party.[36] Moreover Lenin argued that Plekhanov had failed to indicate that the "organization of revolutionaries . . . *direct* the struggle of the proletariat."[37]

In essence Lenin denied that the working class, the proletariat, could ever attain class consciousness without the direct intervention of the professional revolutionary. Furthermore, while he insisted that tactical alliances had to be sought with the peasant and petty-bourgeois elements in Russia, he argued that the "working and exploited masses" could not arouse any popular movement without the specific intercession of the "factory workers"[38] under the direction of the "vanguard of the proletarians, the leadership of the Party." While Marx had maintained that the proletariat, because it was fettered by "radical chains," was the only class capable of rising to the consciousness of the liberating revolution, a revolution it was *compelled* to undertake, Lenin maintained that the proletariat left to itself attained only a trade-union consciousness, and remained forever incapable of waging a victorious struggle against capitalism without the direction of a small coterie of declassed bourgeois intellectuals.

As early as 1899 he held that the professional revolutionary should direct the struggle in the service of "social development," which is even "higher than the interests of the proletariat. . . ."[39] Only such a leadership, perceptive of the ultimate interests of *social development*, can mobilize the elemental strivings of the masses. Such a leadership can support the peasantry—insofar as the peasantry is capable of revolutionary struggle against the survivals of serfdom in general and the autocracy in particular. Such a leadership could support the bourgeoisie and the petty bourgeoisie in such a struggle—with the clear recognition that such support extends only as far as the interests of the party.[40] Years later Lenin said that "morality is what serves to destroy the old exploiting society and to rally all the workers around the proletariat which is building up a new, communist society."[41] Such was the morality which guided his tactical political alliances —not only with the peasantry and the petty bourgeoisie but ultimately with the proletariat who betrayed his vision of the new society. The peasantry, elements of the industrial bourgeoisie, and the petty bourgeoisie could be used in the struggle for Socialism only insofar as they remained subservient to the ultimate interests of the proletarian revolution. And the ultimate interests of the revolution were to be defined by a highly organized cadre of revolutionary intellectuals who directed the proletariat.[42]

By 1903 this seemingly radical innovation in classical Marxism led to critical intraparty discussions in Brussels and London. In

1902 Lenin had published "A Letter to a Comrade on our Organisational Tasks,"[43] in which he outlined the organizational pattern of the party which followed as a natural consequence of his theory of social revolution. The party was to be highly centralized with a hierarchical Central Organ and a Central Committee. The Central Organ would be charged with maintaining the theoretical orthodoxy of the party and the Central Committee would be the executive agency directing the party's activities. Both central bodies should be composed of "people who are in complete harmony with one another."[44] Any new committees working at the local level should be organized only with the co-operation and consent of the Central Organ and the Central Committee. "Strict centralization" was advanced over "the elective principle and decentralization." The defense against betrayal or incompetence was "comradely influence," the central bodies of the party being self-purifying and self-perpetuating. "Purging" was to be the principle of self-governance of the vanguard of the proletariat.

The Congress called at Brussels in 1903 arranged for the reorganization of an All-Russian Social Democratic party. The major political issues which had divided the Social Democrats had been by and large resolved. The advocates of political struggle and Marxist orthodoxy had won over the exponents of "spontaneous economic struggle" and revisionism. But the Congress was called to decide on the rules which would govern the reconstituted party. Lenin's views were well known. He had advanced his view concerning the function of the party with clarity and precision. He had made his view of party organization equally clear. Control was to be hierarchical with ultimate responsibility in the hands of the Central Organ of the party which was, in effect, the editorial board of *Iskra*. The local committees were to be obedient instruments of the top leadership of the party. These committees were to be military commands, transmitting the directives of the two party centers in "all directions" through factory and district subcommittees, and agitational and propaganda groups.

The Congress of 1903 was interesting for a number of reasons. In the first place it gave evidence of Lenin's formidable tactical and political acumen. The Congress had been so arranged that Lenin's faction, the Iskrists, had a clear majority of thirty-three among the fifty-one delegates. In many cases the delegates were

*Iskra* agents whom Lenin had personally sent into Russia. They had been appointed by Lenin and yet were in turn representing the local areas in which they served, thereby establishing the fateful system in which a central committee appointed a "local leadership only to have the latter designated as convention delegates to choose the central body, that is, to confirm the very men who had appointed them in the first place."[45] Lenin, convinced that his faction possessed a clear majority, was prepared for an easy victory on July 30, 1903, when the Congress convened.

The Congress had been called with a conviction that there was substantial unity on theoretical issues, and the delegates had been in part hand-picked by Lenin's faction. Plekhanov delivered the projected party program. Its adoption was a foregone conclusion, and yet the small minority under the leadership of Akimov and Martynov examined every tenet of the proposed program. Akimov, at one point, even leveled a critique at the program's attitude toward the proletariat. "The concepts Party and Proletariat," he argued, "are set in opposition to each other, the first as an active, causative, collective being, the second as a passive medium on which the Party operates. The name of the Party is used throughout as subject . . . the name of the Proletariat as object. . . ."[46]

How trenchant Akimov's criticism was is revealed by the fact that although Lenin took but little part in the discussion concerning the general program of the party, he did intercede when a suggestion was made that the phrase "and the consciousness" be included in the statement that "dissatisfaction, solidarity and numbers of the proletariat" would grow as a consequence of the contradictions inherent in capitalism.[47] Lenin took the floor to declare that the amendment was objectionable. "It would give the idea that the development of consciousness is a spontaneous thing. . . . Aside from the influence of Social Democracy, there is no *conscious* activity of the workers."[48] Martynov could only remind him that of all the Social Democratic programs in existence, the one advanced at the Unity Congress was the only one that neglected to indicate that one of the results of the development of capitalism had been "the development of the class consciousness of the proletariat."[49]

The import of Lenin's change of emphasis became clear only when the Congress came to vote upon the organizational rules of the party. The discussion on the party constitution began with

Article I in which a definition of "party member" was sought. Lenin had proposed a definition that would restrict membership to those who not only recognize and support the party program by material means but by personal participation in one of the party organizations as well. Martov suggested an alternate wording which would have permitted anyone to be enrolled as a party member who rendered personal assistance under the direction of one of the party organizations. Lenin demanded a "narrow" party of selected revolutionaries. Martov sought to broaden the popular base of the party. Trotsky proceeded to side with Martov. Axelrod joined Martov with, "Is not Lenin dreaming of the administrative subordination of an entire party to a few guardians of doctrine?"[50] While Plekhanov sided with Lenin, the rollcall gave the majority of votes to the Martov faction.

Lenin, in order to "bind up" the breach caused by Martov's victory, sought to make the new constitution ultracentralist. At that juncture the delegates of the Jewish Bund, who had been defeated in their attempt to maintain the autonomy of the Jewish Socialist organizations, left the Congress, withdrawing five votes that had been with the Martov faction. Lenin had lost the vote on Article I by six votes. Following up this advantage obtained by the bolt of the Bund delegates, Lenin proposed the dissolution of the theoretical organ *Rabochee Delo* in order to give exclusive party recognition to *Iskra*. The two delegates of the *Rabochee Delo*, offended by the proposal, withdrew from the Congress. They, too, had supported Martov. As a consequence of the change in the disposition of forces, Lenin could command a numerical majority of one or two votes. From that point on he commanded a "majority" of the Congress, and from that day on he advertised his party as Bolshevik, majoritarian.

It was at the Unity Congress of 1903 that Bolshevism took final form. The conviction that class consciousness had to be brought to the proletariat "from without" necessarily led to the demand for a highly centralized party of theoreticians who would direct the party machinery. Without the direction of this select body of intellectuals the revolution could not succeed. These Leninist theses threatened what Martynov maintained to be the recognized tenet of scientific Socialism—that the "development of the proletariat follows the spontaneous laws of nature," and that the hour of the Socialist revolution would strike only when the vast majority of the population had voluntarily come over to the side of the proletariat. In the course of the debates Plekhanov had already admitted that "if the safety of the revolution should demand the temporary limitation of one or another of the democratic principles, it would be a crime to hesitate. . . . If the people, in a moment of revolutionary enthusiasm, should elect a very favorable parliament, naturally we would try to make of it a Long Parliament. But if the elections should turn out badly for the working class, we might try to dissolve it, not at the end of two years, but in two weeks if possible. . . ."[51] Such a tactic could only be justified by committing oneself to the conviction that the vision of the new society, possessed by the leadership of the Social Democratic party, was the ultimate arbiter of a nation's political rights. If the people elect a favorable parliament, a parliament which favored the Socialist revolution as the theoreticians of the party conceived it, it would be permitted to function. Should the parliament elected not accord itself with the program of Marxist theoreticians it would be dissolved.

Only a group of men animated by a faith in the rationality of an inevitable historic process would feel qualified to assume such a responsibility. Only such an "enlightened" minority of men, laboring in the ultimate interest of history, could assume the responsibilities of decisions of this kind against the express wishes of the majority.

Most Socialists felt such a posture to be at stark variance with the fundamental convictions of Marx and Engels. Rosa Luxemburg leveled sharp criticism against the Leninist position. She indicated that Lenin's "ultra-centralist" views concentrated power in the Central Committee of the party and reduced all subsidiary organizations to its executive organs. The "blind obedience" and "mechanical subordination" of the proletariat would contradict the Marxist conviction that the proletariat had or was capable of attaining class consciousness. Marxism could only consistently advance the view that the working masses alone, and not a select few, can be the "ruler of history."[52] Trotsky's criticisms were of the same order. He argued that Lenin's position was that the revolutionary tasks of the proletariat could be performed only by a conspiratorial group of professional revolutionaries. If the advocates of "spontaneity" had failed to *educate* the proletariat, Lenin presumed to *compel* the proletariat to perform its task.

Trotsky argued that the task of the Marxist revolutionary should be to transform the elemental "instincts" of the masses into a conscious striving for political and social self-determination. A proletariat capable of exercising dictatorship over society cannot arise out of a proletariat over whom dictatorship has been exercised.[53]

Both Marx and Engels had held that the world-historical revolution would be a majoritarian, class-conscious proletarian revolution. This seemed to have been their position in the early manuscripts. Certainly it was to be the proletariat *itself* which exercised control and not a self-appointed hierarchy of declassed bourgeois intellectuals.

Yet there was more than a little ambiguity in the position of classical Marxism. Engels, in 1847, had maintained that the revolution would produce the "direct or indirect" mastery of the proletariat: direct in the case of England where the proletariat composed the majority of the population and indirect in the case of France and Germany where the majority consisted of small farmers and the petty bourgeoisie. The form this "indirect" mastery would take was not stipulated.[54] Engels elsewhere indicated that revolution could only be "authoritarian"—one segment of the population imposing, by force of arms, its will upon the remainder.[55] But in the *Manifesto* Marx and Engels had written: "All previous historical movements were movements of minorities, or in the interest of minorities. The proletarian movement is the self-conscious, independent movement of the immense majority, in the interests of the immense majority."[56] The character of the proletarian dictatorship was outlined, as we have seen, in the writings of both Marx and Engels on the Paris Commune. The proletariat would govern itself by electing, through the exercise of the universal franchise, delegates directly controlled by *imperative instructions* and subject to recall upon failure to represent their constituents. The majority of the members of society would possess the vision of the new society, a vision necessarily produced by the economic developments in bourgeois society.

If the proletarian movement of classical Marxism was the self-conscious, independent movement of the immense majority in the interests of the immense majority, Lenin's "majoritarianism," his Bolshevism, was a movement of a self-conscious, independent movement of a revolutionary minority, in the *ultimate* interests of the new society. It was a movement which grew out of the crucial indecisiveness of classical Marxism as to the nature of social consciousness. Neither Marx nor Engels ever clearly decided whether the growth of class consciousness was the spontaneous consequence of socioeconomic development or the labored effect of Socialist education from without. Certainly some quotes could be culled to support either view. But the latter view suggests a voluntarism not consonant with fundamental doctrines of historical inevitability. Yet Engels did argue for a rigid, sometimes minoritarian, authoritarianism in times of revolutionary struggle.

All in all the general impression one receives from classical Marxism is that while revolutions are made by dedicated and autocratic men, the institutions that they would erect on the ruins of the bourgeois state would represent the untrammeled will of at least the working-class majority. The appeal by Marx and Engels to the Paris Commune as a paradigm of the dictatorship of the proletariat is compelling evidence for this thesis. The dictatorship of the proletariat would rest unshakably upon universal suffrage armed with the right to recall elected delegates at any time. Lenin, on the other hand, was disdainful of majority decisions. His conviction was that the "important thing is not the number, but the correct expression of the ideas and policies of the really revolutionary proletariat."[57] And the leadership of the Bolsheviks constituted the *really* revolutionary proletariat. Only the Bolsheviks knew the correct ideas and policies which represented the ultimate interests of the toiling masses. The Bolsheviks alone possessed the "only scientific conception of history."[58] Armed with such a conception, the professional revolutionaries of the Bolshevik party had a mandate from history. While Lenin granted that a revolution could not be made by a minority of conspirators—that it must be the work of an entire people—that specific objective conditions were necessary for revolutionary victory—he argued that a well-organized revolutionary leadership seizes the "elemental, destructive movement" of the people and guides it to fulfillment, to a goal truly perceived only by the theoreticians of scientific Socialism.

As A. G. Meyer indicates, Lenin was torn between two judgments about the proletariat. He was optimistic when the working classes undertook some spontaneous act of revolutionary activity. At the height of the revolutions of 1905 he could write, "The working-class is instinctively, spontaneously, Social Democratic," and further, "The special condition of the proletariat in capitalistic society leads to a striving of workers for socialism; a union of them with the Socialist Party bursts forth with spontaneous force in the very early stages of the movement."[59] Yet his opposing judgment that true class consciousness, an awareness of *ultimate* interests, had to be brought to the proletariat from without seemed to determine his ultimate conception of party organization and revolutionary tactics. The ambiguity of the original theses of classical Marxism produced Lenin's ambivalence toward the consciousness of the working class.

Marx and Engels seemed to see the material realities of life driving the working class into revolutionary activity. That activity would at the same time engender a clear consciousness of its ultimate interests. The consummation of this process would be the proletarian revolution itself, which would be accompanied by a change in "human nature," giving rise to "communist consciousness on a mass scale."[60] Men made history—but only under determinate conditions, and the life conditions of men determined their social consciousness. The consciousness of men, their subjective motives for action, were explicable only by the economics of an epoch. Lenin said as much in the spring and summer of 1894 when he was twenty-four years of age. The theoretical tensions created by the "betrayal" of revolutionary Marxism by German Social Democracy, as well as conditions prevailing in Czarist Russia, found resolution only in his subsequent theory of "vanguardism," which saw true class consciousness as the product of the activity of a small professional class of dedicated revolutionaries forever insulated from revisionism by their conviction in the historical inevitability of Socialist revolution.

Lenin's distinctions between "consciousness" and "spontaneity," between Socialism and working-class movements, were clearly designed to serve as an initial explanation for the missing Western European revolution. We have suggested some of the implications for the history of Russia and for contemporary Soviet ideology. Yet there remained further tensions in the original formulations of classical Marxism. The attempts to resolve the difficulties were to lead to still more portentous modifications in classical Marxism.

## Lenin and Capitalism in Its Final Stage

Lenin's thesis that consciousness must be brought to the working-class movement by Socialist revolutionaries was designed to satisfy the demands of classical Marxism as a theory of history. The objective conditions for revolution obtained in the West and yet revolution was not forthcoming. The responsibility could be charged to a lack of theoretical consistency or to a lack of dedication on the part of the vanguard of the proletariat. Left to its own devices, the proletariat could attain only a trade-union consciousness. Yet it became increasingly apparent that a theoretical conviction that the objective conditions for revolution *should* obtain in Western Europe did not warrant saying that they *did* obtain.

Revolutionary Marxism seemed predicated on the notion of an absolute increase in poverty among the working class. The fall of wages below a subsistence minimum would compel revolution. Yet an objective appraisal of the facts indicated that there was little evidence of such an absolute fall in the standard of living. As early as 1902 Lenin admitted that one could not speak of an absolute increase of poverty among the working class; at best one could refer to the tendency of capitalism to produce such an effect.[61] With such qualifications, and with reservations on the nature and origin of Socialist consciousness, Lenin still retained a substantially classical Marxist position.

Throughout the first decade of the twentieth century Lenin consistently sought to fit the objective facts into the classical Marxist formulae. But orthodox Marxism had not prepared Lenin for the advent of the First World War, in which the proletarian masses of the West would throw themselves into the holocaust of international war with patriotic abandon—at complete variance with Marxist expectations. Classical Marxism had maintained that the proletariat had no objective interest in the international wars provoked by bourgeois competition. As early as 1848 Marx and Engels had maintained that the proletariat had attained the sophistication which made "national chauvinism" impossible. Again during the two months of the Paris Commune the working class had, according to Marx, evidenced its internationalism by renouncing "national interest" as a proletarian concern. Theoretically, war on the scale which broke out in 1914 could be nothing more than the clarion call for proletarian revolution. The working class would not surrender itself as cannon fodder to the industrial bourgeoisie.

Prior to August, 1914, all Marxists were substantially agreed that the advanced material conditions of life in the capitalist economies of the West rendered the working classes increasingly international, increasingly mature, increasingly capable of assuming responsible power. With the outbreak of the world conflict, however, the mass working-class parties of the most advanced capitalist countries were instrumental in throwing millions of workers across national boundaries in a bloody "defense of the Fatherland." The German Social Democratic party, an advanced party of Marxist revolutionaries, voted war credits for the German Emperor. The Socialists of France rose to defend the "democratic war." Even the most active of the Italian Socialists, Mussolini, led an aggressive section of the Italian Socialist party in a program of interventionism.

Lenin was well aware of the implications these events had for theoretical Marxism. At first, he steadfastly refused to believe that the Second International had betrayed its clear and unambiguous stand against any imperialist war. The Stuttgart Congress of 1907, the grandest international display of Socialist unity the world had ever seen, had voted "in a revolutionary spirit" against any imperialist adventures. In 1912 an emergency congress was held at Basel to define the Socialist position on the threatening war. Again the commitment was to oppose war, to make "war against war." Certainly Lenin was not prepared for the reality he had to face after August, 1914. Upon the declaration of war there were joyous celebrations by the proletariat of Vienna, Berlin, Paris, St. Petersburg, and London. Lenin found it impossible to make these events compatible with the classical Marxism he knew. His attempt to find an adequate explanation of these events led to his "creative development" of Marxism and found expression in a brief book entitled *Imperialism: The Highest Stage of Capitalism.*[62]

In the period between 1895—the year of Engels' death—and 1914, Lenin was prepared to make relatively minor modifications in the formulations of classical Marxism, modifications generally supported by a plausible interpretation of the original Marxist texts. But in the traumatic period between 1914 and 1916 Lenin had to undertake an analysis of the entire edifice of classical Marxism to make the theory compatible with facts that could not be explained away. He sought to explain how the "utter betrayal of socialism," the "complete desertion to the side of the bourgeoisie," and "the split in the labor movement" were "bound up with . . . objective conditions. . . ."[63] In this attempt Lenin had recourse to the works of J. A. Hobson, R. Luxemburg, R. Hilferding, and N. Bukharin. All had suggested that capitalism had entered a *new* phase, one which had not been fully anticipated by Marx and Engels. Marx's analysis had been of a capitalist economy in abstraction, and even his final volume of *Capital* had not assessed the impact of the various factors which influenced the tendencies with which he was concerned. Lenin followed his Marxist and non-Marxist predecessors and tried to provide the concreteness history demanded. While he borrowed liberally from them all, he formulated his theses in a rigorous and unique fashion. He was offering an explanation of the most momentous events of his time, which he sought to explain as a consequence of objective conditions. He attempted to explain not only the missing proletarian revolution of the West, but also the betrayal of Socialism by large sections of the working class itself.

Classical Marxism, with its commitment to a logic of history, had at least suggested that the forces of production would inevitably throw off the fetters of capitalism. The revolutionary consciousness of the proletariat would mature in direct proportion with the development of the productive forces. In actual fact, where those forces were most mature, and the proletariat most numerous, the working class was little disposed to revolution. In the backward countries where there was revolutionary potential, primitive economic conditions could not support a Socialist economy. And finally, nationalism continued to inflame that class which, according to classical Marxism, "knew no country." The "contradictions" of capitalism had not proved fatal.

Lenin's theory of imperialism was advanced as an explanation of these apparent discrepancies which history had revealed in the formulations of classical Marxism. In its simplest form Lenin's theory is that "capitalism has grown into a world system of colonial oppression and of the financial strangulation of the overwhelming majority of the people of the world by a handful of 'advanced' countries."[64] The bourgeoisie of these "world marauder" nations employ the "super-profits" plundered from the backward areas to "bribe the labor leaders and the upper stratum of the labor aristocracy" of their own economy, producing a stratum of toilers who "live in more or less petty-bourgeois conditions of life."[65] "This stratum of bourgeoisified workers, or the 'labor aristocracy,' who are quite philistine in their mode of life, in the size of their earnings and in their outlook, serves as the principal prop of the Second International, and, in our days, the principal *social . . . prop of the bourgeoisie.* They are the real *agents of the bourgeoisie in the labor movement,* the labor lieutenants of the capitalist class, real channels of reformism and chauvinism. In the civil war between the proletariat and the bourgeoisie they inevitably, and in no small numbers, stand side by side with the bourgeoisie. . . . Not the slightest progress can be made toward the solution of the practical problems of the Communist movement and of the impending social revolution unless the economic roots of this phenomenon are understood and unless its political and sociological significance is appreciated."[66]

Thus Lenin took up a theme left unresolved by both Marx and Engels—the question of the class consciousness of the proletariat. According to Lenin, Marx and Engels had not been able to analyze the situation because capitalism had not yet appeared in its final stage. Both Marx and Engels were aware that the working class of the advanced countries had become increasingly bourgeois in outlook. Engels had in fact, as early as 1858, given an analysis very similar to that proposed by Lenin. He maintained that the English had produced a "bourgeois proletariat." This seemed appropriate to the most "bourgeois nation" of the world, a nation that "exploited the entire world."[67] But such a thesis remained an anomaly in classical Marxism, its implications not drawn out for Socialist practice. In his *Imperialism* Lenin sought to draw them out.

Lenin indicated that the inevitable process of concentration of industry, anticipated by Marx,[68] had produced combines that dominated capitalist economy. This monopoly capitalism he understood as the essence of imperialism. "Cartels become one of the foundations of the whole of economic life. Capitalism has been transformed into imperialism."[69] These industrial giants combine in order to lessen the perils of anarchy in production. They enter into agreements which mitigate, on the national level, the fluctuations which produce crisis. At the same time the financial institutions of capitalism, hitherto only modest intermediaries in the processes of production, resolve themselves into monopolies controlling the liquid capital and credit resources of the economy. Their control over the available financial resources of the community, as well as their privileged access to the affairs of the various enterprises with which they become connected, permits them increasingly to dominate the whole economy. Finance capital proceeds to exercise control over industrial capital through a variety of means—not the least of which is minority control, a technique increasingly employed in advanced economies where stock companies have become essential. Since small shareholders generally are not disposed, or find it impossible, to attend general meetings, finance capitalists with minority holdings can exercise domination.[70] Through all the techniques which modern capitalism affords, finance capital gains increasing control over the processes of material production. The union of financial and industrial capital ultimately leads to a union between both and the state.

In the economy itself the division between ownership and the management of industrial capital becomes more pronounced. More and more characteristic of monopoly capitalism is the development of a rentier class, a class that lives entirely on income from money capital without exercising any entrepreneurial function. Furthermore, in the most advanced capitalist states this class lends money to the backward areas of the world in order to drain off enormous profits. "Thus, in one way or another, nearly the whole world [becomes] more or less the debtor to the . . . banker countries. . . ."[71] Under the conditions of finance or monopoly capitalism, the export of capital becomes a typical feature. Capitalism becomes overripe. It finds itself burdened by a surplus of investment capital because of the restricted consumer potential of the home market and the consequent capital saturation in industry. Investment capital must find outlets in foreign investment opportunities.[72]

Under such conditions the world is progressively divided up among the principal capitalist combines—the cartels, syndicates, and trusts. These industrial combinations not only impose their control over the national economy but extend their agreements to cover the international consumer and capital investment market. Each such division of the world market seeks to stabilize the international situation. But the division of the world market once effected does not preclude subsequent redivisions. The contradictions of capitalist competition manifest themselves at a higher level. Where competition had hitherto led to local dislocations, even national crises, the necessary policies which attend imperialism lead to international war as each capitalist combine seeks to involve its nation in the protection of its foreign interests. Thus the *forms* of capitalist competition have changed, but their *essence* remains the same. The capitalists of the world are compelled to compete for world markets for their surplus produce as well as for their surplus capital. The division of the available world market is made on the basis of the relative strength of the several capitalist nations. As a consequence the bourgeoisie of each capitalist nation needs an imposing military machine constantly at its disposal.

Monopoly capitalism has solved the immediate contradictions of capitalism by seizing colonies throughout the world as market supplements for its commodities and its capital. This seizure of economic territories further offers a vent for surplus labor. Finally, the profits accrued in the plunder of peripheral areas permit concessions to important strata among the working population, thereby winning them over to capitalism. But the *essence* of capitalist contradictions has not been resolved.

Since each capitalist power bargains from a position of strength, any momentary weakness may be the occasion for a colonial redivision. Any realignment of forces, any temporary internal crisis, may prove the occasion for redistribution. Finance capitalism, in order to secure sources of raw materials and market supplements for its commodities as well as its capital, is driven to seize colonies everywhere in the world. In order to maintain and extend its colonial possessions it is compelled to develop an oppressive military machinery, forever ready to embark on a sanguinary struggle for international booty. Since the turn of the century the world has been completely divided among the major capitalist contenders. The First World War was the first war of redivision.

The fact that large segments of the working class benefit by the profits which accrue to monopoly capitalism involves them in the ideology of imperialism. The increased number of state contracts for the manufacture of arms, the relative economic stability brought about by market supplements in the form of military expenditures and foreign export trade, the reduction of the standing army of surplus labor, all conduce to the development of "two fundamental trends in the working-class movement."[73] One of these is revisionist, apologist, prepared to see in imperialism the resolution of the contradictions of capitalism; the other is revolutionary, possessed of the full consciousness of the economic parasitism of capitalism at the stage of its highest development. "Imperialism, which means the partition of the world, and the exploitation of other countries . . . which means high monopoly profits for a handful of very rich countries, creates the economic possibility of corrupting the upper strata of the proletariat, and thereby fosters, gives form to, and strengthens opportunism."[74] . . . Imperialism has the tendency to create privileged sections even among the workers, and to detach them from the main proletarian masses."[75]

Several conclusions clearly emerge from Lenin's analysis. (1) It is evident that under the conditions of monopoly capitalism revolutionary Socialists can expect support from only a segment of the proletariat of the advanced capitalist countries. (2) Since such is the case, these countries can no longer be conceived as the countries in which the proletarian revolution will necessarily *first* take place. (3) Proletarian revolution, led by a small vanguard of the world proletariat, may well break out in the peripheral, economically backward countries which suffer directly through the exploitative policies of world imperialism.[76]

Lenin maintained that a "privileged layer of the proletariat in the imperialist countries lives partly at the expense of hundreds of millions of uncivilized peoples."[77] Its vested interest in its country's imperialist policies breeds divisiveness among the working people of advanced capitalist nations, further reducing the proletariat's revolutionary potential and its international class solidarity.

Lenin's analysis asserts that capitalism cannot function without producing the social forces which will inevitably lead to its own destruction. Both classical Marxism and Leninism attempt to demonstrate that there are real forces within capitalist society that are inevitably destined to destroy the social relations which constitute capitalism as a system. The distinction is to be found, of course, in the identification of those forces. For classical Marxism the force is the mature and class-conscious proletariat of the advanced capitalist countries, which—spontaneously organized into a revolutionary political party—once having seized power, constructs Socialism upon the elaborate industrial base it has inherited from capitalism. Leninism, on the other hand, sees the most elemental anticapitalist forces arising in the backward nations of the earth where the weight of capitalist exploitation presses most heavily on the toiling masses. But such masses can hardly be conscious of the ultimate interests of the international proletariat and must, necessarily, be led by revolutionary specialists in the *name* of the proletariat. Such revolutions are made by self-conscious leaders, not by self-conscious masses. Such revolutions can serve only as preliminaries to world revolution, for Lenin was sufficiently orthodox to understand that Socialism could never come to an economy resting on a non-capitalist or primitive economic base. Socialism demands the broad base of mature capitalist industry; it could come only when all the potential of capitalism had matured. Thus while revolutionary potential becomes increasingly manifest in the backward nations —the class antagonisms (nations rather than classes becoming protagonists) having been shifted to the international plane— Lenin made no attempt to argue for Socialism in the underdeveloped peripheral areas.

Thus in October, 1917, Lenin argued that revolution was becoming increasingly likely in the "proletarian" or backward nations; and yet as late as the spring of that same year he continued to maintain that such revolutions, should they not spark revolutions in the advanced capitalist countries, must run counter to the logic of history and would be ahistorical accidents.[78]

Marx and Engels, in their own time, had suggested that revolution might break out in a backward locality, and by dint of the same logic, in backward countries. They had not denied the possibility that a small section of the industrial proletariat might carry the mass of "toilers" with it in revolution. In the *German Ideology* they suggested that "big industry does not attain equal levels of development in every locality of a country. This does not, however, retard the class movement of the proletariat, because the proletarians produced by big industry assume leadership over this movement and carry the entire mass with them because the workers who are excluded from large-scale industry are reduced by this exclusion to an even more miserable condition of life than the workers of large-scale industry itself. Furthermore, the countries in which big industry has developed have an impact on the more or less non-industrial countries, insofar as world traffic has dragged them into the universal struggle of competition."[79] But this development would accord with the general classical theory only if the revolutionary activities of the peripheral areas were preliminaries for the worldwide proletarian revolution. Consequently, for Marx, a revolution in Russia seemed to have significance only if it served as a "signal for proletarian revolution in the West. . . ."[80] While Lenin was content to modify classical Marxism to the extent of seeing industrial maturity and revolutionary potential developing in inverse rather than in direct proportion to each other, he was not prepared to maintain that Socialism could arise on a primitive, protocapitalist economic base. All the Marxists of Russia were aware of the economic backwardness of their nation. They had almost universally understood that Socialism presupposes capitalism—a mature productive base, a high productivity of labor, and a class-conscious, skilled, and disciplined working class. Without these necessary conditions there could be no Socialism. Even Lenin had argued in 1905 that the bourgeois revolution in Russia was a necessary historical antecedent,[81] and in his *The Development of Capitalism in Russia*, he outlined the *progressive* character of capitalist industrialization.[82] Socialism could only succeed a mature capitalism.

Everything we know of Lenin's analysis indicates that at least until 1919 he did not consider Socialism in technologically backward Russia as a serious possibility.[83] He sought to justify the Russian Revolution by indicating that it marked a necessary preliminary phase to the world revolution which he felt to be imminent. It was not an "adventure" as his critics charged. The revolution in Russia was to serve as a spark which would ignite a worldwide proletarian conflagration. Only if a Russian revolution signaled a proletarian revolution in the West—which would make the international working class the heir of the economic base developed by capitalism—would Socialism be possible. Thus, in

1918, Lenin argued that the Russian Revolution was justified, since it had caused "a whole group of countries [to be] seized with the flame of workers' revolution. In this respect our efforts and sacrifices . . . have been justified. They have turned out not to be an adventure, as claimed by the slander of our enemy, but a necessary transition to the international revolution. . . ."[84]

It was only in 1920 that Lenin realized that the world revolution might not take the form of an immediate cataclysmic upheaval but rather might be accomplished in the course of a series of wars and revolutions. Yet he continued to conceive Russia as a jumping-off place for international revolution. It is doubtful if he ever conceived of Russia developing by itself an industrial base for Socialism. That this was the case is supported by Stalin's appraisal of Leninism written in May, 1924. "The principal task of socialism—the organization of socialist production—has still to be fulfilled. Can this task be fulfilled, can the final victory of socialism be achieved in one country, without the joint efforts of the proletarians in several advanced countries? No, it cannot."[85]

During the long months of Lenin's final illness and in the period immediately following his death the question of what course the Russian Revolution would take became increasingly urgent. By the end of 1924, less than a year after the death of Lenin, Stalin was already advancing the thesis of Socialism in one country.[86] In 1926 Stalin published a "revised" edition of his *Fundamentals of Leninism*. In May of 1924 he had maintained that a world revolution was a prerequisite for Russian Socialism. Now he announced that the Soviet Union would create, out of its own resources, an economic base for Socialism within the confines of its own territory. Russia was to embark on a program of rapid industrialization to create the "socialist foundation for the national economy."[87] While Lenin had certainly been more and more forced by circumstances to just such a position, it was Stalin who broke with past theory by advancing the conception that the superstructure of society could create its own base! The course of innovations upon the classical theory, at first so minor they caused little stir in the ranks of Russian Social Democracy, finally reached its culmination. Stalin inverted the basic laws of classical Marxism. Political action came to determine economic development; social consciousness was to create social relations;

and man's being was to be a product of his consciousness. For the convenience of the historians of Marxism, Stalin catalogued the changes in classical theory in the series of speeches he made immediately following the death of Lenin. Formerly, Stalin maintained, it was held that the working class undertakes revolution spontaneously with a clear consciousness of its own ultimate purposes. Formerly, the analysis of the prerequisites for the proletarian revolution was approached from the point of view of the economic state of individual countries. Formerly, it was the accepted thing to speak of the existence or absence of objective conditions for proletarian revolution in individual countries, or, to be more precise, in one or another industrially developed country. Formerly, it was held that proletarian revolutions would manifest themselves in countries where "industry is more developed, where the proletariat constitutes the majority, where there is more culture, where there is more democracy." Such views, Stalin announced, were no longer tenable.[88] Many Marxists had no difficulty in recognizing these formerly held views as those of classical Marxism.

## Lenin and the Theory of the State

In 1919 Lenin asserted that the basic question upon which all political issues turned was the question of the state.[89] He maintained that every political question must ultimately turn upon one or another conception of the state, its essence and its significance. In his unfinished work, *The State and Revolution,* interrupted by the October Revolution in Russia, he maintained that because of the world situation the question of the state had acquired particular importance both in theory and in practical politics.[90] In this work Lenin undertook to defend the Marxist theory of the state against the revisions of the "opportunists" and the "social chauvinists" of the Second International, as well as to bring to it the experiences of the Russian revolutions of 1905 and 1917.

In his exposition Lenin employed the theory of the state advanced in the mature writings of classical Marxism, relying primarily on Engels' *Anti-Dühring* of 1876 and the *Origin of the Family, Private Property and the State* of 1884. Lenin understood the state to be a "special group of people whose only occupation is to govern,"[91] a "special category of people who are set apart to rule others and, for the sake and purpose of rule, systematically and permanently to wield a certain apparatus of coercion, an apparatus of violence. . . ."[92] The state is a device specifically designed to secure the control of an armed minority over a class-riven society.

Lenin held that the state arises out of the division of society into classes. "It appears wherever and whenever a division of society into classes appears, whenever exploiters and exploited appear."[93] The state is therefore a historically conditioned phenomenon.[94] But while its form is conditioned by time and circumstance, its essence remains the same. "According to Marx, the state is an organ of class rule, an organ for the *oppression* of one class by another; it is the creation of 'order,' which legalizes and perpetuates this oppression. . . ."[95] During the era of slavery the state, whether it took the form of a monarchy or a republic, whether it was aristocratic or democratic, was a *dictatorship of the slaveholding class*.[96] Similarly, whatever form the capitalist state takes, whether it be monarchical, republican, dictatorial, or democratic, it forever remains a *dictatorship of the bourgeoisie*.[97]

This account relates state, class, and exploitation to one another and summarizes the mature classical Marxist theory of the state. The state is understood as a historical product, the consequence of irreconcilable antagonisms between an exploiting class and an exploited class. The state arises to establish "order," to legalize the property relations established by the oppressors. In a society in which exploitation has become impossible there are no classes. There can consequently be no state.[98]

Lenin's interpretation of the state necessarily involves a conception of the essence of the state as a dictatorship, that is, as the imposition of the will of one class upon another by force "unrestricted by any laws."[99] Any constitution—any laws codified by the state—is a set of rules for securing the class dictatorship. Constitutional law and political rule are ultimately power won and maintained by the violence of one class directed against another. The violence can be directed against the spirit or the flesh. The "conscious hypocrites, the priests and scientists" who defend the bourgeois state, those who have been "bribed" by the dominant class, are subject to a "gentle" but oppressive suasion.[100] The workers themselves, so "crushed by want and poverty" that they cannot concern themselves with political issues, are subject to direct and brutal violence.[101] Even in the most "democratic" of bourgeois states "the fact is that . . . capital dominates, and every attempt of the workers to achieve the slightest real improvement in their condition is immediately met by civil war."[102]

Lenin's position is essentially that the ultimate source of law is the unrestricted power of a class whose dominance is the consequence of developments in the material base of society. The mode of production requires a specific form of social relations. The class representing that specific form must necessarily seize power; it is *compelled* to seize power. Its very life conditions compel its accession to dominance. If there is any "right" which supports the dictatorship of a class, it is the "right" to overthrow the political institutions and productive relations which inhibit the free development of the forces of production.[103] This is the "historic duty" of the revolutionary class.

In this sense Lenin committed himself to the primacy of economics over politics, and in this sense he was consistent with classical Marxism, which criticized Bakunin's and Heinzen's conception that it was the state that created the mode of production rather than the mode of production which created the state.[104] Only when this primacy of the economic over the political is appreciated can the historical fact that minorities have always dominated vast majorities be understood. If political decisions are the ultimate arbiters of economic development, then the revolutionary succession of economic classes becomes inexplicable. We would have to believe that one class would voluntarily call up another to replace it; for if politics is decisive we would have to assume, as Engels suggests, that the dominant class decided to have itself succeeded.[105] The historic evidence is rather that the origins of political power are to be sought in the conditions prevailing in the productive base of society. Control over the instruments and organization of force enables minorities to wrest political control and impose their will by force unrestrained by law. To stabilize their accession they codify laws. The law, Marx and Engels contended, is "the will of a class exalted into statutes, a will which acquires its content from the material conditions of existence of [a specific] class."[106]

Each system of exploitation codified in the laws of the state is based upon the dominance of a specific social and economic class. Since each state is in essence the instrument of a given class, only reforms which do not threaten the vital interests of the dominant class are possible. To expect, Lenin maintained, that reforms would be permitted which threatened the essential class structure of the state would be naive.[107] Consequently the supersession of the bourgeois state by the proletarian state is impossible without a violent revolution.[108] The democratic republic which the capitalist mode of production invariably produces is "the best political shell" for the furtherance of its class interests,[109] and no change of personnel or institutions or parties can alter its essence as a bourgeois tool of exploitation. While the bourgeois democratic state appears to be controlled by the entire population through periodic elections, Lenin understood the actuality to be nothing more than an episodic change of personnel, an opportunity for the proletariat to choose which members of the privileged classes would exercise control.

Capitalist economy is supposedly controlled by a series of competitive exchanges in a free market in which all members of society participate, and bourgeois democracy is supposedly controlled by free elections in which all participate as candidates or through the exercise of suffrage. Lenin, and classical Marxism, held that neither was the case. The individual worker in the capitalist system has as much chance of becoming director of a capitalist combine as he has of becoming president of the republic. Beneath the surface of seeming equality and freedom lie the material constraints and limitations imposed by a class-riven society composed of possessing and propertyless classes.

The state machinery of bourgeois democracy is the perfected tool of class dominance. "All the revolutions which have occurred up to now [have] perfected the state machine," Lenin argued— it is the historic task of the proletariat to smash it.[110] This is what Lenin termed the "chief and fundamental point in the Marxian doctrine of the state."[111]

The proletariat is destined to end the exploitation of man by man. Consequently the proletariat is destined to destroy forever the apparatus of repression, the machinery of that exploitation: the state. "The course of events compels the revolution to 'concentrate all its forces of destruction' against state power, and to set itself the aim, not of perfecting the state machine, but of *smashing and destroying it.*"[112] The interests of both the workers and the peasants, the exploited toiling masses, unites them in the purpose of smashing the state apparatus; it places before them the common task of removing the machinery of the political state and replacing it with something new. That something new was to be "something which is no longer really the state"[113]—a revolutionary organ of the will of the immense majority of working people, something on the order of the Paris Commune.

The revolutionary task of such a popular organ is to remove the special executive and administrative organs of bourgeois dominance—the standing army and the bureaucracy.[114] As early as 1895 Lenin had paid particular attention to the role of the bureaucracy.[115] He understood the bureaucracy to be neither a class nor a part of a class since its members have no special relation to the means of production nor do they derive from any particular class. But like priests, philosophers, economists, and prostitutes, members of the bureaucracy form a social stratum or group drawn from *any* class; their character, interests, and world outlook are determined by those who provide them with their income. They are the intelligentsia whose services are bought by the capitalist class. To eliminate the possibility of such a social group persisting into the proletarian era Lenin proposed the adoption of Marx's formula: the functionaries of the popular will would be "elective, responsible" and their explicit mandates would be "revocable,"[116] "*subject to recall* at the first demand of the people."[117]

In 1917 Lenin held that capitalism had created large-scale production, factories, railways, the postal service, and telephones, all of which had simplified the majority of the functions of the old state power to such a degree that they could be reduced to exceedingly simple operations of registration, filing, and checking —activities that could be performed easily by any literate person at ordinary workmen's wages.[118] Thus the bureaucratic functions were to be stripped of every shadow of privilege and all officials were to be "without exception, elected and subject to recall *at any time,* their salaries reduced to the level of ordinary 'workmen's wages'. . . ."[119]

In essence this was Lenin's vision of the state in 1917. He saw the destruction of the bourgeois state and the banishment of its horde of bureaucratic lackeys. The workers themselves would organize large-scale production on the basis of what capitalism had already created. They would rely on their own experience as workers, voluntarily submitting to the discipline required by production, while the role of the state officials would be reduced to that "of simply carrying out [the workers'] instructions as responsible, revocable, modestly paid 'foremen and bookkeepers' (of course, with the aid of technicians of all sorts, types and degrees)."[120] That was what he construed as the task of the proletariat. Workers so organized would subsequently "voluntarily amalgamate" their "communes" into a nation in a process Lenin called "voluntary centralism."[121] That was what the proletariat must "*start* with in accomplishing the proletarian revolution."[122]

This was not to say that the state would be abolished with the successful revolution. The state, which would not really be a state at all, [123] would take on a "revolutionary and transient form."[124] It would be a residual state which would finally crush the resistance of the bourgeoisie. The proletarian state would ensure the revolution against the forces of counterrevolution. With such a machine, such a "bludegon,"[125] the proletariat would destroy all exploitation. The new type of state, the state of workers', soliders', and peasants' soviets, would suppress counterrevolution during the period of revolution in general and in the period of transition from capitalism to Socialism.[126]

Under the new state's political form, the emancipation of labor would work itself out. This new political form is shorn of many of the functions that had hitherto characterized the state. It is a state markedly diminished in size and complexity, for the "people can suppress the exploiters . . . with a very simple 'machine,' almost without a 'machine,' without a special apparatus. . . ."[127]

The state withers away, finally, when there is no one to suppress. Under Communism there would be no necessity for a state. Individual excesses on the part of persons would be dealt with as simply and as readily as any crowd of civilized people interferes to put a stop to a scuffle or to prevent a woman from being assaulted. Furthermore, crime—whose fundamental cause is exploitation and privation—will be eliminated with the abundance which will attend Communism.

This was Lenin's vision of the good society on the eve of the

Bolshevik Revolution. It was substantially in accord with classical Marxism. The state would gradually wither away as it became more and more fully representative of society as whole, a society in which men, organized in free self-administering productive associations,[128] left the precincts of necessity and entered the realm of freedom. It was a radically democratic vision in which the governance of society was seen to result from the voluntary and rational choice of mature and self-conscious workers who understood not only their own ultimate interests, but also the techniques necessary to control the productive processes inherited from capitalism.

Immediately following Lenin's accession to power in November, 1917, the first Decree on Workers' Control was issued which transferred the control of industry to the workers, who were to administer it directly and locally through elected committees.[129] Lenin was apparently convinced that the course of history would pursue the logic of the reformed materialist conception of history that he had made his own. He saw the immediate future as one in which the proletariat itself would undertake the "positive or creative work of laying down an extremely complex and fine network of new organizational relations, comprising the planned production and distribution of products necessary for the existence of tens of millions of people."[130] All this was to be accomplished under conditions which augured a speedy withering away of the state as an agency of class war and coercion. The Soviet state was to be a "commune-type" state in which the working class would rule itself in a self-administering, voluntarily centralized co-operative enterprise. The decrees on workers' control indicate that Lenin was committed to this conception of "new freedom."[131] In March, 1918, he asked that the workers be given control "over the entire production and distribution of products."

Less than a month later, however, Lenin announced that it would be necessary to "compromise . . . the principles of the Paris Commune and of every proletarian power. . . ."[132] The reasons for the compromise of the principles he had barely laid down were given with candor. While the highest type of state had been introduced in Russia, the most decisive step in the transition to Socialism had not yet been taken. That decisive step was "the organization of the strictest . . . nation-wide accounting and control of production and of the distribution of goods," followed by the "second and equally essential material condition . . . viz., raising the productivity of labor on a national scale."[133]

A scant time before, Lenin had maintained that capitalism in Russia had created the conditions which permitted the working class to "simply" introduce workers' control. In April, 1918, he argued more realistically, "Had our proletariat, after capturing power, quickly solved the problem of accounting, control and organization on a national scale (which was impossible owing to the war and the backwardness of Russia)," then the departure from the principles of the Commune would not have been necessary. In arguing in such a manner Lenin was simply making explicit what every Marxist had long been aware of. Russia was a backward country. It would have been impossible to introduce a "commune-type" proletarian state on its primitive economic base. Lenin was certainly aware of the primitive state of Russian capitalism. Yet in his *State and Revolution* he argued as though capitalism in Russia were mature, as though the base which modern industry had created in Russia were sufficiently broad to permit the introduction of at least the first stage of Socialism.

Both Marx and Engels had argued that the transition from capitalism to Socialism would involve nothing more than stripping away the capitalist integument from the matured productive forces. They maintained that all that needed to be changed after the victorious proletarian revolution were capitalist social relations. Capitalism would have created a Socialist economy and matured the economic potential to the point where the very abundance of commodities would periodically produce a glut, crises of overabundance. Capitalism would have matured the proletariat by disciplining it in the armies of labor and training it in the tasks requisite to industrial efficiency and self-administration. Moreover, Socialism would have already made its appearance within capitalism in the form of co-operatives. Marx indicated that the new mode of production would grow naturally out of the old *"when the development of the material forces of production and of the corresponding forms of social production [had] reached a certain stage."*[134]

Russia had not reached such a stage. What Russia lacked was a material base upon which Socialist relations could be developed. The tasks that faced the newly hatched Soviet state were the organization of industry and the overall increase of productivity. Socialism could come to backward Russia only if Soviet administration could be combined with the "achievements of capitalism."[135] But Russia could only realize the achievements of capitalism under Socialism. The proletariat had captured an unripe economy. It was evident to Lenin that "the use of compulsion" was necessary if the revolution was not to be lost.[136]

"Large scale machine industry," Lenin announced, ". . . calls for absolute and strict unity of will, which directs the joint labors of hundreds, thousands and tens of thousands of people. The technical, economic and historical necessity of this is obvious, and all those who have thought about socialism have always regarded it as one of the conditions of socialism. But how can strict unity of will be ensured?—by thousands subordinating their will to the will of one.

"Given ideal class consciousness and discipline on the part of those taking part in the common work, this subordination would rather remind one of the mild leadership of a conductor of an orchestra. It may assume the sharp forms of a dictatorship if ideal discipline and class consciousness are lacking. . . . Today the . . . revolution demands—precisely in the interests of its development and consolidation, precisely in the interests of socialism—that the masses *unquestioningly obey the single will* of the leaders of the labor process."[137]

The backwardness of the economic conditions in Russia made the organization of industry and an increase in overall productivity essential to the survival of the new Soviet state. But the very backwardness of capitalism in Russia made the "ideal class consciousness" which would have democratically directed this process impossible. In fact, if Lenin is to be taken at his word, "ideal class consciousness" could only be brought to the proletariat by the Bolshevik party, and only if that party controlled all the media of communication for a long time. In any event, the lack of "ideal class consciousness" made "sharp forms of dictatorship" necessary, not for the suppression of class enemies— this was the only purpose Marx and Engels assigned to the dictatorship—but to ensure that thousands would subordinate their will to the will of one leader in the organization and development of Russia's primitive economy. When Lenin had assigned the role of consciousness exclusively to the Bolshevik party, the dictatorship of the proletariat had become the dictatorship *in the name* of the proletariat. But after six months of power, the dictatorship of the proletariat became a dictatorship *over* the proletariat to ensure its submission in the critical task of constructing an economic base for Socialism.

It seemed reasonable to Socialists that the state should use an "iron hand"[138] and "iron rule"[139] against its class enemies. But in 1918 Lenin asserted that the repressive machinery of the state was to be used against the proletariat itself—and that repression was to take the "sharp form of dictatorship." The repressive machinery of the "commune-type" state, which would be exceedingly simple because of the small minority of the class enemies who had to be suppressed, suddenly took on the features of an enormously complex apparatus reaching into every branch of industry to ensure the strict and absolute unity of will of the working class itself.

The features revealed in the pronouncements of April, 1918, were at least foreshadowed in the visionary *State and Revolution* of October, 1917. Behind the anarchosyndicalist utopianisms of the conjectures about the commune-type state there was another image. Lenin had described the "transitional" society in the following way: "The whole of society will have become a single office and a single factory . . ." characterized by "'factory' discipline."[140] "Until the 'higher' phase of Communism arrives, the Socialists demand the *strictest* control of society *and by the State* of the measure of labor and the measure of consumption. . . ."[141] Such a harsh image had been qualified, of course, in October, 1917, by the commitment that such control would be "workers' control." But such control was contingent upon the ability of the workers to solve the "simple" problems of accounting and control,[142] something that the very backwardness of Russian economy, Lenin later admitted, made impossible.

Since the problems of accounting had not been, and under the conditions prevailing in the Russia of the Bolshevik Revolution could not have been, solved, the fact that "all citizens [were] transformed into hired employees of the State"[143] meant in effect that the state had absolute control over the working population. In June, 1918, all parties but the Bolshevik party were made illegal and declared counterrevolutionary.[144] In March, 1919, the structure of the Communist party was made to conform to the organizational ideal for a conspiratorial party advanced by Lenin under the conditions of Czarist autocracy.

Socialists throughout the world were to hold these developments as a betrayal of Marxist ideals. While the Communists were to argue that "objective conditions" had necessitated the abandonment of the ideals of the Paris Commune, those of classical Marxist persuasion were to argue that any competent Marxist should have anticipated such an eventuality. The economic base in backward Russia was far too narrow for proletarian dictatorship. The immature economic conditions in Russia had left the vast majority of the "toiling masses" petty bourgeois in sentiment and interest. The class-conscious proletariat were very few in number. Dictatorship of the proletariat under such conditions could only mean a dictatorship by a minority. Engels had clearly indicated that where the majority of the working population was composed of peasants, control by the proletariat could only be indirect at first, and would become direct only after capitalism had transformed the peasant mass into a proletarian mass. Under any other conditions proletarian rule could only be another in the long history of minoritarian revolutions, maintaining its existence only by the most brutal repressions.

Lenin was certainly aware of such considerations, and it seems that he continued to hope that proletarian revolutions in the advanced capitalist countries would extricate him from the contradictions in which successful revolution had embroiled him. Years later Trotsky revealed that Lenin continued to dwell on the "imminent" revolutions in the West. We have seen that even as late as 1924, months after Lenin's death, Stalin still maintained that Socialism could not come to backward Russia without the successful revolution of the Western proletariat.

Lenin had argued that under the conditions prevailing in the imperialist epoch of capitalism, capitalism might well be thrown off first in the backward, or peripheral, areas. But this revolution could only constitute the beginning of the worldwide proletarian revolution. For a time Lenin believed that the proletariat in the West, under the pressures created by the First World War, would complete their revolution before the Bolsheviks succeeded in theirs. As late as August, 1917, Bukharin and Stalin both felt that the "peasant-proletarian" revolution in Russia might not be completed before the "proletarian" revolution in the West accomplished its purposes.[145]

In arguing against the advisability of Bolshevik insurrection in October, both Zinoviev and Kamenev warned that (1) the majority of the people of Russia did not support the Bolsheviks, and (2) the prospect of international proletarian revolution was remote.[146] Nonetheless Lenin's will prevailed and the Bolsheviks seized power. Under the economic and social conditions which obtained in backward Russia and because the proletarian revolution in the West did not occur, Soviet Russia could only become a historical curiosity.

Lenin had admitted that "so long as the state exists there is no freedom."[147] Yet by March, 1918, he had assigned so many functions to the Soviet state that he could conceive the possibility of its "withering away" only "when the possibility of exploitation no longer exists anywhere in the world." Only then would the state be assigned to the scrap heap.[148]

In October, 1917, Lenin described the prospective Bolshevik state as "a very simple" apparatus for the suppression of class enemies.[149] Its functionaries were to be chosen by direct election and subject to recall at any time by the electorate. There was to be "immediate introduction of control and supervision by all. . . ."[150] It was not, in the proper sense of the word, a state at all. But by March, 1918, the Bolshevik state assumed the responsibility not only of "protecting socialist property" and "suppressing class enemies," but also of controlling accounting, production, and distribution. It had assumed "iron control" over the direction of industry, and there was no further attempt to implement direct election and recall of state functionaries.[151]

The subsequent history of the Soviet state is too well known to warrant any discussion here. A state with the multiplicity of functions assigned to it by Lenin was destined to become a Moloch during Stalin's lifetime. Stalin's Report to the Seventeenth Congress of the Communist party in January, 1934, revealed that all the implications of Lenin's voluntarism had borne fruit. No longer would Marxist theory concern itself with "objective conditions." "The part played by so-called objective conditions," Stalin announced, "has been reduced to a minimum; whereas the part played by our organizations and their leaders has become decisive, exceptional."[152] The classical Marxist thesis of man's consciousness being determined by the conditions governing his life was subverted. The role played by "objective conditions" diminished in significance and that played by the party's organizations and their leaders in the state became "exceptional."

The influence of such "exceptional" leaders could only be effected through the machinery of the state. Stalin chided Marxists who insisted on being "talmudists," who constantly referred to Marx or Engels in their assessment of the nature of the state. Rather they should "further develop the Marxist theory."[153] The Marxian classics, Stalin asserted, written as they were so long ago, could not have "foreseen each and every zigzag of history."[154] Engels' formula on the withering away of the state did not provide an answer to the problems which face the Soviet state.[155] Even Lenin's pronouncements in the *State and Revolution* could not provide a definitive formula. Stalin had indicated that Lenin had planned a further volume: "But what Lenin did not manage to do should be done by his disciples."[156]

Stalin did manage just such a "creative development" of Marxism. His extension of the principle contained in Lenin's modification of *State and Revolution* is contained in his Sixteenth Report to the Communist party of June, 1930. "We stand," he asserted, "for the withering away of the state. At the same time we stand for the strengthening of the dictatorship of the proletariat, which is the mightiest and strongest state power that has ever existed. The highest development of state power with the object of preparing the conditions for the withering away of state power—such is the Marxist formula. Is this 'contradictory'? Yes, it is 'contradictory.' But this contradiction is bound up with life, and it fully reflects Marx's dialectics."[157] The reflection of Marx's dialectics seems to have been purchased at the expense of Marx's thought.

### Leninism and Marxism ·

The history of Leninism is by and large the story of Lenin's theory of the role of consciousness in history, his theory of imperialism, and his conjectures on the state. Each of these components signified departures from classical Marxism. Together they constitute the essentials of contemporary Communism.

Classical Marxism had never resolved, even to its own satisfaction, the question of the role of human consciousness in the making of history. The problem of human initiative as opposed to the domination of objective features of the social and economic environment is one to which Marx and Engels and all subsequent Marxists have returned time and time again. In *The Role of the Individual in History* no less an intelligence than that of Plekhanov labored fruitlessly to produce some solution to that specific problem. Classical Marxism, for all its indecisiveness with respect to the issues involved, seemed to opt for the ultimate decisiveness of the economic factor. Economic circumstances, the development of the material forces of production, created tensions within a specific social order which reflected themselves in the consciousness of men that right had become wrong and reason, unreason. Furthermore, if economic forces generated an awareness of problems, they determined the nature of men's solutions as well, for classical Marxism held that a task arises only when the material conditions for its solution already exist or are at least in the process of formation. Both the problems which beset mankind and their solutions are the product of economic processes and those processes are governed by necessary laws.

But willed change must have as its agents human beings. Classical Marxism seemed to proclaim that not individual man, but a class of men were the agency of change. Yet the will for such a change seemed allotted in different measure to the men of that class. Indeed even classical Marxism had indicated that the clearest consciousness may be possessed by men *not* of that class. Lenin's innovation was not so marked a departure from classical Marxism. It grew out of a theoretical weakness in the system. Lenin maintained that some men were possessed of the gift of class consciousness while others were not. The acquisition of such a consciousness was not a simple matter of reflecting objective conditions. His suggestion that the proletariat, as a class, was forever incapable of attaining class consciousness without the intercession of bourgeois intellectuals was portentous. The repository of class consciousness was no longer a class of men produced by objective economic and social circumstances. The bearers of consciousness were a select group who were to bring consciousness to the blind and elemental strivings of the restive and destructive revolutionary masses. Such select groups are the chosen ones of history; they use the masses as a lever with which to overturn the world. Martov, Axelrod, Martynov, Luxemburg, Kautsky, and even Plekhanov, all ultimately understood the implications of this change of emphasis. The proletariat was not to mature to responsibility; it was to be marshaled to it. It was not to take up its tasks; its tasks were to be imposed upon it. It was not to come to know; it was to be told its purpose. It might come to appreciate its *immediate* interest, but only the revolutionary cadre could understand its *ultimate* interest. Rosa Luxemburg early divined that Lenin's implicit intention was to impose upon the proletariat the discipline of a military camp.

Under the conditions which prevailed in autocratic Russia, the hierarchical and centralist organization of the Bolsheviks seemed an expediency. Its conspiratorial character seemed required by the circumstances. Nonetheless, many Marxists were to point out the anomaly of awakening an entire class, the ultimate bearers of self-directed power, to consciousness through the medium of such an organization. Enlightened self-consciousness could only be the product of maturation in the social system itself, which would impose tasks demanding more and more self-discipline and a greater and greater maturity of the working class. Rational self-consciousness could not be "brought to them from without" in mechanical fashion through a chain of command carrying out the imperatives of party leaders.

Such were the circumstances which surrounded Marxism as a theory of social change at the outbreak of the First World War. With the advent of the war, and the shock of what he conceived as the betrayal of the international interests of the proletariat, Lenin introduced his second and more far-reaching modification of classical Marxism. Lenin did not "hesitate . . . to replace some of the propositions and conclusions of Marx and Engels, which had become outdated, with new propositions and conclusions corresponding to the new historical era."[158] The new propositions to which Soviet Marxists refer concern the possibility of revolution in the peripheral areas of the world. Lenin maintained that the peculiar features of capitalism led to the creation of revolutionary conditions in the backward economies of the world rather than in the areas of advanced industrialism. The weight of industrialism pressed heavily on the areas of the world subject to brazen imperialist exploitation. The booty of exploitation was used, in part, to bribe the proletariat of the advanced nations. Lenin's revision of classical Marxism saw in the restive masses of the underdeveloped nations the principal agents of world history. The proletarian revolution would erupt first in the backward areas of the world. Such an analysis committed Marxism to a revolutionary struggle in areas where class consciousness could not conceivably be developed because the objective economic conditions which could produce a general, enlightened consciousness did not exist. The purpose, the strategy, and the day-to-day tactics of revolution would have to be imposed upon the revolutionary situation from without. Revolutionary masses were to be manipulated in the service of ends they could not possibly understand. Lenin became more and more emphatic in his appraisal of the changed character of revolution in our century. His eyes were turned to the faceless masses of Asia and the non-industrial world. There the possibilities of successful revolution were infinitely better than in the advanced industrial countries of the West. A small privileged class held down a seething elemental mass of unrest. The prospects of success for a small, well-disciplined, highly centralized and aggressive revolutionary coterie were enormously enhanced under such circumstances, and Bolshevik organization lent itself admirably well to such situations.

In such a conception some of the basic components of classical Marxism are sacrificed. The revolution which both Marx and Engels anticipated was a revolution that could only come when the "masses themselves . . . have grasped what is at stake," for what was demanded was a "complete transformation of the social organization," which could not be "carried through by small conscious minorities at the head of unconscious masses."[159] The original theory could be salvaged only if the revolution in such areas precipitated the worldwide proletarian revolution. Certainly Lenin continued to believe that such a revolution was necessary. For some time he held it to be imminent; only slowly did he begin to realize that such an eventuality was a hope which might not be realized for decades. As late as 1917 he had not prepared for such a possibility. He continued to speak of the theory of the state in classical Marxist terms as though the objective conditions it necessarily presumed would, in fact, obtain after successful revolution. The peasant and proletariat revolution in Russia inaugurated a new type of state, a state which was not a state in the proper sense of the word. It would be a very simple state in which the functionaries were to be elected by universal ballot and their mandate revocable at any time by the electorate. It was to be a form of state which would see the advent of what Engels had called "one great union," a free association of workers who, on their own initiative, would work out plans for the organization of co-operative societies and who would voluntarily federate into an enormous collective enterprise attuned to one vast productive task.[160] What was necessarily entailed in such a vision was the adequate training and the enlightened class consciousness of the vast majority of the working population. It implied the existence of the fully matured economic base which would serve such a population. The one was, of course, the precondition of the other. The working class achieved conscious maturity only after all the economic potential of capitalist society had itself achieved maturity. The working class was required by history but to strip off the outgrown skin of the old order. Capitalism was supposed to have created not only the material conditions, but also the revolutionary consciousness for the future society.

With the awareness that the saving revolution in the West might not be immediately forthcoming, Lenin was faced with the responsibility of solving the problems of having made a revolution in an "unripe" country. He was compelled to compromise the principles of the classical Marxist theory of the state. Owing to the absence of class consciousness among the proletariat and the prevalence of petty-bourgeois disposition among the peasant masses, the decrees granting workers' control over the processes of production were quickly rescinded and a "sharp dictatorship" imposed instead. Lenin, like Marx before him, recognized that while the peasants could serve as allies for revolution, their mentality was impossibly petty-bourgeois. "The lower middle-classes, the small manufacturers, the shopkeepers, the artisan, the peasant, all these fight against the bourgeoisie, to save from extinction their existence as fractions of the middle-class. . . . [They] are [therefore] reactionary, for they try to roll back the wheel of history." This was Marx's judgment in the *Manifesto* of 1848 and he repeated it in 1867.[161] Not only was the vast majority of the Russian population petty-bourgeois in sentiment, but even the proletariat itself had not developed a class consciousness which, in classical Marxist terms, would have qualified it to rule. The only repository of class consciousness was the highly centralized, aggressive Bolshevik minority.

The maintenance of control under such circumstances required a repressive machinery of enormous complexity. The Soviet state was born. Stalin made no apology for its existence but heralded it as the realization of the aspirations of Karl Marx and Friedrich Engels. Not only was the state to exist as a repressive political power, but it was to burgeon into the most imposing state power that has ever existed. And, unless the entire world became Communist in the interim, it was to persist into the epoch of the Communist society itself.[162]

A most singular inversion of classical Marxism had taken place. No longer was historical development determined "on the basis of the given economic situation." The part played by "objective conditions" was reduced to a minimum. History was determined by the "exceptional" leaders and their state organizations. By implication, the theoretical roots of the "cult of personality" and the absolute state lay firmly rooted in Lenin's first innovation in the original Marxist conception of history. Finally Stalin contended that exceptional men, hitherto the products of objective conditions, were to create the objective conditions themselves. Being did not determine consciousness; consciousness determined being. The economic base was not to be the source of Socialist social consciousness but was to be its product. It was to be created by a unique band of men whose responsibilities after became greater than they had been before and during the revolution. "The proletariat needs the Party not only to achieve the dictatorship; it needs it still more to maintain the dictatorship, to consolidate and expand it in order to achieve the complete victory of socialism."[163]

The development taken by Leninism has run a curious course. In the pious attempt to resolve some difficulties in the theoretical structure of classical Marxism, Lenin introduced a change of emphasis in some of the elementary propositions of the material conception of history. The ambiguities surrounding the nature of consciousness and the motive force of historical development inaugurated some modest changes in the classical Marxist explanation.

At the base of the materialist conception of history is the conception that the logic of history proceeds independently of the will of man. The material productive forces, the ultimate determinants of the material conditions of life, seem possessed of an immanent logic. Their progress, in some ultimate sense, seems independent of man's will and consciousness. The socioeconomic conditions which they produce are somehow reflected in the consciousness of man. The processes of history pursue an inevitable course. Lenin was preoccupied with these problems in a real and intimate way. As early as 1894 he outlined the classical conception of history. Productive relations determined all other relations and the relations of production necessarily corresponded to the stage of development of the material productive forces. From this vantage point materialism carried the "analysis deeper . . . and its conclusion that the course of ideas depends on the course of things is the only one compatible with scientific psychology."[164] Only in such fashion could the necessary logic of history be argued with any credibility.

Around just such issues some of the most fundamental problems of the materialist conception of history have collected. Lenin remained forever concerned with them, and in the course of his life he materially assisted those who promised, or seemed to promise, their definitive resolution. Lenin was perhaps vaguely aware that the tactical innovations he had introduced did violence to the original theory. Whatever the case might be, these theoretical innovations in the theory were to provide the subject for the further development of Marxism as a theory of history.

# 7 Contemporary Marxism
## as a Theory of History:
## A Brief Survey of Problems

The modifications which Lenin introduced into the classical theory of history literally inverted the theory. Beginning with changes of emphasis, continuing with a reassessment of essential features, Lenin was ultimately to introduce the qualifications which Stalin employed to justify perhaps the most onerous dictatorship in the history of mankind. The excesses of the "Stalin era" will probably never be fully known, but enough is known to indicate that something frightening had happened to the Marxism of Marx and Engels. Originally a doctrine committed to the liberation of man it was pressed into the service of man's enslavement. Originally a doctrine of radical democracy, seeing the true society as an association of free producers in voluntary combination, it metamorphosed into a doctrinal facade for coercion on so vast a scale as to beggar description. From a doctrine which saw revolution as a leap into the realm of freedom, it became a doctrine in which the revolutionary atmosphere, insistence on ideological conformity, political and social orthodoxy, economic and institutional centralism did not cease after the revolution but on the contrary became more and more intensified. From a conception of revolutionary dynamics which saw the social movement as the action of the immense majority of the citizenry, it became a commitment to a minoritarian revolution led by a self-selecting, self-perpetuating leadership.

Lenin's insistence that the consciousness which motivated revolutionary ardor had to be brought to the masses by a few professional revolutionaries laid the basis for state control by a minority party. His conception of revolution in the backward areas made such control almost an inevitability. Where the vast majority of people are non-proletarian, leadership, direction, and control must reside in a privileged caste. Leninism has seized power not where economic conditions have made Socialist control a necessity but rather where the immaturity of society and the economy, where war and civil strife have brought about almost complete disintegration. Leninism has come to power only under such exceptional conditions, and as a consequence has always had to assume dictatorial power if any semblance of order was to be restored. Leninism has nowhere inherited the material base classical Marxism saw as its heritage. Leninism has had to create such a base. It has become a doctrine for rapid industrialization of backward economies. To effect such a program it has had to use violence, coercion, and absolute state control. It has had to telescope into a single generation two centuries of economic maturation. Such a program involves the sacrifice not only of liberty but of life as well. Such sacrifices have become the price of rapid industrial transformation. And yet to the backward countries of the world Leninism is the promise of national advance and industrial growth that has characterized the West. At the same time it permits a renunciation of the West, long identified with colonialism and imperialism. Leninism has provided the rationale for the one-party states which have begun to characterize our century, and it has very little real relationship to the classical Marxism of Marx and Engels. Engels' admonition that the working class must not lose control of the state, that it must "safeguard itself against its own deputies and officials, by declaring them all, without exception, subject to recall at any moment,"[1] has never been known to be effectively heeded in any Leninist state. The conditions under which Leninism can come to power make such a safeguard impossble.

The results of the transformation of classical Marxism into Leninism are too well known to history to require elaboration here. We have been concerned with the process of transformation.

## Contemporary Marxism and Biology

Like all scientific hypotheses, historical materialism is subject to revision. In some cases the revisions have been of such fundamental character that the expectations aroused by the modified theory stand at direct variance to those of the classical theory. Classical Marxism had maintained that the elements of the new society would mature in the womb of the old, that "no social order ever perishes before all the productive forces for which there is room in it have developed," and that "new, higher relations of production never appear before the material conditions of their existence have matured in the womb of the old society itself."[2] Leninism claims confirmation of these theses in the developments in backward Russia and feudal China. Classical Marxism had claimed as a necessary law the increasing impoverishment of the working classes under capitalism. Leninism claims that this thesis has been confirmed by the increase in real wages, the bribery of the upper stratum of the working class in the advanced countries, and by the wretched living conditions which prevail in noncapitalist economies.

More important for the purposes of this inquiry is the fact that Soviet Marxism has found it necessary to supplement the materialist conception of history with biological and psychological theories of suspect merit. In the course of our discussion it was indicated that Engels had found it necessary to attempt to accommodate the general theories of organic and social evolution associated with Darwinism within the theoretical confines of classical Marxism. Darwin's appropriation of the time scale of geology had cast the brief written history of man into a new perspective. The classical Marxists themselves could no longer talk meaningfully of the mode of production and the class struggle as determining *all* of man's social history. In the first instance man, for an incredibly long time, lived without a "mode of production" distinguishable from that of his primate congeners. Yet, he, like them, enjoyed elaborate social relations, well-defined mating practices,[3] a sense of territoriality, and presumably a disposition to organize his society on hierarchical lines. All social animals, in fact, seem to evince these traits. Engels made at least one of these traits, the governance of breeding practices in accordance with well-articulated rules, an independent determinant of man's social history. In the *Origin of the Family, Private Property and the State*, he argued that the "determining factor in history is, in the last resort, the production and reproduction of immediate life," which was of "two-fold character," the production of the means of subsistence on the one hand and the production of human beings, the propagation of the species, on the other. To call these *two* demonstrably different elements *the* "determining factor" can hardly obscure the fact that a new variable has been introduced. Soviet social theorists have consistently recognized the threat Engels' innovation posed to their system. In a rare display of critical assessment, contemporary Soviet commentators have held that "Engels is . . . guilty of inexactitude by citing the propagation of the species alongside the production of the means of subsistence as causes determining the development of society and social institutions."[4] For Soviet Marxists the theoretical system of classical Marxism seems to remain, in certain critical areas, inflexible. The ultimate determining factor governing the development of society and social institutions *must* remain the "mode of production."

There seems little doubt that Engels felt that a modification of the original thesis was required by the development of the historical and social sciences. Soviet social philosophers, on the other hand, seem wedded to what is essentially a monocausal theory of history. Their assessment of classical Marxist and contemporary scientific theories seems structured by this antecedent commitment. This seems evident in the Soviet treatment of Engels' modification of the original classical Marxist thesis. When this modification threatens to introduce a new causal determinant, Engels is rejected. Engels' less credible suggestions concerning the inheritance of acquired characteristics, on the other hand, have been accepted and have had a doleful impact upon contemporary Marxist social theory.

In the effort to eliminate the non-economic factors with which the theory of organic evolution threatened the Marxist theory of history, Engels insisted that individual and group variations in inventiveness, for example, could be admitted as a determinant only with the understanding that such variations were in turn determined by prevailing material conditions of life. Variations arise within a species as a consequence of demands made by the external environment, and these variations are subsequently fixed by the altered heredity of the race.[5] This would be consistent with the monocausal theory of history. As a consequence the Lamarckian notion of the inheritance of induced variation has been explicitly accepted by contemporary Marxists and is essential to what is called Soviet Darwinism.

Lenin, hardly a specialist in biology, early and eagerly took up the cause of the advocates of the inheritance of acquired characteristics and hybrid vigor. During the first years of the Soviet regime he espoused the cause of Paul Kammerer, the Austrian naturalist whose heterodox views concerning the inheritance of acquired traits[6] had made him suspect to the science of the West. Kammerer claimed, by virtue of a series of protracted experiments, to have altered the inheritance in *Salamandra maculosa* and *Salamandra atra* by subjecting the organisms to altered environmental conditions.[7] When the specimens which purported to substantiate his contentions underwent expert scrutiny by G. K. Noble and Hans Przibram, it was found that all had been "improved upon," *post mortem*, with coloring matter. Kammerer committed suicide.[8] Nonetheless, he continued to be touted in the Soviet Union as the "enemy of reaction," a "hero of Soviet science," and an advocate of a "consistent, monistically materialist position."[9]

Even during the critical days of the Civil War, Lenin had given evidence of his inordinate interest in these problems by supporting the work of I. V. Michurin, whose biological speculations rested upon the conviction that acquired traits could be systematically inherited.[10] That this obscure agronomist captured his attention is evidence of the significance Lenin attributed to this particular biological tenet. At the height of the struggle to establish the Soviet state in 1921–1922, Lenin took the time to provide measures to assist Michurin in his work.[11] The notion of the inheritance of acquired characteristics was subsequently elevated by Soviet theoreticians to the rank of "one of the greatest achievements in the history of biological science."[12] It was conceived as "the root question of biology."[13]

Like his followers, who have collected beneath the standard of T. D. Lysenko, Michurin explicitly identified himself with Marxism as a theory of history,[14] and his remarkable speculations have been clearly recognized by party theoreticians in the Soviet Union as providing the necessary "scientific" supplement to historical materialism.[15] These speculations have been systematized into a body of doctrine which in our own time has become known as "creative" or "Soviet" Darwinism.[16]

In making place for this supplement, the Soviet Union has had to devise a special "genetics" involving the inheritance of acquired characteristics and a special anthropology predicated on Engels' "labor theory of anthropogenesis."[17] Not only has no conclusive evidence for the inheritance of acquired traits been forthcoming and Soviet Lamarckianism been proved singularly lacking in explanatory force, but Soviet "genetics" has succeeded in becoming increasingly bizarre in the effort to accommodate a theory of organic evolution to the monocausal conception of history advanced by Marx and Engels.[18]

The question here is whether science, the search for knowledge that can meet the test of public and specifiable criteria, can operate in an environment which requires that the empirical investigator make an anterior commitment to some particular system of transempirical "truth." Contemporary Marxism seems to require such an anterior commitment, particularly with respect to sensitive issues directly related to the essentials of the theory which provides the rationale for the Soviet Marxist *Weltanschauung*. Among those commitments is the disposition to read a "logic" into history, to see its development as an upward and onward progress, caused *ultimately* by the material mode of production. Such a view commits its proponents to conceive human consciousness as a by-product of an inevitable development independent of their will and consciousness. For an enterprise that pretends to scientific stature such commitments have ominous portent.

### Contemporary Marxism and Psychology

We have briefly considered the influence of doctrinal preconceptions on the theory of organic evolution. A much more compelling instance of their influence is displayed in the construction of psychological theory. In this regard the negative impact of doctrinal constraints becomes obvious. Any assessment of Marxism as a scientific system would be incomplete without at least a cursory treatment of contemporary Marxism's unique contribution to the study of human psychology. For if there is one problem that illustrates the baleful effects upon science of anterior doctrinal commitment, it is the problem of specifying with some kind of precision the manner in which man's consciousness can be said to be determined by his Being. Neither Marx nor Engels gave an exhaustive treatment to what are essentially the psychological premises involved in such a conception. In their early writings there was a naive conviction that consciousness was simply "determined" by the material conditions of life. Later they provided considerable evidence that the material conditions of life could not be simply "reflected" in consciousness in a one-to-one relationship. In some way consciousness was determined by Being—precisely how, they never attempted to explicate.

Lenin's treatment of the role of consciousness in history left much to be desired. On the one hand he looked suspiciously voluntaristic. He seemed to accord considerable place to will and determination in the dynamic social situation in which he found himself; and yet, in theory, he seemed unequivocally committed to a notion of historical progression which saw one order of things "inevitably [growing] out of the preceding one regardless of whether men believe in it or not, whether they are conscious of it or not."[19] He advanced, as we have seen, the thesis that "the course of ideas depends on the course of things" as "the only one compatible with scientific psychology."[20]

Contemporary Soviet Marxists argue that the physiopsychological work of Ivan P. Pavlov provides an important theoretical addendum to the original theory.[21] Among the most recent Soviet discussions are still contentions that Pavlov "laid a sound scientific basis for an understanding of human mental activity."[22]

Pavlov's "nervism" is a non-Marxist and peculiarly Soviet innovation in the sense that the founders of classical Marxism nowhere proposed a formal psychological or psychophysiological theory. In fact, a case can be made for the thesis that Pavlovianism is "mechanistic" rather than "dialectical," having mechanically "reduced" complex human behavior to reflex responses. But this much having been said, it is the case that Pavlov's theory of "higher nervous activity" forms a significant component of the Marxist-Leninist theory of man and history, and requires assessment as such. It is a peculiarly Marxist-Leninist addendum to the corpus of "Marxism at a higher level of development."

The claims of Pavlov's general theory of higher nervous activity are relatively clear. The theory constitutes an audacious attempt to "reduce" psychic activity to "purely" physiological dimensions. The total behavior of the higher animals and man, observed as the sum of automatic and voluntary movements, is conceived as nothing other than a complex of reflexes. This complex rests, ultimately, upon a base of native, or unconditioned, reflexes. Each such reflex is a three-phase process commencing with stimulation originating in the external (or internal) environment, passing to the spinal cord or the brain and transmission outward to the muscles, precipitating activity.[23] Unconditioned reflexes are found in the deeper levels of the central nervous system. On the foundation of these involuntary, native reflexes the voluntary movements arise by virtue of a process of conditioning which begins to affect the organism on the very first day of life. These conditioned reflexes establish themselves in the cerebral hemispheres.

Every act of man, "voluntary" or "involuntary," is conceived to be a simple or complex reflex[24] whose function is to secure a more perfect adaptation of the organism to the environment.[25] The central explanatory concept employed by Pavlov was therefore, as it had been earlier for Sechenov,[26] the reflex, a determined neurodynamic response of the central nervous system to excitation. Each response is strictly determined,[27] so the human organism is a "strictly determined" homeostatic machine[28] which adjusts itself by reflex mechanisms to its environment.[29]

Within such a context neurophysiology serves as a "primary discipline" for the reduction of terms employed in psychological propositions. Terms which figure in psychological accounts are explicitly and exhaustively definable in neurophysiological terms. In accordance with the system of his "reductionism," Pavlov carefully proscribed the use of "subjective" terms native to psychology. Expressions like "will," "motivation," "interest," and "drive" were systematically avoided. In fact, Pavlov went so far as to fine students for employing expressions such as "conscious" or "voluntary."[30]

Clearly such notions have no place in a theoretical system which reduces "psychic" activity to temporary conditioned cortical connections, incredibly specialized and complicated, adjusting the organism to peripheral excitations. In such a system notions such as "volition," "choice," and "deliberation" refer, in some obscure way, to the fact that the higher nervous activity of the human organism is fraught with "contradictions, conflict and struggles" in which "some processes sometimes overwhelm others, sometimes unite with them. . . ."[31]

Thus Pavlov's work, though physiological in the strictest sense, was in the tradition of "objective" psychology—a tradition which had its origins in the physiopsychology of the nineteenth century and which formed the theoretical core of the early behaviorist movement in the United States. That enormous benefits have accrued as a consequence of the decision by a determined body of investigators to thus pursue their research "objectively" cannot be gainsaid. We shall only try to indicate here that the theory of higher nervous activity as it is espoused today in the Soviet Union seems to create as many problems as it solves.

The reflex, according to Pavlov and his followers, is a "clearly defined, strictly scientific" notion which provides a universally applicable sketch of simple determinism.[32] Armed with so powerful a concept, the "objective" scientist observes animal behavior as an astronomer or chemist might follow events in order to divine "exact and constant connections."[33] He knows that the ultimate cause of the activity of an organism is the "impact" of the external world upon its nervous system.[34] The behavior of the organism thus "proceeds lawfully" since it is "precisely determined."[35]

And yet, when we seek to fit these "clear lines of reflex determination" to random samples of animal behavior, their clarity diminishes with astonishing rapidity. The "clear lines" become increasingly tenuous, and their determination becomes contingent. We find, for one thing, a most curious "reflex" among Pavlov's repertoire of reflexes—the "orientating" or "what-is-it?" reflex, which is elicited by an change in the intensity of illumination (flickering of a lamp, a momentary shadow), by any new odor, by a chance warm or cold current of air, by something touching the subject's skin, by any sound or movement, or by any of a thousand different stimuli.[36] Nor is the "reflex behavior" itself any more precise. It can range from furious activity to sleep. More than that, this strange "reflex" is *extinguished* by reinforcement. The more frequently the organism is subjected to the same stimulus the weaker the response—in direct contradiction to the prescribed method for establishing and maintaining a reflex.[37]

Not content with this most singular "reflex," Pavlov proceeded to introduce a host of *ad hoc* and equally curious "reflexes," among which are numbered those of "freedom," of "slavery," and of "purpose." If a subject is constrained and makes motions which to an uncommitted observer bespeak impatience, irritability, and discomfort, the "objective" scientist records activity attendant upon the "reflex of freedom."[38] An unpredictable chaos of responses evoked by an unspecified number of stimuli are lumped together under the category of the "reflex of freedom."

The Pavlovians are sometimes given to "interpreting" the behavior of characters in fiction from the vantage point of their theory. Pavlov offers his insight into the psychodynamics leading to the suicide in Kuprin's *River of Life*. Pavlov informs us that the unfortunate, "tormented by his conscience after having betrayed his companions to the police," was driven to self-destruction not by despair, compunction, or remorse, but by the "reflex of slavery" which he had inherited from his mother![39]

But perhaps the most fascinating of all these strange and sundry "reflexes" (which, we must remember, are clear responses of the organism to specific excitation) is the "reflex of purpose." We have been told, on the one hand, that the "fundamental law of life," governing all the reflex activities of the organism, is "equilibration with surrounding nature."[40] Now, on the other hand, we are told that "the reflex of purpose is of great and vital importance; it is the fundamental form of the life energy of us all. Life is beautiful and strong only to him who during his whole existence strives toward the always desirable but *ever inaccessible goal*. . . .[41] All life, all its improvement and progress, all its culture, are effected through the reflex of purpose, are realized only by those who strive to put into life a purpose."[42] But the "reflex of purpose," "the fundamental form of life energy," thus understood, is clearly at odds with the "fundamental law of life." The "fundamental law" seeks adaptation and equilibration, while the fundamental form of "life energy" aspires to an ever inaccessible goal.

Under these circumstances even the layman can legitimately protest that the concept "reflex" has lost all scientific and commonsensical import. The notion of "reflex" is pressed into service to cover the most complex and disparate of phenomena—the "reflex of purpose" covering everything from the random activity of a hound investigating an alien environment to the cultural and political eminence of one nation over another (the Anglo-Saxons have a stronger "reflex of purpose" than have other nationalities!).[43]

As early as 1931, K. Lashley wrote, "In order that the concept of stimulus-response should have any scientific value it must convey a notion of how a particular stimulus elicits a particular response and no other. . . ."[44] When employing a reasonably precise notion of reflex, certain relatively well-defined initial and terminal points in the course of the organism's activity are fixed. For example, with a human subject at rest (initial point) a blow is struck at the patellar tendon (stimulus) which results in a reflex flexion (terminal point). What, on the other hand, are the initial and terminating loci for the "reflexes" of "purpose," of "freedom," of "orientation," and of "slavery"?

This seems to be but one of many difficulties inherent in the theory of higher nervous activity. When we attempt to explain behavior "neurodynamically" we are employing a notion in which the organism is conceived as an irritable, reactive mechanism subject to constant peripheral agitation. Afferent impulses constantly assail the central nervous system. The question is, Why is one connection established, leading to a given action, rather than another? How does the organism come to "deliberate" and then set itself in motion?

An enormous number of sensory (interoceptive, proprioceptive, and external) stimuli excite the terminal receptors as a consequence of which a certain complex behavior is elicited. All that takes place between stimuli and response is appraised almost exclusively from a hypothetical point of view.[45] We can expect, as a consequence, that speculative elements will abound in any detailed discussion of the neurophysiology of human behavior. Pavlovianism has the dubious distinction of entertaining more of such speculations than almost any other system.[46] To "explain" the irregularity of response to specific excitation, "desires" are suddenly introduced which, we are informed, inhibit predicted reflex reaction.[47] Or, stimuli which escape the notice of the physiologist may be invoking obscure "reflexes." Another explanation of differential responses to identical stimuli is offered in the form of a hypothesis of innate typological differences, e.g., the organism may be "choleric," or "sanguine," or "melancholic."[48] These *ad hoc* causes of error are introduced to explain the discrepancy between predicted and observed "reflex" behavior. But there is something very peculiar about a theory whose explanations in principle, have force only *post factum*. Nature seems to have so conspired that this mechanism, the animal organism, behaves for all the world like the physical embodiment of consciousness and free will.

The apparently uncritical extension of the concept "reflex" to cover all the behavior of higher organisms confounds any attempt to distinguish between what laymen are wont to call "voluntary" as distinct from "involuntary" behavior.[49] We cherish a tolerably well-conceived notion of what constitutes voluntary as distinct from involuntary behavior. The difference between "voluntary" and "involuntary" is the difference between "Did the person do it?" and "Was it done to him?"

Any serious attempt to explain the behavior of the higher animal organism, particularly that of man, must adequately consider the role of "mental dispositions" in influencing voluntary behavior. To maintain that planning, deliberation, preference, choice, volition, pleasure, pain, displeasure, love, hatred, attention, vigilance, enthusiasm, grief, indignation, expectation, remembrance, hope, and desire are not among the effective causal agencies which determine human behavior is to discredit the most common-sense evidence and to employ language in a curious and unjustifiable way. Ordinary language distinguishes between involuntary reactions (e.g., pupillary response), where the subject is acted upon, and "voluntary" control upon the issuance of "self-commands" or "self-instruction."

By way of illustration we can consider the case where a conditioned stimulus (a bell) was associated with an unconditioned stimulus (a light) thereby calling forth an unconditioned reflex (a pupillary contraction). Once established as a conditioned stimulus the bell reguarly causes pupillary contraction. The subject who observes this sequence is aware of something being done to him, rather than of doing something. Ordinary language would characterize this act as "involuntary."

Now consider the case where a local stimulus is substituted for the unconditioned stimulus. Contraction of the pupil can be initiated by the command "contract!" The subject "internalizes" the command stimulus and can self-initiate contraction. It seems meaningful to say that each such act is in some sense voluntary. (It is interesting to note, in passing, that such "voluntary" reflex control can be extended over a wider range of somatic activity than physiologists had previously thought possible. Moreover such "self-initiated" commands can "supplant, suppress and replace" unconditioned, inborn reflexes[50] and do not suffer the experimental extinction to which "involuntary" conditioned responses are subject.) Unless appropriate distinctions between voluntary and involuntary activities are drawn, and a more sophisticated analysis is forthcoming, the theory of higher nervous activity threatens to bog down in the most uncritical of simplisms.[51] In one place Pavlov argued, "The movement of plants toward the light and the seeking of truth through a mathematical analysis— are these not phenomena belonging to the same order?"[52]

The question here is not one of sundering the "psyche," "will," or "volition" from the neurophysiological apparatus of the central nervous system.[53] Rather it is a question of whether the higher animal organism can be conceived of, in any significant sense, as the initiator of its own activity. Sechenov's early answer had the virtue of being explicit. "All psychical acts without exception . . . develop by way of reflex. Hence, all conscious movements resulting from these acts and usually described as voluntary, are reflex movements in the strict sense of the term."[54] In Soviet intellectual circles the question has undergone reconsideration several times. R. Bauer, for example, was convinced, as late as 1952, that the trend in the Soviet Union was toward increased emphasis upon "autogenic," "self-initiating" behavior, and away from the concept of man as a passive, "equilibrating" homeostat.[55] As a matter of fact, precisely the reverse seems to be the case.[56]

In 1946 the Five Year Plan for Medicine could still allude to the highly speculative nature of Pavlovian "physiopsychology," and S. Rubinschtein could still write (with all the ardor of an unreconstructed voluntarist), "The freedom of a voluntary act consists in its independence of the impulse of the immediate situation, and means that the behavior of man is not determined directly by his immediate surroundings. . . ."[57] Earlier still, it had been proclaimed that "for Marxist psychology it is equally unacceptable to reduce psychic process to either the conception of 'reaction' or 'reflex.' Such concepts," ran the argument, "presuppose the reduction of all of man's complex behavior and thoughts to simple reactions to external stimuli. . . . Finally, such concepts 'are based on the theory of equilibrium and ignore completely the problem of autogenic movement.' "[58] L. Orbeli had pointed out in 1935 that the presumed "connective filaments" which joined external stimuli with "determined" responses were of an entirely speculative character.[59] Similarly Beritaschivili (Beritov) maintained that the hypothetical "connections" postulated by the physiology of the cerebral cortex could not provide an exhaustive explanation of "voluntary" activity.[60] Physiology must be supplemented by psychological insights, among which, it was suggested, should be numbered the notion of "states of internal excitement" through which the animal might initiate "voluntary" activity.[61]

These constituted the principal unorthodoxies of the "Beritov-Orbeli-Anokhin clique" which Bykov, Ivanov-Smolensky, and Asratyan dedicated themselves to "stamping out" after the "Scientific Session on the Physiological Teachings of Pavlov" in 1950, in "full accordance with the wishes of J. V. Stalin"[62] that "titan of science."[63] The most objectionable of the heterodoxies was the notion of spontaneous, or voluntary, activity of the organism,[64] for such a notion was at odds with the dogma of the "reflex" as a "determined response of the organism to specific excitation of the peripheral receptors." "All in all (and this should be especially noted)," wrote E. A. Asratyan, "the entire activity of the brain is determined by its environment."[65] "All movements known in physiology as voluntary are reflex movements in the strictest sense of the word."[66] All psychic activity is "mechanical,"[67] "looked upon as machine like."[68] "Under similar external and internal conditions man must act in the same way. The choice of one of many possible ends of the same psychical reflex is definitely impossible, and its apparent possibility is only an illusion of our consciousness. . . . The real sense of every human activity lies outside man."[69]

At best all this is programmatic. It represents a commitment rather than an empirical fact. Investigations conducted on the lines of such programmatic bias enjoy no more predictive fruitfulness than do those pursued in accordance with "purely psychological" techniques, and most of the *post factum* explanations offered by the theory of higher nervous activity are *ad hoc*.

In the West, learning theory has become embroiled in enormous difficulties in the past by attempting to employ the conditioned reflex per se as explanatory of adult behavior. Conditioning in adults was found to be systematically obstructed by "conscious" controls effected by the subject. To talk of a "struggle of reflexes," the outcome of which strictly determines the activity of the organism, is to offer, at best, a pseudo-explanation, for the question then becomes what determines the outcome of the "struggle." The theory of higher nervous activity is largely supported by the promissory notes of hypotheticals: if the initial state of the organism could be exhaustively known . . . if the past history of the organism could be established in detail . . . if the environment could be fully analyzed. . . . Such schemata are so vague and indeterminate that they do not lend themselves to empirical confirmation or disconfirmation. They represent a metaphysical apologetic rather than serious scientific inquiry.

Ultimately these problems were reduced to the still more complex one of "free will" versus "determinism," and in this area discussion has regularly generated more heat than light. But if, as "nervism" contends, introspective awareness of "choice" can be exhaustively explicated by reference to the neurodynamic process of varying predominance of electrical potentials of the several cerebral circuits of which it is an "epiphenomenon,"[70] it is difficult to imagine how ascriptions of praise or blame can properly be made.[71] If "voluntary" behavior is as much the result of the electrical state of a neural circuit as is "involuntary" behavior, it is as improper to assign responsibility for the one as it is for the other. If peripheral excitation necessarily evokes behavior which the agent can no more inhibit than foster, it seems impossible to meet at least the necessary condition for the ascription of moral responsibility, i.e., that one could have done, or could do, something other than one did do or is doing.

Consistent with these considerations, Soviet law was, for a time, based not upon principles of moral responsibility, but upon social utility. Because of the commitment to determinism, the concept of "guilt" was deemed inappropriate.[72] "Socially dangerous act" functioned in place of the term "crime" in Soviet penal codes, and "measure of social defense" assumed the place of the term "punishment." But Soviet penologists, legal theorists, and psychologists have been no happier with these notions than the intelligent layman would be. To date, however, Soviet physiologists and philosophers have been unwilling, or unable, to offer an alternate, more satisfying interpretation.

Much of the responsibility for these difficulties can be traced directly back to Pavlov. He cautioned, on many occasions, against the uncritical extension to man of experimental findings in the study of animal behavior.[73] Nonetheless, he himself was guilty of such practices. He conjured up ill-conceived and ill-contrived "reflexes" to explain complex human behavior in an effort to remain faithful to the exceedingly obscure doctrines of "hard" determinism and mechanical rationalism.[74] So dedicated was he to the doctrine of extreme environmentalism that he committed himself to the notion of the inheritance of learned behavior[75] on the strength of carelessly conducted experiments by his pupils, which later controlled investigations proved to be without substance.[76] While he made haste to admit his original error,[77] he continued to entertain the conviction that acquired conditioned reflexes could become hereditary and "remained true to it to the end."[78]

Pavlov's ascription of "consciousness" to areas of optimum excitability of the cerebral surface seems disconfirmed by subsequent empirical investigation.[79] His insistence that conditioned reflexes could only be established in the cortex seems belied by conditioned reflexes observed in decorticated animals (reflexes apparently being mediated at the collicular and bulbar-subcortical level). Finally, his strict determinism creates untold problems for all of us concerned with the apt appraisal of human conduct.

That neurophysiology per se aspires to provide, one day, neurodynamic correlates for psychic states is perfectly legitimate. At present, of course, the provision of such correlates remains an aspiration. Whether, in the final analysis, such a mapping would even then solve the mind-body problem is a supposition which is at least dubious. Certainly the theory of higher nervous activity meets, for the time being, neither the requirements of the aspiration nor of the supposition.

Since "de-Stalinization" began there has been a tendency in the Soviet Union to permit a reconsideration of at least the most outrageous propositions of "nervism." But when a conference in Moscow during May of 1962 convened to discuss the philosophical problems of psychology and the physiology of higher nervous activity, it criticized the Pavlov conference of 1950, not for having given a wrong direction to Soviet psychology, but only for its dogmatism and its excesses in properly directing it.[80] Pavlovianism, in the Soviet Union, is still understood to provide the "strictly scientific basis"[81] for the classical Marxist pronouncement that man's consciousness is a product of his being. It is also conceived as an exhaustive explication of Lenin's "copy theory" of perception.[82] That the theory of higher nervous activity is conceived by Soviet theoreticians as playing some vital role in the formulation of contemporary Marxist philosophy and the theory of history is obviously the case. As a consequence it is made to carry a theory load for which it was not designed. That such a supplement should be pressed into service to provide at least part of the basis for Marxism would—we may guess—hardly have been other than an acute embarrassment to Karl Marx.

The addenda to Marxist theory for which Engels was, at least in part, responsible, seem to supplement weaknesses in the original formulations. These addenda drive Marxism further in the direction of a strict economic determinism. In the case of the "Darwinist supplement," man's creativity is explained by his economic environment. His brain, the organ of creativity, develops with the increased availability of special foodstuffs and as the consequence of increasingly complex productive activity. Co-operative labor *necessitates* the development of speech, so that an appropriate organ *must be created* and the brain further developed. In a complex feedback relationship the original impetus is provided by conditions in the economic environment. The inheritance of acquired characteristics is the theoretical device which serves to organize these conjectures into some kind of system. Both Michurinism (or Lysenkoism) and Pavlovianism are emphatic in their commitment to the inheritance of acquired traits. The biological notion of heterosis, hybrid vigor, which played a minor role in Engels' original speculations, is occasionally pressed into service as a non-economic factor in explaining the course of man's historical development.

Pavlovianism, furthermore, sees man as a reflex mechanism developing in response to his environmental conditioning. Since the concrete sociohistorical conditions in which the individual finds himself are, in the last analysis, the consequence of developments in the economic base, the social consciousness of man is understood as a reflection of the economy of his epoch.[83] "The causes of psychological facts," it is maintained, "are influences

emanating from without, primarily influences of social character."[84] The conditioned reflexes of a given historical period
are induced changes which are inherited and which provide the
point of departure for subsequent changes in the succeeding
epoch.

Besides being scientifically impoverished these contemporary
supplements to Marxism as a theory of history seem to be at
considerable variance with the thought of Marx and Lenin. They
constitute forms of reductionism to which Marx could hardly
have subscribed. The Pavlovian addendum seems also to make
much of Lenin's conception of the role of consciousness in the
dynamics of the revolutionary situation "unscientific." Lenin *did*
seem to ascribe considerable responsibility to conscious determination. Yet "nervism" would make determination, will, sacrifice,
little other than complex reflex action to which we could not
*meaningfully* ascribe all the high honors which Soviet society
lavishes on the heroes of Socialism. That contemporary Soviet
thinkers have not seen fit to renounce these supplements to Marxist thought, supplements for which Stalin was by and large responsible, indicates that both Michurinism and Pavlovianism, irrespective of the scientific objections to which they are evidently subject, serve contemporary Marxism in a critical ideological capacity.
Under the dictatorship of Stalin both became, literally by decree,
components of Marxism as a conception of historical development.
Both add to its scope and complexity but do little for its scientific
stature. Their inclusion seems to be the consequence of seeing
history in terms of artificial schematisms. The extensive use of
metaphor, serious methodological impairments, and the indis-
position to divest itself of preconceptions lend contemporary
Marxism the species traits of a "metaphysics of history" (in its
pejorative sense), rather than a scientific enterprise.

## Historical Materialism as Science

The most authoritative contemporary texts devoted to Marxism
as a theory of history advance the claim that "historical materialism is the science of the general laws which govern the development of society," "the only certain, scientific solution to the most

cardinal, the most general theoretic and methodological problems of social science. . . . It conceives the history of society as a coherent process governed by laws. . . ."[85] The claim is explicit: historical materialism is a *science* concerned with the general laws of social development.

Marxists contend that historical materialism qualifies as a science of history and not as a philosophy of history. In general they have denied historical materialism the title "philosophy of history" because such an assignation implies "history conceived as schemes or tendencies and designs . . . based on syllogisms, demonstrations and deductions,"[86] a "fantastic and artificial" schematism.[87]

Contemporary Marxists in the Soviet Union advertise historical materialism as an empirical science of the general laws of history and, as such, identical in content with Marxist sociology.[88] Soviet Marxists make a distinction, in practice, between a historian who uses archival material to reconstruct past history and a sociologist who investigates contemporary society in order to provide a theoretical account of its dynamics, but the general underlying principle in the two cases is identical. In essence both possess a "theory of history," a systematic body of general laws understood to govern social dynamics. These laws take on the character of "dominant trends" which are distinguished from the confused mass of individual cases and non-essential deviations.[89] Thus "laws" are understood to express "tendencies," which under given conditions might be temporarily counteracted by other tendencies or forces.[90] In expressing his general laws, Marx regularly referred to them as "tendencies."[91] "Law, therefore," he advised, "shows itself only as a tendency, whose effects become clearly marked only under certain conditions and in the course of long periods."[92] In practice such "laws" always display "counteracting tendencies,"[93] which obscure the operation of the "law."

Engels also employed the notion of "law" in the study of historical development to mean "tendency." In his criticism of Paul Barth's *The Philosophy of History of Hegel and the Hegelians*,[94] Engels indicated that Marx analyzed the influence of political events within history's "*general* dependence upon economic conditions,"[95] and he himself believed that a multiplicity of component factors in history exert counterinfluences, against which "economic necessity" only *ultimately* asserts itself.[96] Once any historical element has been brought into the universe of historical events by other, ultimately economic causes, it can influence events within that universe even to the extent of acting upon those causes that have given rise to it.[97] Political, juridical, philosophical, religious, literary, and artistic development are based on economic development; and yet they can, individually or in conjunction, react upon the base and upon each other.[98] As residues from an anterior economic epoch, some of these intersecting variables may ultimately have "only a negative economic basis." To the extent that they form an independent element their influence acts upon the economic base.[99] The entire process "goes on in the form of interaction—though of very unequal forces, the economic movement being by far the strongest, most primeval, most decisive. . . ."[100] Yet even so, "everything is relative and nothing absolute."[101] Under specific conditions the decisive power of the economic base can be completely nullified by effective political power.[102]

The best that such a theory of history, committed to the ultimate decisiveness of the economic factor, can deliver by way of confirmation is the conviction that if one were to plot the axis of the curve of any independent sphere of human activity one would find that "the axis of this curve will run more and more nearly parallel to the axis of the curve of economic development the longer the period considered and the wider the field dealt with."[103]

Such a claim is relatively modest, but it has much to recommend it as a working hypothesis. It must be recognized, however, that such a hypothesis is impaired by the fact that the broader the area and the longer the temporal range of investigation to which a hypothesis must appeal for confirmation, the weaker such confirmation is. The broader the range of phenomena the easier it is to discover "tendencies." There is, for example, a general correlation between cranial capacity and civilization. What this specifically implies is difficult to say. Most physical anthropologists and psychologists today would say that it tells us nothing either about the innate capacity for civilization enjoyed by whole races of presapiens man or about the innate capacity for civilization possessed by whole races and individual men today. Yet there is a "tendency" for cranial size to increase with the complexity of society. The axis of the one curve, plotted over a sufficiently long period of time, corresponds remarkably well with the other. Can the absolute increase in the size of the brain, then, be legitimately conceived to operate as the decisive factor in determining the increased complexity of society?

Curiously enough Engels admitted that if the temporal reach of the curve he proposed were extended far enough into the past there would be a *negative correlation* between the economic base and social relations. The decisive factor determining those relations, until a few thousand years ago, were the rules governing breeding groups and sex relations.[104] Apparently confirmation for the hypothesis can only be obtained by plotting the curves within an arbitrarily specified historical period, for countertrends make their appearance within too brief *and* too broad a range.

The assertion that the economic factor is the ultimately decisive factor can qualify only as a weak claim. The "laws" of history are, at best, tendencies and could only operate as such. Each specific historical period must be assessed by employing a number of general laws which interact in a complex and obscure way. Any given period may defy any or all of the general laws of historical materialism. The failure of historical materialism to predict any particular historical event is sufficient evidence of its low predictive power.

Beside these qualifications concerning the "laws" of historical materialism, there is another and perhaps more serious consideration. Many of the "laws" or "tendencies" of historical materialism are couched in terms that are so loose that it is difficult to divine when, in fact, they are confirmed or disconfirmed. For example, one of the tendencies attributed to the capitalist epoch is the "law of the increasing misery of the working class." Critics of historical materialism are quick to indicate that such a tendency has not been realized. In its defense J. Gillman can still say that Marx "never spoke of the growing poverty of the working class" but rather of its increasing "pauperization," its increasing "misery."[105] Apparently the wording of some of the "laws" and their various formulations over a generation of literary activity have left sufficient room for such varied opinions about their meaning that even specialists are confused as to their intent. When Marx and Engels speak of the modern laborer sinking "deeper and deeper below the conditions of existence" and of the capitalist class not being competent "to assure an existence" to its wage-slaves,[106] this is not to be understood to mean, according to some interpretations, that there will be "growing poverty" among the working classes. When Marx writes that "eventually wages, which have already been reduced to a minimum, must be reduced yet further," a reduction which "necessarily leads to revolution,"[107] he is to be understood by some to mean a "relative" not "absolute" decline in the workers' standard of living.[108]

At least some of this confusion originates in the work of Marx himself. He employs the concepts of *relative* and *absolute* decline in the workers' standard of living, on occasion, without distinguishing between the two. Thus in the essay "Wage Labor and Capital" he speaks of a real rise in wages at a time when the "power of the capitalist class has grown." He illustrates the use of the relative fall in the standard of living by arguing that a worker's house hitherto felt to be adequate becomes inadequate when a palace arises next door.[109] Immiseration would therefore be relative immiseration. Nevertheless, at the end of the same work, Marx contends that under capitalism, "the forest of uplifted arms demanding work becomes ever thicker, while the arms themselves ever thinner."[110] Immiseration seems to be spoken of, in this context, as absolute.

While the draft program of the Russian Social Democratic party of 1902 included the "growth of poverty" in its indictment of capitalism,[111] Lenin, familiar with the criticism of German revisionism, had reservations on that formulation.[112] He did not propose to speak of "the absolute growth of poverty. . . ."[113] Yet one of the most recent texts out of the Soviet Union speaks of the relative *and* absolute increase in "pauperization" and decline in the "standard of living."[114] Other authorities maintain that "the absolute impoverishment of the working and other toiling masses is expressed in the continuous decline of real wages. . . ."[115] Khrushchev, in turn, speaks of a "very slight" increase in real wages in the advanced capitalist countries but a general worsening of conditions in the underdeveloped areas.[116]

If the "tendencies" governing a historical epoch are so vague that the proponents of the theory are in doubt concerning its specific implications it is difficult to understand under what conditions such a tendency is confirmed. When Engels identified Marx's discovery of the "law of the development of human history" as meaning nothing more than that he had revealed the "simple fact, hitherto concealed by an overgrowth of ideology, that mankind must first of all eat, drink, have shelter and clothing, before it can pursue politics, science, art, religion, etc.,"[117] he was certainly not formulating a "law" in any meaningful sense. That if men do not eat they will ultimately die is hardly to be classified as a discovery of any particular significance. Engels adds to this pronouncement a "therefore" in proceeding to tell us that man's social consciousness must be explained in the light of the production of the immediate means of subsistence. But the use of "therefore" is not warranted, for he has not advanced an argument. When he uses metaphors which maintain that state institutions "arise" from an economic "foundation" it is almost impossible to determine what is implied. One simply does not know how to go about confirming such "laws." How, for example, does one "prove" that the United States Supreme Court "arose" out of an economic "foundation"? Certainly Engels realized that one ran the risk of making oneself "ridiculous" if one attempted to explain in terms of economics the existence of every small state in Germany.[118] The difficulty seems to be in determining when it would not be ridiculous to attempt, in terms of economics, the explanation of any given historic event or series of historic events. Laws, even tendencies, have to be stipulated with sufficient precision so that we can determine when and under what conditions they are in fact verified. Certainly most of the laws and tendencies of historical materialism are so vague that they elude empirical assessment.

More important than all this is the fact that it was possible in Marx's day to speak of a theory which advanced general laws of historical motion as "scientific" although its laws were characterized as "inevitable" and "inexorable." The prevailing science of his day was essentially a materialistic determinism. In our own time, however, it has become apparent that scientific laws do not exemplify necessity. Empirical laws are probability statements of a higher or lower order—but probability statements nonetheless. Even if the laws of historical materialism could be formalized in such a way that the countertrends would not threaten to always behave as *ad hoc* causes of error whenever a prediction failed to materialize, it would still not be possible to speak of such laws as necessary and their working out as inevitable. Necessity can only be applied to a closed class; and empirical predictions, referring as they do to the future, cannot have a closed class as a referent, not unless one were a prophet or a Hegel. Prophets can refer to future events as instances of a closed class, because they have privileged access to the future. They pretend to have access to future events as immediately as we have access to past and present events. Hegel could be sure that the succession of events would be in accord with a predetermined pattern because his Idealism rested on an identity between mind and history. According to Hegel one can *deduce* future events, for the development of Spirit is a logical development and logical connections are necessary connections. Since man and Spirit share a common substance in Reason, human logic shares a common substance with the logic of history. Only by thus turning history into a logic could "inevitability" be ascribed to its course.

Historical materialism surrendered its right to speak in terms of inevitabilities when it abandoned Hegel's Idealism. Any theory of history which speaks of necessity must entail some form of idealism. Any system which seriously maintains that the world is a complex of material processes reflected in the mind of man must necessarily treat laws as empirical generalizations. Such laws enjoy no "iron necessity," nor can they be spoken of as inexorable. Empirical generalizations include sets of conditions which must be present if an event or a series of events is to occur. As such they are probability statements.

The use of locutions appropriate to logic, that is, the contention that the laws discovered by historical materialism are necessary and inevitable, threatens to make of it a philosophy of history which "deduces" the future. We have indicated that Engels frequently treated the future as though it could be deduced with mathematical precision. Contemporary Soviet Marxists insist on speaking of the "necessary internal connection" between events,[119] Khrushchev speaking, for example, of the "inevitability of the victory of the working class . . . the law-bound character of historical progress and the inevitability of the victory of socialism. . . ."[120]

There are certainly elements of a philosophy of history in the materialist conception of history. It possesses much of the character of theodicy, an explaining away of "evil." If historical progression is inevitable, then every past event was necessary and had to occur just as it did. It could be neither good nor evil. Hence for historical materialism slavery was "necessary" to the course of history.[121] Engels went so far as to say, "Without the slavery of antiquity no modern socialism."[122] He seemed convinced that each historical event formed a link in "the chain of mankind's universal progress"[123] in which "there is no great historical evil without a compensating historical progress."[124] Not much can be said for such convictions. They do not lend themselves to cognitive refutation, for they are articles of faith. At its worst historical materialism is a faith in history.

At its best it offers us probability statements which taken together offer us a pattern which may or may not serve as an analytic tool in the study of complex phenomena. It may serve as an illuminating principle for interpreting historical events. But as an empirical generalization of limited probability its pattern is obscured by an accumulation of detail in "an interaction of all . . . elements" and "amid all the endless host of accidents. . . ."[125] In empirical science when a "law" or a "tendency" is so obscured, verification may be accomplished if we can construct and execute a crucial experiment. Unfortunately, history does not lend itself to such an enterprise. Consequently there seem to be a multitude of possible patterns to history, a variety of intersecting tendencies. When Marx undertook to analyze exhaustively any particular period of history, the explanatory force of the specific general laws of historical materialism was certainly not so compelling that an alternative interpretation might not have with equal plausibility been substituted. To maintain that historical materialism is the *only* scientific technique available for the study of human society is so broad a claim that it can hardly be taken seriously.

But even as one scientific technique among others, historical materialism seems impaired by a multitude of shortcomings. The measure of credibility of any scientific thesis is its susceptibility to confirmation. The propositions of any empirical science should be framed in such a way that some empirical facts can either directly or indirectly verify them. We have indicated that some of the propositions of historical materalism defy any such confirmation. When Engels holds that historical materialism *had* to be discovered, he is advancing a thesis that no empirical investigation could ever confirm. When he maintains that had Napoleon not existed someone else would have performed his historic tasks, we have a transempirical thesis subject to no known scientific test. Lenin, by introducing variables unknown or incompletely known to the founders of classical Marxism, wrought such changes in the original theses that what would have been held, prior to his revision, to be a disproof of Marxism became its confirmation. The proliferation of the administrative organs of the state, its absolute growth in size and complexity, are all cited by Soviet Marxists as evidence of the success of Marxian Socialism, where a reading of Marx and Engels would suggest that just such facts were indicative of its failure. But since some contemporary Marxists, including Stalin, have argued that Marxism admits "contradictions" within its calculations, such apparent contradictions confirm the hypothesis in question. The only objection that could be raised would be, What would then *not* confirm the hypothesis? It seems that the thesis is confirmed by any event. If so, it is vacuous.

In many cases theses are advanced which can neither be proved nor disproved because they are loosely framed and/or technical difficulties make them impossible to investigate. Thus Lenin argued that the "exploitation of the masses, their want and their poverty" are the direct cause of crime.[126] With the elimination of want under Socialism excesses "will inevitably" begin to "wither away." Lenin adds that "we do not know how quickly and in what succession, but we know that they will wither away." There is no direct evidence that crime has begun to "wither away" in the Soviet Union. The difficulties of obtaining adequate statistics (statistics on crime are a state secret in the Soviet Union) and changing concepts of what constitutes crime make confirmation of Lenin's thesis impossible. But the fact that Soviet law includes elaborate criminal codes and has restored the death penalty for certain "socially dangerous acts," if it is indicative of anything at all, suggests that the Soviet Union expects crime to continue into the foreseeable future.[127] But since no time specifications confine the range in which confirmation might be forthcoming the thesis is never threatened. Many of the "inevitabilities" of historical materialism operate in some such fashion: anything confirms the thesis, or confirmation is technically impossible, or confirmation can always be postponed to some future time.

## Marxism Today

Marxism as a theoretical device for explaining historical and sociological phenomena has had an enormous impact on both historians and sociologists. There are few specialists in either discipline who are not familiar with at least the basic tenets of Marxism. Almost all have been directly or indirectly influenced by the thought of Karl Marx. Some have developed aspects of Marx's sociological system to the ultimate enrichment of science. Men such as Max Weber, Karl Mannheim, and Ferdinand Tönnies have been directly influenced by classical Marxism in one or another form. American scholars of the stature of Thorstein Veblen, Charles Beard, and C. Wright Mills have been similarly influenced. There is much in the rich heritage of Marxism that is suggestive of lines of inquiry and techniques for study. It is in this respect that contemporary Marxism is of most interest and importance for the science of human society. We often confuse the abundance Marx and Engels left us as part of our nineteenth-century legacy with the political system which rules today in the East. The history of Marxism is part of the intellectual history of the nineteenth century and as such it is part of our own intellectual history. But Marxism is also the source of the vocabulary employed by twentieth-century politicians. When we hear the cry of Socialism from some primitive African community, it can only be interpreted to mean that a demand has arisen for rapid industrialization. Such rapid industrialization almost inevitably means enormous human effort and sacrifice, which can only be ensured through coercion and violence exercised by a monolithic political organization that we have come to identify with "Communism." In primitive areas, force and violence become the conditions for development and industrial progress. For classical Marxism force and violence were at times a contingent, transitory evil and a means to the revolution which would usher in the new Socialist order of society. Marxism-Leninism, on the other hand, which seeks to construct the economic base beneath a "Socialist" society—an economic base which Marx thought Socialism would simply inherit—has elevated the use of force to the rank of a necessary condition of "progress."

It has become incumbent upon the West to distinguish the two faces of Marxism, the theory of classical Marxism, which is part of our heritage and for which we should show no shame—and a political tradition which is fundamentally not of Western provenience. All too often no such distinction is made.

For all of his efforts to be a practical revolutionary, Marx remained forever a scholar. Among the works of the nineteenth century, his are valuable additions to our intellectual stock. As such they can be inspected and, where suitable, employed in a free and honest contest of ideas. The West has matured to the point where the contest of alternative hypotheses has become one of the most profitable techniques for the advancement of knowledge. In this contest much of classical Marxism has been found wanting. Its most serious shortcoming is its evident addiction to Hegelianism. The addiction became increasingly pronounced as an increased number of causes of error and countertrends were introduced into the original formulations. More and more, recourse was had to "essences" that were behind "appearances." The more apparent the conditioned and conditioning circumstances, the more mysterious the "immanent laws" became. By the time Marx wrote the third volume of *Capital*, the processes governing human society had become recondite, and the clear consciousness of the dynamics governing social life could come to man only through the medium of select men. Where in the early manuscripts the working class was driven to the truth by the evident simplicity of the laws operating in society, in the final manuscripts such knowledge could only come to those who devoted their entire lives to the study of political economy. But the laws themselves, hidden though they were, were "essential," "immanent," "necessary," and "inexorable."

Lenin followed a similar course. Although initially convinced that the truth of Marxism was evident for all men to see, he later contended that only a thorough study of Hegel could permit one to understand even the first part of Marxism. There are but few men, we might add, who have the potential or the stamina for such a study. If Marx is difficult, Hegel is all but impossible.

Marxism as a science of society began a course of sure development when the dialectic of concepts ceased to be employed to deduce conclusions about existential affairs and was employed instead as a means of arriving at a hypothesis applicable to particulars. It gave evidences of decline when the concepts and categories began to appear in materialist guise, particularly in the writings of Engels. With Lenin the process reached its culmination in a literal restoration of Hegelianism, with all its categories and essences, operating behind the world, forever independent of any empirical verification.

# A Postscript in Lieu

# of Conclusions

We have concluded our brief survey of Marxism. In it we have
been primarily concerned with the thought of the three men who
have made contemporary Marxism what it is. We have distinguished the philosophy from the theory of history, treating each
as separate and distinct from the other. There is ample justification
for such a distinction. Marx himself never began any of his mature
works with an exposition of his "philosophy." He employed, rather,
certain methodological principles and advanced certain hypothetical constructs in the analysis of historical and economic
phenomena. It was Engels who introduced "dialectical materialism" as a necessary philosophical antecedent to Marxism as a
system. Lenin, in his turn, only began to employ "dialectical
materialism" as a preliminary to a discussion of Marxism in his
essay "Karl Marx," written in 1914 after he began reading Hegel.
His wife indicated, at the time, that this was unusual for him. This
departure from his usual practice, prompted by his introduction
to Hegel, nonetheless, derives specifically from Engels. Every
reference in the sections "Philosophical Materialism" and
"Dialectics" cites a work by Engels. Only when Lenin begins to
discuss historical materialism is Marx introduced as an authority.
Similarly, Stalin's work on *Dialectical and Historical Materialism*,
which set the standard for the treatment of Marxism in the Soviet
Union and which argued for the intrinsic connection between
dialectical and historical materialism, advances as dialectical

materialism that philosophy for which Engels is almost exclusively responsible.

We have indicated that the position assumed by the young Karl Marx was an anthropological realism which would accord well with the historical materialism of his mature years. He never explicitly abandoned his earlier position nor did he explicitly assume that of Friedrich Engels. At the present time there is a growing sentiment among Marxists, even within the Socialist nations, to reconsider the possibility of substituting Marx's early epistemology and his philosophy of natural science for the confused and confusing speculation of Engels' dialectical materialism. Certainly Marx's early writings are more defensible than those of the mature Engels. Equally certain is the fact that there is no necessary connection between the dialectical materialism of Engels and historical materialism as Marx understood it. The latter is as defensible, or as indefensible, with it as it is without it. The only trait shared by all the elements of Marxism is a tendency to confuse logical and empirical matters, but this is a failing common to much of the speculation of the nineteenth century. The belief was that the terms "scientific" and "deterministic" were, if not synonymous, at least inseparably connected. That empirical laws should be "inevitable" and "necessary" was a common prejudice from which our century has not yet completely liberated itself.[1] A shared disposition to use such expressions is not compelling evidence that Marx shared Engels' neo-Hegelianism. The form of Hegelianism found in Marx's mature writing is perfectly compatible with the anthropological realism of his youth couched in the terms of scientific determinism of his time. One need but read the modern works of George Herbert Mead to realize that a form of "social Hegelianism" can be made compatible with empirically oriented sociology. It is Engels' neo-Hegelianism, his applied effort to Hegelianize the natural sciences, which is so much at variance with contemporary Western thought. Lenin's confusion of materialism and Hegelianism seems to have even less to recommend it.

Contemporary Soviet philosophers have made some considerable gains in eliminating some of the more outrageous confusions which afflicted dialectical materialism, but there is little indication that they are prepared to abandon either the writings of Engels or Lenin as canonical in specifically philosophic concerns.

For the foreseeable future their work will probably be confined to attempts to make those writings seem more coherent. As the various Socialist states redefine their relationship to the Soviet Union there is the possibility that scholars in the various countries (should a new relationship permit increased freedom from the direct control of Moscow) will seek a more substantial philosophic base for their system in the early works of Karl Marx. We have indicated that some Polish philosophers have argued just such a theme. Certainly, for Western scholars the early Marx manuscripts are infinitely more interesting than the turgid philosophical works of Engels or Lenin. Karl Marx, even in his youth, was a student of philosophy in the literal sense of the word, something which cannot be said of either Engels or Lenin.

If historical materialism is conceived as a theory of history, independent of the neo-Hegelianism of both Engels and Lenin, it can be judged within the context of empirical science. Its claims can then be confirmed or disconfirmed in practice. In any event, whatever the judgments of science, historiography and social science in general owe an inestimable debt to Marxism. Social science can never return to its pre-Marxian forms. Whether Marxism per se is exclusively responsible for this does not concern us here. Whatever may be the case, contemporary thinkers can no more do without a knowledge of Marxist social science than they can do without a knowledge of Darwinism.

The theses advanced by Marxism as a theory of history are interesting and important. In many cases a connected account of a historical period can seemingly be given only in terms of a quasi-Marxist analysis. This is, of course, not to pretend that historical materialism is the only analytic and conceptual tool available to social science. We have tried to indicate some of the shortcomings of historical materialism as a scientific theory of history. Where Marxists have argued for Marxism as a philosophy of history, where they would infuse history with a purpose and a goal, a technique for inducing among men "a sense of mission and dedication,"[2] they have often shown themselves to be lamentably ignorant of the distinction between values and means to the realization of values. Unless such a distinction is made there is the real possibility that means may become ends in themselves. Such seems to have been the case with Lenin. The means to the Socialist society were elevated finally to ends in themselves—at the expense of the explicit values which Marxism entertained. Marx and Engels were both dedicated to the full liberation of man. To them revolution seemed a necessary means to that end. Lenin's insistence upon revolution at any cost and under any condition was the consequence both of a poor assessment of objective fact and a seeming lack of commitment to values which animated the thought of the founders of Marxism. The excesses of Stalinism can be, at least in part, charged to Lenin. That Soviet thinkers have themselves recognized the enormities committed by Stalin is gratifying. Their insistence that such enormities are no longer possible under a Socialist system[3] would be more reassuring if they could give some evidence that the hierarchical and centralist principles of Leninism had been significantly relaxed. To date there are but few indications that such is to be the case.[4] Yugoslavia, on the other hand, may seriously have such a "democratization" in mind.[5] Whatever the case, the values to which Marx and Engels were committed are relatively clear. And historical materialism is animated by values held in common with the Western tradition. Few would object to those values. In general our objections are to the scientific analysis of historical and social change, and consequently to the means Marxism conceives as essential to the attainment of its ends. The latter are factual considerations and can be significantly discussed in the cognitive language of fact. It is with those issues that we have been concerned. We are all, by and large, committed to values such as the "liberation" of man from false consciousness, to an economy characterized as an "association of free producers," to "distributive justice," to broad "democracy." But such values become substantial only when a course is undertaken to implement them. Then they have real consequences which demand regular reassessment and value judgment.

Most propositions concerning "values" can be unpacked to indicate that facts are, in some sense, involved in them. In most cases it will be found that arguments about "ends" are substantially arguments about facts—the attitudinal biases, the emotive components of such propositions are frequently shared in common by all parties in the discussion. Thus we all object to war and favor peace. What we may significantly argue about is whether one course rather than another better assures peace. When we find ourselves arguing with an opponent who explicitly favors war and destruction as a value, there doesn't seem to be any way to resolve our differences. If one prefers war and destruction to peace and construction, there does not seem to be any way in which we can disabuse him of his preference short of psychotherapy. But, fortunately, most men, Marxist or non-Marxist, seem committed to essentially the same values. Differences are differences which turn on facts, concerns with how best to achieve the truly human social order, how to ensure peace, prosperity, and a future for mankind.

This book has been concerned with Marxism's answers to these questions, and thus with cognitive issues. In principle, these are subject to reasoned resolution. No pretense is made that this book has *resolved* the issues. It has undertaken an assessment—one among many. All or any of its theses may be questioned; and its expositions of the basic ideas of Marxism may be found to err. It is hoped that at least some of it will stand the test of scrutiny. It is offered in the conviction that the only legitimate technique for the resolution of differences which divide men of good will is reasoned discourse.

# Notes and References

References have been made to editions of the works of Marx, Engels, and Lenin that would be most accessible to the reader. For this reason the early Marx and Engels material is cited in the new German edition, the Marx, Engels *Werke* rather than the older Marx, Engels *Gesamtausgabe*. While the latter is a more definitive edition, the former is more easily obtained, and the publication in English of much of the early Marx material omitted from the new collection justifies its use.

*The following abbreviations have been used in the notes:*

AD  F. Engels, *Anti-Dühring: Herr Eugen Dühring's Revolution in Science* (Moscow, 1962).

CRP  I. P. Pavlov, *Conditioned Reflexes and Psychiatry* (New York, 1941).

CW  F. Engels, *The Condition of the Working-Class in England in 1844* (London, 1950).

DI  K. Marx and F. Engels, *Die deutsche Ideologie*, in *Werke*, Vol. III (Berlin, 1958).

DN  F. Engels, *Dialectics of Nature* (Moscow, 1954).

EPM  K. Marx, *Economic and Philosophic Manuscripts* (Moscow, n.d.).

FD  G. Gentile, *Fondamenti della filosofia del diritto con aggiunti due studi sulla filosofia di Marx* (Florence, 1955).

HF  K. Marx and F. Engels, *The Holy Family or Critique of Critical Critique* (Moscow, 1956).

LCR  I. P. Pavlov, *Lectures on Conditioned Reflexes* (New York, 1928).

LCW  V. I. Lenin, *Collected Works* (Moscow, 1960–    ).

*LF* F. Engels, *Ludwig Feuerbach and the End of Classical German Philosophy,* in K. Marx and F. Engels, *Selected Works in Two Volumes,* Vol. II (Moscow, 1955), pp. 357–401.

*LP* *Die Lehre I. P. Pawlows und die philosophischen Fragen der Psychologie* (Berlin, 1955).

*LSW* V. I. Lenin, *Selected Works in Two Volumes* (Moscow, 1950–1951).

*MEC* V. I. Lenin, *Materialism and Empiriocriticism: Critical Comments on a Reactionary Philosophy,* in *Collected Works,* Vol. XIV (Moscow, 1962).

*MESW* K. Marx and F. Engels, *Selected Works in Two Volumes* (Moscow, 1955).

*MEW* K. Marx and F. Engels, *Werke* (Berlin, 1957– ).

*PN* V. I. Lenin, *Philosophical Notebooks,* in *Collected Works,* Vol. XXXVIII (Moscow, 1961).

*PP* K. Marx, *The Poverty of Philosophy* (Moscow, n.d.).

*PSW* I. P. Pavlov, *Selected Works* (Moscow, 1955).

*SE* K. Marx, *Selected Essays* (London, n.d.).

*SSW* J. V. Stalin, *Works* (Moscow, 1952–1955).

*SW* L. Feuerbach, *Ludwig Feuerbachs sämmtliche Werke* (Leipzig, 1846–1866).

# CHAPTER ONE

1 Cf. A. Voden, "Talks with Engels," *Reminiscences of Marx and Engels* (Moscow, n.d.), pp. 330–331.

2 R. Dunayevskaya, *Marxism and Freedom* (New York, 1958), pp. 290–325.

3 I have used the first complete English edition of the *Economic and Philosophic Manuscripts of 1844* provided by the Foreign Languages Publishing House of Moscow in an undated edition. Since that time Moscow has made a second edition available, dated 1961. In 1964 International Publishers of New York made a revised translation of the Russian edition available under the same title. The McGraw-Hill Book Company of New York made a new translation available in 1964 in the volume *Karl Marx: Early Writings,* translated and edited by T. B. Bottomore.

4 Cf. J. Lindsay, *Marxism and Contemporary Science* (London, 1949), pp. 19–27.

5 Cf. A. Cornu, *Karl Marx: Die ökonomisch-philosophischen Manuskripte*

(Berlin, 1955), and his *Karl Marx und die Entwicklung des modernen Denkers* (Berlin, 1950), pp. 99–107.

6 Cf. Dunayevskaya, *op. cit.*, pp. 53–66; E. Fromm, *Marx's Concept of Man* (New York, 1961), pp. 1–83.

7 D. Bell, "The Debate on Alienation," in L. Labedz, ed., *Revisionism: Essays on the History of Marxist Ideas* (New York, 1962), pp. 195–211; R. Tucker, *Philosophy and Myth in Karl Marx* (Cambridge, England, 1962); R. Mondolfo, *Marx y Marxismo: Estudios historicocriticos* (Buenos Aires, 1960); H. Popitz, *Der entfremdete Mensch* (Basel, 1953); K. H. Breuer, *Der junge Marx: sein Weg zum Kommunismus* (Cologne, 1954); P. Bigo, *Marxismo e umanismo* (Milan, 1963); J. Calvez, *La pensée de Karl Marx* (Paris, 1956).

8 *FD;* see particularly the appendix entitled "La filosofia di Marx."

9 Cf. A. J. Gregor, "Giovanni Gentile and the Philosophy of the Young Karl Marx," *Journal of the History of Ideas*, XXIV, 2 (1963), 213–230.

10 For the purpose of this discussion no distinction is made between *entäussern* and *entfremden*. Cf. Translator's Note on Terminology in *EPM*, pp. 10–13.

11 For an excellent discussion of this period, cf. M. Rossi, *Marx e la dialettica hegeliana* (Rome, 1963), II, pt. 1.

12 Cf. "Marx' Brief an seinen Vater vom 10. November 1837," in S. Landshut, ed., *Die Frühschriften* (Stuttgart, 1953), p. 7.

13 Cf. H. Adams, *Karl Marx in His Earlier Writings* (London, 1940), pp. 23 ff.

14 See K. Marx, Preface to "Differenz der demokritischen und epikureischen Naturphilosophie im Allgemeinen," in F. Mehring, *Aus dem literarischen Nachlass von Karl Marx, Friedrich Engels und Ferdinand Lassalle* (Stuttgart, 1902), I, 68; cf. Breuer, *op. cit.*, p. 62.

15 L. von Stein, *Der Socialismus und Communismus des heutigen Frankreichs* (Leipzig, 1842).

16 *LF*, pp. 358, 366–367.

17 K. Marx, "Luther als Schiedsrichter zwischen Strauss und Feuerbach," *MEW*, I, 27.

18 Cf. *HF*, pp. 15, 56, 124 ff.

19 A. Labriola, *Studio su Marx* (Naples, 1926), p. 60.

20 Marx, "Vorarbeiten zur Dissertation," *Marx, Engels, Historische-Kritische Gesamtausgabe. Werke/Schriften/Briefe* (Berlin, 1927), I, pt. 1, 119.

21 "Zur Kritik der Hegelschen Philosophie," *SW*, II, 230–231.

22 "Vorläufige Thesen zur Reform der Philosophie," *SW*, II, 246.

23 Cf. "Grundsätze der Philosophie der Zukunft," *SW*, II, 270.

24 L. Feuerbach, *The Essence of Christianity* (New York, 1957), p. 14.

25 *Ibid.*, p. 25.

26 "Grundsätze . . ." SW, II, 273.

27 "Vorläufige Thesen . . ." SW, II, 248.

28 "Grundsätze . . ." SW, II, 304–305.

29 "Vorläufige Thesen . . ." SW, II, 246.

30 *Ibid.*, pp. 247–248.

31 "Zur Kritik . . ." SW, II, 227.

32 *Ibid.*, p. 222.

33 "Grundsätze . . ." SW, II, 332.

34 Feuerbach, *Essence* . . . , p. xxxv.

35 *Ibid.*, pp. xxxiv–xxxv. Cf. SW, VII, 10, 12.

36 *EPM*, p. 17.

37 *EPM*, p. 145.

38 G. della Volpe, *Rousseau y Marx y otros ensayos de critica materialista* (Buenos Aires, 1963), pp. 101–102.

39 *MEW*, I, 209, 224.

40 *Ibid.*, p. 233.

41 *Ibid.*, p. 213.

42 "A Criticism of the Hegelian Philosophy of Right," SE, p. 11. Retranslated from the German.

43 Marx to Ruge, September, 1843, *MEW*, I, p. 346.

44 *Ibid.*, 206.

45 *MEW*, I, 224; cf. p. 215.

46 *EPM*, pp. 149–150.

47 "Vorläufige Thesen . . ." SW, II, 266–267.

48 *HF*, pp. 78–83.

49 *HF*, p. 124.

50 *EPM*, p. 146.

51 *EPM*, p. 148.

52 *EPM*, p. 151.

53 *EPM*, p. 153.

54 *EPM*, p. 155.

55 *EPM*, p. 166.

56 K. Marx, *Capital* (Moscow, 1954), I, 19.

57 *EPM*, pp. 155–156.

58  *HF,* p. 107.

59  *HF,* p. 59.

60  Marx to Annenkov, December 28, 1846, *MESW,* II, 447.

61  *PP,* p. 122.

62  *PP,* p. 128.

63  *PP,* p. 129.

64  *DI,* pp. 28, 25.

65  *DI,* p. 26.

66  Engels, in "Outlines of a Critique of Political Economy," *EPM,* p. 187.

67  *HF,* p. 56.

68  Marx, *Grundrisse der Kritik der politischen Ökonomie, Rohentwurf 1857–1858* (Berlin, 1953), pp. 21–29.

69  *Capital,* I, 72.

70  *Ibid.*

71  *Ibid.,* p. 76.

72  *EPM,* p. 146.

73  *EPM,* p. 145.

74  *PP,* p. 122.

75  *DI,* pp. 20–21.

76  *DI,* p. 27.

77  *DI,* pp. 26–27.

78  Marx, "Theses on Feuerbach," Thesis Four, *MESW,* II, 403; cf. *DI,* p. 42, where Marx speaks of the "embryos capable of development" to be found in Feuerbach's thought.

79  Cf. F. Olgiati, *Carlo Marx* (Milan, 1918), pp. 152 ff.

80  Cf. M. Rosental, *Die Dialektik in Marx' "Kapital"* (Berlin, 1959), p. 385.

81  "Vorläufige Thesen . . ." *SW,* 266–267.

82  Cf. K. Löwith, *Von Hegel zu Nietzsche* (Stuttgart, 1953), pp. 333–334.

83  Feuerbach, *Briefwechsel und Nachlass,* ed. K. Grün (Heidelberg, 1874), I, 409.

84  "Criticism . . ." *SE,* p. 39.

85  "Zur Kritik . . ." *SW,* II, 192, 207, 231; cf. W. Chamberlain, *Heaven Wasn't His Destination: The Philosophy of Ludwig Feuerbach* (New York, 1940), p. 30.

86  *SW,* II, 236, 258.

87 "Feuerbach explains the Hegelian dialectic . . . from the positive, from sense certainty . . ." *EPM*, p. 145; cf. p. 111.

88 "Subjects and objects do not come together to create human activity: they are ever changing distinctions within it." S. Hook, *From Hegel to Marx: Studies in the Intellectual Development of Karl Marx* (Ann Arbor, 1962), p. 259.

89 "Vorläufige Thesen . . ." *SW*, II, 252–253; Chamberlain, *op. cit.*, p. 184.

90 "Über den 'Anfang der Philosophie,'" *SW*, II, 235 ff.

91 "Is the object nothing more than an object? Surely it is the other of the ego [*das Andere des Ich*], but could I not say the obverse: the ego is the other, the object of the object . . . ?" *Ibid.*, p. 237.

92 Cf. Hegel, *Phenomenology of Mind*, trans. Baillie (New York, 1949), pp. 154–155.

93 "Zur Kritik . . ." *SW*, II, 214.

94 "Über den 'Anfang der Philosophie,'" *SW*, II, 239–240.

95 F. Jodl, *Ludwig Feuerbach* (Stuttgart, 1908), p. 40.

96 "The doubts that theory leaves unresolved are resolved for you in practice." "Fragmente zur Charakteristik meines philosophischen *curriculum vitae*," *SW*, II, 411.

97 Cf. Hook, *op. cit.*, p. 229.

98 "The transition from the ideal to the real has its place only in practical philosophy." "Vorläufige Thesen . . ." *SW*, II, 254.

99 "Only there . . . where I suffer arises the idea of an activity outside myself, that is, objectivity." "Grundsätze . . ." *SW*, II, 322.

100 Cf. "Vorläufige Thesen . . ." *SW*, II, 264.

101 ". . . out of the essence and the traits of the object one concludes the essence and traits of the subject." "Grundsätze . . ." *SW*, II, 275.

102 Hook, *op. cit.*, p. 237.

103 "Vorläufige Thesen . . ." *SW*, II, 263.

104 "Matter comes to be known and recognized only in opposition to the spirit. Matter exists only for a being other than matter, more correctly a being which distinguishes itself from matter, just as darkness exists only for a being who has sight, who is not blind." "Kritik des Idealismus," *SW*, II, 147.

105 Cf. M. Adler, *Lehrbuch der materialistischen Geschichtsauffassung* (Berlin, 1930), I, 96 ff. Marx understood this: ". . . the old contradiction between spiritualism and materialism has been . . . overcome once and for all by Feuerbach." *HF*, p. 126.

106 Cf. "Vorläufige Thesen . . ." *SW*, II, 264.

107 "The measure of the species is the absolute measure, law, and criterion of man." Feuerbach, *Essence* . . . p. 16.

108 "Man . . . is to himself the measure of all things, of all reality." *Ibid.*, p. 22.

109 "I have regarded *man* as the criterion of truth. . . ." *Ibid.*, p. xlii.

110 "Zur Kritik . . ." *SW*, II, 230.

111 Feuerbach, *Essence* . . . p. 5.

112 *Ibid.*, p. 4.

113 ". . . the object itself is nothing other than the objective ego [*gegenständliche Ich*]." "Anfang . . ." *SW*, II, 231.

114 Feuerbach, *Essence* . . . p. 11.

115 *Ibid.*, p. 12.

116 *Ibid.*, p. 8.

117 Cf. *Ibid.*, p. 7.

118 "Every speculation which pretends to transcend nature and man is vain." "Anfang . . ." *SW*, II, 231.

119 "Whatever the world is, it at least is what it looks like to man and his body. It is no less real nor more real than what it appears to those creatures who see with different eyes, touch with different 'hands' . . . save that the whole comparison is fantastic, for we can never know how things appear to other organisms." Hook, *op. cit.*, p. 258.

120 "Every object becomes known and understood by men only as a consequence of its relationship to men—even in science . . ." "Über Philosophie und Christum," *SW*, II, 181.

121 "Anfang . . ." *SW*, II, 234.

122 Cf. "Grundsätze . . ." *SW*, II, 323. Cf. *FD*, p. 205; Hook, *op. cit.*, pp. 222, 229. "Men have capabilities in that in which they are interested. The mystics and scholastics of the Middle Ages had no capabilities and skill in natural science because they had no interest in nature." "Grundsätze . . ." *SW*, II, 290.

123 Cf. "Beleuchtung einer theologischen Recension vom 'Wesen des Christenthums,'" *SW*, I, 207–208.

124 "Only that is real, at least for men, which is the object of real, practical activity." "Grundsätze . . ." *SW*, II, 289.

125 ". . . limited understanding . . . values the limited nature whose understanding it is. Each is exactly adapted to the other. . . . The eye of the brute sees no farther than its needs and its nature no farther than its needs." Feuerbach, *Essence* . . . p. 8.

126 "I consider Feuerbach a subjective absolutist because the principle of his world view and his standpoint, in his explicit view, the Absolute

or the Divine, is the subject or the essence of mankind. The subjective absolute or the species consciousness of mankind is therefore the world divinity, that is the principle and the essence of the objective world . . ." A. Cornill, *Ludwig Feuerbach und seine Stellung zur Religion und Philosophie* (Frankfurt am Main, 1851), pp. 55–56.

127 Cf. Hook, *op. cit.*, p. 257.

128 Cf. "Zur Kritik . . ." *SW*, II, 231.

129 *EPM*, pp. 113–114, 148–149.

130 *EPM*, pp. 109, 145.

131 *HF*, p. 56.

132 "Man as an objective, sensuous being is therefore a *suffering* being— and because he feels what he suffers, a *passionate* being. Passion is the essential force of man energetically bent on its object." *EPM*, p. 158.

133 ". . . the resolution of the *theoretical* antitheses is *only* possible *in a practical way*, by virtue of the practical energy of men. Their resolution is therefore by no means merely a problem of knowledge, but a *real* problem of life, which *philosophy* could not solve precisely because it conceived this problem as *merely* a theoretical one." *EPM*, p. 109.

134 "*The alienation of self-consciousness* establishes *thinghood.* . . . it *is* not *real* Man, nor therefore *Nature*—Man being *human* Nature—who as such is made the subject, but only the abstraction of man—self-consciousness . . ." *EPM*, p. 155.

135 *EPM*, p. 156.

136 ". . . nature appears as *his* work and his reality. The object of labor is, therefore, the *objectification of man's species life;* for he duplicates himself not only, as in consciousness, intellectually, but also actively, in reality, and therefore he contemplates himself in a world that he has created." *EPM*, p. 76. Man creates "an *objective world* by his practical activity . . ." *EPM*, p. 75.

137 Cf. *EPM*, p. 107.

138 ". . . industry . . . is the *exoteric* revelation of man's *essential powers,* we . . . (therefore) gain an understanding of the *human* essence of nature or the *natural* essence of man. In consequence, natural science will lose its abstractly material—or rather, its idealistic—tendency, and will become the basis of *human* science, as it has already become the basis of actual human science . . ." *EPM*, p. 110.

139 *EPM*, p. 169.

140 "Reality, therefore according to [Marx], is a subjective production of man; a production however of sensory activity (*sinnliche Thätigkeit*); not of thought as Hegel and the other Idealists imagined." *FD*, p. 216.

**141** "Neither nature objectively nor nature subjectively is directly given a form adequate to the *human* being." *EPM*, p. 158.

**142** Cf. *EPM*, p. 76.

**143** "Here we see how consistent naturalism or humanism distinguishes itself both from idealism and materialism, constituting at the same time the unifying truth of both." *EPM*, p. 156.

**144** "In practice I can relate myself to a thing humanly only if the thing relates itself to the human being humanly." *EPM*, p. 107, n. 1. ". . . it is only when the objective world becomes everywhere for man in society the world of man's essential powers—human reality, and for that reason the reality of his *own* essential powers—that all *objects* become for him the *objectification* of himself . . . become *his* objects . . ."*EPM*, p. 107.

**145** "For this reason it [the human world] is just as highly varied as the determination of human *essence* and *activities.*" *EPM*, p. 106, n. 1. "Man appropriates his total essence in a total manner, that is to say, as a whole man. Each of his *human* relations to the world—seeing, hearing, smelling, tasting, feeling, thinking, being aware, sensing, wanting, acting, loving—in short, all the organs of his individual being, like those organs which are directly social in their form, are in their *objective* orientation or in their *orientation to the object,* the appropriation of that object, the appropriation of the *human* world; their orientation to the object is the *manifestation of the human world;* it is human *efficaciousness* and *human suffering . . .*" *EPM*, p. 106.

**146** "When you ask about the creation of nature and man, you are abstracting, in so doing, from man and nature. You postulate them as *non-existent,* and yet you want me to prove them to you as *existing.* Now I say to you: Give up your abstraction and you will also give up your question. Or if you want to hold on to your abstraction, then be consistent, and if you think of man and nature as *non-existent,* then think of yourself as non-existent, for you too are surely nature and man. Don't think, don't ask me, for as soon as you think and ask, your *abstraction* from the existence of nature and man has no meaning." *EPM*, p. 113.

**147** ". . . it is only when the objective world becomes everywhere for man in society the world of man's essential powers—human reality, and for that reason the reality of his *own* essential powers—that all *objects* become for him the *objectification of himself* . . . become *his* objects . . ." *EPM*, p. 107.

**148** "In a system which posits as a fundamental thesis the intimate interrelation between the subject and the object, and which makes of one the product of the other, it becomes meaningless to ask if thought achieves objective reality." C. Scalia, *Il Materialismo Storico e il Socialismo* (Milan, 1920), p. 16; cf. Labriola, *op. cit.*, p. 38.

149 "Thinking and being are thus no doubt *distinct*, but at the same time they are in *unity* with each other." *EPM*, p. 105.

150 *EPM*, p. 76.

151 "The chief defect of all hitherto existing materialism—that of Feuerbach included—is that the object, reality, sensuousness, is conceived only in the form of the *object* or datum of *contemplation* but not as *human sensuous activity, practice*, not subjectively. Thus it happened that the active side, in opposition to materialism, was developed by idealism—but only abstractly, since, of course, idealism does not know real sensuous activity as such. Feuerbach wants sensuous objects, really differentiated from the thought objects, but he does not conceive human activity itself as activity *through objects*. Consequently, in the *Essence of Christianity*, he regards the theoretical attitude as the only genuinely human attitude, while practice is conceived and fixed only in its dirty-Jewish form of appearance. Hence he does not grasp the significance of 'revolutionary,' or practical-critical, activity." Marx, "Theses on Feuerbach," Thesis One, *MESW*, II, 402.

152 Marx, *Capital* (Moscow, 1962), III, 259.

153 Cf. Fromm's introductory essay, *op. cit.*, pp. v–89; A. J. Gregor, "Erich Fromm and the Young Karl Marx," *Studies on the Left*, III, 1 (1962), 85–92.

154 As a living whole, nature is a total process or Idea; as contingency and externality, it is the same Idea in its otherness or self-estrangement." Hegel, *Encyclopedia of Philosophy*, trans. G. Mueller (New York, 1959), p. 166; cf. *HF*, pp. 188–189. "The Idea—the final cause and teleological process of the whole—gains existence in the life of nature but is also estranged from itself." Hegel, *Encyclopedia*, p. 181.

155 Cf. Marx's discussion in *PP*, pp. 117–118.

156 Cf. Hegel, *Encyclopedia*, p. 270.

157 Cf. *LF*, pp. 362, 385. This is how Engels in his maturity refers to "alienation."

158 "The principle of *Development* involves also the existence of a latent germ of being—a capacity or potentiality striving to realize itself." Hegal, *The Philosophy of History* (New York, 1956), p. 54. "Spirit is only that which it attains by its own efforts . . ." *Ibid.*, p. 55.

159 *Ibid.*, pp. 73–74.

160 *Ibid.*, pp. 37, 55.

161 ". . . spirit . . . is always one and the same, but . . . unfolds . . . its one nature in the phenomena of the World's existence. This must, as before stated, present itself as the ultimate result of history. But we have to take the latter as it is. We must proceed historically—empirically." *Ibid.*, p. 10.

162 "What Spirit really strives for is the realization of its Ideal being; but in doing so, it hides that goal from its own vision, and is proud and well satisfied in this alienation from it." *Ibid.*, p. 55.

163 Hegel, *The Phenomenology of Mind*, pp. 251–267.

164 Marx, *MEW*, I, 286.

165 ". . . the moment we cease to pursue the historical movement of production relations, of which the categories are but the theoretical expression, the moment we want to see in these categories no more than ideas, spontaneous thoughts, independent of real relations, we are forced to attribute the origin of these thoughts to the movement of pure reason. How does pure, eternal, impersonal reason give rise to these thoughts? How does it proceed in order to produce them? If we had M. Proudhon's intrepidity in the matter of Hegelianism we should say: it is distinguished in itself from itself. What does this mean? Impersonal reason, having outside itself neither a base on which it can pose itself, nor an object to which it can oppose itself, nor a subject with which it can compose itself, head over heels, in posing itself, opposing itself and composing itself—position, opposition, composition. Or, to speak Greek—we have thesis, antithesis and synthesis. For those who do not know the Hegelian language, we shall give the consecrating formula:—affirmation, negation and negation of the negation. It is certainly not Hebrew (with due apologies to M. Proudhon); but it is the language of this pure reason, separate from the individual. Instead of the ordinary individual with his ordinary manner of speaking and thinking we have nothing but this ordinary manner in itself—without the individual." *PP*, pp. 117–118; see also p. 121.

166 Marx to P. V. Annenkov, December 28, 1846, *MESW*, II, 441–452.

167 *EPM*, p. 136.

168 *EPM*, p. 148.

169 *HF*, p. 78.

170 *PP*, p. 118.

171 *DI*, pp. 48 ff.

172 *EPM*, p. 76.

173 *EPM*, p. 129.

174 *EPM*, p. 105.

175 *Ibid.*

176 *EPM*, p. 80

177 *EPM*, p. 110.

178 *EPM*, p. 80.

179  *EPM*, p. 82.

180  *EPM*, p. 80.

181  *EPM*, pp. 151–152.

182  *EPM*, p. 135.

183  *EPM*, pp. 105 ff.

184  *EPM*, p. 114.

185  *EPM*, p. 102.

186  Marx, "Marx über sein Verhältnis zu Hegel und Feuerbach," *MEW*, III, 536.

187  Marx, "Aus I. Feuerbach," *MEW*, III, 540.

188  This compares with the various, i.e., ontological and empirical, usages found in the writings of Hess. Cf. "Über das Geldwesen," in *Philosophische und sozialistische Schriften, 1837–1850*, ed. A. Cornu and W. Mönke (Berlin, 1962), pp. 330–331.

189  *EPM*, pp. 73–74.

190  *EPM*, p. 74.

191  *EPM*, p. 79.

192  *EPM*, p. 78. Emphasis supplied.

193  "Private property thus results by analysis from the concept of alienated labor. . . ." *EPM*, p. 80.

194  Marx, *MESW*, I, 364.

195  Cf. Editor's introduction to *Die deutsche Ideologie* (Berlin, 1958), p. 6.

196  *DI*, p. 19.

197  "The family which to begin with is the only social relationship, becomes later, when increased needs create new social relations and the increased population new needs, a subordinate one (except in Germany), and must then be treated and analyzed according to the existing empirical data, not according to 'the concept of the family,' as is the custom in Germany." *DI*, p. 29.

198  *DI*, p. 38.

199  *DI*, pp. 28–35.

200  *DI*, p. 38.

201  Marx, Engels, "Manifesto . . ." *MESW*, I, 58.

202  Marx, "Aus I. Feuerbach," *MEW*, III, 540.

203  Marx, *MESW*, I, 362.

204  Cf. *HF*, p. 51.

205  *HF*, p. 73; cf. p. 111.

**206** *PP*, p. 128.

**207** The Soviet Marxist editors of the *Manuscripts* insist that this is the only use of alienation: "By 'estrangement,' or 'alienation,' Marx means the forced labor of the laborer for the capitalist, the appropriation by the capitalist of the product of a worker's labor and the separation of the laborer from the means of production which, being in the capitalist's possession, confront the laborer as an alien, enslaving power." *EPM*, p. 8. This would make alienation the consequence of private property rather than its cause.

**208** *EPM*, p. 69.

**209** *EPM*, p. 15.

**210** "Our conception of history depends on our ability to expound the real process of production, starting out from the simple material production of life, and to comprehend the form of intercourse connected with this and created by this . . . as the basis of all history; further, to show it in its action as state, and so, from this starting point, to explain the whole mass of different theoretical products and forms of consciousness, religion, philosophy, ethics, etc. . . ." *DI*, pp. 37–38.

**211** Cf. M. Adler, *Engels als Denker* (Berlin, 1925), pp. 37–49.

**212** Cf. Engels' writings of the period in *MEW*, I, pp. 454–592, particularly Engels' *The Condition of the Working Class in England in 1844*, written during 1844.

**213** Engels, "On the History of the Communist League," *MSEW*, II, p. 343; cf. R. Mondolfo, *Il materialismo storico in Federico Engels* (Genoa, 1912), p. 132.

**214** Engels to Marx, November 19, 1844, in A. Bebel and E. Bernstein, eds., *Der Briefwechsel zwischen Friedrich Engels und Karl Marx, 1844 bis 1883* (Stuttgart, 1913), I, 7. Later Engels was to characterize the method of "pure ideology" as that which deduces "reality not from itself, but from a concept." *AD*, p. 134. In 1886 he characterized the materialistic dialectic as comprehending "the concepts in our heads once more materialistically—as images of real things instead of regarding the real things as images of this or that stage of the absolute concept." *LF*, p. 386.

**215** Marx, *Grundrisse der Kritik der politischen Ökonomie*, pp. 715–717.

**216** *Ibid.*, p. 715. Emphasis supplied.

**217** Compare here Engels' account of "alienation" in his "Outline of a Critique of Political Economy": "The immediate consequence of private property was the split of production into two opposing sides— the natural and the human sides, the soil which without fertilization by man is dead and sterile, and human activity, whose first condition is that very soil. Furthermore we have seen how human activity in its turn was dissolved into labor and capital, and how these two sides antagonistically confronted each other." *EPM*, p. 193.

218 *Capital*, I, 571.

219 *Ibid.*, p. 432.

220 *Ibid.*, pp. 645–646.

221 As it is to Engels; cf. *AD*, pp. 372, 376, 386.

222 Feuerbach, *Essence* . . . p. 26.

223 *EPM*, p. 70.

224 Cf. Hess, "Philosophie der That," in *Philosophische und Sozialistische Schriften*, pp. 224–225.

225 Cf. Marx, "Thesen über Feuerbach," Thesis Six, *MEW*, III, 6.

226 E. Buggenhagen, *Die Stellung zur Wirklichkeit bei Hegel und Marx* (Marburg, 1933), pp. 8, 18.

227 Marx, *MEW*, I, 224.

228 Cf. E. Thier, "Etappen der Marxinterpretation," *Marxismusstudien* (Tübingen, 1954), p. 27.

229 Marx to Engels, May 31, 1873, *Briefwechsel* . . . IV, 346.

## CHAPTER TWO

1 Cf. G. Mayer, *Friedrich Engels: A Biography* (New York, 1936), and Y. Stepanova, *Frederick Engels* (Moscow, 1958).

2 Cf. Marx, "Die Verhandlungen des 6. rheinischen Landtags: Debatten über das Holzdiebstahlsgesetz," *MEW*, I, 109–147.

3 Engels, "Briefe aus dem Wuppertal," *MEW*, I, 413–432.

4 Mayer, *op. cit.*, p. 12.

5 Cf. Tucker, *Philosophy and Myth in Karl Marx*, p. 73.

6 Engels, "Die Lage Englands. 'Past and Present' by Thomas Carlyle, London, 1843," *MEW*, I, 546–547.

7 Hess, "Die europäische Triarchie," *op. cit.*, pp. 77–166.

8 Hess, "Philosophie der That," *op. cit.*, p. 221.

9 Cf. Hess, "Einundzwanzig Bogen aus der Schweiz," *op. cit.*, pp. 200, 210–211.

10 "One word more about giving instruction as to what the world ought to be. Philosophy in any case always comes on the scene too late to give it. As the thought of the world, it appears only when actuality is already there cut and dried after its process of formation has been completed. . . . The owl of Minerva spreads its wings only with the

falling of dusk." Hegel, *Philosophy of Right,* trans. T. M. Knox (Oxford, 1942), pp. 12–13.

11  Mayer, *op. cit.,* p. 27.

12  Hess, "Über das Geldwesen," *op. cit.,* p. 333.

13  Cf. Engels, "Die Lage Englands: Das achtzehnte Jahrhundert," *MEW,* I, 552.

14  Engels, "Outlines . . ." in *EPM,* pp. 175–209.

15  Cornu and Moenke, introduction to M. Hess, *Philosophische und socialistische Schriften,* pp. xlii–xliii.

16  Engels, "Outlines . . ." in *EPM,* pp. 178, 183.

17  Engels, "Fortschritte der Sozialreform auf dem Kontinent," *MEW, I,* 494.

18  *AD,* pp. 16–17.

19  *MEW,* I, 549.

20  Cf. *MEW,* I, 552.

21  Engels, *The Peasant War in Germany* (New York, 1926), p. 27.

22  *LF,* p. 401.

23  Engels to Marx, July 14, 1858, *Briefwechsel* . . . II, 279; cf. *AD,* p. 85. *Naturphilosophie* refers to a section in Hegel's *Encyclopedia.*

24  *AD,* p. 38; cf. *LF,* p. 384.

25  *DN,* p. 330.

26  *AD,* p. 32, n. 2.

27  *AD,* pp. 195–196.

28  *AD,* pp. 452–453.

29  *AD,* p. 458.

30  Engels to Marx, November 23, 1882, *Briefwechsel* . . . IV, 492.

31  *AD,* p. 16.

32  *AD,* p. 515. "Causa Finalis—Matter and Its Inherent Motion," *DN,* p. 322.

33  *AD,* p. 93; *DN,* pp. 93, 325.

34  *DN,* p. 337.

35  Cf. *LF,* pp. 371–372.

36  *DN,* p. 51.

37  *DN,* p. 406.

38  *DN,* p. 278. Engels adds "whenever the conditions for it . . . are present." This qualification is important and reduces the warrant for the rest of the claim.

39  *DN,* p. 54.

40  *DN*, p. 262.

41  *DN*, p. 322.

42  *LF*, p. 386.

43  *AD*, p. 464.

44  *DN*, p. 92; cf. p. 83.

45  *DN*, pp. 27, 83; cf. *AD*, pp. 174–177, 182–191, 193–195.

46  *AD*, p. 36.

47  *DN*, p. 280.

48  Cf. *LF*, pp. 371–372.

49  *AD*, p. 55.

50  *DN*, p. 299.

51  *LF*, p. 386.

52  *DN*, p. 271; cf. *LF*, p. 362.

53  *DN*, pp. 352–353.

54  *AD*, pp. 36–37.

55  *AD*, pp. 17–18.

56  *AD*, p. 21.

57  *AD*, p. 19.

58  *LF*, p. 389.

59  *AD*, p. 191.

60  *LF*, p. 389; *AD*, p. 40.

61  *AD*, pp. 457–458; *DN*, pp. 64 65.

62  *DN*, p. 83.

63  *DN*, p. 83.

64  *DN*, p. 84.

65  Cf. *LF*, p. 388.

66  *AD*, p. 462.

67  *DN*, p. 41; *LF*, p. 388.

68  *DN*, p. 40.

69  *LF*, p. 388; *AD*, p. 36.

70  *DN*, p. 43.

71  *DN*, p. 61.

72  *DN*, p. 62.

73  Cf. *DN*, p. 64.

74  *AD*, p. 37, n. 1.

75  Cf. *AD*, p. 38.
76  Cf. *AD*, pp. 174–175.
77  *DN*, p. 293.
78  *DN*, p. 282.
79  *DN*, p. 284.
80  *DN*, p. 387.
81  *AD*, p. 166.
82  *AD*, p. 474.
83  *AD*, p. 166.
84  *AD*, p. 166.
85  *AD*, p. 475.
86  *DN*, p. 280.
87  *LF*, pp. 362, 373.
88  *DN*, p. 275.
89  Cf. *AD*, pp. 54–55.
90  *DN*, pp. 298–299.
91  *AD*, p. 186.
92  *AD*, pp. 186–187.
93  Cf. *LF*, p. 364.
94  *AD*, p. 85.
95  *AD*, p. 165.
96  *DN*, p. 397.
97  *DN*, pp. 280–281.
98  *AD*, p. 467.
99  *DN*, p. 97.
100  *DN*, p. 282.
101  Cf. *LF*, p. 361.
102  *AD*, p. 193.
103  *AD*, p. 193.
104  *DN*, p. 294.
105  *LF*, p. 362.
106  Engels, "Socialism: Utopian and Scientific," *MESW*, II, 100.
107  *Ibid.*, pp. 100–101.
108  *LF*, p. 370.
109  *DN*, p. 305.

110 *DN*, p. 304.

111 *DN*, p. 304.

112 ". . . the correct reflection of nature is extremely difficult . . ." *AD*, p. 474.

113 *AD*, p. 57; cf. *DN*, p. 320.

114 Engels, "Socialism: Utopian and Scientific," *MESW*, II, 100.

115 *LF*, p. 362; Engels, "Socialism: Utopian and Scientific," *MESW*, II, 100; *AD*, pp. 38, 36–37, 474; *DN*, pp. 285, 280, 271.

116 *LF*, p. 362.

117 *AD*, p. 55.

118 *AD*, p. 55.

119 *AD*, p. 166.

120 *LF*, p. 376.

121 I am indebted to Professor Z. A. Jordan for the preceding argument.

122 *DN*, p. 54.

123 Cf. S. Hook, *Reason, Social Myths and Democracy* (New York, 1950), pp. 199–200. Much of the subsequent discussion follows that of Professor Hook.

124 Cf. H. Feigl, "Notes on Causality," *Readings in the Philosophy of Science*, H. Feigl and M. Brodbeck, eds. (New York, 1953), p. 408.

125 *DN*, pp. 295–296.

126 *DN*, p. 296.

127 *DN*, p. 296.

128 *AD*, p. 173.

129 *AD*, p. 174.

130 Engels, of course, is not guilty of this. Cf. *DN*, pp. 334–335.

131 Cf. *DN*, p. 334.

132 *DN*, p. 84.

133 *DN*, p. 61.

134 *AD*, p. 193.

135 *DN*, p. 388.

136 *AD*, p. 166.

137 *DN*, p. 84.

138 "It is obvious that I do not say anything concerning the *particular* process of development of, for example, a grain of barley from germination to the death of the fruit bearing plant . . ."*AD*, pp. 193–194.

139 *AD*, p. 195.

140 *AD*, p. 475.

141 *AD*, p. 194.

142 *AD*, p. 194.

143 *AD*, pp. 475–476.

144 Cf. Hegel, *The Phenomenology of Mind*, p. 139.

145 *DN*, p. 257.

146 *AD*, p. 186.

147 Cf. *AD*, p. 185.

148 *AD*, p. 193.

149 *AD*, p. 504.

150 "Forms of thought also partly inherited by development (self-evidence, for instance, of mathematical axioms for Europeans . . .)" *AD*, p. 461.

151 *DN*, p. 340.

152 Cf. particularly Adler, *Engels als Denker*.

153 Adler, *Lehrbuch*, I, 102; *DN*, p. 337.

154 *DN*, p. 312.

155 *DN*, p. 272.

156 *DN*, p. 274.

157 Adler, *Lehrbuch*, I, 101–102. Mondolfo, *Il materialismo storico in Federico Engels*, provides a discussion of Engels' views.

158 *DN*, p. 322.

159 *AD*, p. 17.

160 *AD*, p. 14.

161 Engels to Marx, May 30, 1873, *Briefwechsel* . . . IV, 344–345.

162 Marx to Engels, July 4, 1864, *ibid.*, III, 173.

163 *Capital*, I, 19.

164 *DI*, pp. 26–27.

CHAPTER THREE

1 Cf. B. Wolfe, *Three Who Made a Revolution* (Boston, 1948), p. 499.

2 *LF*, pp. 389, 399.

3 A. von Weiss, "Fundamente und Wirksamkeit der 'Bolschewistischen Ideologie,'" *Ost Europa*, VIII (March, 1958), 171.

4 Cf. *MEC*, pp. 27–28, 308. Cf. K. Hager, "Wissenschaft und Weltanschauung," *Einheit*, XIII (January, 1958), 38–39.

5 The epistemological work of the young Karl Marx and Engels' notebooks, the *Dialectics of Nature*, were unknown to him.

6 F. Chasschatschich, *Materie und Bewusstsein* (Berlin, 1957), pp. 19–20.

7 R. Garaudy, *Contribution à la théorie matérialiste de la connaissance* (Paris, 1954), p. 1; Adler, *Lehrbuch*, I, 119.

8 *MEC*, pp. 69–70; cf. D. Guest, *Textbook of Dialectical Materialism* (New York, 1939), p. 30.

9 Cf. M. Cornforth, *Dialectical Materialism* (London, 1954), III, foreword, pp. 5–6; G. Lukacs, *Existentialismus oder Marxismus* (Berlin, 1951), p. 128.

10 *MEC*, p. 51; cf. H. Levy, *A Philosophy for a Modern Man* (London, 1938), pp. 21–22; Cornforth, *Dialectical Materialism*, III, p. 175.

11 "*'Objective truth'* . . . means nothing else than the existence of objects (i.e. 'things in themselves') truly reflected by thinking." *MEC*, pp. 104–105. "What is truth? An idea or a concept of an object must be understood as true which gives a true reflection, a true 'copy' of this object." M. Rosental, *Was ist marxistische Erkenntnistheorie?* (Berlin, 1956), p. 21.

12 *MEC*, p. 134; F. Oelssner, *Der Marxismus der Gegenwart und seine Kritiker* (Berlin, 1952), p. 23.

13 *MEC*, pp. 136–137; Chasschatschich, *op. cit.*, p. 15.

14 J. Bocheński, *Der sowjetrussische Dialektische Materialismus* (Bern, 1950), p. 102. An English edition of Bocheński's book is available as *Soviet Russian Dialectical Materialism* (Dordrecht, 1963).

15 *MEC*, p. 261.

16 ". . . matter [is] neither created nor destroyed, but is forever undergoing through its own inherent motion, infinite change and transformation." H. Selsam, *Philosophy in Revolution* (New York, 1957), p. 55; Chasschatschich, *op. cit.*, p. 19; A. Buchholz, "Das naturwissenschaftlich-ideologische Weltbild der Sowjetunion," *Ost Europa*, VII (February, 1957), p. 78; H. Ley, "Materialität der Welt—Grundlage für den wissenchaftlich-atheistischen Charakter unserer Weltanschauung," *Einheit*, XIII, 5 (May, 1958), 630.

17 Cf. P. T. Below, *Über den primären Charakter der Materie und den sekundären Charakter des Bewusstseins* (Berlin, 1955), pp. 22 ff.; Cornforth, *Dialectical Materialism*, III, 13.

18 *MEC*, pp. 26, 108, 130, 160.

19 Chasschatschich, *op. cit.*, p. 133.

20 Cf. Cornforth, *Dialectical Materialism*, III, 151.

21 *Ibid.*, p. 152.

22 Cf. Adler, *Lehrbuch*, I, 131–132.

23 Cf. M. Adler, *Marxistische Probleme* (Stuttgart, 1913), pp. 66–67, *Kant und der Marxismus* (Berlin, 1925), p. 167.

24 Cf. P. Jordan, *Physics of the 20th Century* (New York, 1944), p. 26; A. Ushenko, *Philosophy of Relativity* (London, 1937), pp. 13 ff.; E. Schrödinger, *Science and Humanism* (Cambridge, Mass., 1952), pp. 11 ff.; B. Russell, *Understanding History* (New York, 1957), p. 106; W. Heisenberg, *Physics and Philosophy* (New York, 1958), pp. 66–67.

25 Cf. Adler, *Lehrbuch*, I, 144; V. Sheen, *Philosophy of Science* (Milwaukee, 1934), p. 32.

26 Cf. L. de Broglie, *Matter and Light* (New York, 1939), p. 228, *Physics and Microphysics* (New York, 1955), p. 109.

27 Heisenberg, *Physics and Philosophy*, pp. 47–48.

28 W. Heisenberg, *Philosophic Problems of Nuclear Physics* (New York, 1952), p. 38.

29 Cf. B. Russell, *Analysis of Matter* (New York, 1954), p. 26; Heisenberg, *Physics and Philosophy*, p. 58.

30 Heisenberg, *Physics and Philosophy*, p. 58; de Broglie, *Physics and Microphysics*, p. 130; Cohen's introduction to Hertz, *op. cit.*

31 Heisenberg, *Physics and Philosophy*, p. 41; de Broglie, *Physics and Microphysics*, p. 134; cf. Ushenko, *op. cit.*, pp. 19–21; de Broglie, *Physics and Microphysics*, p. 130.

32 Cf. P. Duhem, *The Aim and Structure of Physical Theory* (Princeton, 1954), pp. 9–10, 19.

33 Cf. C. Joad, *Philosophical Aspects of Modern Science* (London, 1948), pp. 20–21; Sheen, *op. cit.*, pp. 32–33; Heisenberg, *Physics and Philosophy*, p. 70.

34 Heisenberg, *Philosophic Problems*, p. 56.

35 "I keep to what I said earlier in a more general context: it is certainly an *adequate* picture; but as regards its *truth* the appropriate question to ask is not whether it is true or not, but whether it is at all capable of being either true or false. Probably it is not. Probably we cannot ask for more than just adequate pictures capable of synthesizing in a comprehensible way all observed facts and giving a reasonable expectation on new ones we are out for." Schrödinger, *Science and Humanism*, p. 24; Cf. Murphy's Introduction to Schrödinger, *Science, Theory and Man* (New York, 1957), p. xviii; P. Frank, ed., *The Validation of Scientific Theories* (Boston, 1956), p. 14.

36 De Broglie, *Revolution in Physics* (New York, 1953), p. 37, *Matter and Light*, p. 229.

37 Cf. Heisenberg, *Physics and Philosophy*, p. 49.

38 "The salient point is that according to Bohr every state or arrangement can be 'interpreted' by particles; but he does not claim that particles 'exist.'" P. Frank, *Philosophy of Science* (Englewood, N.J., 1957), p. 244.

39 "Nature, in the aspects which the physicist investigates, behaves *as if* there were atoms and *as if* they had the properties which we now claim for them. . . . Some people might be inclined to go further, and claim a definite reality for atoms, electrons, and other ultimate particles, and for the scheme of atomic structure which has been worked out. The great point is that whether the man of science regards his atoms as having an ultimate reality or not does not affect the validity of the theory; the theory is just as useful in introducing order and promoting discovery if they are merely polite fictions as if they were desperate realities, and two men who hold different views on this point will, if they are equally adequate as mathematicians and equally capable as physicists, both be able to make the same predictions based on theory, and to derive the same satisfaction from experimental verification." E. Andrade, *An Approach to Modern Physics* (New York, 1957), pp. 4–5; Frank, *Philosophy of Science*, pp. 143–144.

40. "If a phenomenon is susceptible of one mechanical explanation, it is susceptible of an infinite number of others which would account equally well for all the features revealed by experience. . . . How are we to choose . . . ? The day will come, perhaps, when physicists will lose interest in these questions, which are admittedly inaccessible to positive methods and abandon them to metaphysicians." Poincaré, as cited in T. Dantzig, *Henri Poincaré, Critic of Crisis* (New York, 1954), pp. 10–11; Russell, *Analysis*, pp. 8–9.

41 Frank, *Philosophy of Science*, pp. 237, 355 ff., 187.

42 Cf. Bocheński, *op. cit.*, p. 69.

43 ". . . transmental Reality can be God, or, as it is with Hegel, Spirituality which develops from the elementary beginnings to human self-consciousness; it can be the Will of Schopenhauer, or it could also be a multiplicity of Spirits or Demons; in short the recognition of a Reality outside of consciousness is not identical with the thesis that that Reality is Matter . . ." Adler, *Lehrbuch*, I, 149; cf. Bocheński, *op. cit.*, p. 89.

44 *MEC*, pp. 260–261; cf. Lukacs, *op. cit.*, p. 139.

45 *MEC*, p. 261; cf. J. Lewis, *Marxism and the Irrationalists* (London, 1955), p. 42; Garaudy, *op. cit.*, p. 14; cf. Lukacs, *op. cit.*, p. 138.

46 H. Selsam, *Philosophy in Revolution*, p. 55.

47 Cf. *MEC*, pp. 175–176; Stalin, *Dialectical and Historical Materialism* (New York, 1940), p. 15.

48 "Dialectical Materialism has other elements; but all that constitutes the essence of classical materialism is contained in it." Bocheński, *op. cit.*,

pp. 106–107. Cf. H. Koch, "Sowjetideologie als Weltanschauung und Wissenschaft," *Ost Europa,* VII (January, 1957), 13.

49 Cf. *MEC,* pp. 175–176.

50 *MEC,* p. 262.

51 *MEC,* p. 262.

52 V. Afanasyev, *Marxist Philosophy: A Popular Outline* (Moscow, n.d.), p. 61; Ley, *op. cit.,* p. 637.

53 Cf. Hoepfner, *op. cit.,* pp. 453–454.

54 "Thus to the irritation of many, the assertions of science tend to keep away from the use of words like 'real' and 'ultimate'. . . . Knowledge of science and practice of it and interest in it neither compel nor deny the belief that the changing phenomena of the actual world are illusion, that only the unchanging and permanent ideas are real." F. Oppenheimer, *Science and the Common Understanding* (New York, 1954), pp. 6–7. ". . . whole statements and even intelligent-sounding deeply disturbing questions . . . turn out to be meaningless . . . Here are a few examples: 'Which is really at rest, the sun or the earth?' 'Will this table cease to exist while it is not being observed?' 'Is light made of corpuscles only or waves only?' " G. Holton, *Introduction to Concepts and Theories in Physical Science* (Cambridge, Mass., 1952), p. 225; cf. Sheen, *op. cit.,* p. 15.

55 "As for our scientific ideas and theories, you are well aware that an entirely pragmatic conception of their value and truth had already developed among natural scientists before the birth of pragmatism in philosophy. Molecules and atoms, ions and electrons, ether and its vibrations . . . are the creations of our mind in its efforts to orient itself amid the chaos of facts, to understand or 'explain' and to foretell the facts of sensible experience. They are not absolute truths or the adequate expression of objective realities . . ." T. Flournoy, *The Philosophy of William James* (New York, 1917), pp. 57–58; Einstein, *op. cit.,* p. 61, cf. p. 93.

56 *MEC,* pp. 260, 261; Frank, *Philosophy of Science,* p. 178.

57 Cf. Rosental, *Was ist marxistische Erkenntnistheorie?* p. 6.

58 "Science does not doubt that the substance it is investigating exists in three-dimensional space and hence, that the particles of that substance, although they be so small that we cannot see them, must also 'necessarily' exist in this three dimensional space." *MEC,* pp. 180–181.

59 Cf. Moore, "Influence of Political Creeds on the Acceptance of Theories," in Frank, ed., *Validation* . . . p. 33.

60 Cf. J. Jeans, *The Mysterious Universe* (New York, 1948), pp. 89, 139.

61 Cf. S. Müller-Markus, *Einstein und die Sowjetphilosophie* (Dordrecht, 1960).

62  Cf. V. Weiss, "Logischer Positivismus und Kybernetik im Blickfeld der bolschewistischen Kritik," *Freiburger Zeitschrift für Philosophie und Theologie*, II, pp. 292–293.

63  Cf. M. Cohen, *Reason and Nature* (Glencoe, 1931), p. 225.

64  *MEC*, p. 92; cf. Chasschatschich, *op. cit.*, p. 53.

65  *MEC*, p. 46.

66  Cf. Adler, *Lehrbuch*, I, 142 ff.

67  Chasschatschich, *op. cit.*, p. 127.

68  *MEC*, p. 51.

69  *MEC*, p. 130.

70  Chasschatschich, *op. cit.*, p. 133.

71  *MEC*, p. 108. Emphasis supplied.

72  *MEC*, p. 160. Emphasis supplied.

73  *MEC*, p. 26. Emphasis supplied.

74  *MEC*, p. 130. Emphasis supplied.

75  Chasschatschich, *op. cit.*, p. 138.

76  Cf. Bocheński, *op. cit.*, p. 92; G. Wetter, *Dialectical Materialism: A Historical and Systematic Survey of Philosophy in the Soviet Union* (New York, 1963), p. 503.

77  Cf. "We ask, is a man given objective reality when he sees something red . . . ? If you hold that it is not given . . . you inevitably sink to subjectivism and agnosticism. . . . If you hold that it is given, a philosophical concept is needed for this objective reality, and this concept has been worked out long, long ago. This concept is *matter*. Matter is a philosophical category designating the objective reality which is given to man by his sensations, and which is copied, photographed and reflected by our sensations . . ." *MEC*, pp. 129–130. "If color is a sensation dependent upon the retina (as natural science compels you to admit) then the light rays falling on the retina produce the sensation of color. That means that independent of us and our consciousness there exists vibrations of matter, or ether waves of a certain length and certain velocity which, acting upon the retina, produce in us the sensation of one color or another. That is how natural science regards it. The various sensations of one color or another are explained by science in terms of various lengths of light waves . . . Such is the view of materialism . . ." *MEC*, p. 55.

78  Cf. Chasschatschich, *op. cit.*, p. 20.

79  *MEC*, pp. 105–106.

80  Hobbes, *Leviathan*, bk. I, ch. i.

81  Cf. T. Hobbes, *De Corpore*, bk. I, ch. vi, par. 10.

82  In E. Erdmann, *Die philosophischen Grundlagen von Helmholtz Wahrnehmungstheorie* (Berlin, 1921), p. 38.

83  Cornforth, *Dialectical Materialism*, III, 33.

84  D. Chaplin, "Challenge and Meaning of Modern Marxism," *European*, IX, 4 (June, 1957), 215.

85  *MEC*, pp. 232, 234.

86  *MEC*, p. 235; Chasschatschich, *op. cit.*, p. 153. Epicurus, as a consistent materialist, was aware of a similar danger should sense perception be brought into question. As a consequence he maintained a strict, naive materialism and a copy theory of perception. Cf. *Letter to Herodotus*, 52; Cicero, *De finibus*, I, vii, 22, and *De natura deorum*, I, 25, 70.

87  E. Albrecht, *Darstellung und Kritik der erkenntnistheoretischen Grundlage, der Kausalitätsauffassung und der Ethik des Neopositivismus* (Rostock, 1948), pp. 75–76.

88  Chasschatschich, *op. cit.*, p. 135.

89  *Ibid.*, p. 136.

90  *Ibid.*, p. 145.

91  *Ibid.*, p. 149.

92  *Ibid.*, p. 151.

93  *Ibid.*, p. 23.

94  Cf. Hobbes, *De Corpore*, bk. I, ch. vi, par. 5.

95  Chasschatschich, *op. cit.*, pp. 135–136.

96  Hobbes, *De Corpore*, bk. IV, ch. xxv, par. 1.

97  *MEC*, p. 235; Garaudy, *op. cit.*, p. 26.

98  Chasschatschich, *op. cit.*, p. 140.

99  *Ibid.*

100  Marx seems to suggest something like this when he complains that the early materialists had taken the "bloom" out of sensuousness. *HF*, p. 173.

101  Adler so interprets the position advanced by Marx and Engels. The immediately given (sense-data) enjoy a primary and fundamental status while scientific entities are characterized by a derived and secondary status, as *"blosse Denkbegriffe"* in quite the positivistic sense. Cf. Adler, *Lehrbuch*, I, pp. 101–102.

102  Leonov, *Grundriss des dialektischen Materialismus*, as cited in Wetter, *op. cit.*, p. 504.

103  Mitin, as cited in *ibid.*

104  *MEC*, pp. 216, 262.

105  Cf. F. Schiller, *Logic for Use* (New York, 1930), pp. 127 ff.; cf. Paul, "Lenin's Theory of Perception," *Philosophy and Analysis,* A. Flew, ed. (Oxford, 1954), pp. 283, 286.

106  "Knowledge can be useful . . . only when it reflects an objective truth independent of man." *MEC,* pp. 139–140.

107  *MEC,* p. 137; Chasschatschich, *op. cit.,* p. 191.

108  *MEC,* pp. 104–105.

109  "What is truth? Under truth must be understood an idea or a concept of an object which is a true reflection, a true 'copy' of that object." Rosental, *Was ist marxistische Erkenntnistheorie?* p. 21.

110  Chasschatschich, *op. cit.,* pp. 194–195; Lukacs, *op. cit.,* p. 143.

111  Chasschatschich, *op. cit.,* p. 199.

112  Cf. J. Lewis, *Marxism and the Open Mind* (New York, 1957), p. 8; Chasschatschich, *op. cit.,* p. 203.

113  Chasschatschich, *op. cit.,* p. 189.

114  ". . . while the form of expression of truth and the limits of its approximation to objective reality depend on us, its content, what it is about, the objective reality to which it corresponds, does not depend on us. In this sense there is an element of both relativity and absoluteness, of subjectivity and objectivity, in every truth. Truth is relative inasmuch as it is expressed in terms dependent upon the particular circumstances, experience and means of arriving at truth of the people who formulate it. It is absolute inasmuch as what is expressed or reproduced in these terms is objective reality, existing independently of man's knowledge of it." Cornforth, *Dialectical Materialism,* III, 156–157; cf. *MEC,* p. 175.

115  Cf. *MEC,* pp. 134 ff.

116  "From the standpoint of modern materialism, i.e., Marxism, the limits of approximation of our knowledge to the objective, absolute truth are historically conditioned, but the existence of such truth is unconditional and the fact that we are approaching nearer to it is also unconditional. The contours of the picture are historically conditioned, but the fact that this picture depicts an objectively existing model is unconditional." *MEC,* p. 136; cf. Lukacs, *op. cit.,* pp. 140–141, 146.

117  Chasschatschich, *op. cit.,* p. 194.

118  *Ibid.,* p. 199.

119  Cf. Cornforth, *Dialectical Materialism,* III, 156–157.

120  Cf. Chasschatschich, *op. cit.,* p. 195.

121  *MEC,* p. 185; V. Adoratsky, *Dialectical Materialism* (New York, 1934), p. 70.

122  Cornforth, *Dialectical Materialism,* III, 151–152.

123 Chasschatschich, *op. cit.*, p. 190.

124 ". . . *all* our cognitions are simply approximations of reality in its totality; in thus far is knowledge always relative." Lukacs, *op. cit.*, p. 146. ". . . all knowledge is relative." Lewis, *Marxism and the Open Mind*, p. 8. ". . . all knowledge . . . [is] of relative character . . ." Lewis, *Marxism and the Irrationalists*, p 16.

125 "Although cosmologists, like many others, very often talk as if there is such an object ('the universe as a whole') and that it is with it that they are concerned, an examination of their actual procedures discloses that what they in fact do is not in any way altered if one surrenders this belief or assumption. For what they . . . do is to construct a symbolic scheme which they employ with reference to the empirical data which they possess. And an examination of . . . [what goes into the stipulation of the meanings assigned to] the several conceptual parts of this symbolic scheme reveals that these do not in fact depend either for the individual parts of the scheme taken singly, or their combined use as a systematic unity upon the assumption that there is some object to which they refer and with which they can be made to correspond." M. Munitz, *Space, Time and Creation. Philosophical Aspects of Scientific Cosmology* (Glencoe, 1957), pp. 66–67.

126 ". . . the attitude at that time . . . was different from what it is now, it was still a little too naive. While asserting that any model we may conceive is sure to be deficient and would surely be modified sooner or later, one still had at the back of one's mind the thought that a true model exists . . . that we approach to it gradually, without perhaps ever reaching it. This attitude has now been abandoned." Schrödinger, *Science and Humanism*, p. 25.

127 *MEC*, p. 137.

128 Engels, in a manuscript that could not have been known to Lenin at the time of the writing of *Materialism and Empiriocriticism*, was not as convinced of the existence of ether. Cf. *DN*, pp. 93, 323.

129 Cf. Holton, *op. cit.*, p. 506.

130 Cf. Frank, *Philosophy of Science*, p. 178.

131 Schrödinger, *Science and Humanism*, pp. 24–25; cf. Einstein, *op. cit.*, p. 93.

132 Cf. the editors' Introduction to *PN*, p. 18.

133 *MEC*, p. 160.

134 *MEC*, pp. 129–130.

135 *PN*, p. 372.

136 *PN*, p. 319.

137 *PN*, p. 159.

138 *PN*, p. 380; Lenin is referring to Marx's comment on Leibniz in a letter, Marx to Engels, May 10, 1870, *Briefwechsel* . . . IV, 283.

139 Cf. H. Fleischer, "The Materiality of Matter," *Studies in Soviet Thought*, II, 1 (March, 1962), 13.

140 *MEC*, pp. 156–157.

141 *PN*, p. 153.

142 *PN*, p. 151.

143 *PN*, p. 152.

144 *PN*, p. 285.

145 *PN*, p. 146.

146 *PN*, p. 256.

147 *PN*, p. 93.

148 Cf. *PN*, p. 93.

149 *PN*, p. 147.

150 *PN*, pp. 146–147.

151 O. W. Kuusinen, *Fundamentals of Marxism-Leninism* (Moscow, 1961), p. 15.

152 Leonov, as cited, T. J. Blakeley, *Soviet Scholasticism* (Dordrecht, 1961), p. 93, n. 46.

153 F. V. Konstantinov, *Los fundamentos de la filosofia Marxista* (Mexico City, 1959), p. 164. J. Bocheński has made a synopsis of this work available as *The Dogmatic Principles of Soviet Philosophy* (Dordrecht, 1963).

154 *Ibid.*, p. 165.

155 *Ibid.*, p. 166.

156 *Ibid.*, p. 179.

157 Rosental, *Was ist marxistische Erkenntnistheorie?* p. 22.

158 *Ibid.*, p. 30.

159 Cf. M. Rosental and G. M. Straks, *Categorias del Materialismo Dialectico* (Mexico City, 1960), pp. 62–63.

160 V. S. Tiukhtin, "On the Process of Reflecting Reality in Cognition," *Soviet Studies in Philosophy*, I, 2 (Fall, 1962), p. 47. "To reduce to physical similarity the concept of similarity between the reflection and the thing reflected not only narrows the sphere of the reflected properties and leads to agnostic conclusions, but also limits the possibilities of the reflective action." *Ibid.*, p. 45.

161 *Ibid.*

162 *Ibid.*, p. 48.

163 Chasschatschich, *op. cit.*, p. 127.

164 Cf. Rosental, *Was ist marxistische Erkenntnistheorie?* p. 23.

165 Cf. Rosental and Straks, *op. cit.*, p. 2.

166 Konstantinov, *Los fundamentos* . . . p. 170; cf. Afanasyev, *op. cit.*, pp. 79 ff.

167 *PN*, p. 171.

168 Rosental, *Was ist marxistische Erkenntnistheorie?* pp. 33–34.

169 Rosental and Straks, *op. cit.*, p. 2.

170 *Ibid.*, pp. 15 ff.

171 *HF*, p. 173.

172 *DN*, p. 337.

173 *PN*, p. 99.

174 ". . . the *individual* is the *universal.*" "Every individual is (in one way or another) a universal. Every universal is (a fragment, or an aspect, or the essence of) an individual." *PN*, p. 361.

175 *PN*, p. 180.

176 M. Rosental and P. Iudin, *Diccionario de filosofia y sociologia Marxista* (Buenos Aires, 1959), p. 13. Rosental and Iudin published a *Brief Philosophical Dictionary* in several editions. Selections from the earlier edition have been translated under the title *Diccionario de filosofia y sociologia Marxista* by Editorial Seneca in Buenos Aires. The latest edition, in its entirety, has been published by Ediciones Pueblos Unidos under the title *Diccionario filosofico abreviado* (Montevideo, 1959). Cf. H. Fleischer, "On Categories in Soviet Philosophy: A Survey," *Studies in Soviet Thought*, I, 64–73; Afanasyev, *op. cit.*, chap. viii.

177 Rosental and Straks, *op. cit.*, p. 44.

178 Rosental and Straks, *op. cit.*, pp. 316–317.

179 Rosental, *Die Dialektik in Marx' Kapital*, p. 406.

180 *Ibid.*, p. 407.

181 Chasschatschich, *op. cit.*, p. 170.

182 Rosental and Straks, *op. cit.*, p. 319.

183 Marx, *Contribution to the Critique of Political Economy* (Chicago, 1918), pp. 292–293.

184 *PN*, p. 319.

185 *PN*, p. 143.

186 *PN*, pp. 146–147.

187 Lenin, "The Agrarian Question and the 'Critics of Marx,'" *LCW*, V, 147.

188 *PN*, p. 361.

189 "If *everything* develops, does not that apply also to the most general *concepts* and *categories* of thought?" *PN*, p. 256.

190 Wetter, *op. cit.*, p. 540.

191 Cf. K. Zweiling, *Der Leninsche Materiebegriff und seine Bestätigung durch die moderne Atomphysik* (Berlin, 1957), p. 17.

192 *Ibid.*, p. 16.

193 F. T. Arjiptsev, *La materia como categoria filosofica* (Mexico City, 1962), p. 132.

194 "For a definition to reflect the development of an object, it is necessary to discover its contradictions." Rosental and Straks, *op. cit.*, p. 323.

195 *Ibid.*, p. 129.

196 *PN*, p. 152.

197 *AD*, p. 123.

198 Konstantinov, *Los fundamentos* . . . p. 291.

199 Adoratsky, *op. cit.*, p. 27.

200 Konstantinov, *Los fundamentos* . . . p. 633.

## CHAPTER FOUR

1 K. Kautsky, *Die materialistische Geschichtsauffassung*, Vol. I.

2 E. Bernstein, *Die Voraussetzungen des Sozialismus und die Aufgaben der Sozialdemokratie*, trans. into English as *Evolutionary Socialism* (New York, 1961). The English translation omits much of Bernstein's criticisms of the Hegelianism which found its way into Marxism. See also the Italian translation *Socialismo e Socialdemocrazia* (Rome, n.d.).

3 J. Dietzgen, *Philosophical Essays* (Chicago, 1917), and *The Positive Outcome of Philosophy* (Chicago, 1906); E. Untermann, *Die logischen Mängel des engeren Marxismus* (Munich, 1910); H. Roland-Holst, *Josef Dietzgens Philosophie* (Munich, 1910).

4 Among the French, Georges Sorel, of course, occupies a central place: cf. his *Saggi di critica del Marxismo* (Milan, 1903), and his "The Decomposition of Marxism," in I. L. Horowitz, *Radicalism and the Revolt Against Reason: The Social Theories of Georges Sorel* (New York, 1961). In Italy the early works of Arturo Labriola, particularly his *Studio su Marx*, are interesting; those of Antonio Labriola are good statements of classical Marxist orthodoxy. *Vide* his *Essays on the Materialist Conception of History* (Chicago, 1904), *Socialism and Philosophy* (Chicago, 1934), and *Lettere a Engels* (Rome, 1949).

**5** G. Plekhanov, *Selected Philosophical Works* (Moscow, n.d.); *vide* also Trotsky, *Marxism and Science* (Colombo, Ceylon, 1949) and the works of A. Deborin, A. Bogdanov, and N. Bukharin; for brief sketches of these men cf. Labedz, *Revisionism: Essays on the History of Marxist Ideas*, T. Anderson, *Masters of Russian Marxism* (New York, 1963), and Wetter, *op. cit.*, chs. vi, vii, viii.

**6** Cf. M. N. Roy, *Materialism: An Outline of the History of Scientific Thought* (Calcutta, 1951).

**7** Cf. D. Joravsky, *Soviet Marxism and Natural Science, 1917–1932* (New York, 1961), pp. 66–67.

**8** *Ibid.*, p. 87.

**9** M. Lange, *Marxismus, Leninismus, Stalinismus* (Stuttgart, 1955), pp. 104 ff.

**10** Joravsky, *op. cit.*, p. 98.

**11** *Ibid.*, pp. 170–171.

**12** *Foundations of Leninism*, SSW, VI, 71–196.

**13** Lange, *Marxismus* . . . pp. 107–108; cf. *LF*, p. 388.

**14** V. I. Lenin's "Testament," *The New Communist Manifesto and Related Documents*, ed. D. N. Jacobs (New York, 1962), p. 133.

**15** Cf. H. Koch, *op. cit.*, p. 11.

**16** J. V. Stalin's *Dialectical and Historical Materialism* was originally a chapter in the official Soviet history of the Communist party.

**17** SSW, I, 297–372; cf. also appendix, pp. 373–391.

**18** J. V. Stalin, *Economic Problems of Socialism in the U.S.S.R.* (New York, 1952).

**19** Stalin, *Dialectical and Historical Materialism*, p. 7.

**20** *Ibid.*

**21** *Ibid.*, p. 8.

**22** *Ibid.*, p. 11.

**23** Cf. H. H. Dahm, "Ontologische Aspekte der sowjetischen Dialektik," *Ost Europa*, VII, 4 (April, 1957), 235.

**24** As cited in *ibid.*, p. 236.

**25** *PN*, pp. 226–227.

**26** Cf. M. Lange, *Wissenschaft im totalitären Staat* (Stuttgart, 1955), pp. 197–198.

**27** Rosental and Iudin, *Diccionaria de filosofia* . . . p. 54; cf. pp. 11, 79, 109.

**28** *Ibid.*, p. 39.

29  Cf. Lange, *Marxismus, Leninismus, Stalinismus*, pp. 100–103, *Wissenschaft* . . . pp. 45–46.

30  Lange, *Wissenschaft* . . . p. 201.

31  Cf. the editorial "Zum Abschluss der Diskussion über die formale Logik," *Einheit*, VIII, 2 (February, 1953), 3.

32  F. V. Konstantinov, *Basis and Superstructure* (Moscow, 1955), pp. 18–19.

33  In, *Die Bedeutung der Arbeiten des Genossen Stalin über den Marxismus und die Fragen der Sprachwissenschaft für die Entwicklung der Wissenschaften* (Berlin, 1952), p. 47.

34  As cited in Dahm, *op. cit.*, p. 243.

35  Cf. Bocheński, *Der sowjetrussische Dialektische Materialismus*, pp. 55–56; cf. the English ed., pp. 38–39.

36  Marx felt that when economics was associated with the class struggle, it ceased to be a science and became a "prize fighter" in the service of class interests. *Capital*, I, 15.

37  *MEC*, pp. 342–343.

38  Konstantinov, *Los fundamentos* . . . p. 529, n. 1.

39  Cf. Müller-Markus, *op. cit.*, pp. 78–86.

40  Cf. H. Koch, pp. 13–14.

41  Cf. V. Stern, *Erkenntnistheoretische Probleme der modernen Physik* (Berlin, 1952), pp. 11–76.

42  Cf. Müller-Markus, *op. cit.*, pp. 350–351, 444.

43  Rosental and Iudin, *Diccionario de filosofia* . . . p. 72. Emphasis supplied.

44  Kuusinen, *op. cit.*, p. 17.

45  *Ibid.*, p. 18.

46  For Einstein's appraisal of Engels' dialectical materialism, cf. Hook, *Reason, Social Myths and Democracy*, p. 222; see also Appendix 5: "Einstein on Engels," pp. 224–226.

47  G. Plekhanov, *Fundamental Problems of Marxism* (New York, n.d.), p. 116.

48  *Ibid.*, pp. 112–113.

49  *PN*, pp. 97–100; cf. Lenin, "Once Again on the Trade Unions," *New Economic Policy—Socialist Construction* (New York, 1937), p. 66.

50  *PN*, p. 177.

51  Rosental and Iudin, *Diccionario de filosofia* . . . p. 61; cf. V. Stern, *Zu einigen Fragen der Marxistischen Philosophie* (Berlin, 1954), pp. 42–43.

52  J. Stalin, *Marxism and Linguistics* (New York, 1951).

53  *Ibid.*, p. 11; cf. Stern, *Zu einigen Fragen* . . . p. 59, n. 8.

54  Cf. Dahm, "Renaissance der formalen Logik," *Ost-Probleme*, VIII (1957), 254–267; J. M. Bocheński, "Soviet Logic," *Studies in Soviet Thought*, I (1961), 29–38.

55  Cf. "Protokoll der philosophischen Konferenze über Fragen der Logik am 17. und 18. November 1951 in Jena," *Deutschen Zeitschrift für Philosophie*, I (1953), 4.

56  Cf. "Zum Abschluss der Diskussion über die formale Logik," *Einheit*, VIII (1953), 197.

57  Cf. Z. Jordan, "The Development of Philosophy and Marxism-Leninism in Poland Since the War," *Studies in Soviet Thought*, I (1961), 88–99; for an excellent and exhaustive account of the discusssion surrounding formal logic in Poland see Z. Jordan, *Philosophy and Ideology: The Development of Philosophy and Marxism-Leninism in Poland Since the Second World War* (Dordrecht, 1963), pt. 4.

58  G. Kueng, "Mathematical Logic in the Soviet Union (1917–1947 and 1947–1957)," *Studies in Soviet Thought*, I (1961), 39–43.

59  Cf. Blakeley, *Soviet Scholasticism*, pp. 30–31.

60  *Ibid.*, p. 31n.; Wetter, *op. cit.*, p. 529.

61  *PN*, p. 319.

62  Cf. N. Lobkowicz, "The Principle of Contradiction in Recent Soviet Philosophy," *Studies in Soviet Thought*, I (1961), 44–51.

63  Cf. E. Kolman, "Die materielle Grundlage des Widerspruchs und sein Abbildung im Denken," in N. Lobkowicz, ed., *Das Widerspruchsprinzip in der neueren sowjetischen Philosophie* (Dordrecht, 1959), pp. 45 ff.

64  *Ibid.*, pp. 54–55.

65  *Ibid.*, p. 55.

66  *Ibid.*, pp. 55–56.

67  F. V. Konstantinov, *Los fundamentos* . . . p. 289.

68  Rosental and Iudin, *Diccionario filosofico abreviado* (Montevideo, 1959), p. 299.

69  S. Meliujin, *Dialectica del desarrollo en la naturaleza inorganica* (Mexico City, 1963), p. 105.

70  *Ibid.*, pp. 105–106.

71  *Ibid.*

72  Jordan, *Philosophy and Ideology*, pp. 302 ff.

73  Cf. Lobkowicz, "The Principle of Contradiction . . ." *op. cit.*, p. 48.

74  Kolman, "Die materielle Grundlage . . ." *op. cit.*, pp. 54–56.

75  Meliujin, *op. cit.*, p. 106.

**76** Kuusinen, *op. cit.*, pp. 99–100.

**77** Lange, *Wissenschaft* . . . ch. ix.

**78** J. Bocheński, "The Three Components of Communist Ideology," *Studies in Soviet Thought*, II, 1 (1962), 7–11.

**79** Cf. S. Meliujin, *El problema de lo finito y lo infinito* (Mexico City, 1960).

**80** Cf. H. Fleischer, "On Categories in Soviet Philosophy: A Survey," *Studies in Soviet Thought*, I (1961), 64–77.

**81** "The entire course of world history for the last century irrefutably proves the truthfulness of the principles of Marxism-Leninism and of the laws revealed by it." Konstantinov, *Los fundamentos* . . . p. 9; cf. Kuusinen, *op. cit.*, pp. 17–21; cf. Blakeley, *Soviet Scholasticism*, pp. 34–35.

**82** Konstantinov, *Los fundamentos* . . . p. 39.

**83** Cf. Blakeley, *Soviet Scholasticism*, pp. 59–65.

**84** "Nor did [Lenin] hesitate, proceeding from the substance of Marxism to replace some of the propositions and conclusions of Marx and Engels, which had become outdated, with new propositions and conclusions corresponding to the new historical era." Stepanova, *op. cit.*, p. 262.

**85** Konstantinov, *Los fundamentos* . . . p. 122.

**86** Cf. Z. A. Jordan's exhaustive *Philosophy and Ideology: The Development of Philosophy and Marxism in Poland Since the Second World War.*

**87** *Ibid.*, ch. xviii.

**88** Cf. L. Kolakowski, "Karl Marx and the Classical Definition of Truth," *Revisionism*, ch. xii.

**89** Cf. A. Schaff, "Studies of the Young Marx: A Rejoinder," *ibid.*, ch. xiii; cf. also his "Marxism and Existentialism," *Monthly Review*, XIV, 1 (May, 1962), 12–18, and his *A Philosophy of Man* (New York, 1963).

**90** Czechoslovakia has shown some independence as well; cf. N. Lobkowicz, "Marxism-Leninism in Czechoslovakia," *Studies in Soviet Thought*, I (1961), 106–107.

**91** Kuusinen, *op. cit.*, p. 14.

**92** *Capital*, I, 19–20.

**93** *Ibid.*, p. 19.

**94** *PN*, p. 180.

**95** Dunayevskaya, *op. cit.*, p. 171.

**96** V. I. Lenin, *Marx, Engels, Marxism* (Moscow, 1947), pp. 15–49.

**97** *Ibid.*, p. 23.

**98** Lange, *Marxismus, Leninismus, Stalinismus*, p. 65.

CHAPTER FIVE

1 As cited in H. Cunow, *Die Marxsche Geschichts-, Gesellschafts- und Staatstheorie* (Berlin, 1920), I, 143.

2 Engels' letter to Starkenburg, January 25, 1894, *MESW*, II, 505; cf. G. Plekhanov, *The Development of the Monist View of History* (Moscow, 1956), chs. i, ii, iii; Labriola, *Essays on the Materialistic Conception of History*, pp. 35–36.

3 As cited in O. J. Hammen, "The Spectre of Communism in the 1840's," *Journal of the History of Ideas*, XIV, 3 (June, 1953), 409.

4 T. B. Bottomore and M. Rubel, Introduction to *Karl Marx: Selected Writings in Sociology and Social Philosophy* (Harmondsworth, 1961), pp. 24–25.

5 *Ibid.*, p. 25.

6 Cf. *ibid.*, pp. iv–v, ix, 3.

7 *Ibid.*, p. 34.

8 *MESW*, II, 452.

9 As cited, R. Michels, *La teoria di C. Marx sulla miseria crescente e le sue origini* (Turin, 1922), pp. 11, 64. The discussion in this section is much indebted to that of Michels.

10 *Capital*, I, 646, n. 2; cf. p. 616, n. 2.

11 F. Nebenius, *Bemerkungen über den Zustand Grossbritanniens in staatswissenschaftlicher Hinsicht* (Karlsruhe-Baden, 1818), pp. 10, 64–65.

12 G. Parisi, *Della condizione economica delle Nazioni* (Milan, 1840), p. 96.

13 *Ibid.*, pp. 40–41.

14 Cf. Michels, *op. cit.*, pp. 85–86.

15 Cf. M. Hamburger, *Reason and Energy: Studies in German Literature* (New York, 1957), p. 187.

16 Hess, "Über eine in England bevorstehende Katastrophe," *Rheinische Zeitung*, 177 (June 26, 1842), in Hess, *op. cit.*, pp. 183–184.

17 A. Ferguson, *An Essay on the History of Civil Society* (Basel, 1789), p. 277.

18 Hess, *Die heilige Geschichte der Menschheit* (Stuttgart, 1837), in *op. cit.* p. 62.

19 Hess, "Über das Geldwesen," in *op. cit.*, pp. 333, 336.

20 Cf. R. Garaudy, *Die französischen Quellen des wissenschaftlichen Sozialismus* (Berlin, 1954), ch. i.

21 Ferguson, *op. cit.*, p. 279.

22 Cf. Michels, *op. cit.*, pp. 100–101.

23 Cf. Marx, "Der Kommunismus und die Augsburger 'Allgemeine Zeitung,'" *MEW*, I, 108.

24 Tscherkesoff, *Pages d'histoire socialiste: Doctrines et actes de la Socialdémocratie* (Paris, 1896).

25 Cf. Arturo Labriola, *Contro G. Plekanoff e per il Sindacalismo* (Pescara, 1909), p. 72; K. Kautsky, "Das kommunistische Manifest ein Plagiat?" *Neue Zeit*, XXIV, Vol. II, no. 47 (1906).

26 Cited in Garaudy, *Die französische Quellen* . . . pp. 148–149.

27 Cf. G. Gurvitch, "La sociologie du jeune Marx," *Cahiers Internationaux de Sociologie*, IV (1948), 3–47; G. Lichtheim, *Marxism: An Historical and Critical Study* (New York, 1962), pt. 1; E. Hammacher, *Das philosophisch-ökonomische System des Marxismus* (Leipzig, 1909), pp. 53–54.

28 "Manifesto of the Communist Party," *MESW*, I, 54.

29 J. J. Rousseau, *Du Contrat ou Principes du Droit Politique* (Paris, 1933), p. 24.

30 W. Sombart, *Der proletarische Sozialismus*, I, 363, cited in L. Schwarzschild, *The Red Prussian: The Life and Legend of Karl Marx* (London, 1948), p. 153.

31 Cf. Engels, *The Peasant War in Germany*, p. 28; *HF*, pp. 176–177; *AD*, pp. 349–364.

32 *LF*, p. 392.

33 *MESW*, II, 452.

34 Cf. *EPM*, pp. 21–36; *Capital*, I, 46, n. 1; *Theories of Surplus Value* (Moscow, n.d.), pt. 1, p. 70; H. W. B. Joseph, *The Labour Theory of Value in Karl Marx* (London, 1923), pp. 9–11; G. D. H. Cole, *The Meaning of Marxism* (Ann Arbor, 1964), pp. 211–215.

35 T. Ramm, "The Utopian Tradition," *The Future of Communist Society*, ed. W. Laqueur and L. Labedz (New York, 1962), p. 98.

36 Engels, Preface to the "Communist Manifesto," German ed. of 1883, *MESW*, I, 24–25.

37 *AD*, pp. 365–366.

38 Cf. I. Fetscher, "Das Verhältnis des Marxismus zu Hegel," *Marxismusstudien*, III (Tübingen, 1960), 66–169.

39 *LF*, pp. 359–366.

**40** Marx's letter to his father, November 10, 1837, in Marx, *Die Frühschriften*, pp. 3, 7.

**41** *MESW*, I, 362; cf. *DI*, p. 36.

**42** G. Hegel, *Philosophy of Right*, pars. 190–192, pp. 127–128.

**43** *Ibid.*, par. 201, p. 130.

**44** *Ibid.*, pars. 243–246, pp. 149–151.

**45** "Vorläufige Thesen . . ." *SW*, II, 254.

**46** Marx, "Der leitende Artikel in Nr. 179 der 'Kölnischen Zeitung.' " *MEW*, I, 97.

**47** *Ibid.*, p. 103.

**48** Marx, "Debatten über das Holzdiebstahlsgesetz," *MEW*, I, 126.

**49** *Ibid.*, p. 143.

**50** Marx, "Rechtfertigung des ++-Korrespondenten von der Mosel," *MEW*, I, 177; cf. also p. 195. Emphasis supplied.

**51** *PP*, p. 122.

**52** Cf. *Capital*, I, 9–10.

**53** Marx, "Kritik . . ." *MEW*, I, 229.

**54** *Ibid.*, p. 231; cf. p. 286.

**55** *Ibid.*, p. 233.

**56** *EPM*, p. 145.

**57** Marx, "Theses on Feuerbach," Thesis Six, *MESW*, II, 403.

**58** "Vorlesungen über das Wesen der Religion," *SW*, VIII, 397–398.

**59** "Criticism . . ." *SE*, p. 27.

**60** *Ibid.*, p. 29.

**61** *Ibid.*, pp. 37–38.

**62** Marx, letter to Ruge, September, 1843, *MEW*, I, 345.

**63** *HF*, pp. 52–53. Emphasis supplied in first sentence.

**64** *EPM*, p. 22.

**65** *EPM*, pp. 24, 26.

**66** *EPM*, p. 26.

**67** *EPM*, p. 66.

**68** Engels, "Outlines . . ." in *EPM*, pp. 178–179.

**69** Engels, "Die Lage Englands: Das achtzehnte Jahrhundert," *MEW*, I, 568.

**70** Engels, "Outlines . . ." in *EPM*, p. 192.

**71** Engels, *ibid.*, p. 198.

72 Cf. Engels, "Lage der arbeitenden Klasse in England," *MEW*, I, 464.

73 *CW*, p. 132.

74 Engels, "Briefe aus London," *MEW*, I, 468.

75 Engels, "Die Lage Englands: Die englische Konstitution," *MEW*, I, 577.

76 *Ibid.*, p. 592.

77 Marx, *MESW*, I, 362–363.

78 *PP*, p. 122.

79 Marx, "Wage Labor and Capital," *MESW*, I, 90; cf. ". . . the development of the forces of production . . . in the last resort, determines the development of all social relations . . ." G. Plekhanov, *Fundamental Problems of Marxism*, p. 36.

80 ". . . scientific analysis of the capitalist mode of production demonstrates that it is a peculiar mode of production, specifically defined by historical development; that it, like any other definite mode of production, is conditioned upon a certain stage of social productivity and upon the historically developed form of the forces of production. . . . The conditions of distribution are essentially identical with these conditions of production, being their reverse side . . ." *Capital*, III, 856. Some changes in translation have been made to better accord with the original German.

81 ". . . my view [is] . . . that the mode of production determines the character of the social, political and intellectual life generally . . ." *Capital*, I, 82n.

82 Marx, letter to Annenkov, December 28, 1846, *MESW*, II, 442.

83 "Marx . . . reduces the whole problem of the development of economic structure to the problem of the causes that determine the evolution of the productive forces . . ." Plekhanov, *Fundamental Problems* . . . pp. 31–32.

84 Cf. Plekhanov, *The Development of the Monist View of History*, p. 264.

85 Cf. M. Tugan-Baranowsky, *Theoretische Grundlagen des Marxismus* (Leipzig, 1905), pp. 4–5.

86 J. Turner, *Challenge to Karl Marx* (New York, 1941), p. 181.

87 A. Thalheimer, *Introduction to Dialectical Materialism* (New York, 1936), p. 193.

88 Stalin, *Dialectical and Historical Materialism*, p. 28.

89 H. Lefebvre, *Il Marxismo* (Milan, 1954), pp. 56–57.

90 Cunow, *op. cit.*, II, 158.

91 G. Plekhanov, *The Materialist Conception of History* (New York, n.d.), p. 18.

92  *Capital*, I, 178.

93  *DI*, p. 31.

94  Cf. Kautsky, *Die materialistische Geschichtsauffassung*, I, 577; S. Dange, *India from Primitive Communism to Slavery: A Marxist Study of Ancient History in Outline* (New Delhi, 1955), p. 32.

95  Cf. *Capital*, I, 178 ff.; "Critique of the Gotha Program," *MESW*, II, 18–19.

96  "Each new productive force . . . brings . . . a further development of the division of labor." *DI*, p. 22.

97  *Capital*, I, 180.

98  Cf. Stalin, *Dialectical and Historical Materialism*, p. 25.

99  ". . . classes [are] determined by the division of labor . . ." *DI*, pp. 30 ff.; cf. Marx to Weydemeyer, March 5, 1852, *MESW*, II, 452; *AD*, p. 386.

100  Engels, "Outlines . . ." *EPM*, p. 188.

101  Cf. Engels to Starkenburg, January 25, 1894, *MESW*, II, 504.

102  *DI*, p. 28.

103  "Marx discovered the law of development of human history: the simple fact . . . that mankind must first of all eat, drink, have shelter and clothing. . . ." Engels, "Graveside Speech," *MESW*, II, 167.

104  *Capital*, I, 179.

105  *Ibid.*

106  *Ibid.*, p. 372, n. 3.

107  *Ibid.* Emphasis supplied.

108  *Ibid.*, pp. 179–180.

109  *Ibid.*, p. 394, cf. p. 376; cf. Engels, "Grundsätze . . ." *MEW*, IV, 363.

110  *CW*, p. 1; cf. pp. 4, 7.

111  *PP*, p. 122.

112  *MESW*, I, 37.

113  "Steam and the new tool-making machinery were . . . revolutionizing the whole foundation of bourgeois society." *AD*, p. 356.

114  Dange, *op. cit.*, p. 33.

115  Konstantinov, *Los fundamentos* . . . pp. 387–388.

116  Stalin, *Dialectical and Historical Materialism*, p. 31.

117  Plekhanov, *The Development of the Monist View of History*, p. 155.

118  Marx seems to think in terms of instruments of production when he speaks of dynamic change in the mode of production. "These social

relations into which the producers enter with one another, the conditions under which they exchange their activities and participate in the whole act of production, will naturally vary according to the character of the means of production. With the invention of *a new instrument* of warfare, firearms, the whole internal organization of the army necessarily changed . . ." Marx, "Wage Labor and Capital," *MESW*, I, 89. Emphasis supplied.

119 K. Federn, *The Materialist Conception of History* (London, 1939), pp. 16–17.

120 *Capital*, I, 386.

121 Cf. M. Bober, *Karl Marx's Interpretation of History* (Cambridge, England, 1948), pp. 8–9.

122 Marx to Annenkov, December 28, 1846, *MESW*, II, 442.

123 "To a large extent . . . needs . . . are determined by the nature of the implements with which [man] subjugates nature . . ." Plekhanov, *The Materialist Conception of History*, p. 18.

124 *DI*, p. 28; Labriola describes the process as one in which men, "not by free choice, but because they could not act otherwise, satisfy first certain elementary needs, which, in their turn, give rise to others in their upward development. . . . For the satisfaction of their needs . . . they employ and invent certain means and certain tools and associate themselves in certain fashions . . ." Labriola, *Essays on the Materialist Conception of History*, p. 99.

125 Plekhanov, *Fundamental Problems of Marxism*, p. 90.

126 *CW*, p. 5.

127 *Capital*, I, 9.

128 *Ibid.*, 8–9.

129 *Ibid.*, p. 763.

130 *CW*, p. 18.

131 *AD*, p. 351.

132 *AD*, p. 372.

133 Cf. B. Croce, *Materialismo storico ed economia marxista* (Bari, 1921), p. 5.

134 Marx to Engels, March 25, 1868, *Briefwechsel* . . . IV, 30.

135 Kuusinen, *op. cit.*, p. 145.

136 Cf. Bottomore and Rubel, *op. cit.*, ch. ii.

137 *CW*, pp. 296–297.

138 *CW*, p. 18.

139 Marx approved this interpretation: *vide Capital*, I, 18.

140 Engels to Bloch, September 21–22, 1890, *MESW*, II, 488.

141 Engels to Starkenburg, January 25, 1894, *MESW*, II, 505.

142 Engels to Schmidt, October 27, 1890, *MESW*, II, 496.

143 Engels, "Outlines . . ." *EPM*, p. 178.

144 Engels to Danielson, October 17, 1893, *MESW*, II, 503.

145 Engels to Starkenburg, January 25, 1894, *MESW*, II, 505. Yet elsewhere Engels maintains that without Marx "the theory would not be
by far what it is today." *LF*, p. 385, n. 1.

146 *AD*, p. 367.

147 *AD*, p. 37.

148 *AD*, p. 38.

149 *AD*, p. 351.

150 Marx, *MESW*, I, 363.

151 *Capital*, I, 10.

152 Engels, "Outlines . . ." *EPM*, p. 183.

153 *LF*, pp. 389–390.

154 Engels to Schmidt, August 5, 1890, *MESW*, II, 487.

155 Engels, "Socialism: Utopian and Scientific," *MESW*, II, 102.

156 *LF*, pp. 388–389; cf. L. Woltmann, *Die darwinsche Theorie und
der Sozialismus* (Düsseldorf, 1899), pp. 6, 20–21; cf. C. Zirkle,
*Evolution, Marxian Biology and the Social Scene* (Philadelphia,
1959), p. 85.

157 Engels, *Manifesto . . . MESW*, I, 34, n.b.; cf. Engels, "The Origin
of the Family . . ." *MESW*, II, 171.

158 Cf. Engels' preface to "The Origin of the Family . . ." *MESW*, II,
170–171; C. Resek, *Lewis Henry Morgan: American Scholar* (Chicago,
1960), pp. 160 ff.

159 Engels to Marx, December 8, 1882, *Briefwechsel . . .* IV, 495.

160 *MESW*, II, 80–92; *DN*, pp. 228–246.

161 Emphasis supplied.

162 Engels, "The Origin of the Family . . ." *MESW*, II, 170–171.

163 Cf. Cunow, *op. cit.*, II, 140.

164 Emphasis supplied.

165 Engels, "The Origin of the Family . . ." *MESW*, II, 171.

166 "Just as Darwin discovered the law of development of organic nature,
so Marx discovered the law of development of human history: the
simple fact, hitherto concealed by an overgrowth of ideology, that mankind must first of all eat, drink, have shelter and clothing, before it

can pursue politics, science, art, religion, etc.; that therefore the production of the immediate material means of subsistence and consequently the degree of economic development attained by a given people or during a given epoch form the foundation upon which the state institutions, the legal conceptions, art, and even the ideas on religion, of the people concerned have been evolved, and in the light of which they must, therefore, be explained . . ." Engels, "Speech at the Graveside of Karl Marx," *MESW*, II, 167; cf. "Karl Marx," *MESW*, II, 164.

**167** Cf. L. Woltmann, *Der historische Materialismus* (Düsseldorf, 1900), p. 221.

**168** Cf. Masaryk, *op. cit.*, p. 334, n. 1.

**169** Cf. Cunow, *op. cit.*, II, 140–141.

**170** This is G. Plekhanov's position; *vide The Development of the Monist View of History*, pp. 168–170.

**171** Cf. Scalia, *op. cit.*, p. 67; Kuusinen, *op. cit.*, p. 145.

**172** ". . . history rests, before all else, upon the development of technique . . . the successive discovery of tools . . ." Labriola, *Essays* . . . p. 121, cf. pp. 119–120; Stalin, *Dialectical and Historical Materialism*, pp. 28, 31.

**173** Marx was aware of this fact, but never succeeded in following through its implications. *EPM*, p. 75; *DI*, p. 21.

**174** Cf. Woltmann, *Der historische Materialismus*, pp. 222–223, *Die darwinsche Theorie* . . . pp. 26–27, 239; Masaryk, *op. cit.*, pp. 333, 342–343.

**175** Engels to Schmidt, August 5, 1890, *MESW*, II, 486; Engels to Bloch, September 21–22, 1890, *ibid.*, pp. 488–489.

**176** Engels, "The Part Played by Labor . . ." *MESW*, II, 80; cf. Afanasyev, *op. cit.*, p. 84.

**177** Engels, *ibid.*, pp. 81–82.

**178** Emphasis supplied.

**179** Engels, *ibid.*, pp. 82–83; cf. Afanasyev, *op. cit.*, p. 86.

**180** Engels, *ibid.*, p. 86.

**181** Engels, "Origin of the Family . . ." *MESW*, II, 189.

**182** "The plentiful meat and milk diet among the Aryans and the Semites . . . may, perhaps, explain the superior development of these two races." *Ibid.*

**183** Engels to Starkenburg, January 25, 1894, *MESW*, II, 504.

**184** Engels, quoting with approval the words of Lewis H. Morgan, "Origin of the Family . . ." *MESW*, II, 207.

**185** Engels, "Die innern Krisen," *MEW*, I, 459.

**186** Engels, "Grundsätze . . ." *MEW*, IV, 369.

187  *Ibid.*, p. 372.

188  *CW*, p. 212.

189  *CW*, p. 295.

190  Engels, "Die innern Krisen," *MEW*, I, 459–460.

191  *EPM*, p. 66.

192  Engels, "Der europäische Krieg," *MEW*, X, 8; cf. Marx, "The Class Struggles in France 1848–1850," *MESW*, I, 143.

193  *CW*, pp. 295–296.

194  *PP*, p. 195.

195  *AD*, p. 367.

196  *MESW*, I, 31.

197  *AD*, pp. 362–363.

198  *PP*, p. 13; cf. *AD*, p. 365.

199  Cf. *LF*, p. 393.

200  *AD*, p. 379.

201  *Ibid.*

202  *HF*, p. 73.

203  *HF*, p. 52.

204  *DI*, pp. 26–27.

205  "Moralizing Criticism and Critical Morality: A Polemic Against Karl Heinzen," *SE*, pp. 160–161. Emphasis supplied.

206  "On the King of Prussia and Social Reform," *SE*, p. 123.

207  Engels, "Stellung der politischen Partei," *MEW*, I, 461.

208  *CW*, p. 219.

209  *MESW*, I, 42.

210  *Ibid.*, p. 51.

211  *Ibid.*, p. 62.

212  Engels, "Grundsätze . . ." *MEW*, IV, 372.

213  Engels, "Stellung der politischen Partei," *MEW*, I, 461.

214  Engels, "Briefe aus London," *MEW*, I, 468.

215  Marx, "The Class Struggles in France 1848–1850," *MESW*, I, 211.

216  *Ibid.*

217  Both these quotations are cited in L. Krieger, "Marx and Engels as Historians," *Journal of the History of Ideas*, XIV, 3 (June, 1953), 393–394. The immediately preceding discussion follows Krieger's account.

218  Engels to Marx, November 18, 1868, *Briefwechsel . . .* IV, 113.

**219** *CW,* pp. 237–238.

**220** Cf. H. Mayo, *Introduction to Marxist Theory* (New York, 1960), pp. 60 ff.

**221** Cf. Krieger, *op. cit.,* p. 397.

**222** Engels to Marx, October 7, 1858, *Briefwechsel* . . . II, 290.

**223** Cf. Mehring, *op. cit.,* pp. 494, 514.

**224** Engels, Introduction to "The Class Struggles in France 1848–1850," *MESW,* I, 119.

**225** *Capital,* III, 863. The passage has been retranslated from the German.

**226** *Ibid.,* p. 135.

**227** *Ibid.,* p. 231; cf. *AD,* p. 375.

**228** *Capital,* III, 251, cf. pp. 237, 239, 261, 428, 472–473; cf. *AD,* pp. 377–378, 387, 393; *LF,* p. 373.

**229** *Capital,* III, 244.

**230** *Ibid.,* p. 328; *AD,* p. 376.

**231** *Capital,* III, 259; cf. Marx, "Inaugural Address," *MESW,* I, 377–385.

**232** Compare *Capital,* III, 427–431, and *AD,* pp. 369–370, 380.

**233** Engels to Bloch, September 21–22, 1890, *MESW,* II, 488–489.

**234** Labriola, *Essays on the Materialist Conception of History,* p. 124.

**235** *Capital,* III, 862. This passage is retranslated from the German.

**236** Marx, "Der leitende Artikel in Nr. 179 der 'Kölnischen Zeitung,' " *MEW,* I, 103.

**237** ". . . die Philosophie interpretiert die Rechte der Menschheit, sie verlangt, dass der Staat der Staat der menschlichen Natur sei." *Ibid.,* p. 102.

**238** Marx, "Kritik . . ." *MEW,* I, 233.

**239** Marx, "Verhandlungen . . ." *MEW,* I, 121.

**240** Cf. Breuer, *op. cit.,* pp. 78–91.

**241** Marx, "Kritik . . ." *MEW,* I, 283.

**242** *HF,* p. 162.

**243** Marx, "Der leitende Artikel . . ." *MEW,* I, 104.

**244** Marx, "M. an R., May, 1843," *MEW,* I, 338–339; cf. *SE,* pp. 57–59; F. Pappenheim, *The Alienation of Modern Man* (New York, 1959), pp. 81–83.

**245** "On the Jewish Question," *SE,* p. 67.

**246** *Ibid.,* p. 59.

**247** "Das Wesen des Glaubens im Sinne Luthers," *SW,* I, 260.

248 *Ibid.*, p. 262.

249 *Ibid.*, p. 260.

250 *Ibid.*

251 *Ibid.*

252 *Ibid.*, p. 264.

253 *SE*, p. 12.

254 *Ibid.*, pp. 12–13.

255 *Ibid.*, p. 25.

256 Marx, "Kritik . . ." *MEW*, I, 224–225; cf. H. Röhr, *Pseudoreligiöse Motive in den Frühschriften von Karl Marx* (Tübingen, 1962), pp. 42 ff.

257 Marx, "Kritik . . ." *MEW*, I, 233.

258 "On the Jewish Question," *SE*, p. 51.

259 *Ibid.*, pp. 55–56.

260 *Ibid.*, p. 59.

261 *Ibid.*, p. 67.

262 *Ibid.*, pp. 74, 76.

263 *HF*, p. 162.

264 *HF*, p. 56.

265 *HF*, p. 162.

266 "On the Jewish Question," *SE*, p. 66.

267 *Ibid.*, p. 83.

268 *HF*, p. 163.

269 "On the Jewish Question," *SE*, p. 60.

270 "On the King of Prussia and Social Reform," *SE*, p. 117; cf. also the identical conception in *DI*, p. 33.

271 *Ibid.*, p. 119.

272 *Ibid.*, p. 130.

273 "Moralizing Criticism and Critical Morality: A Polemic Against Karl Heinzen," *SE*, p. 137.

274 *Ibid.*

275 "On the Jewish Question," *SE*, p. 92.

276 *Ibid.*, p. 95.

277 *EPM*, p. 161.

278 *EPM*, p. 165.

279 "On the Jewish Question," *SE*, p. 73.

280 *Ibid.*, pp. 79 f.

281 *Ibid.*, p. 82.

282 "The King of Prussia . . ." *SE*, p. 116.

283 *Ibid.*, p. 117.

284 *Ibid.*, p. 118.

285 "In England labor distress is not partial but universal, not confined to the factory districts, but co-extensive with the country districts." *Ibid.*, pp. 104 f.

286 *Ibid.*, p. 130.

287 Hegel, *Philosophy of Right,* par. 241, pp. 148 f.

288 "The King of Prussia . . ." *SE*, p. 118.

289 "Criticism . . ." *SE*, p. 37.

290 "The King of Prussia . . ." *SE*, p. 110.

291 "Moralizing Criticism . . ." *SE*, p. 160.

292 *Ibid.*, p. 143.

293 *Ibid.*, p. 156.

294 *Ibid.*, p. 160.

295 Marx and Engels, "Manifesto . . ." *MESW*, I, 54.

296 "On the Jewish Question," *SE*, pp. 84–85.

297 Marx and Engels, "Manifesto . . ." *MESW*, I, 53.

298 *Ibid.*

299 *Ibid.*, p. 54.

300 *PP*, p. 197.

301 Marx and Engels, "Manifesto . . ." *MESW*, I, 44.

302 *MEW*, IV, 372.

303 Cf. Engels, "Die Lage Englands: Die englische Konstitution," *MEW*, I, 591–592.

304 *MESW*, I, 485.

305 *MESW*, I, 22.

306 Engels, "The Origin of the Family . . ." *MESW*, II, 321.

307 Cf. *ibid.*, p. 318.

308 *AD*, p. 391.

309 *AD*, pp. 382–398.

310 Engels, "The Origin of the Family . . ." *MESW*, II, 316–317.

311 *AD*, pp. 403–404.

312 *DI*, pp. 32–33.

313 *AD*, pp. 406–407.

314 Cf. Engels, Introduction to "The Civil War in France," *MESW*, I, 485.

315 *Ibid.*, p. 483.

316 Marx, "The Civil War in France," *MESW*, I, 519–523.

317 Marx, "Critique of the Gotha Programme," *MESW*, II, 32–33.

318 Engels, Introduction to "The Civil War in France," *MESW*, I, 485.

319 Engels, "On Authority," *MESW*, I, 635–636.

320 *Ibid.*, p. 636: Cf. Engels to Lafargue, December 30, 1871, in F. Engels, P. and L. Lafargue, *Correspondence* (Moscow, 1959), I, 34–35.

321 Marx saw in the "co-operative factories of the laborers themselves . . . the first beginnings of the new" society. *Capital*, III, 431.

322 *AD*, p. 434.

323 *AD*, p. 391.

324 *AD*, pp. 434–435.

325 Marx, "Über die Nationalisierung des Grund und Bodens," *MEW*, XVIII, 62.

326 Engels to Bebel, March 18–28, 1875, *MESW*, II, 42.

327 Marx, "Critique of the Gotha Programme," *MESW*, II, 20. Emphasis supplied.

328 Marx and Engels, "Manifesto . . ." *MESW*, I, 34 n. a.

329 *PP*, p. 196.

330 *Ibid.*

331 Engels, Introduction to "The Class Struggles in France 1848–1850," *MESW*, I, 134.

332 *Ibid.*, p. 136.

333 Cf. *Manual de economia politica*, ed. K. V. Ostrovitianov (Mexico City, 1961), pp. 260–261.

334 Cf. Marx and Engels, "Manifesto . . ." *MESW*, I, 57–58; *AD*, pp. 351, 362–363.

335 *Capital*, I, 10; cf. I. T. Martov's views, in T. Anderson, *Masters of Russian Marxism*, pp. 90–119.

336 *AD*, p. 386.

## CHAPTER SIX

1 "Criticism . . ." *SE*, p. 34.

2 Cf. C. Gneuss, "The Precursor: Eduard Bernstein," in *Revisionism*, pp. 31–41.

3 Marx, "Inaugural Address," *MESW*, I, 384.

4 Cf. *MESW*, I, 46.

5 *Ibid.*, p. 43.

6 As cited in L. H. Haimson, *The Russian Marxists and the Origins of Bolshevism* (Cambridge, England, 1955), p. 45. The discussion here follows that of Haimson. Cf. R. Kindersley, *The First Russian Revisionists* (Oxford, 1962).

7 Plekhanov, *Fundamental Problems* . . . pp. 92–93.

8 "What the 'Friends of the People' Are . . ." *LCW*, I, 137–138.

9 *Ibid.*, pp. 139–140.

10 *Ibid.*, p. 141.

11 *Ibid.*, p. 159.

12 *Ibid.*, p. 166.

13 Cf. Haimson, *op. cit.*, pp. 78–79.

14 "The Urgent Tasks of Our Movement," *LCW*, IV, 368.

15 "Where to Begin," *LCW*, V, 18.

16 "A Talk with Defenders of Economism," *LCW*, V, 316.

17 *Ibid.*

18 *Ibid.*, p. 318.

19 "What Is to Be Done?" *LSW*, I, pt. 1, 219.

20 *Ibid.*, p. 227.

21 *Ibid.*, p. 232.

22 *Ibid.*, pp. 233–234. Emphasis supplied.

23 *Ibid.*, p. 242.

24 Kautsky, as cited by Lenin, *ibid.*, p. 243.

25 *Ibid.*, pp. 244–245.

26 Cf. *ibid.*, pp. 248, 268.

27 *Ibid.*, p. 258.

28  "Class political consciousness can be brought to the workers *only from without* . . ." *ibid.*, p. 287.

29  *Ibid.*, pp. 323, 348–349.

30  *Ibid.*, pp. 315, 320, 336.

31  *Ibid.*, pp. 352–353.

32  *Ibid.*, p. 353.

33  *Ibid.*, p. 390.

34  As cited in Haimson, *op. cit.*, p. 98.

35  "Notes on Plekhanov's First Draft Programme," *LCW*, VI, 19.

36  *Ibid.*, p. 22.

37  *Ibid.*, p. 25.

38  Cf. "Additional Remarks on the Committee's Draft Programme," *LCW*, VI, 76.

39  "A Draft Programme for Our Party," *LCW*, IV, 236.

40  *Ibid.*, pp. 242–243.

41  Lenin, "The Tasks of the Youth Leagues," *On Socialist Ideology and Culture* (Moscow, n.d.), p. 53.

42  Cf. Lukacs, *Geschichte und Klassenbewusstsein* (Berlin, 1927), pp. 53–54.

43  *LCW*, VI, 235–252.

44  *Ibid.*, p. 236.

45  Wolfe, *op. cit.*, p. 231; cf. N. K. Krupskaya, *Reminiscences of Lenin* (Moscow, 1959), p. 94.

46  As cited in Wolfe, *op. cit.*, p. 235.

47  Cf. "The Program of the Russian Social Democratic Labor Party," *The Communist Blueprint for the Future,* ed. T. Whitney (New York, 1962), p. 67.

48  As cited in Wolfe, *op. cit.*, p. 239.

49  As cited in Haimson, *op. cit.*, p. 172.

50  As cited in Wolfe, *op. cit.*, p. 241; cf. L. Trotsky, *Lenin* (London, 1925), pp. 65–66. For a Soviet account, cf. *Vladimir Lenin: A Political Biography* (New York, 1943), pp. 67–68.

51  As cited in Wolfe, *op. cit.*, p. 236.

52  Cf. R. Luxemburg, *Leninism or Marxism* (Glasgow, 1935), pp. 6–7, 17–23.

53  Trotsky, *Our Political Tasks,* in *A Documentary History of Communism,* ed. R. V. Daniels (New York, 1962), I, 30–32.

54  Engels, "Grundsätze . . ." *MEW*, IV, 372–373; cf. S. W. Moore,

*Three Tactics: The Background in Marx* (New York, 1963), for an excellent discussion of these issues.

55 Cf. "The Proletarian Revolution and the Renegade Kautsky," *LSW*, II, pt. 2, 46.

56 *MESW*, I, 44; cf. also *DI*, p. 69.

57 As cited in A. G. Meyer, *Leninism* (New York, 1962), p. 35. The subsequent discussion follows Meyer.

58 "What the 'Friends of the People' Are . . ." *LCW*, I, 142.

59 As cited in Dunayevskaya, *op. cit.*, p. 182; cf. A. G. Meyer, *Communism* (New York, 1962), ch. iv.

60 *DI*, p. 70.

61 "Notes on Plekhanov's Second Draft Programme," *LCW*, VI, 48.

62 Lenin, *Imperialism: The Highest Stage of Capitalism* (New York, 1939).

63 *Ibid.*, p. 7.

64 *Ibid.*, pp. 10–11.

65 *Ibid.*, pp. 12–13; cf. also "The Program of the All-Russian Communist Party—1919," in *The Communist Blueprint* . . . p. 78.

66 Lenin, *Imperialism* . . . p. 14.

67 Engels to Marx, October 7, 1858, *Briefwechsel* . . . II, 290.

68 Lenin, *Imperialism* . . . p. 20.

69 *Ibid.*, p. 22.

70 *Ibid.*, pp. 48–49.

71 *Ibid.*, p. 61.

72 *Ibid.*, p. 63.

73 *Ibid.*, p. 102.

74 *Ibid.*, p. 104.

75 *Ibid.*, p. 106.

76 Cf. Stalin, *Problems of Leninism* (Moscow, 1953), p. 19.

77 As cited in Meyer, *Leninism*, p. 245.

78 Cf. *ibid.*, p. 253; cf. Trotsky, *The Revolution Betrayed* (Garden City, 1937), Appendix: "Socialism, in One Country," pp. 291–308.

79 *DI*, p. 61.

80 Marx, Preface to the "Communist Manifesto," Russian Edition of 1882, *MESW*, I, 24.

81 Cf. "Two Tactics of Social Democracy in the Democratic Revolution," *LCW*, IX, 84–85.

82 Cf. *The Development of Capitalism in Russia, LCW*, III, 548–549.

83 Cf. Meyer, *Leninism*, pp. 220–221.

84 As cited in *ibid.*, p. 227.

85 Cited in "Concerning Questions of Leninism," *SSW*, VIII, 65.

86 "The October Revolution and the Tactics of the Russian Communists," *SSW*, VI, 394.

87 "The Economic Situation of the Soviet Union and the Policy of the Party," *SSW*, VIII, 124.

88 "The Foundations of Leninism," *SSW*, VI, 99–100.

89 Lenin, *The State* (Moscow, 1951), p. 31.

90 "State and Revolution," *LSW*, II, pt. 1, 199.

91 Lenin, *The State*, p. 14.

92 *Ibid.*, p. 13.

93 *Ibid.*, p. 12; cf. pp. 14–15, 18.

94 *Ibid.*, p. 10; "State and Revolution," *LSW*, II, pt. 1, 281.

95 "State and Revolution," *LSW*, II, pt. 1, 204.

96 Lenin, *The State*, p. 22.

97 "State and Revolution," *LSW*, II, pt. 1, 234; "The Program of the All-Russian Communist Party—1919," in *The Communist Blueprint . . .* p. 79.

98 Lenin, *The State*, p. 38.

99 "The Proletarian Revolution and the Renegade Kautsky," *LSW*, II, pt. 2, 41.

100 Lenin, *The State*, p. 35.

101 "State and Revolution," *LSW*, II, pt. 1, 289.

102 Lenin, *The State*, p. 36; cf. "Proletarian Revolution . . ." *LSW*, II, pt. 2, 50–51.

103 Cf. "A Letter to the Members of the Central Committee," *LSW*, II, pt. 1, 197.

104 Cf. "Moralizing Criticism . . ." *SE*, pp. 136–137.

105 *AD*, p. 226.

106 Marx and Engels, "Manifesto . . ." *MESW*, I, 49.

107 Cf. "The Economic Content of Narodism," *LCW*, I, 425–426; "Two Tactics of Social Democracy in Democratic Revolution," *LSW*, I, pt. 2, 24–25.

108 "State and Revolution," *LSW*, II, pt. 1, 220.

109 "The Tasks of the Proletariat in Our Revolution," *LSW*, II, pt. 1, 37; "State and Revolution," *LSW*, II, pt. 1, 211.

110 "State and Revolution," *LSW*, II, pt. 1, 226.

111 *Ibid.*, p. 227.

112 *Ibid.*, pp. 229–230.

113 *Ibid.*, p. 242.

114 *Ibid.*, pp. 241 ff.

115 Cf. "The Economic Content of Narodism," *LCW*, I, 421–422.

116 "State and Revolution," *LSW*, II, pt. 1, 241–242.

117 "On the Dual Power," *LSW*, II, pt. 1, 21.

118 "State and Revolution," *LSW*, II, pt. 1, 249.

119 *Ibid.*, p. 244.

120 *Ibid.*, p. 250.

121 *Ibid.*, p. 254.

122 *Ibid.*, p. 250.

123 "Tasks of the Proletariat in Our Revolution," *LSW*, II, pt. 1, 37.

124 "State and Revolution," *LSW*, II, pt. 1, 261.

125 Lenin, *The State*, p. 38.

126 "Tasks . . ." *LSW*, II, pt. 1, 37.

127 "State and Revolution," *LSW*, pt. 1, 293.

128 Cf. Lenin, "Thesis on Bourgeois Democracy and the Dictatorship of the Proletariat," *The Paris Commune* (New York, 1934), p. 54.

129 Cf. J. Bunyan and H. Fisher, *The Bolshevik Revolution, 1917–1918* (Stanford, 1934), pp. 308 ff.

130 "The Immediate Tasks of the Soviet Government," *LSW*, II, pt. 1, 450.

131 Cf. H. Cambre, *El Marxismo en la Union Sovietica* (Madrid, 1960), pp. 78–79.

132 "Immediate Tasks . . ." *LSW*, II, pt. 1, 459.

133 *Ibid.*, p. 455.

134 *Capital*, III, 431. Emphasis supplied. Retranslated from the German.

135 "Immediate Tasks . . ." *LSW*, II, pt. 1, 471.

136 *Ibid.*

137 *Ibid.*, pp. 481–482.

138 *Ibid.*, p. 477.

139 *Ibid.*, p. 478.

140 "State and Revolution," *LSW*, II, pt. 1, 305.

141 *Ibid.*, p. 300.

142 *Ibid.*, p. 304.

143 *Ibid.*

144 Cf. J. Bunyan, *Intervention, Civil War, and Communism in Russia, April–December, 1918* (Baltimore, 1936), p. 191.

145 Cf. Daniels, *A Documentary History* . . . I, 96.

146 *Ibid.*, p. 116.

147 "State and Revolution," *LSW*, II, pt. 1, 299.

148 Lenin, *The State*, p. 38.

149 "State and Revolution," *LSW*, II, pt. 1, 293.

150 *Ibid.*, p. 314.

151 The right of recall was referred to in the 1919 program. Cf. *The Communist Blueprint* . . . p. 81. Cf. H. Duncker, *Introduction to Marxism* (Leipzig, 1962), p. 167.

152 "Report to the Seventeenth Party Congress," *SSW*, XIII, 374.

153 Stalin, "Report to the Eighteenth Congress of the Communist Party," *Problems of Leninism*, p. 792.

154 *Ibid.*, p. 794.

155 *Ibid.*, p. 793.

156 *Ibid.*, p. 795.

157 "Political Report of the Central Committee to the Sixteenth Congress," *SSW*, XII, 381.

158 Stepanova, *op. cit.*, p. 262.

159 Engels, Introduction to *The Class Struggles in France, 1848–1850, MESW*, I, 134.

160 *Ibid.*, p. 479.

161 *Capital*, I, 764, n. 1.

162 Stalin, "Report to the Eighteenth Congress," *Problems of Leninism*, p. 797.

163 "Foundations of Leninism," *SSW*, VI, 187.

164 "What the 'Friends of the People' Are . . ." *LCW*, I, 139–140.

## CHAPTER SEVEN

1 Engels, Introduction to "The Civil War in France," *MESW*, I, 483.

2 Marx, *MESW*, I, 363.

3 Engels, "Origin of the Family . . ." *MESW*, II, 194–195.

4 *Ibid.*, p. 171, editor's note 1.

5 Cf. T. Lysenko, "Engels and Certain Problems of Darwinism," *Agrobiology* (Moscow, 1954), pp. 340–345; *DN*, p. 353.

6 P. Kammerer, *The Inheritance of Acquired Characteristics* (New York, 1924).

7 Cf. J. Segal, *Michurin, Lysenko e il problema dell'eredità* (Milan, 1952), pp. 87–88; cf. N. Belenky, in *The Situation in Biological Science: Proceedings of the Lenin Academy of Agricultural Sciences of the U.S.S.R., July 31–August 7, 1948* (New York, 1949), pp. 93 ff.

8 Cf. C. Zirkle, *Dealth of a Science in Russia* (Philadelphia, 1949), pp. 18–19.

9 Cf. Joravsky, *op. cit.*, p. 300; R. Cook, "Lysenko's Marxist Genetics," *Journal of Heredity*, XL, 7 (July, 1949), 174.

10 I. V. Michurin, "Some Problems of Method," *Selected Works* (Moscow, 1949), pp. 269–270; A. Bakharev, *I. V. Michurin: The Great Remaker of Nature* (Moscow, 1954), pp. 9, 69, 84–85, 137.

11 "In the early days of the Soviet regime, Lenin, one of mankind's greatest geniuses, revealed to our country and to the working people of all the world a man who at that time was little known, namely, I. V. Michurin." T. Lysenko, "The Creator of Soviet Agrobiology," *Agrobiology* (Moscow, 1954), p. 257. "The first to direct attention to Michurin's work was V. I. Lenin." Yakovlev, Preface to I. V. Michurin, *Selected Works*, p. xvii. "Lenin was the first to estimate correctly the value of Michurin's contribution to science. The civil war was still raging in the country when Lenin adopted radical measures to provide normal conditions for Michurin's work. For this purpose Lenin sent his closest assistants to the town of Kozlov, now Michurinsk, commissioning them to find out under what conditions the scientist was working and to do everything they could to provide him with all that was necessary for normal research." V. Stoletov, *The Fundamentals of Michurin Biology* (Moscow, 1953), p. 22.

12 T. Lysenko, in *The Situation in Biological Science* . . . p. 25.

13 I. Prezent, in *ibid.*, p. 575.

14 I. Michurin, "Answers to Questions," *Selected Works*, p. 487.

15 Cf. F. Skaskin and R. Lerman, *T. D. Lysenko: Leben und Werk* (Berlin, 1951), pp. 8, 13.

16 Cf. T. Lysenko in *The Situation in Biological Science* . . . pp. 19, 47; Belenky, in *ibid.*, pp. 87–88.

17 Cf. M. Nesturkh, *The Origin of Man* (Moscow, 1959).

18 The body of literature devoted to the exposition and criticism of Soviet "genetics" is extensive. Besides the works herein cited, the most

readily accessible literature, representing both sides of the controversy, includes: A. Morton, *Soviet Genetics* (London, 1951); J. Fyfe, *Lysenko Is Right* (London, 1950); T. Lysenko, *Heredity and Its Variability* (New York, 1949); J. Huxley, *Soviet Genetics and World Science* (London, 1949); P. Hudson and R. Richens, *The New Genetics in the Soviet Union* (Cambridge, England, 1946); G. Wetter, *op. cit.*, pp. 455–469. For a bibliographic survey see M. C. Leikind, "The Genetics Controversy in the U.S.S.R.," *Journal of Heredity*, XL, 7 (July, 1949), pp. 203–208.

19  "What the 'Friends of the People' Are . . ." *LCW*, I, 166.

20  *Ibid.*, pp. 139–140.

21  Cf. Rosental and Straks, *op. cit.*, pp. 100–101, 142; Kuusinen, *op. cit.*, pp. 40–43; Konstantinov, *Los fundamentos* . . . pp. 156–162; Below, *op. cit.*, pp. 38–39.

22  Kuusinen, *op. cit.*, p. 42.

23  "'Pure Physiology' of the Brain," *PSW*, p. 222.

24  J. Wortis, *Soviet Psychiatry* (Baltimore, 1950), p. 28.

25  "Behavior . . . is always an active adaptation of the organism to the environment." Petruschewski, "I. P. Pawlow's Kampf für den Materialismus in Physiologie und Psychologie," *LP*, pp. 43–44.

26  I. Sechenov, *Selected Physiological and Psychological Works* (Moscow, n.d.).

27  "The behavior of an organism, no matter how complicated it may appear, is always a determined response to concrete external influences. . . ." Petruschewski, in *LP*, p. 40. Each "psychic" process proceeds, "not capriciously, not accidentally," but rather is the "determined product of the structure of the brain, which arises as a consequence of external and internal material influences." *Ibid.*, p. 46.

28  Referring to patients of the psychiatric clinic, Pavlov said: "Machines . . . machines and nothing more. An apparatus, a damaged apparatus." As cited in Wetter, *op. cit.*, p. 478.

29  "All willed movements . . . of men, the simplest as well as the most complex, are nothing other than learned or conditioned reflexes." Seliwanow, "Zur Frage des sogennanten willkürlichen Verhaltens," in *LP*, pp. 316–317.

30  L. Kubie, "Pavlov, Freud and Soviet Psychology," *Monthly Review*, IX (March, 1958), 359.

31  A. Ivanov-Smolensky, "Lines of Development of I. P. Pavlov's Ideas in the Pathophysiology of the Higher Nervous Activity," *Scientific Session on the Physiological Teachings of Academician I. P. Pavlov* (Moscow, 1953), p. 127; "Physiology and Psychology in the Study of the Higher Nervous Activity of Animals," *PSW*, pp. 401 ff.

32  Pavlov, as cited by Rubinschtein, "Pawlows Lehre und Probleme der Psychologie," in *LP*, p. 168; cf. "Reflex of Purpose," *LCR*, p. 275.

33  Petruschewski, in *LP*, p. 41.

34  *Ibid.*, p. 48.

35  Pavlov, as cited in *ibid.*, p. 52.

36  "The Task and the Arrangement of a Laboratory for the Study of the Normal Activity of the Highest Parts of the Central Nervous System in the Higher Animals," *LCR*, pp. 133–134.

37  Cf. E. Straus, *Vom Sinn der Sinne: Ein Beitrag zur Grundlegung der Psychologie* (Berlin, 1956), p. 71.

38  "The Reflex of Freedom," *LCR*, pp. 282–286.

39  *Ibid.*, p. 286.

40  "The Task and the Arrangement of a Laboratory . . ." *LCR*, p. 131; "Natural Science . . ." *PSW*, p. 218.

41  Emphasis supplied.

42  "The Reflex of Purpose," *LCR*, p. 279.

43  *Ibid.*, p. 280.

44  K. Lashley, "Cerebral Control Versus Reflexology: A Reply to Professor Hunter," *Journal of General Psychology*, V (1931), 14.

45  Cf. "Problem of Higher Nervous Activity," *Soviet Five-Year Plan for Medicine* (1946–1950), sec. 6a.

46  Straus, *op. cit.*, p. 35.

47  "Experimental Psychology . . ." *LCR*, p. 57.

48  "Conditioned Reflexes," *PSW*, pp. 259–260.

49  Cf. B. Babkin, *Pavlov: A Biography* (Chicago, 1949), p. 329.

50  H. Wells, *Ivan P. Pavlov: Toward a Scientific Psychology and Psychiatry* (New York, 1956), pp. 90 ff.

51  *Vide* Pavlov's conjecture on the frontal lobes as the "organ" of "purely human mentality." *Psychopathology and Psychiatry* (Moscow, n.d.), p. 297.

52  *LCR*, p. 59.

53  Seliwanow, in *LP*, pp. 302, 313.

54  Sechenov, "Reflexes of the Brain," in *Selected Physiological and Psychological Works*, p. 110.

55  R. Bauer, *The New Man in Soviet Psychology* (Cambridge, England, 1952), p. 137.

56  Cf. Von Kultschytsky, "Die marxistische-sowjetische Konzeption des Menschen in Lichte der westlichen Psychologie," *LP*, pp. 98–99.

57 As cited in Bauer, *op. cit.*, p. 133.

58 *Ibid.*, pp. 96–97.

59 Orbeli, *Lectures on the Physiology of the Nervous System*, p. 232, as cited in Ivanov-Smolensky, "Lines of Development . . ." *Scientific Session . . .* p. 123.

60 Beritov, *Über die Grundformen der nervalen und psychonervalen Tätigkeit*, pp. 4, 98, as cited by Seliwanow, in *LP*, p. 305.

61 Kupalov, *Bulletin of Experimental Biology and Medicine*, II (1950), 87.

62 Ivanov-Smolensky, "Reply to the Discussion," *Scientific Session . . .* p. 153.

63 Bykov, "Reply to the Discussion," *ibid.*, p. 164.

64 Cf. Seliwanow, in *LP*, pp. 301, 305; Petruschewski, in *LP*, pp. 70–71.

65 Asratyan, in *Scientific Session . . .* p. 147.

66 Babkin, *op. cit.*, p. 286.

67 P. Popowski, *I. P. Pawlow: Aus dem Leben und Werken des grossen russischen Gelehrten* (Berlin, 1948), p. 14.

68 Babkin, *op. cit.*, p. 287.

69 *Ibid.*, p. 291; Petruschewski, in *LP*, p. 48.

70 "Consciousness is but a reflection of underlying physiological processes. It is true . . . that persons have a subjective feeling of freedom, but this is illusory. It is the task of science to reduce this area of illusion and demonstrate the determinate nature of all phenomena." Bauer, *op. cit.*, p. 68; cf. *CRP*, p. 126; *PSW*, pp. 421–422.

71 Cf. Taylor, "Determinism and the Theory of Agency," *Freedom and Determinism in the Age of Modern Science*, ed. S. Hook (New York, 1958), p. 209; Hart, "Legal Responsibility and Excuses," *ibid.*, pp. 82–83, n. 1B; Edwards, "Hard and Soft Determinism," *ibid.*, p. 113.

72 Bauer, *op. cit.*, p. 36.

73 Cf. Babkin, *op. cit.*, p. 328.

74 Cf. Straus, *op. cit.*, p. 36.

75 Asratyan, *Scientific Session . . .* p. 96; Petruschewski, in *LP*, p. 51; Ivanov-Smolensky, "Lines of Development . . ." *Scientific Session . . .* pp. 77–78.

76 Cf. T. Morgan, *Evolution and Genetics* (Princeton, 1925), pp. 158–159.

77 Cf. Gantt, Introduction to *LCR*, p. 23.

78 Asratyan, in *Scientific Session . . .* p. 97; cf. Below, *op. cit.*, p. 48.

79 Cf. W. Penfield, *Archives of Neurology and Psychiatry*, XL (1938), 417–418.

80 Cf. R. Tucker, *The Soviet Political Mind* (New York, 1963), p. 118.

81 Cf. "I. P. Pavlov," in Rosental and Iudin, *Diccionario filosofico abreviado*, p. 402.

82 Konstantinov, *Los fundamentos* . . . pp. 158–159.

83 Cf. F. V. Konstantinov, *The Role of Socialist Consciousness in the Development of Soviet Society* (Moscow, 1951), pp. 23 ff.

84 As cited in Tucker, *The Soviet Political Mind*, p. 109.

85 F. V. Konstantinov, *El materialismo historico* (Mexico City, 1960), pp. 1–2. For a recent Soviet discussion *vide* G. Glezerman, *The Laws of Social Development* (Moscow, n.d.).

86 Labriola, *Essays* . . . p. 127.

87 Cf. Croce, *Materialismo storico* . . . pp. 2–3.

88 M. N. Rutkevich and L. N. Kogan, "Methodology in Sociological Studies," *Soviet Sociology*, I, 1 (Summer, 1962), 3. For a discussion of sociology in the Soviet Union *vide* G. Fischer, *Science and Politics: The New Sociology in the Soviet Union* (Ithaca, 1964).

89 P. P. Maslov, "Model Building in Sociological Research," *Soviet Sociology*, I, 1 (Summer, 1962), p. 11.

90 Cf. J. Gillman, *The Falling Rate of Profit* (New York, 1958), p. 1.

91 *Capital*, III, 227.

92 *Ibid.*, p. 233.

93 *Ibid.*, p. 241.

94 P. Barth, *Die Geschichtsphilosophie Hegels und der Hegelianer* (Leipzig, 1890).

95 Engels to Schmidt, October 27, 1890, *MESW*, II, 496.

96 Engels to Starkenburg, January 25, 1894, *MESW*, II, 504.

97 Engels to Mehring, July 14, 1893, *MESW*, II, 499.

98 Engels to Starkenburg, January 25, 1894, *MESW*, II, 504.

99 Engels to Schmidt, October 27, 1890, *MESW*, II, 495.

100 *Ibid.*, p. 496.

101 *Ibid.*

102 *Ibid.*, p. 493.

103 Engels to Starkenburg, January 25, 1894, *MESW*, II, 506.

104 Cf. Engels to Marx, December 8, 1882, *Briefwechsel* . . . IV, 495.

105 Gillman, *op. cit.*, pp. 146–147; cf. R. L. Meek, "Marx's Doctrine of Increasing Misery," *Science and Society*, XXVI, 4 (1962), 422–441.

106 Marx and Engels, "Manifesto . . ." *MESW*, I, 45.

107 *EPM*, p. 66.

108 Gillman, *op. cit.*, p. 148.

109 Marx, "Wage Labor and Capital," *MESW*, I, 93–94.

110 *Ibid.*, p. 104.

111 Cf. "Remarks on the Committee's Draft Programme," *LCW*, VI, 65.

112 *Ibid.*, pp. 65–66.

113 *Ibid.*, p. 48.

114 *Manual de economia politica*, pp. 133–138.

115 A. Alekseyev, *The Basic Economic Law of Modern Capitalism* (Moscow, 1955), p. 29; cf. P. Nikitin, *Fundamentals of Political Economy* (Moscow, n.d.), pp. 79–80.

116 Khrushchev, *Report to the Twenty-second Congress of the CPSU* (New York, 1961), I, 23.

117 Engels, "Speech at the Graveside of Karl Marx," *MESW*, II, 167.

118 Engels to Bloch, September 21–22, 1890, *MESW*, II, 489.

119 Konstantinov, *El materialismo historico*, p. 10.

120 As cited in Blakeley, *Soviet Scholasticism*, p. 149, n. 550.

121 *AD*, pp. 249 ff.

122 *AD*, p. 250.

123 Engels, "Outlines . . ." *EPM*, p. 183.

124 Engels to Danielson, October 17, 1893, *MESW*, II, 503.

125 Engels to Bloch, September 21–22, 1890, *MESW*, II, 488.

126 "State and Revolution," *LSW*, II, pt. 1, 294.

127 H. J. Berman, "The Dilemma of Soviet Law Reform," in *Contemporary Communism: Theory and Practice*, ed. H. R. Swearer and R. P. Longaker (Los Angeles, 1963), pp. 73–82.

# A POSTSCRIPT IN LIEU OF CONCLUSIONS

Cf. K. Popper, *The Open Society and Its Enemies* (New York, 1963), II, 81–88.

Cf. Lewis, *Marxism and the Open Mind*, pp. 24 ff.

Rosental and Iudin, *Diccionario filosofico abreviado*, p. 482.

4 Cf. L. Schapiro, "The Party and the State," in *The Future of Communist Society*, pp. 111–116.

5 Cf. C. McVicker, *Titoism: Pattern for International Communism* (New York, 1957); for an opposing view, cf. C. Zalar, *Yugoslav Communism: A Critical Study of Its Socioeconomic, Legal, and Political Aspects* (Washington, D.C., 1961).

# Suggestions for Further Reading

This selected bibliography is designed to guide the reader toward further works devoted to the subjects discussed in this book. I have not attempted to list every work of merit. The literature devoted to Marxism is far too abundant for such an undertaking. What has been attempted is a listing of good books in English which are relatively easy to obtain and which will assist the student in understanding Marxism as a philosophical system. For the more advanced student who has reading facility in one or another European language, a perusal of the notes will suggest pertinent foreign-language material. Where necessary I have identified the book with a brief description in order to indicate its major emphasis and help the reader distinguish between Marxist and non-Marxist authors.

## 1 / Anthologies

Marx, Karl and Friedrich Engels. *Selected Works in Two Volumes.* Moscow: Foreign Languages Publishing House. Several editions. This collection contains a substantial part of the mature works of Marx and Engels including *The Communist Manifesto* and its various prefaces, Marx's *Wage Labor and Capital, The Class Struggles in France, The Eighteenth Brumaire of Louis Bonaparte, Critique of the Gotha Program, Value Price and Profit,* and *The Civil War in France* in their entirety. It also includes Engels' *The Origin of the Family, Private Property and the State,* and *Ludwig Feuerbach and the End of Classical German Philosophy* in their entirety. There are selections from other works as well.

Lenin, V. I. *Selected Works in Two Volumes.* Moscow: Foreign Languages

Publishing House, 1950–1951. This collection is published in four parts and includes a substantial part of Lenin's mature work: *Two Tactics of Social Democracy in the Democratic Revolution; The Right of Nations to Self-Determination; Imperialism, The Highest Stage of Capitalism; What the "Friends of the People" Are and How They Fight the Social-Democrats; What Is to Be Done?; One Step Forward, Two Steps Back; The Proletarian Revolution and the Renegade Kautsky; "Left-Wing" Communism, An Infantile Disorder; The Tasks of the Proletariat in Our Revolution; The Impending Catastrophe and How to Combat It; The Tasks of the Revolution; The State and Revolution;* and *The Immediate Tasks of the Soviet Government.* The selection includes brief essays and a number of speeches as well.

Stalin, J. *Problems of Leninism.* Moscow: Foreign Languages Publishing House, 1953.

Selsam, Howard and H. Martel (eds.). *Reader in Marxist Philosophy.* New York: International Publishers, 1964. This collection provides a serviceable selection of passages from the works of Marx, Engels, and Lenin as they bear specifically on philosophical issues.

Bottomore, T. B. and M. Rubel (eds.). *Karl Marx: Selected Writings in Sociology and Social Philosophy.* Harmondsworth: Penguin Books, 1963. A collection of passages from the writings of Marx bearing specifically on sociology and social philosophy. Many of the passages are original translations from manuscripts unavailable to students who have access only to English-language material.

Meek, R. (ed.). *Marx and Engels on Malthus: Selections from the Writings of Marx and Engels Dealing with the Doctrines of Thomas Robert Malthus on Population and Economic Theory and Their Relation to Darwinism.* New York: International Publishers, 1954. This collection provides selections from a number of sources difficult to obtain.

## 2 / Selection of Works by Marx and Engels Available in English

Marx, K. *Economic and Philosophic Manuscripts of 1844.* Moscow: Foreign Languages Publishing House, n.d. A more amply annotated edition of this volume is available through International Publishers, edited and with an Introduction by Dirk J. Struik.

————. *Capital.* 3 vols. Moscow: Foreign Languages Publishing House, 1954–1962.

————. *Selected Essays.* London: Leonard Parsons, 1926. These essays include some of the early essays of Marx which date from 1844 to 1850. While the translation itself leaves something to be desired these essays are essential to an appreciation of the philosophy of the young Marx.

————. *Early Writings.* New York: McGraw-Hill, 1964. This collection includes "On the Jewish Question," "Contribution to the Critique of Hegel's Philosophy of Right," and the "Economic and Philosophical Manuscripts of 1844."

———. *The Poverty of Philosophy.* Moscow: Foreign Languages Publishing House, n.d.

———. *A Contribution to the Critique of Political Economy.* Chicago: Charles H. Kerr, 1918.

**Engels, F.** *The Condition of the Working-Class in England in 1844.* London: George Allen & Unwin, 1950.

———. *Anti-Dühring: Herr Eugen Dühring's Revolution in Science.* Moscow: Foreign Languages Publishing House, 1962.

———. *Dialectics of Nature.* Moscow: Foreign Languages Publishing House, 1954.

——— and Paul and Laura Lafargue. *Correspondence.* 3 vols. Moscow: Foreign Languages Publishing House, 1959–1960.

**Marx, K. and Friedrich Engels.** *The Holy Family or Critique of Critical Critique.* Moscow: Foreign Languages Publishing House, 1956.

———. *The German Ideology.* Parts 1 and 3. New York: International Publishers, 1939.

———. *Selected Correspondence.* Moscow: Foreign Languages Press, n.d.

## 3 / Suggested Supplementary Commentaries by Chapters

### CHAPTER ONE

**Adams, H. P.** *Karl Marx in His Earlier Writings.* London: George Allen & Unwin, 1940. Interpretive chapters devoted to the early writings of Marx. This volume provides an account of Marx's earlier works as yet unavailable in English.

**Dunayevskaya, R.** *Marxism and Freedom . . . from 1776 Until Today.* New York: Bookman Associates, 1958. Chapter iii. In this chapter Miss Dunayevskaya interprets the early manuscripts as the thought of the "true" Marx.

**Fromm, E.** *Marx's Concept of Man.* New York: Frederick Ungar, 1961. A preliminary essay, which should be critically evaluated, precedes a partial translation of Marx's *Manuscripts of 1844.*

**Hook, S.** *From Hegel to Marx: Studies in the Intellectual Development of Karl Marx.* Ann Arbor: University of Michigan Press, 1962. An excellent survey of the intellectual background of Karl Marx.

**Marcuse, H.** *Reason and Revolution: Hegel and the Rise of Social Theory.* New York: Humanities Press, 1954. Part 2. This selection provides a stimulating discussion of particularly the Hegelian background and content of Marx's *Economic and Philosophic Manuscripts.*

**Pappenheim, F.** *The Alienation of Modern Man: An Interpretation based on Marx and Tönnies.* New York: Monthly Review Press, 1959.

**Tucker, R.** *Philosophy and Myth in Karl Marx.* New York: Cambridge University Press, 1961. An attempt at a psychological interpretation of the philosophical enterprise of the young Marx in relation to his predecessors, particularly Hegel and Feuerbach.

## CHAPTER TWO

Hook, S. *Reason, Social Myths and Democracy.* New York: Humanities Press, 1950. Chapters ix, x, xi. These chapters provide a searching critique of the dialectic, particularly as it is found in the works of Engels.

## CHAPTERS THREE AND FOUR

Adoratsky, V. *Dialectical Materialism: The Theoretical Foundations of Marxism-Leninism.* New York: International Publishers, 1934. An early Soviet exposition of Marxism-Leninism.

Afanasyev, V. *Marxist Philosophy: A Popular Outline.* Moscow: Foreign Languages Publishing House, n.d. This is the most recent translation from the Russian of the modern synthesis of Marx-Engels-Lenin.

Blakeley, T. J. *Soviet Scholasticism.* Dordrecht: D. Reidel, 1961. An analysis of philosophical methodology employed in the Soviet Union.

Bocheński, J. M. *Soviet Russian Dialectical Materialism [Diamat].* Dordrecht: D. Reidel, 1963. A standard survey of contemporary Soviet philosophy.

Joravsky, D. *Soviet Marxism and Natural Science, 1917–1932.* New York: Columbia University Press, 1961. A scholarly treatment of the relationships between Marxism-Leninism and the natural sciences.

Somerville, J. *Soviet Philosophy: A Study of Theory and Practice.* New York: Philosophical Library, 1946. A sympathetic account of philosophy in the Soviet Union.

*Soviet Studies in Philosophy: Selected Articles from Soviet Scholarly Journals in English Translation.* Edited by John Somerville. Published by International Arts and Sciences Press, New York.

*Studies in Soviet Thought: A Quarterly of the Institute of East-European Studies at the University of Fribourg, Switzerland.* Edited by J. M. Bocheński and T. J. Blakeley. Critical articles by various specialists on aspects of Marxist-Leninist thought in the Soviet Union.

Wetter, G. A. *Dialectical Materialism: A Historical and Systematic Survey of Philosophy in the Soviet Union.* New York: Frederick A. Praeger, 1958. A detailed treatment of the development of philosophy in the Soviet Union.

## CHAPTER FIVE

Bober, M. *Karl Marx's Interpretation of History.* Cambridge, England: Cambridge University Press, 1948. An excellent critical analysis.

Boudin, B. *The Theoretical System of Karl Marx.* Chicago: C. H. Kerr, 1907. A good, early, and rather sympathetic account devoted substantially to the theory of history of Marx and Engels.

**Bukharin, N.** *Historical Materialism: A System of Sociology.* New York: International Publishers, 1925. A work by one of the most important Soviet theoreticians in the period immediately following the Russian Revolution.

**Cole, G. D. H.** *The Meaning of Marxism.* Ann Arbor: University of Michigan Press, 1964. This work is largely devoted to an interpretation of the theory of history of Marx and Engels in the effort to render its language more comprehensible to contemporary readers.

**Croce, B.** *Historical Materialism and the Economics of Karl Marx.* New York: Macmillan, 1914. A collection of brief critical essays by one of Italy's leading philosophers.

**Federn, K.** *The Materialist Conception of History: A Critical Analysis.* London: Macmillan, 1939.

**Kautsky, K.** *Foundations of Christianity.* New York: S. A. Russell, 1953. This constitutes an attempt by one of Marxism's foremost theoreticians to interpret early Christianity with the use of Marxist techniques.

**Labriola, Antonio.** *Essays on the Materialist Conception of History.* Chicago: C. H. Kerr, 1904. This is a substantial early work by an Italian Marxist.

**Meyer, A. G.** *Marxism: The Unity of Theory and Practice.* Ann Arbor: University of Michigan Press, 1963. An excellent interpretive essay of the theory of history of classical Marxism.

**Plekhanov, G.** *Selected Philosophical Works.* Vol. I. Moscow: Foreign Languages Press, n.d. This collection of works by one of Russia's foremost prerevolutionary Marxists contains *The Development of the Monist View of History*, one of the best of the orthodox expositions of the Marxist theory of history.

————. *Art and Social Life.* London: Lawrence and Wishart, 1953. This is an application of the Marxist theory of history to the problems of aesthetics.

**Seligman, E. R. A.** *The Economic Interpretation of History.* New York: Columbia University Press, 1961. A revised edition of an early work that provides a good introduction to Marxism as a theory of history.

**Venable, V.** *Human Nature: The Marxist View.* New York: A. A. Knopf, 1946. A competent and interesting interpretation of the theory of history of classical Marxism.

CHAPTER SIX

**Berdyaev, N.** *The Origin of Russian Communism.* Ann Arbor: University of Michigan Press, 1960. A suggestive discussion of early influences on the development of Lenin's theory of history.

————. *The Russian Revolution.* Ann Arbor: University of Michigan Press, 1961. A suggestive work that should be critically read: it attempts to identify influences which modified classical Marxism as a theory of history.

**Kautsky, K.** *The Dictatorship of the Proletariat.* Ann Arbor: University of Michigan Press, 1964. This work is a criticism of Lenin's interpretation of the proletarian revolution by one of the foremost thinkers of the Second International.

Luxemburg, R. *The Russian Revolution* and *Leninism or Marxism*. Ann Arbor: University of Michigan Press, 1961. These two essays are criticisms of Leninism by one of the foremost Marxists of the first quarter of the century.

McNeal, R. H. *The Bolshevik Tradition: Lenin, Stalin, Khrushchev*. Englewood Cliffs: Prentice-Hall, 1963.

Meyer, A. G. *Leninism*. New York: Frederick A. Praeger, 1962. This is perhaps the best single work on Lenin's conception of history.

Moore, S. W. *The Critique of Capitalist Democracy: An Introduction to the Theory of the State in Marx, Engels, and Lenin*. New York: Paine Whitman Publishers, 1957. This is a scholarly interpretation of the theory of the state as found in the mature works of Marx, Engels, and Lenin. There is no attempt to trace the development of the theory of the state in the early writings of Marx and Engels in order to distinguish it from the more mature expression.

————. *Three Tactics: The Background in Marx*. New York: Monthly Review Press, 1963. An excellent analysis of the various elements found in classical Marxism which led to the development of divergent tactics among contemporary Marxists.

Wolfe, B. D. *Three Who Made a Revolution: A Biographical History*. Boston: Beacon Press, 1948. An account which places Lenin in a historical context and renders many of his innovations in the classical Marxist theory of history comprehensible as tactical necessities.

CHAPTER SEVEN

Bakharev, A. N. *I. V. Michurin, The Great Remaker of Nature*. Moscow: Foreign Languages Publishing House, 1954. A Soviet account of the work of I. V. Michurin and an exposition of his theory of the inheritance of acquired traits.

Bykov, K. M. *The Cerebral Cortex and the Internal Organs*. Moscow: Foreign Languages Publishing House, 1959. Chapter i. An interesting discussion of the methodology of Pavlovian research.

Fischer, G. *Science and Politics: The New Sociology in the Soviet Union*. Ithaca: Center for International Studies, 1964. An account of the current situation in Soviet sociology.

Fyfe, J. *Lysenko Is Right*. London: Lawrence & Wishart, 1950. A defense of Lysenko's theories by a botanist.

Glezerman, G. *The Laws of Social Development*. Moscow: Foreign Languages Publishing House, n.d. The most recent translation out of Russian of a work devoted to the contemporary Soviet theory of history.

Huxley, J. *Soviet Genetics and World Science: Lysenko and the Meaning of Heredity*. London: Chatto and Windus, 1949. A critical appraisal of the genetics controversy in the Soviet Union by an internationally recognized geneticist.

Kuusinen, O. W. (ed.) *Fundamentals of Marxism-Leninism*. Moscow: Foreign Languages Publishing House, 1961. A translation of a contemporary Soviet text which provides a survey of Marxist-Leninist social theories.

**Lyensko, T.** *Agrobiology.* Moscow: Foreign Languages Publishing House, 1954.

———. *Heredity and Its Variability.* New York: King's Crown Press, 1946.

**Michurin, I. V.** *Selected Works.* Moscow: Foreign Languages Publishing House, 1949.

**Morton, A. G.** *Soviet Genetics.* London: Lawrence & Wishart, 1951. A Marxist account of Michurin's and Lysenko's theories of the inheritance of acquired traits.

**Nesturkh, M.** *The Origin of Man.* Moscow: Foreign Languages Publishing House, 1959. Chapter i. A discussion of the development of man, employing Engels' concept of the "labor theory of anthropogenesis."

**Pavlov, I. P.** *Lectures on Conditioned Reflexes.* New York: International Publishers, 1928.

———. *Selected Works.* Moscow: Foreign Languages Publishing House, 1955.

———. *Conditioned Reflexes and Psychiatry.* New York: International Publishers, 1941.

———. *Psychopathology and Psychiatry.* Moscow: Foreign Languages Publishing House, n.d.

*The Situation in Biological Science: Proceedings of the Lenin Academy of Agricultural Sciences of the U.S.S.R. July 31–August 7, 1948. Complete Stenographic Report.* New York: International Publishers, 1949. A complete stenographic report of the famous genetics controversy in the Soviet Union.

*Soviet Sociology: Selected Articles from Soviet Scholarly Journals in English Translation.* Edited by S. P. Dunn and M. Yanowitch. Published by the International Arts and Sciences Press, New York.

**Stoletov, V.** *The Fundamentals of Michurin Biology.* Moscow: Foreign Languages Publishing House, 1953.

**Tucker, R.** *The Soviet Political Mind: Studies in Stalinism and Post-Stalin Change.* New York: Frederick A. Praeger, 1963. Chapter v. A discussion of the circumstances surrounding psychology in the contemporary Soviet Union.

**Wells, H.** *Ivan P. Pavlov: Toward a Scientific Psychology and Psychiatry.* New York: International Publishers, 1956. A scholarly Marxist account of the theories of Pavlov.

**Winn, R. B.** (ed.) *Psychotherapy in the Soviet Union.* New York: Grove Press, 1961. A collection of essays by therapists in the Soviet Union, some of whom employ Pavlovian concepts in therapy.

**Zirkle, C.** *Death of a Science in Russia.* Philadelphia: University of Pennsylvania Press, 1949. A detailed discussion of the genetics controversy in the Soviet Union.

## 4 / General Commentaries and Biographies

### A. MARXISM AND MARXISM-LENINISM
### AS PHILOSOPHY

Brameld, T. B. H. *A Philosophic Approach to Communism.* Chicago: Chicago University Press, 1933. A general introduction to Marxism and Marxism-Leninism as philosophy.

Cornforth, M. *In Defence of Philosophy Against Positivism and Pragmatism.* New York: International Publishers, 1950. A Marxist-Leninist attempt to defend Marxism-Leninism from more contemporary trends.

————. *Science and Idealism: An Examination of "Pure Empiricism" and Modern Logic.* New York: International Publishers, 1947. A defense of Marxism-Leninism against modern philosophical schools.

————. *Dialectical Materialism: An Introductory Course.* 3 vols. New York: International Publishers, 1953–1954. A Marxist-Leninist introduction to dialectical materialism. The volume contains no discussion of contemporary developments in Marxism-Leninism.

————. *Philosophy for Socialists.* London: Lawrence & Wishart, 1959. A brief introduction to Marxism-Leninism by a Marxist-Leninist.

Guest, D. A. *Lectures on Marxist Philosophy.* New York: International Publishers, 1963. A republication of an account of Marxism-Leninism written by a Marxist-Leninist in 1939.

Jordan, Z. A. *Philosophy and Ideology: The Development of Philosophy and Marxism-Leninism in Poland Since the Second World War.* Dordrecht: D. Reidel, 1963. An excellent and exhaustive account. Contains an excellent analysis of Engels' epistemology and a discussion of the logical problems of dialectical materialism.

Selsam, H. *What Is Philosophy? A Marxist Introduction.* New York: International Publishers, 1963. A republication of a good, standard introduction to Marxist philosophy written by a Marxist-Leninist in 1938.

————. *Philosophy in Revolution.* New York: International Publishers, 1957. A Marxist-Leninist survey of Marxism-Leninism as philosophy.

### B. MARXISM AND MARXISM-LENINISM
### IN GENERAL

Carew Hunt, R. N. *The Theory and Practice of Communism: An Introduction.* New York: Macmillan, 1957.

Eastman, M. *Marxism: Is It Science?* New York: Norton, 1940. A searching criticism of Marxism and Marxism-Leninism.

Lichtheim, G. *Marxism: An Historical and Critical Study.* New York: Frederick A. Praeger, 1962. An excellent historical survey of Marxism and its further development in the theories of Lenin.

Mayo, H. B. *Introduction to Marxist Theory*. New York: Oxford University Press, 1960.

Mills, C. W. *The Marxists*. New York: Dell, 1962. This is a work by an internationally celebrated sociologist. Selections from the works of the classics and contemporary texts are provided with a knowledgeable interpretive commentary.

Popper, K. R. *The Open Society and Its Enemies*. 2 vols. New York: Harper & Row, 1963. Vol. II. A searching criticism of Marxism as a theory of history by a philosopher of science.

Ulam, A. B. *The Unfinished Revolution: An Essay on the Sources and Influence of Marxism and Communism*. New York: Random House, 1964. An interesting interpretive account of Marxism and its contemporary development.

## C. BIOGRAPHIES

Berlin, I. *Karl Marx: His Life and Environment*. New York: Oxford University Press, 1949. A good standard biography.

Mehring, F. *Karl Marx: The Story of His Life*. John Lane, The Bodley Head, 1936. The standard Social Democratic account of Marx's life and work.

Ruhle, O. *Karl Marx: His Life and Work*. New York: The Viking Press, 1935.

*Reminiscences of Marx and Engels*. Moscow: Foreign Languages Publishing House, n.d. A collection of contemporary recollections of Marx and Engels.

Mayer, G. *Friedrich Engels: A Biography*. New York: A. A. Knopf, 1936. The only adequate biography of Engels in English.

Stepanova, Y. *Frederick Engels*. Moscow: Foreign Languages Publishing House, 1958. A Soviet biography.

Fischer, L. *The Life of Lenin*. New York: Harper & Row, 1964. Most of this interesting biography is devoted to Lenin's later life.

Fotieva, L. *Pages from Lenin's Life*. Moscow: Foreign Languages Publishing House, 1960. This volume is an account of Lenin written by his secretary.

Krupskaya, N. K. *Lenin*. Moscow: Foreign Languages Publishing House, 1959. The biography of Lenin written by his wife.

Payne, R. *The Life and Death of Lenin*. New York: Simon and Schuster, 1964.

Trotsky, L. *Lenin*. London: George C. Harrap, 1925. An account of Lenin by the man who helped him make the Russian Revolution.

*Vladimir Lenin: A Political Biography*. New York: International Publishers, 1943. A standard Soviet biography.

Trotsky, L. *Stalin: An Appraisal of the Man and His Influence*. New York: Grosset and Dunlap, 1941.

Deutscher, I. *Stalin: A Political Biography*. New York: Random House, 1960. The best biography of Stalin in English.

# Index

# A SURVEY OF MARXISM

*Problems in Philosophy and the Theory of History*

**by A. James Gregor**

*A Survey of Marxism* is a brief but thorough exposition of Marxism as it developed within the work of Marx and Engels and through the writings of their followers. Professor Gregor deals with the evolution of Marxism as a philosophy and then with its development as a theory of history. An extremely useful guide in depth for students of modern philosophy, history, and political science.